HANDBOOK
LITERARY A[N]
BOOK II

HOW TO EVALUATE
PROSE FICTION, DRAMA, AND POETRY
Illustrated Edition

James P. Stobaugh

New York
Harvard Square Editions
www.harvardsquareeditions.org
2013

HANDBOOK FOR LITERARY ANALYSIS: How to Evaluate Prose Fiction, Drama, and Poetry, Illustrated Edition

Published in the United States by
Harvard Square Editions
ISBN: 978-0-9833216-8-2
Harvard Square Editions web address: www.HarvardSquareEditions.org
This is an educational publication printed in the United States of America.

Special thanks to my students including John Micah Braswell, Alouette Greenidge, Daniel Greenidge, Anna Grace Knudtsen, Claire Atwood, Chris Lloyd, Callie Lloyd, and Joseph Stahl, for their diligent work and generosity in allowing me to use their essays as samples.
Thanks to David Garber, Julie Atwood, Julie Braswell, and Karen Stobaugh for editing my manuscript.

Cover photo, Boy with Books © Jupiterimages
Layout by Daphnide McDermet

Special note: The present tense is appropriately used to refer to memorable works of the past and to narrate a fictional work's plot. "Characters in books, plays, and films do things." — *Chicago Manual of Style*, 16th edition

For further information:
James Stobaugh, 510 Swank Rd., Hollsopple, PA 15935 (814-479-7710)
E-mail: jim@forsuchatimeasthis.com
Website: http://www.harvardsquareeditions.org and
http://www.forsuchatimeasthis.com
Facebook: http://www.facebook.com/jpstobaugh
Twitter: http://twitter.com/jamespstobaugh

Fantastic Praise for Jim Stobaugh's

Handbook for Literary Analysis

"Dr. Stobaugh's Handbook of Literary Criticism is an outstanding resource for educators and the students. Over the past several decades, the influence of literature produced by Christians has significantly declined. From my perspective as a Christian culture influencer, I believe we must reverse that trend. We need more effective authors who are producing world class literature framed in the Christian worldview. I see Dr. Stobaugh's handbook to be essential to reverse that trend. I highly recommend it."

—Ray Traylor, Homeschool Dad, Author *True Riches*
(2010) & *Besetting Sin* (2013)

"This book is appropriate for junior high students through adults. You can work through the book sequentially or selectively, depending upon your need. The book reads like a literature text with plentiful use of literary excerpts, including many from Scripture, as examples. It also should help familiarize readers with some great literary works. There are no questions or assignments as you would find in a course. Instead, it is expected that the reader will be using it for self-directed education. Parents might assign particular sections for the student lacking self-direction, then follow up with a discussion regarding what they have read."

—Cathy Duffy, "Guru" of Homeschool Reviews

"I've recommended all Jim Stobaugh's curricula because they have been so important to our home school. His guidance through his curriculum helped us instill in our sons solid academic knowledge and a strong Christian worldview."

—Christine Gallegos, Homeschool Mom

"Jim Stobaugh has not only discipled my son as a writer but has inspired him... I believe that writing is possibly the most important skill necessary to a successful college experience and I am beginning to relax knowing that when the time comes my son will be prepared."

—Julie Braswell, Homeschool Mom

"Dr. Stobaugh's Handbook for Literary Analysis has been an unspeakably beneficial addition to my education. Before taking the course, my writing was defined by numerous different formulas that left my style rigid and unconvincing. Dr. Stobaugh's course not only freed my writing, but also greatly increased my appreciation of literature. By encouraging careful analysis of great authors' literary styles, I traveled from abridged versions of Alice in Wonderland and The Jungle Book to unabridged copies of Call of the Wild and Uncle Tom's Cabin in one exciting year. Now, writing assignments thrill me, and I face requests for written material with anticipation, not dread. I whole-heartedly recommend Handbook for Literary Analysis as an ineffably valuable educational tool for any blossoming writer."

—John-Micah Braswell, Student

About the Author

 **James P. Stobaugh** and his wife, Karen, have four homeschooled adult children. They have a growing ministry, For Such a Time As This Ministries, committed to challenging this generation to change its world for Christ. His academic credentials include the following: BA, cum laude, Vanderbilt University; Teacher Certification, Peabody College for Teachers; MA, Rutgers University; MDiv, Princeton Theological Seminary; Merrill Fellow, Harvard University; DMin, Gordon-Conwell Theological Seminary.

Dr. Stobaugh's books include the following:

The SAT and College Preparation Course for the Christian Student
The ACT and College Preparation Course for the Christian Student
Encouraging Thoughtful Christians to be World Changers (series)
    Handbook for Literary Analysis
    Skills for Rhetoric
    American Literature
    British Literature
    World Literature
High School History Courses (series)
    American History
    British History
    World History
    Epoch I–IV History
    Companion to 50 Classics
Devotions for Thoughtful Christians (series)
    Fire That Burns But Does Not Consume
    A Gathered Inheritance

TABLE OF CONTENTS

Background

Arps and Johnson, in their compelling book *Literature: Structure, Sound, and Sense*, argue, "The theme of a piece of fiction is its controlling idea or its central insight. It is the unifying generalization about life stated or implied by the story. To derive the theme of a story, we must determine what its central purpose is: what view of life it supports or what insight into life it reveals." Within the concept of a theme is the concept of worldview, the ubiquitous, intangible philosophy/theology that drives the thematic engine in every literary piece.

Suggested Literary Works

Austen, Jane. Pride and Prejudice.
Conrad, Joseph. Heart of Darkness.
Dostoyevsky, Fyodor. Crime and Punishment.
Eliot, George. Silas Marner.
Fitzgerald, F. Scott. The Great Gatsby.
Goldman, William. Lord of the Flies.
Hemingway, Ernest. The Old Man and the Sea.
Hurston, Zora Neale. Their Eyes Were Watching God.
Lewis, C. S. The Screwtape Letters.
London, Jack. "To Light a Fire."
O'Neill, Eugene. Emperor Jones.
Plato. Republic.
Swift, Jonathan. Gulliver's Travels.
Tolkien, J. R. R. Lord of the Rings trilogy.
Virgil. Aeneid.
Wells, H. G. The Time Machine.

Themes

The story may differ, the characters might change, or not, but the basic themes or motifs in literature remain more or less the same over the centuries. The theme of fate in Homer's *Iliad* (800 BCE) is quite similar to the theme in *A Separate Peace* (1959), by John Knowles.

What are themes in literature? Well, a theme can be defined as the basic idea—not a moral—exhibited in a piece of literature. Themes are created through the story, plot, and setting. It is rarely stated overtly by the writer.

Here is a list of themes in literature, which more or less appear in every serious dramatic narrative:

The individual in nature
The individual in society
An individual's relation to the cosmos

Of course, most literary works have multiple themes.

Terms

Alongside the term *theme*, a similar concept or word is *motif*. A motif is any recurring image that has symbolic significance in a story. Through its repetition, a motif affects other narrative aspects such as theme or mood.

A *moral* is a message conveyed or a lesson to be learned from a story or event. The moral may be left to readers to determine for themselves, or may be explicitly encapsulated in an aphorism. A moral, as contrasted to a theme, is a subjective, partisan behavioral bent that is advanced through the literary elements of a story.

Satire is a thematic approach where shortcomings are held up to ridicule and caricature, ideally with the intent of teasing individuals, and society itself, into improvement. Although satire is usually meant to be funny, it can be quite vitriolic. A common feature of satire is strong *irony* or *sarcasm*. One critic explains, "In satire, irony is militant." *Parody* is a mild form of satire and is never meant to be a caustic allusion. This "militant" *irony* or *sarcasm*, tongue in cheek, often mockingly embraces the very things the satirist wishes to attack.

"The Dream," by John Donne: Love as a Theme

> Dear love, for nothing less than thee
> Would I have broke this happy dream;
> It was a theme
> For reason, much too strong for fantasy,
> Therefore thou wak'd'st me wisely; yet
> My dream thou brok'st not, but continued'st it.
> Thou art so true that thoughts of thee suffice
> To make dreams truths, and fables histories;
> Enter these arms, for since thou thought'st it best,
> Not to dream all my dream, let's act the rest.

The Individual in Nature

The first theme explored here is the individual in nature. Prime examples are available in Jack London, Emerson, and the Bible.

"To Build a Fire," by Jack London

In this story nature is foreboding, powerful, and ubiquitous. The dog is more in tune with reality than the man because he is more in tune with nature.

Day had broken cold and grey, exceedingly cold and grey, when the man turned aside from the main Yukon trail and climbed the high earth-bank, where a dim and little-travelled trail led eastward through the fat spruce timberland. It was a steep bank, and he paused for breath at the top, excusing the act to himself by looking at his watch. It was nine o'clock. There was no sun nor hint of sun, though there was not a cloud in the sky. It was a clear day, and yet there seemed an intangible pall over the face of things, a subtle gloom that made the day dark, and that was due to the absence of sun. This fact did not worry the man. He was used to the lack of sun. It had been days since he had seen the sun, and he knew that a few more days must pass before that cheerful orb, due south, would just peep above the sky-line and dip immediately from view.

The man flung a look back along the way he had come. The Yukon lay a mile wide and hidden under three feet of ice. On top of this ice were as many feet of snow. It was all pure white, rolling in gentle undulations where the ice-jams of the freeze-up had formed. North and south, as far as his eye could see, it was unbroken white, save for a dark hair-line that curved and twisted from around the spruce-covered island to the south, and that curved and twisted away into the north, where it disappeared behind another spruce-covered island. This dark hair-line was the trail—the main trail—that led south five hundred miles to the Chilcoot Pass, Dyea, and salt water; and that led north seventy miles to Dawson, and still on to the north a thousand miles to Nulato, and finally to St. Michael on Bering Sea, a thousand miles and half a thousand more.

But all this—the mysterious, far-reaching hair-line trail, the absence of sun from the sky, the tremendous cold, and the strangeness and weirdness of it all—made no impression on the man. It was not because he was long used to it. He was a newcomer in the land, a *chechaquo*, and this was his first winter. The trouble with him was that he was without imagination. He was quick and alert in the things of life, but only in the things, and not in the significances. Fifty degrees below zero meant eighty odd degrees of frost. Such fact impressed him as being cold and uncomfortable, and that was all. It did not lead him to meditate upon his frailty as a creature of temperature, and upon man's frailty in general, able only to live within certain narrow limits of heat and cold; and from there on it did not lead him to the conjectural field of immortality and man's place in the universe. Fifty degrees below zero stood for a bite of frost that hurt and that must be guarded against by the use of mittens, ear-flaps, warm moccasins, and thick socks. Fifty degrees below zero was to him just precisely fifty degrees below zero. That there should be anything more to it than that was a thought that never entered his head.

As he turned to go on, he spat speculatively. There was a sharp, explosive crackle that startled him. He spat again. And again, in the air, before it could fall to the snow, the spittle crackled. He knew that at fifty below spittle crackled on the snow, but this spittle had crackled in the air. Undoubtedly it was colder than fifty below — how much colder he did not know. But the temperature did not matter. He was bound for the old claim on the left fork of Henderson Creek, where the boys were already. They had come over across the divide from the Indian Creek country, while he had come the roundabout way to take a look at the possibilities of getting out logs in the spring from the islands in the Yukon. He would be in to camp by six o'clock; a bit after dark, it was true, but the boys would be there, a fire would be going, and a hot supper would be ready. As for lunch, he pressed his hand against the protruding bundle under his jacket. It was also under his shirt, wrapped up in a handkerchief and lying against the naked skin. It was the only way to keep the biscuits from freezing. He smiled agreeably to himself as he thought of those biscuits, each cut open and sopped in bacon grease, and each enclosing a generous slice of fried bacon.

He plunged in among the big spruce trees. The trail was faint. A foot of snow had fallen since the last sled had passed over, and he was glad he was without a sled, travelling light. In fact, he carried nothing but the lunch wrapped in the handkerchief. He was surprised, however, at the cold. It certainly was cold, he concluded, as he rubbed his numbed nose and cheek-bones with his mittened hand. He was a warm-whiskered man, but the hair on his face did not protect the high cheek-bones and the eager nose that thrust itself aggressively into the frosty air.

At the man's heels trotted a dog, a big native husky, the proper wolf-dog, grey-coated and without any visible or temperamental difference from its brother, the wild wolf. The animal was depressed by the tremendous cold. It knew that it was no time for travelling. Its instinct told it a truer tale than was told to the man by the man's judgment.

In reality, it was not merely colder than fifty below zero; it was colder than sixty below, than seventy below. It was seventy-five below zero. Since the freezing-point is thirty-two above zero, it meant that one hundred and seven degrees of frost obtained. The dog did not know anything about thermometers. Possibly in its brain there was no sharp consciousness of a condition of very cold such as was in the man's brain. But the brute had its instinct. It experienced a vague but menacing apprehension that subdued it and made it slink along at the man's heels, and that made it question eagerly every unwonted movement of the man as if expecting him to go into camp or to seek shelter somewhere and build a fire. The dog had learned fire, and it wanted fire, or else to burrow under the snow and cuddle its warmth away from the air.

The frozen moisture of its breathing had settled on its fur in a fine powder of frost, and especially were its jowls, muzzle, and eyelashes whitened by its crystalled breath. The man's red beard and moustache were likewise frosted, but more solidly, the deposit taking the form of ice and increasing with every warm, moist breath he exhaled. Also, the man was chewing tobacco, and the muzzle of ice held his lips so rigidly that he was unable to clear his chin when he expelled the juice. The result was that a crystal beard of the color and solidity of amber was increasing its length on his chin. If he fell down it would shatter itself, like glass, into brittle fragments. But he did not mind the appendage. It was the penalty all tobacco-chewers paid in that country, and he had been out before in two cold snaps. They had not been so cold as this, he knew, but by the spirit thermometer at Sixty Mile he knew they had been registered at fifty below and at fifty-five.

He held on through the level stretch of woods for several miles, crossed a wide flat of niggerheads [meadow], and dropped down a bank to the frozen bed of a small stream. This was Henderson Creek, and he knew he was ten miles from the forks. He looked at his watch. It was ten o'clock. He was making four miles an hour, and he calculated that he would arrive at the forks at half-past twelve. He decided to celebrate that event by eating his lunch there.

The dog dropped in again at his heels, with a tail drooping discouragement, as the man swung along the creek-bed. The furrow of the old sled-trail was plainly visible, but a dozen inches of snow covered the marks of the last runners. In a month no man had come up or down that silent creek. The man held steadily on. He was not much given to thinking, and just then particularly he had nothing to think about save that he would eat lunch at the forks and that at six o'clock he would be in camp with the boys. There was nobody to talk to and, had there been, speech would have been impossible because of the ice-muzzle on his mouth. So he continued monotonously to chew tobacco and to increase the length of his amber beard.

Once in a while the thought reiterated itself that it was very cold and that he had never experienced such cold. As he walked along he rubbed his cheek-bones and nose with the back of his mittened hand. He did this automatically, now and again changing hands. But rub as he would, the instant he stopped his cheek-bones went numb, and the following instant the end of his nose went numb. He was sure to frost his cheeks; he knew that, and experienced a pang of regret that he had not devised a nose-strap of the sort Bud wore in cold snaps. Such a strap passed across the cheeks, as well, and saved them.

But it didn't matter much, after all. What were frosted cheeks? A bit painful, that was all; they were never serious.

Empty as the man's mind was of thoughts, he was keenly observant, and he noticed the changes in the creek, the curves and bends and timber-jams, and always he sharply noted where he placed his feet. Once, coming around a bend, he shied abruptly, like a startled horse, curved away from the place where he had been walking, and retreated several paces back along the trail. The creek he knew was frozen clear to the bottom—no creek could contain water in that arctic winter—but he knew also that there were springs that bubbled out from the hillsides and ran along under the snow and on top the ice of the creek. He knew that the coldest snaps never froze these springs, and he knew likewise their danger. They were traps. They hid pools of water under the snow that might be three inches deep, or three feet. Sometimes a skin of ice half an inch thick covered them, and in turn was covered by the snow. Sometimes there were alternate layers of water and ice-skin, so that when one broke through he kept on breaking through for a while, sometimes wetting himself to the waist.

That was why he had shied in such panic. He had felt the give under his feet and heard the crackle of a snow-hidden ice-skin. And to get his feet wet in such a temperature meant trouble and danger. At the very least it meant delay, for he would be forced to stop and build a fire, and under its protection to bare his feet while he dried his socks and moccasins. He stood and studied the creek-bed and its banks, and decided that the flow of water came from the right. He reflected awhile, rubbing his nose and cheeks, then skirted to the left, stepping gingerly and testing the footing for each step. Once clear of the danger, he took a fresh chew of tobacco and swung along at his four-mile gait.

In the course of the next two hours he came upon several similar traps. Usually the snow above the hidden pools had a sunken, candied appearance that advertised the danger. Once again, however, he had a close call; and once, suspecting danger, he compelled the dog to go on in front. The dog did not want to go. It hung back until the man shoved it forward, and then it went quickly across the white, unbroken surface. Suddenly it broke through, floundered to one side, and got away to firmer footing. It had wet its forefeet and legs, and almost immediately the water that clung to it turned to ice. It made quick efforts to lick the ice off its legs, then dropped down in the snow and began to bite out the ice that had formed between the toes. This was a matter of instinct. To permit the ice to remain would mean sore feet. It did not know this. It merely obeyed the mysterious prompting that arose from the deep crypts of its being. But the man knew, having achieved a judgment on the subject, and he removed the mitten from his right hand and helped tear out the ice-particles. He did not expose his fingers more than a minute, and was astonished at the swift numbness that smote them. It certainly was cold. He pulled on the mitten hastily, and beat the hand savagely across his chest.

At twelve o'clock the day was at its brightest. Yet the sun was too far south on its winter journey to clear the horizon. The bulge of the earth intervened between it and Henderson Creek, where the man walked under a clear sky at noon and cast no shadow. At half-past twelve, to the minute, he arrived at the forks of the creek. He was pleased at the speed he had made. If he kept it up, he would certainly be with the boys by six. He unbuttoned his jacket and shirt and drew forth his lunch. The action consumed no more than a quarter of a minute, yet in that brief moment the numbness laid hold of the exposed fingers. He did not put the mitten on, but, instead, struck the fingers a dozen sharp smashes against his leg. Then he sat down on a snow-covered log to eat. The sting that followed upon the striking of his fingers against his leg ceased so quickly that he was startled. He had had no chance to take a bite of biscuit. He struck the fingers repeatedly and returned them to the mitten, baring the other hand for the purpose of eating. He tried to take a mouthful, but the ice-muzzle prevented. He had forgotten to build a fire and thaw out. He chuckled at his foolishness, and as he chuckled he noted the numbness creeping into the exposed fingers. Also, he noted that the stinging which had first come to his toes when he sat down was already passing away. He wondered whether the toes were warm or numbed. He moved them inside the moccasins and decided that they were numbed.

He pulled the mitten on hurriedly and stood up. He was a bit frightened. He stamped up and down until the stinging returned into the feet. It certainly was cold, was his thought. That man from Sulphur Creek had spoken the truth when telling how cold it sometimes got in the country. And he had laughed at him at the time! That showed one must not be too sure of things. There was no mistake about it, it *was* cold. He strode up and down, stamping his feet and threshing his arms, until reassured by the returning warmth. Then he got out matches and proceeded to make a fire. From the undergrowth, where high water of the previous spring had lodged a supply of seasoned twigs, he got his firewood. Working carefully from a small beginning, he soon had a roaring fire, over which he thawed the ice from his face and in the protection of which he ate his biscuits. For the moment the cold of space was outwitted. The dog took satisfaction in the fire, stretching out close enough for warmth and far enough away to escape being singed.

When the man had finished, he filled his pipe and took his comfortable time over a smoke. Then he pulled on his mittens, settled the ear-flaps of his cap firmly about his ears, and took the creek trail up the left fork. The dog was disappointed and leaned back toward the fire. This man did not know cold. Possibly all the generations of his ancestry had been ignorant of cold, of real cold,

 of cold one hundred and seven degrees below freezing-point. But the dog knew; all its ancestry knew, and it had inherited the knowledge. And it knew that it was not good to walk abroad in such fearful cold. It was the time to lie snug in a hole in the snow and wait for a curtain of cloud to be drawn across the face of outer space whence this cold came. On the other hand, there was keen intimacy between the dog and the man. The one was the toil-slave of the other, and the only caresses it had ever received were the caresses of the whip-lash and of harsh and menacing throat-sounds that threatened the whip-lash. So the dog made no effort to communicate its apprehension to the man. It was not concerned in the welfare of the man; it was for its own sake that it yearned back toward the fire. But the man whistled, and spoke to it with the sound of whip-lashes, and the dog swung in at the man's heels and followed after.

The man took a chew of tobacco and proceeded to start a new amber beard. Also, his moist breath quickly powdered with white his moustache, eyebrows, and lashes. There did not seem to be so many springs on the left fork of the Henderson, and for half an hour the man saw no signs of any. And then it happened. At a place where there were no signs, where the soft, unbroken snow seemed to advertise solidity beneath, the man broke through. It was not deep. He wet himself halfway to the knees before he floundered out to the firm crust.

He was angry, and cursed his luck aloud. He had hoped to get into camp with the boys at six o'clock, and this would delay him an hour, for he would have to build a fire and dry out his foot-gear. This was imperative at that low temperature—he knew that much; and he turned aside to the bank, which he climbed. On top, tangled in the underbrush about the trunks of several small spruce trees, was a high-water deposit of dry firewood—sticks and twigs principally, but also larger portions of seasoned branches and fine, dry, last-year's grasses. He threw down several large pieces on top of the snow. This served for a foundation and prevented the young flame from drowning itself in the snow it otherwise would melt. The flame he got by touching a match to a small shred of birch-bark that he took from his pocket. This burned even more readily than paper. Placing it on the foundation, he fed the young flame with wisps of dry grass and with the tiniest dry twigs.

He worked slowly and carefully, keenly aware of his danger. Gradually, as the flame grew stronger, he increased the size of the twigs with which he fed it. He squatted in the snow, pulling the twigs out from their entanglement in the brush and feeding directly to the flame. He knew there must be no failure. When it is seventy-five below zero, a man must not fail in his first attempt to build a fire—that is, if his feet are wet. If his feet are dry, and he fails, he can run along the trail for half a mile and restore his circulation. But the circulation of wet and freezing feet cannot be restored by running when it is seventy-five below. No matter how fast he runs, the wet feet will freeze the harder.

All this the man knew. The old-timer on Sulphur Creek had told him about it the previous fall, and now he was appreciating the advice. Already all sensation had gone out of his feet. To build the fire he had been forced to remove his mittens, and the fingers had quickly gone numb. His pace of four miles an hour had kept his heart pumping blood to the surface of his body and to all the extremities. But the instant he stopped, the action of the pump eased down. The cold of space smote the unprotected tip of the planet, and he, being on that unprotected tip, received the full force of the blow. The blood of his body recoiled before it. The blood was alive, like the dog, and like the dog it wanted to hide away and cover itself up from the fearful cold. So long as he walked four miles an hour, he pumped that blood, willy-nilly, to the surface; but now it ebbed away and sank down into the recesses of his body. The extremities were the first to feel its absence. His wet feet froze the faster, and his exposed fingers numbed the faster, though they had not yet begun to freeze. Nose and cheeks were already freezing, while the skin of all his body chilled as it lost its blood.

But he was safe. Toes and nose and cheeks would be only touched by the frost, for the fire was beginning to burn with strength. He was feeding it with twigs the size of his finger. In another minute he would be able to feed it with branches the size of his wrist, and then he could remove his wet foot-gear, and, while it dried, he could keep his naked feet warm by the fire, rubbing them at first, of course, with snow. The fire was a success. He was safe. He remembered the advice of the old-timer on Sulphur Creek, and smiled. The old-timer had been very serious in laying down the law that no man must travel alone in the Klondike after fifty below. Well, here he was; he had had the accident; he was alone; and he had saved himself. Those old-timers were rather womanish, some of them, he thought. All a man had to do was to keep his head, and he was all right. Any man who was a man could travel alone. But it was surprising, the rapidity with which his cheeks and nose were freezing. And he had not thought his fingers could go lifeless in so short a time. Lifeless they were, for he could scarcely make them move together to grip a twig, and they seemed remote from his body and from him. When he touched a twig, he had to look  and see whether or not he had hold of it. The wires were pretty well down between him and his finger-ends.

All of which counted for little. There was the fire, snapping and crackling and promising life with every dancing flame. He started to untie his moccasins. They were coated with ice; the thick German socks were like sheaths of iron halfway to the knees; and the moccasin strings were like rods of steel all twisted and knotted as by some conflagration. For a moment he tugged with his numbed fingers, then, realizing the folly of it, he drew his sheath-knife.

But before he could cut the strings, it happened. It was his own fault or, rather, his mistake. He should not have built the fire under the spruce tree. He should have built it in the open. But it had been easier to pull the twigs from the brush and drop them directly on the fire. Now the tree under which he had done this carried a weight of snow on its boughs. No wind had blown for weeks, and each bough was fully freighted. Each time he had pulled a twig he had communicated a slight agitation to the tree — an imperceptible agitation, so far as he was concerned, but an agitation sufficient to bring about the disaster. High up in the tree one bough capsized its load of snow. This fell on the boughs beneath, capsizing them. This process continued, spreading out and involving the whole tree. It grew like an avalanche, and it descended without warning upon the man and the fire, and the fire was blotted out! Where it had burned was a mantle of fresh and disordered snow.

The man was shocked. It was as though he had just heard his own sentence of death. For a moment he sat and stared at the spot where the fire had been. Then he grew very calm. Perhaps the old-timer on Sulphur Creek was right. If he had only had a trail-mate he would have been in no danger now. The trail-mate could have built the fire. Well, it was up to him to build the fire over again, and this second time there must be no failure. Even if he succeeded, he would most likely lose some toes. His feet must be badly frozen by now, and there would be some time before the second fire was ready.

Such were his thoughts, but he did not sit and think them. He was busy all the time they were passing through his mind. He made a new foundation for a fire, this time in the open, where no treacherous tree could blot it out. Next, he gathered dry grasses and tiny twigs from the high-water flotsam. He could not bring his fingers together to pull them out, but he was able to gather them by the handful. In this way he got many rotten twigs and bits of green moss that were undesirable, but it was the best he could do. He worked methodically, even collecting an armful of the larger branches to be used later when the fire gathered strength. And all the while the dog sat and watched him, a certain yearning wistfulness in its eyes, for it looked upon him as the fire-provider, and the fire was slow in coming.

When all was ready, the man reached in his pocket for a second piece of birch-bark. He knew the bark was there, and, though he could not feel it with his fingers, he could hear its crisp rustling as he fumbled for it. Try as he would, he could not clutch hold of it. And all the time, in his consciousness, was the knowledge that each instant his feet were freezing. This thought tended to put him in a panic, but he fought against it and kept calm. He pulled on his mittens with his teeth, and threshed his arms back and forth, beating his hands with all his might against his sides. He did this sitting down, and he stood up to do it; and all the while the dog sat in the snow, its wolf-brush of a tail curled around warmly over its forefeet, its sharp wolf-ears pricked forward intently as it watched the man. And the man, as he beat and threshed with his arms and hands, felt a great surge of envy as he regarded the creature that was warm and secure in its natural covering.

After a time he was aware of the first faraway signals of sensation in his beaten fingers. The faint tingling grew stronger till it evolved into a stinging ache that was excruciating, but which the man hailed with satisfaction. He stripped the mitten from his right hand and fetched forth the birch-bark. The exposed fingers were quickly going numb again. Next he brought out his bunch of sulphur matches. But the tremendous cold had already driven the life out of his fingers. In his effort to separate one match from the others, the whole bunch fell in the snow. He tried to pick it out of the snow, but failed. The dead fingers could neither touch nor clutch. He was very careful. He drove the thought of his freezing feet, and nose, and cheeks, out of his mind, devoting his whole soul to the matches. He watched, using the sense of vision in place of that of touch, and when he saw his fingers on each side the bunch, he closed them — that is, he willed to close them, for the wires were drawn, and the fingers did not obey. He pulled the mitten on the right hand, and beat it fiercely against his knee. Then, with both mittened hands, he scooped the bunch of matches, along with much snow, into his lap. Yet he was no better off.

After some manipulation he managed to get the bunch between the heels of his mittened hands. In this fashion he carried it to his mouth. The ice crackled and snapped when by a violent effort he opened his mouth. He drew the lower jaw in, curled the upper lip out of the way, and scraped the bunch with his upper teeth in

Nature is foreboding, relentless, neutral if not evil, and it is conquering the man.
Photo by Douglas Brown

order to separate a match. He succeeded in getting one, which he dropped on his lap. He was no better off. He could not pick it up. Then he devised a way. He picked it up in his teeth and scratched it on his leg. Twenty times he scratched before he succeeded in lighting it. As it flamed he held it with his teeth to the birch-bark. But the burning brimstone went up his nostrils and into his lungs, causing him to cough spasmodically. The match fell into the snow and went out.

The old-timer on Sulphur Creek was right, he thought in the moment of controlled despair that ensued: after fifty below, a man should travel with a partner. He beat his hands, but failed in exciting any sensation. Suddenly he bared both hands, removing the mittens with his teeth. He caught the whole bunch between the heels of his hands. His arm-muscles not being frozen enabled him to press the hand-heels tightly against the matches. Then he scratched the bunch along his leg. It flared into flame, seventy sulphur matches at once! There was no wind to blow them out. He kept his head to one side to escape the strangling fumes, and held the blazing bunch to the birch-bark. As he so held it, he became aware of sensation in his hand. His flesh was burning. He could smell it. Deep down below the surface he could feel it. The sensation developed into pain that grew acute. And still he endured it, holding the flame of the matches clumsily to the bark that would not light readily because his own burning hands were in the way, absorbing most of the flame.

At last, when he could endure no more, he jerked his hands apart. The blazing matches fell sizzling into the snow, but the birch-bark was alight. He began laying dry grasses and the tiniest twigs on the flame. He could not pick and choose, for he had to lift the fuel between the heels of his hands. Small pieces of rotten wood and green moss clung to the twigs, and he bit them off as well as he could with his teeth. He cherished the flame carefully and awkwardly. It meant life, and it must not perish. The withdrawal of blood from the surface of his body now made him begin to shiver, and he grew more awkward. A large piece of green moss fell squarely on the little fire. He tried to poke it out with his fingers, but his shivering frame made him poke too far, and he disrupted the nucleus of the little fire, the burning grasses and tiny twigs separating and scattering. He tried to poke them together again, but in spite of the tenseness of the effort, his shivering got away with him, and the twigs were hopelessly scattered. Each twig gushed a puff of smoke and went out. The fire-provider had failed. As he looked apathetically about him, his eyes chanced on the dog, sitting across the ruins of the fire from him, in the snow, making restless, hunching movements, slightly lifting one forefoot and then the other, shifting its weight back and forth on them with wistful eagerness.

The sight of the dog put a wild idea into his head. He remembered the tale of the man, caught in a blizzard, who killed a steer and crawled inside the carcass, and so was saved. He would kill the dog and bury his hands in the warm body until the numbness went out of them. Then he could build another fire. He spoke to the dog, calling it to him; but in his voice was a strange note of fear that frightened the animal, who had never known the man to speak in such way before. Something was the matter, and its suspicious nature sensed danger—it knew not what danger, but somewhere, somehow, in its brain arose an apprehension of the man. It flattened its ears down at the sound of the man's voice, and its restless, hunching movements and the liftings and shiftings of its forefeet became more pronounced; but it would not come to the man. He got on his hands and knees and crawled toward the dog. This unusual posture again excited suspicion, and the animal sidled mincingly away.

The man sat up in the snow for a moment and struggled for calmness. Then he pulled on his mittens, by means of his teeth, and got upon his feet. He glanced down at first in order to assure himself that he was really standing up, for the absence of sensation in his feet left him unrelated to the earth. His erect position in itself started to drive the webs of suspicion from the dog's mind; and when he spoke peremptorily, with the sound of whip-lashes in his voice, the dog rendered its customary allegiance and

The last image of the short story is the dog, the animal, whose primeval instincts rule.

came to him. As it came within reaching distance, the man lost his control. His arms flashed out to the dog, and he experienced genuine surprise when he discovered that his hands could not clutch, that there was neither bend nor feeling in the fingers. He had forgotten for the moment that they were frozen and that they were freezing more and more. All this happened quickly, and before the animal could get away, he encircled its body with his arms. He sat down in the snow, and in this fashion held the dog, while it snarled and whined and struggled.

But it was all he could do, hold its body encircled in his arms and sit there. He realized that he could not kill the dog. There was no way to do it. With his helpless hands he could neither draw nor hold his sheath-knife nor throttle the animal. He released it, and it plunged wildly away, with tail between its legs, and still snarling. It halted forty feet away and surveyed him curiously, with ears sharply pricked forward. The man looked down at his hands in order to locate them, and found them hanging on the ends of his arms. It struck him as curious that one should have to use his eyes in order to find out where his hands were. He began threshing his arms back and forth, beating the mittened hands against his sides. He did this for five minutes, violently, and his heart pumped enough blood up to the surface to put a stop to his shivering. But no sensation was aroused in the hands. He had an impression that they hung like weights on the ends of his arms, but when he tried to run the impression down, he could not find it.

A certain fear of death, dull and oppressive, came to him. This fear quickly became poignant as he realized that it was no longer a mere matter of freezing his fingers and toes, or of losing his hands and feet, but that it was a matter of life and death with the chances against him. This threw him into a panic, and he turned and ran up the creek-bed along the old, dim trail. The dog joined in behind and kept up with him. He ran blindly, without intention, in fear such as he had never known in his life. Slowly, as he ploughed and floundered through the snow, he began to see things again, — the banks of the creek, the old timber-jams, the leafless aspens, and the sky. The running made him feel better. He did not shiver. Maybe, if he ran on, his feet would thaw out; and, anyway, if he ran far enough, he would reach camp and the boys. Without doubt he would lose some fingers and toes and some of his face; but the boys would take care of him, and save the rest of him when he got there. And at the same time there was another thought in his mind that said he would never get to the camp and the boys; that it was too many miles away, that the freezing had too great a start on him, and that he would soon be stiff and dead. This thought he kept in the background and refused to consider. Sometimes it pushed itself forward and demanded to be heard, but he thrust it back and strove to think of other things.

It struck him as curious that he could run at all on feet so frozen that he could not feel them when they struck the earth and took the weight of his body. He seemed to himself to skim along above the surface and to have no connection with the earth. Somewhere he had once seen a winged Mercury, and he wondered if Mercury felt as he felt when skimming over the earth.

His theory of running until he reached camp and the boys had one flaw in it: he lacked the endurance. Several times he stumbled, and finally he tottered, crumpled up, and fell. When he tried to rise, he failed. He must sit and rest, he decided, and next time he would merely walk and keep on going. As he sat and regained his breath, he noted that he was feeling quite warm and comfortable. He was not shivering, and it even seemed that a warm glow had come to his chest and trunk. And yet, when he touched his nose or cheeks, there was no sensation. Running would not thaw them out. Nor would it thaw out his hands and feet. Then the thought came to him that the frozen portions of his body must be extending. He tried to keep this thought down, to forget it, to think of something else; he was aware of the panicky feeling that it caused, and he was afraid of the panic. But the thought asserted itself, and persisted, until it produced a vision of his body totally frozen. This was too much, and he made another wild run along the trail. Once he slowed down to a walk, but the thought of the freezing extending itself made him run again.

And all the time the dog ran with him, at his heels. When he fell down a second time, it curled its tail over its forefeet and sat in front of him, facing him, curiously eager and intent. The warmth and security of the animal angered him, and he cursed it till it flattened down its ears appeasingly. This time the shivering came more quickly upon the man. He was losing in his battle with the frost. It was creeping into his body from all sides. The thought of it drove him on, but he ran no more than a hundred feet, when he staggered and pitched headlong. It was his last panic. When he had recovered his breath and control, he sat up and entertained in his mind the conception of meeting death with dignity. However, the conception did not come to him in such terms. His idea of it was that he had been making a fool of himself, running around like a chicken with its head cut off—such was the simile that occurred to him. Well, he was bound to freeze anyway, and he might as well take it decently. With this new-found peace of mind came the first glimmerings of drowsiness. A good idea, he thought, to sleep off to death. It was like taking an anæsthetic. Freezing was not so bad as people thought. There were lots worse ways to die.

He pictured the boys finding his body next day. Suddenly he found himself with them, coming along the trail and looking for himself. And, still with them, he came around a turn in the trail and found himself lying in the snow. He did not belong with himself any more, for even then he was out of himself, standing with the boys and looking at himself in the snow. It certainly was cold, was his thought. When he got back to the States he could tell the folks what real cold was. He drifted on from this to a vision of the old-timer on Sulphur Creek. He could see him quite clearly, warm and comfortable, and smoking a pipe.

"You were right, old hoss; you were right," the man mumbled to the old-timer of Sulphur Creek.

Then the man drowsed off into what seemed to him the most comfortable and satisfying sleep he had ever known. The dog sat facing him and waiting. The brief day drew to a close in a long, slow twilight. There were no signs of a fire to be made, and, besides, never in the dog's experience had it known a man to sit like that in the snow and make no fire. As the twilight drew on, its eager yearning for the fire mastered it, and with a great lifting and shifting of forefeet, it whined softly, then flattened its ears down in anticipation of being chidden by the man. But the man remained silent. Later, the dog whined loudly. And still later it crept close to the man and caught the scent of death. This made the animal bristle and back away. A little longer it delayed, howling under the stars that leaped and danced and shone brightly in the cold sky. Then it turned and trotted up the trail in the direction of the camp it knew, where were the other food-providers and fire-providers.

"The Snow-Storm," by Ralph Waldo Emerson

Emerson the Romantic views snow and cold quite different than does naturalist Jack London.

Announced by all the trumpets of the sky,
Arrives the snow, and, driving o'er the fields,
Seems nowhere to alight: the whited air
Hides hills and woods, the river, and the   heaven,
And veils the farm-house at the garden's end.
The sled and traveller stopped, the courier's feet
Delayed, all friends shut out, the housemates sit
Around the radiant fireplace, enclosed
In a tumultuous privacy of storm.
Come see the north wind's masonry.
Out of an unseen quarry evermore
Furnished with tile, the fierce artificer

Curves his white bastions with projected roof
Round every windward stake, or tree, or door.
Speeding, the myriad-handed, his wild work
So fanciful, so savage, nought cares he
For number or proportion. Mockingly,
On coop or kennel he hangs Parian wreaths;
A swan-like form invests the hidden thorn;
Fills up the farmer's lane from wall to wall,
Maugre the farmer's sighs; and, at the gate,
A tapering turret overtops the work.
And when his hours are numbered, and the world
Is all his own, retiring, as he were not,
Leaves, when the sun appears, astonished Art
To mimic in slow structures, stone by stone,
Built in an age, the mad wind's night-work,
The frolic architecture of the snow.

Individual and Nature in the Bible

Moses and the Red Sea: Exodus 14:10–31

As Pharaoh approached, the Israelites looked up, and there were the Egyptians, marching after them. They were terrified and cried out to the LORD. They said to Moses, "Was it because there were no graves in Egypt that you brought us to the desert to die? What have you done to us by bringing us out of Egypt? Didn't we say to you in Egypt, 'Leave us alone; let us serve the

Egyptians'? It would have been better for us to serve the Egyptians than to die in the desert!"

Moses answered the people, "Do not be afraid. Stand firm and you will see the deliverance the LORD will bring you today. The Egyptians you see today you will never see again. The LORD will fight for you; you need only to be still."

Then the LORD said to Moses, "Why are you crying out to me? Tell the Israelites to move on. Raise your staff and stretch out your hand over the sea to

divide the water so that the Israelites can go through the sea on dry ground. I will harden the hearts of the Egyptians so that they will go in after them. And I will gain glory through Pharaoh and all his army, through his chariots and his horsemen. The Egyptians will know that I am the LORD when I gain glory through Pharaoh, his chariots and his horsemen."

Then the angel of God, who had been traveling in front of Israel's army, withdrew and went behind them. The pillar of cloud also moved from in front and stood behind them, coming between the armies of Egypt and Israel. Throughout the night the cloud brought darkness to the one side and light to the other side; so neither went near the other all night long.

Then Moses stretched out his hand over the sea, and all that night the LORD drove the sea back with a strong east wind and turned it into dry land. The waters were divided, and the Israelites went through the sea on dry ground, with a wall of water on their right and on their left.

The Egyptians pursued them, and all Pharaoh's horses and chariots and horsemen followed them into the sea. During the last watch of the night the LORD looked down from the pillar of fire and cloud at the Egyptian army and threw it into confusion. He jammed the wheels of their chariots so that they had difficulty driving. And the Egyptians said, "Let's get away from the Israelites! The LORD is fighting for them against Egypt."

Then the LORD said to Moses, "Stretch out your hand over the sea so that the waters may flow back over the Egyptians and their chariots and horsemen." Moses stretched out his hand over the sea, and at daybreak the sea went back to its place. The Egyptians were fleeing toward it, and the LORD swept them into the sea. The water flowed back and covered the chariots and horsemen — the entire army of Pharaoh that had followed the Israelites into the sea. Not one of them survived.

But the Israelites went through the sea on dry ground, with a wall of water on their right and on their left. That day the LORD saved Israel from the hands of the Egyptians, and Israel saw the Egyptians lying dead on the shore. And when the Israelites saw the mighty hand of the LORD displayed against the Egyptians, the people feared the LORD and put their trust in him and in Moses his servant.

Jesus Calms the Storm: Matthew 8:23–27

Then he got into the boat and his disciples followed him. Suddenly a furious storm came up on the lake, so that the waves swept over the boat. But Jesus was sleeping. The disciples went and woke him, saying, "Lord, save us! We're going to drown!"

He replied, "You of little faith, why are you so afraid?" Then he got up and rebuked the winds and the waves, and it was completely calm.

The men were amazed and asked, "What kind of man is this? Even the winds and the waves obey him!"

Feeding the Five Thousand: John 6:1–14

Sometime after this, Jesus crossed to the far shore of the Sea of Galilee (that is, the Sea of Tiberias), and a great crowd of people followed him because they saw the signs he had performed by healing the sick. Then Jesus went up on a mountainside and sat down with his disciples. The Jewish Passover Festival was near.

When Jesus looked up and saw a great crowd coming toward him, he said to Philip, "Where shall we buy bread for these people to eat?" He asked this only to

test him, for he already had in mind what he was going to do.

Philip answered him, "It would take more than half a year's wages to buy enough bread for each one to have a bite!"

Another of his disciples, Andrew, Simon Peter's brother, spoke up, "Here is a boy with five small barley loaves and two small fish, but how far will they go among so many?"

Jesus said, "Have the people sit down." There was plenty of grass in that place, and they sat down (about five thousand men were there). Jesus then took the loaves, gave thanks, and distributed to those who were seated as much as they wanted. He did the same with the fish.

When they had all had enough to eat, he said to his disciples, "Gather the pieces that are left over. Let nothing be wasted." So they gathered them and filled twelve baskets with the pieces of the five barley loaves left over by those who had eaten.

After the people saw the sign Jesus performed, they began to say, "Surely this is the Prophet who is to come into the world." Jesus, knowing that they intended to come and make him king by force, withdrew again to a mountain by himself.

Jesus Walks on the Water: John 6:16–24

When evening came, his disciples went down to the lake, where they got into a boat and set off across the lake for Capernaum. By now it was dark, and Jesus had not yet joined them. A strong wind was blowing and the waters grew rough. When they had rowed about three or four miles, they saw Jesus approaching the boat, walking on the water; and they were frightened. But he said to them, "It is I; don't be afraid." Then they were willing to take him into the boat, and immediately the boat reached the shore where they were heading. The next day the crowd that had stayed on the opposite shore of the lake realized that only one boat had been there, and  that Jesus had not entered it with his disciples, but that they had gone away alone. Then some boats from Tiberias landed near the place where the people had eaten the bread after the Lord had given thanks. Once the crowd realized that neither Jesus nor his disciples were there, they got into the boats and went to Capernaum in search of Jesus.

The Star of Bethlehem: Matthew 2:1–9

After Jesus was born in Bethlehem in Judea, during the time of King Herod, Magi from the east came to Jerusalem and asked, "Where is the one who has been born king of the Jews? We saw his star when it rose and have come to worship him."

When King Herod heard this he was disturbed, and all Jerusalem with him. When he had called together all the people's chief priests and teachers of the law, he asked them where the Messiah was to be born. "In Bethlehem in Judea," they replied, "for this is what the prophet has written:

"'But you, Bethlehem, in the land of Judah,

    are by no means least among the rulers of Judah;

    for out of you will come a ruler

    who will shepherd my people Israel.'"

Then Herod called the Magi secretly and found out from them the exact time

the star had appeared. He sent them to Bethlehem and said, "Go and search carefully for the child. As soon as you find him, report to me, so that I too may go and worship him."

After they had heard the king, they went on their way, and the star they had seen when it rose went ahead of them until it stopped over the place where the child was.

The Individual and Society

Following are selections showing how famous authors develop *themes* about how the individual relates with society.

Crime and Punishment, by Fyodor Dostoyevsky

Themes

Man struggling in society. Raskolnikov, the protagonist, commits two murders, yet Dostoyevsky asks readers to sympathize with him. Raskolnikov is part cold-blooded killer and part compassionate human being. The struggle between those two parts of Raskolnikov's character — his dual personality — is the central theme of the novel. At the same time, as Raskolnikov struggles with his growing sense of remorse, fed by Sonia, he begins to struggle with society itself.

Falling in love. The novel *Crime and Punishment* is a love story, or rather several love stories. When Raskolnikov is at last able to admit his love for Sonia and to accept her Christian beliefs, he begins his journey to salvation. In contrast, when his sister Dunya repels the advances of Svidrigailov, he commits suicide. As one critic explains, "Dostoyevsky suggests that human love is an expression of divine love, with the power to save or d---."

The wages of sin is death; forgiveness brings life. Dostoyevsky analyzes the effect of criminal behavior, both on the perpetrator and on the people around him. Sinners are doomed to isolation and failure. But there is forgiveness too. Raskolnikov murders, but through Sonia he finds his way to the cross and is saved. But Raskolnikov learns that he must admit his bad choices publicly before he can be saved.

Rehabilitative aspects of suffering. At first, Sonia and Raskolnikov think differently about suffering. She believes suffering ameliorates a person and that it can be endured because God will reward the sufferer. She has a strong sense of God's Sovereign Grace. At first, Raskolnikov insists that suffering is wasted misery. He's impatient and skeptical of the notion that God cares.

Objective morality. Dostoyevski believes that humans must live by an objective ethical standard. Things are either right or they are wrong. Ethics are not relative. Raskolnikov, notwithstanding his virginal naïveté in the universe, had no right to murder the old ladies. Men do not break the laws of God; the laws of God break men.

Yet, at the same time, he suggests that immoral and even illegal behavior can be forgiven. Sonia's prostitution doesn't keep her from God; Dunya's lies to shield her mother from Raskolnikov's trial are justifiable.

Providence. Raskolnikov says over and over that Fate caused his actions. Yet the author rejects this notion of Fate as the power that predetermines events. Dostoyevsky understands that a loving, benevolent God is in control of the universe.

In the book's last chapter (below), Sonia has followed Raskolnikov to Siberia and to prison. She loves him unconditionally, but he still does not understand.

Raskolnikov is once more sick, but it is psychological. He believes that he made a huge mistake, he does admit—but anybody could have done that. Worse yet, he feels he's got nothing left to live for.

Raskolnikov does realize that people hate him and that Sonia is loved. But he can't understand what it is about her that makes people feel that way.

It is now Easter, and a new feeling is discovered: worry and compassion. Sonia is sick and Raskolnikov is worried.

When Sonia recovers enough to come to see him, a miracle occurs. Raskolnikov weeps and then kneels before her. He loves Sonia, and he loves her God. He is saved. In their faces glow "the dawn of a new future, a perfect resurrection into a new life." Jesus Christ has raised them from the death of sin and judgment! As one critic explains, "It is the love of God that has shown through Sonia and her suffering. Loving her, Raskolnikov is also ready to love God."

Dostoyevsky ends the novel on a note of hope and joy. With Christ as one's Savior, the past is expiated, and the future holds infinite possibility!

Epilogue, Chapter 2, Paragraphs 1, 11–30

He was ill a long time. But it was not the horrors of prison life, not the hard labor, the bad food, the shaven head, or the patched clothes that crushed him. What did he care for all those trials and hardships! He was even glad of the hard work. Physically exhausted, he could at least reckon on a few hours of quiet sleep. And what was the food to him — the thin cabbage soup with beetles floating in it? In the past as a student he had often not had even that. His clothes were warm and suited to his manner of life. He did not even feel the fetters. Was he ashamed of his shaven head and parti-colored coat? Before whom? Before Sonia? Sonia was afraid of him, how could he be ashamed before her? And yet he was ashamed even before Sonia, whom he tortured because of it with his contemptuous rough manner. But it was not his shaven head and his fetters he was ashamed of: his pride had been stung to the quick. It was wounded pride that made him ill. Oh, how happy he would have been if he could have blamed himself! He could have borne anything then, even shame and disgrace. But he judged himself severely, and his exasperated conscience found no particularly terrible fault in his past, except a simple blunder which might happen to anyone. He was ashamed just because he, Raskolnikov, had so hopelessly, stupidly come to grief through some decree of blind fate, and must humble himself and submit to "the idiocy" of a sentence, if he were anyhow to be at peace. . . .

In prison, of course, there was a great deal he did not see and did not want to see; he lived as it were with downcast eyes. It was loathsome and unbearable for him to look. But in the end there was much that surprised him and he began, as it were involuntarily, to notice much that he had not suspected before. What surprised him most of all was the terrible impossible gulf that lay between him and all the rest. They seemed to be a different species, and he looked at them and they at him with distrust and hostility. He felt and knew the reasons of his isolation, but he would never have admitted till then that those reasons were so deep and strong. There were some Polish exiles, political prisoners, among them. They simply looked down upon all the rest as ignorant churls; but Raskolnikov could not look upon them like that. He saw that these ignorant men were in many respects far wiser than the Poles. There were some Russians who were just as contemptuous, a former officer and two seminarists. Raskolnikov saw their mistake as clearly. He was disliked and avoided by everyone; they even began to hate him at last—why, he could not tell. Men who had been far more guilty despised and laughed at his crime.

"You're a gentleman," they used to say. "You shouldn't hack about with an axe; that's not a gentleman's work."

The second week in Lent, his turn came to take the sacrament with his gang. He went to church and prayed with the others. A quarrel broke out one day, he did not know how. All fell on him at once in a fury.

"You're an infidel! You don't believe in God," they shouted. "You ought to be killed."

He had never talked to them about God nor his belief, but they wanted to kill him as an infidel. He said nothing. One of the prisoners rushed at him in a perfect frenzy. Raskolnikov awaited him calmly and silently; his eyebrows did not quiver, his face did not flinch. The guard succeeded in intervening between him and his assailant, or there would have been bloodshed.

There was another question he could not decide: why were they all so fond of Sonia? She did not try to win their favour; she rarely met them, sometimes only she came to see him at work for a moment. And yet everybody knew her, they knew that she had come out to follow him, knew how and where she lived. She never gave them money, did them no particular services. Only once at Christmas she sent them all presents of pies and rolls. But by degrees closer relations sprang up between them and Sonia. She would write and post letters for them to their relations. Relations of the prisoners who visited the town, at their instructions, left with Sonia presents and money for them. Their wives and sweethearts knew her and used to visit her. And when she visited Raskolnikov at work, or met a party of the prisoners on the road, they all took off their hats to her. "Little mother Sofya Semyonovna, you are our dear, good little mother," coarse branded criminals said to that frail little creature. She would smile and bow to them and everyone was delighted when she smiled. They even admired her gait and turned round to watch her walking; they admired her too for being so little, and, in fact, did not know what to admire her most for. They even came to her for help in their illnesses.

He was in the hospital from the middle of Lent till after Easter. When he was better, he remembered the dreams he had while he was feverish and delirious. He dreamt that the whole world was condemned to a terrible new strange plague that had come to Europe from the depths of Asia. All were to be destroyed except a very few chosen. Some new sorts of microbes were attacking the bodies of men, but these microbes were endowed with intelligence and will. Men attacked by them became at once mad and furious. But never had men considered themselves so intellectual and so completely in possession of the truth as these sufferers, never had they considered their decisions, their scientific conclusions, their moral convictions so infallible. Whole villages, whole towns and peoples went mad from the infection. All were excited and did not understand one another. Each thought that he alone had the truth and was wretched looking at the others, beat himself on the breast, wept, and wrung his hands. They did not know how to judge and could not agree what to consider evil and what good; they did not know whom to blame, whom to justify. Men killed each other in a sort of senseless spite. They gathered together in armies against one another, but even on the march the armies would begin attacking each other, the ranks would be broken and the soldiers would fall on each other, stabbing and cutting, biting and devouring each other. The alarm bell was ringing all day long in the towns; men rushed together, but why they were summoned and who was summoning them no one knew. The most ordinary trades were abandoned, because everyone proposed his own ideas, his own improvements, and they could not agree. The land too was abandoned. Men met in groups, agreed on something, swore to keep together, but at once began on something quite different from what they had proposed. They accused one another, fought and killed each other. There were conflagrations and famine. All men and all things were involved in destruction. The plague spread and moved further and further. Only a few men could be saved in the whole world. They were a pure chosen people, destined to found a new race and a new life, to renew and purify the earth, but no one had seen these men, no one had heard their words and their voices.

Raskolnikov was worried that this senseless dream haunted his memory so miserably, the impression of this feverish delirium persisted so long. The second week after Easter had come. There were warm bright spring days; in the prison ward the grating windows under which the sentinel paced were opened. Sonia had only been able to visit him twice during his illness; each time she had to obtain permission, and it was difficult. But she often used to come to the hospital yard, especially in the evening, sometimes only to stand a minute and look up at the windows of the ward.

One evening, when he was almost well again, Raskolnikov fell asleep. On waking up he chanced to go to the window, and at once saw Sonia in the distance at the hospital gate. She seemed to be waiting for someone. Something stabbed him to the heart at that minute. He shuddered and moved away from the window. Next day Sonia did not come, nor the day after; he noticed that he was expecting her uneasily. At last he was discharged. On reaching the prison he learnt from the convicts that Sofya Semyonovna was lying ill at home and was unable to go out.

He was very uneasy and sent to inquire after her; he soon learnt that her illness was not dangerous. Hearing that he was anxious about her, Sonia sent him a penciled note, telling him that she was much better, that she had a slight cold and that she would soon, very soon come and see him at his work. His heart throbbed painfully as he read it.

Again it was a warm bright day. Early in the morning, at six o'clock, he went off to work on the river bank, where they used to pound alabaster and where there was a kiln for baking it in a shed. There were only three of them sent. One of the convicts went with the guard to the fortress to fetch a tool; the other began getting the wood ready and laying it in the kiln. Raskolnikov came out of the shed on to the river bank, sat down on a heap of logs by the shed and began gazing at the wide deserted river. From the high bank a broad landscape opened before him, the sound of singing floated faintly audible from the other bank. In the vast steppe, bathed in sunshine, he could just see, like black specks, the nomads' tents. There was freedom, there other men were living, utterly unlike those here; there time itself seemed to stand still, as though the age of Abraham and his flocks had not passed. Raskolnikov sat gazing, his thoughts passed into day-dreams, into contemplation; he thought of nothing, but a vague restlessness excited and troubled him. Suddenly he found Sonia beside him; she had come up noiselessly and sat down at his side. It was still quite early; the morning chill was still keen. She wore her poor old burnous [one-piece cloak] and the green shawl;

her face still showed signs of illness, it was thinner and paler. She gave him a joyful smile of welcome, but held out her hand with her usual timidity. She was always timid of holding out her hand to him and sometimes did not offer it at all, as though afraid he would repel it. He always took her hand as though with repugnance, always seemed vexed to meet her and was sometimes obstinately silent throughout her visit. Sometimes she trembled before him and went away deeply grieved. But now their hands did not part. He stole a rapid glance at her and dropped his eyes on the ground without speaking. They were alone, no one had seen them. The guard had turned away for the time.

How it happened he did not know. But all at once something seemed to seize him and fling him at her feet. He wept and threw his arms round her knees. For the first instant she was terribly frightened and she turned pale. She jumped up and looked at him trembling. But at the same moment she understood, and a light of infinite happiness came into her eyes. She knew and had no doubt that he loved her beyond everything and that at last the moment had come. . . .

They wanted to speak, but could not; tears stood in their eyes. They were both pale and thin; but those sick pale faces were bright with the dawn of a new future, of a full resurrection into a new life. They were renewed by love; the heart of each held infinite sources of life for the heart of the other. They resolved to wait and be patient. They had another seven years to wait, and what terrible suffering and what infinite happiness before them! But he had risen again and he knew it and felt it in all his being, while she — she only lived in his life.

On the evening of the same day, when the barracks were locked, Raskolnikov lay on his plank bed and thought of her. He had even fancied that day that all the convicts who had been his enemies looked at him differently; he had even entered into talk with them and they answered him in a friendly way. He remembered that now, and thought it was bound to be so. Wasn't everything now bound to be changed?

He thought of her. He remembered how continually he had tormented her and wounded her heart. He remembered her pale and thin little face. But these recollections scarcely troubled him now; he knew with what infinite love he would now repay all her sufferings. And what were all, all the agonies of the past! Everything, even his crime, his sentence and imprisonment, seemed to him now in the first rush of feeling an external, strange fact with which he had no concern. But he could not think for long together of anything that evening, and he could not have analyzed anything consciously; he was simply feeling. Life had stepped into the place of theory and something quite different would work itself out in his mind.

Under his pillow lay the New Testament. He took it up mechanically. The book belonged to Sonia; it was the one from which she had read the raising of Lazarus to him. At first he was afraid that she would worry him about religion, would talk about the gospel and pester him with books. But to his great surprise she had not once approached the subject and had not even offered him the Testament. He had asked her for it himself not long before his illness and she brought him the book without a word. Till now he had not opened it.

He did not open it now, but one thought passed through his mind: "Can her convictions not be mine now? Her feelings, her aspirations at least. . . ."

She too had been greatly agitated that day, and at night she was taken ill again. But she was so happy—and so unexpectedly happy—that she was almost frightened of her happiness. Seven years, only seven years! At the beginning of their happiness at some moments they were both ready to look on those seven years as though they were seven days. He did not know that the new life would not be given him for nothing, that he would have to pay dearly for it, that it would cost him great striving, great suffering.

But that is the beginning of a new story—the story of the gradual renewal of a man, the story of his gradual regeneration, of his passing from one world into another, of his initiation into a new unknown life. That might be the subject of a new story, but our present story is ended.

Comments on Crime and Punishment

Ralph Harper reflects on Raskolnikov's inward debate: "He represses pity as long as it gets in the way of the egoism that his rational crime is fed by. But he never denies the necessity of pity. "Pain and suffering are always inevitable for a large intelligence and a deep heart. The really great men must, I think, have great sadness on earth." Not only does he never deny pity, he is constantly tortured by his Titanic pride. He has an instinct within him that solemnly condemns him even while he refuses to listen. Time after time Raskolnikov's pity produces works of compassion, charity, and self-sacrifice. *Crime and Punishment* is the story of the half-conscious debate of inwardness rising slowly and surely to a fully conscious plane. Raskolnikov confesses to the police, not because he has failed or been caught, but because he knows he cannot resolve the torment of his questionableness or suppress the inward debate."

Pride and Prejudice, by Jane Austen

Themes

Poise and manners. While Jane Austen approves of the correct forms of social behavior and protocol, she makes fun of them when they are carried to excess, and she does not approve of them as substitutes for decent, just behavior.

Privilege and responsibility. The English gentry and nobility were highly privileged people. When Darcy is criticized for being proud, Charlotte Lucas comes to his defense. Privilege brings with it responsibilities, which good characters like Darcy take seriously. For example, his housekeeper tells of his fair treatment of his servants and tenants. And later, Darcy rescues Lydia and Wickham. Darcy's sense of responsibility impresses Elizabeth and finally wipes away her prejudice against him. Darcy is a poster boy for the English gentry, a decent sort of fellow.

Human relationships. Jane Austen is known for her perceptive depiction of parlor scenes and romances. Thus one critic explains: "In *Pride and Prejudice*, for example, she shows us all kinds of marriages, no two of them alike: Mr. and Mrs. Bennet, Charlotte and Mr. Collins, Lydia and Wickham, Jane and Bingley, and, finally, Elizabeth and Darcy. She also shows us other kinds of relationships: the sisterly relationship of Jane and Elizabeth, the aunt and niece relationship of Elizabeth and Mrs. Gardiner. Finally, there are the friendships: Elizabeth and Charlotte enjoy a friendship of equals, even though they do not always agree. Darcy and Bingley, on the other hand, have an odd relationship in which Bingley confesses himself to be in awe of Darcy, and Darcy, the stronger character, has taken on a responsibility for his friend's welfare—to the point of manipulating him away from courting Jane. At the end of the novel, when Darcy and Elizabeth are married, Darcy's sister Georgiana is amazed that Elizabeth can tease Darcy and make him laugh at himself—a privilege, as Jane Austen points out, that a wife may have but not a younger sister. In this final subtle touch Jane Austen shows her mastery of the art of relationships."

Chapter 1

It is a truth universally acknowledged, that a single man in possession of a good fortune, must be in want of a wife.

However little known the feelings or views of such a man may be on his first entering a neighbourhood, this truth is so well fixed in the minds of the surrounding families, that he is considered the rightful property of some one or other of their daughters.

"My dear Mr. Bennet," said his lady to him one day, "have you heard that Netherfield Park is let at last?"

Mr. Bennet replied that he had not.

"But it is," returned she; "for Mrs. Long has just been here, and she told me all about it."

Mr. Bennet made no answer.

"Do you not want to know who has taken it?" cried his wife impatiently. "You want to tell me, and I have no objection to hearing it."

This was invitation enough.

"Why, my dear, you must know, Mrs. Long says that Netherfield is taken by a young man of large fortune from the north of England; that he came down on Monday in a chaise and four to see the place, and was so much delighted with it, that he agreed with Mr. Morris immediately; that he is to take possession before Michaelmas, and some of his servants are to be in the house by the end of next week."

"What is his name?"

"Bingley."

"Is he married or single?"

"Oh! Single, my dear, to be sure! A single man of large fortune; four or five thousand a year. What a fine thing for our girls!"

"How so? How can it affect them?"

"My dear Mr. Bennet," replied his wife, "how can you be so tiresome! You must know that I am thinking of his marrying one of them."

"Is that his design in settling here?"

"Design! Nonsense, how can you talk so! But it is very likely that he may fall in love with one of them, and therefore you must visit him as soon as he comes."

"I see no occasion for that. You and the girls may go, or you may send them by themselves, which perhaps will be still better, for as you are as handsome as any of them, Mr. Bingley may like you the best of the party."

"My dear, you flatter me. I certainly have had my share of beauty, but I do not pretend to be anything extraordinary now. When a woman has five grown-up daughters, she ought to give over thinking of her own beauty."

"In such cases, a woman has not often much beauty to think of."

"But, my dear, you must indeed go and see Mr. Bingley when he comes into the neighbourhood."

"It is more than I engage for, I assure you."

Notice Austen's skillful use of dialogue.

"But consider your daughters. Only think what an establishment it would be for one of them. Sir William and Lady Lucas are determined to go, merely on that account, for in general, you know, they visit no newcomers. Indeed you must go, for it will be impossible for us to visit him if you do not."

"You are over-scrupulous, surely. I dare say Mr. Bingley will be very glad to see you; and I will send a few lines by you to assure him of my hearty consent to his marrying whichever he chooses of the girls; though I must throw in a good word for my little Lizzy."

"I desire you will do no such thing. Lizzy is not a bit better than the others; and I am sure she is not half so handsome as Jane, nor half so good-humoured as Lydia. But you are always giving her the preference."

"They have none of them much to recommend them," replied he; "they are all silly and ignorant like other girls; but Lizzy has something more of quickness than her sisters."

"Mr. Bennet, how can you abuse your own children in such a way? You take delight in vexing me. You have no compassion for my poor nerves."

"You mistake me, my dear. I have a high respect for your nerves. They are my old friends. I have heard you mention them with consideration these last twenty years at least."

"Ah, you do not know what I suffer."

"But I hope you will get over it, and live to see many young men of four thousand a year come into the neighbourhood."

"It will be no use to us, if twenty such should come, since you will not visit them."

"Depend upon it, my dear, that when there are twenty, I will visit them all."

Mr. Bennet was so odd a mixture of quick parts, sarcastic humour, reserve, and caprice, that the experience of three-and-twenty years had been insufficient to make his wife understand his character. Her mind was less difficult to develop. She was a woman of mean understanding, little information, and uncertain temper. When she was discontented, she fancied herself nervous. The business of her life was to get her daughters married; its solace was visiting and news.

The Individual and Society in the Bible

The Sermon on the Mount: Matthew 5–6

Now when Jesus saw the crowds, he went up on a mountainside and sat down. His disciples came to him, and he began to teach them.

He said:

"Blessed are the poor in spirit, for theirs is the kingdom of heaven.

Blessed are those who mourn,

for they will be comforted.

Blessed are the meek,

for they will inherit the earth.

Blessed are those who hunger and thirst for righteousness,

for they will be filled.

Blessed are the merciful,

for they will be shown mercy.

Blessed are the pure in heart,

for they will see God.

Blessed are the peacemakers,

for they will be called children of
God.

Blessed are those who are persecuted
because of righteousness,

for theirs is the kingdom of
heaven.

"Blessed are you when people insult you, persecute you and falsely say all kinds of evil against you because of me. Rejoice and be glad, because great is your reward in heaven, for in the same way they persecuted the prophets who were before you.

"You are the salt of the earth. But if the salt loses its saltiness, how can it be made salty again? It is no longer good for anything, except to be thrown out and trampled underfoot.

"You are the light of the world. A town built on a hill cannot be hidden. Neither do people light a lamp and put it under a bowl. Instead they put it on its stand, and it gives light to everyone in the house. In the same way, let your light shine before others, that they may see your good deeds and glorify your Father in heaven.

"Do not think that I have come to abolish the Law or the Prophets; I have not come to abolish them but to fulfill them. For truly I tell you, until heaven and earth disappear, not the smallest letter, not the least stroke of a pen, will by any means disappear from the Law until everything is accomplished. Therefore anyone who sets aside one of the least of these commands and teaches others accordingly will be called least in the kingdom of heaven, but whoever practices and teaches these commands will be called great in the kingdom of heaven. For I tell you that unless your righteousness surpasses that of the Pharisees and the teachers of the law, you will certainly not enter the kingdom of heaven.

"You have heard that it was said to the people long ago, 'You shall not murder, and anyone who murders will be subject to judgment.' But I tell you that anyone who is angry with a brother or sister will be subject to judgment. Again, anyone who says to a brother or sister, 'Raca,' is answerable to the court. And anyone who says, 'You fool!' will be in danger of the fire of hell.

"Therefore, if you are offering your gift at the altar and there remember that your brother or sister has something against you, leave your gift there in front of the altar. First go and be reconciled to them; then come and offer your gift.

"Settle matters quickly with your adversary who is taking you to court. Do it while you are still together on the way, or your adversary may hand you over to the judge, and the judge may hand you over to the officer, and you may be thrown into prison. Truly I tell you, you will not get out until you have paid the last penny.

"You have heard that it was said, 'You shall not commit adultery.' But I tell you that anyone who looks at a woman lustfully has already committed adultery with her in his heart. If your right eye causes you to stumble, gouge it out and throw it away. It is better for you to lose one part of your body than for your whole body to be thrown into hell. And if your right hand causes you to stumble, cut it off and throw it away. It is better for you to lose one part of your body than for your whole body to go into hell.

"It has been said, 'Anyone who divorces his wife must give her a certificate of divorce.' But I tell you that anyone who divorces his wife, except for sexual immorality, makes her the victim of adultery, and anyone who marries a divorced woman commits adultery.

"Again, you have heard that it was said to the people long ago, 'Do not break your oath, but fulfill to the Lord the vows you have made.' But I tell you, do not swear an oath at all: either by heaven, for it is God's throne; or by the earth, for it is his footstool; or by Jerusalem, for it is the city of the Great King. And do not swear by your head, for you cannot make even one hair white or black. All you need to say is simply 'Yes' or 'No'; anything beyond this comes from the evil one.

"You have heard that it was said, 'Eye for eye, and tooth for tooth.' But I tell you, do not resist an evil person. If anyone slaps you on the right cheek, turn to them the other cheek also. And if anyone wants to sue you and take your shirt, hand over your coat as well. If anyone forces you to go one mile, go with them two miles. Give to the one who asks you, and do not turn away from the one who wants to borrow from you.

"You have heard that it was said, 'Love your neighbor and hate your enemy.' But I tell you, love your enemies and pray for those who persecute you, that you may be children of your Father in heaven. He causes his sun to rise on the evil and the good, and sends rain on the righteous and the unrighteous. If you love those who love you, what reward will you get? Are not even the tax collectors doing that? And if you greet only your own people, what are you doing more than others? Do not even pagans do that? Be perfect, therefore, as your heavenly Father is perfect.

Jesus represents a radical departure from Hellenistic (Greek) and even from the usual Jewish ethics. He calls his disciples to radical obedience and dependence on God. His followers must be meek, go beyond the letter of the law to its spirit, not retaliate, love their enemies, do what is right when no one sees, depend on God for their needs, pursue God's purposes rather than their own, and leave judgment to God. In short, true people of the kingdom live for God, not for themselves. A very tall order!

"Be careful not to practice your righteousness in front of others to be seen by them. If you do, you will have no reward from your Father in heaven.

"So when you give to the needy, do not announce it with trumpets, as the hypocrites do in the synagogues and on the streets, to be honored by others. Truly I tell you, they have received their reward in full. But when you give to the needy, do not let your left hand know what your right hand is doing, so that your giving may be in secret. Then your Father, who sees what is done in secret, will reward you.

"And when you pray, do not be like the hypocrites, for they love to pray standing in the synagogues and on the street corners to be seen by others. Truly I tell you, they have received their reward in full. But when you pray, go into your room, close the door and pray to your Father, who is unseen. Then your Father, who sees what is done in secret, will reward you. And when you pray, do not keep on babbling like pagans, for they think they will be heard because of their many words. Do not be like them, for your Father knows what you need before you ask him.

"This, then, is how you should pray:
"'Our Father in heaven,
hallowed be your name,
your kingdom come,
your will be done,
    on earth as it is in heaven.
Give us today our daily bread.
And forgive us our debts,
    as we also have forgiven our debtors.
And lead us not into temptation,
    but deliver us from the evil one.'

For if you forgive other people when they sin against you, your heavenly Father will also forgive you. But if you do not forgive others their sins, your Father will not forgive your sins.

For if you forgive other people when they sin against you, your heavenly Father will also forgive you.

"When you fast, do not look somber as the hypocrites do, for they disfigure their faces to show others they are fasting. Truly I tell you, they have received their reward in full. But when you fast, put oil on your head and wash your face, so that it will not be obvious to others that you are fasting, but only to your Father, who is unseen; and your Father, who sees what is done in secret, will reward you.

"Do not store up for yourselves treasures on earth, where moths and vermin destroy, and where thieves break in and steal. But store up for yourselves treasures in heaven, where moths and vermin do not destroy, and where thieves do not break in and steal. For where your treasure is, there your heart will be also.

"The eye is the lamp of the body. If your eyes are healthy, your whole body will be full of light. But if your eyes are unhealthy, your whole body will be full of darkness. If then the light within you is darkness, how great is that darkness!

"No one can serve two masters. Either you will hate the one and love the other, or you will be devoted to the one and despise the other. You cannot serve both God and money.

"Therefore I tell you, do not worry about your life, what you will eat or drink; or about your body, what you will wear. Is not life more than food, and the body more than clothes? Look at the birds of the air; they do not sow or reap or store away in barns, and yet your heavenly Father feeds them. Are you not much more valuable than they? Can any one of you by worrying add a single hour to your life?

"And why do you worry about clothes? See how the flowers of the field grow. They do not labor or spin. Yet I tell you that not even Solomon in all his splendor was dressed like one of these. If that is how God clothes the grass of the field, which is here today and tomorrow is thrown into the fire, will he not much more clothe you—you of little faith? So do not worry, saying, 'What shall we eat?' or 'What shall we drink?' or 'What shall we wear?' For the pagans run after all these things, and your heavenly Father knows that you need them. But seek first his kingdom and his righteousness, and all these things will be given to you as well. Therefore do not worry about tomorrow, for tomorrow will worry about itself. Each day has enough trouble of its own.

The Cost of Discipleship, by Dietrich Bonhoeffer

Cheap grace means grace sold on the market like a cheapjack's wares. The sacraments, the forgiveness of sin, and the consolations of religion are thrown away at cut-rate prices. Grace is represented as the Church's inexhaustible treasury, from which she showers blessings with generous hands, without asking questions or fixing limits. Grace without price; grace without cost! And the essence of grace, we suppose, is that the account has been paid in advance; and, because it has been paid, everything can be had for nothing. Since the cost was infinite, the possibilities of using and spending it are infinite. What would grace be, if it were not cheap? . . . In such a Church the world finds a cheap covering for its sins; no contrition is required, still less any real desire to be delivered from sin. . . .

Cheap grace means the justification of sin without the justification of the sinner. Grace alone does everything, they say, and so everything can remain as it was before. . . . Cheap grace is the preaching of forgiveness without requiring

repentance, baptism without church discipline, Communion without confession, absolution without personal confession. Cheap grace is grace without discipleship, grace without the cross, grace without Jesus Christ, living and incarnate.

Costly grace is the treasure hidden in the field; for the sake of it a man will gladly go and sell all that he has. It is the pearl of great price to buy [for] which the merchant will sell all his goods. It is the kingly rule of Christ, for whose sake of one will pluck out the eye which causes him to stumble; it is the call of Jesus Christ at which the disciple leaves his nets and follows him. Costly grace is the gospel which must be sought again and again, the gift which must be asked for, the door at which a man must knock. Such grace is costly because it calls us to follow, and it is grace because it calls us to follow Jesus Christ.

It is costly because it costs a man his life, and it is grace because it gives a man the only true life. It is costly because it condemns sin, and grace because it justifies the sinner. Above all, it is costly because it cost God the life of his Son: "Ye were bought at a price," and what has cost God much cannot be cheap for us. Above all, it is grace because God did not reckon his Son too dear a price to pay for our life, but delivered him up for us. . . .

Grace is costly because it compels a man to submit to the yoke of Christ and follow him; it is grace because Jesus says: "My yoke is easy and my burden light."

Dietrich Bonhoeffer was an exceptional person, a Christian who challenged Hitler publicly (even returning to Germany after having escaped for a time first to England and then to America). The Nazis arrested him in 1943, and the SS chief Himmler himself ordered him hanged in April 1945, just a few weeks before the allies liberated his prison.

An Individual's Relation to the Cosmos

Lord of the Flies, by William Golding

Themes

Good versus evil. Jack and his hooligans fight Ralph and his civilized tribe. Goldman makes a few naturalist statements about evil overcoming good in this unnerving drama.

Original sin. As the veneer of civilization disappears, the boys revert to savagery.

† † †

Jack leapt on to the sand.

"Do our dance! Come on! Dance!"

He ran stumbling through the thick sand to the open space of rock beyond the fire. Between the flashes of lightning the air was dark and terrible; and the boys followed him, clamorously. Roger became the pig, grunting and charging at Jack, who side-stepped. The hunters took their spears, the cooks took spits, and

41

the rest clubs of firewood. A circling movement developed and a chant. While Roger mimed the terror of the pig, the littluns ran and jumped on the outside of the circle. Piggy and Ralph, under the threat of the sky, found themselves eager to take a place in this demented but partly secure society. They were glad to touch the brown backs of the fence that hemmed in the terror and made it governable.

"Kill the beast! Cut his throat! Spill his blood!"

The movement became regular while the chant lost its first superficial excitement and began to beat like a steady pulse. Roger ceased to be a pig and became a hunter, so that the center of the ring yawned emptily. Some of the littluns started a ring on their own; and the complementary circles went round

and round as though repetition would achieve safety of itself. There was the throb and stamp of a single organism.

The dark sky was shattered by a blue-white scar. An instant later the noise was on them like the blow of a gigantic whip. The chant rose a tone in agony.

"Kill the beast! Cut his throat! Spill his blood!"

Now out of the terror rose another desire, thick, urgent, blind.

"Kill the beast! Cut his throat! Spill his blood!"

Again the blue-white scar jagged above them and the sulphurous explosion beat down. The littluns screamed and blundered about, fleeing from the edge of the forest, and one of them broke the ring of biguns in his terror.

"Him! Him!"

The circle became a horseshoe. A thing was crawling out of the forest.

It came darkly, uncertainly. The shrill screaming that rose before the beast was like a pain. The beast stumbled into the horseshoe.

"Kill the beast! Cut his throat! Spill his blood!"

The blue-white scar was constant, the noise unendurable. Simon was crying out something about a dead man on a hill.

"Kill the beast! Cut his throat! Spill his blood! Do him in!"

The sticks fell and the mouth of the new circle crunched and screamed.

The beast was on its knees in the center, its arms folded over its face. It was crying out against the abominable noise something about a body on the hill. The beast struggled forward, broke the ring and fell over the steep edge of the rock to the sand by the water. At once the crowd surged after it, poured down the rock, leapt on to the beast, screamed, struck, bit, tore. There were no words, and no movements but the tearing of teeth and claws.

"Maybe there is a beast. . . . Maybe it's only us." — William Golding

Then the clouds opened and let down the rain like a waterfall. The water bounded from the mountain-top, tore leaves and branches from the trees, poured like a cold shower over the struggling heap on the sand. Presently the heap broke up and figures staggered away. Only the beast lay still, a few yards from the sea. Even in the rain they could see how small a beast it was; and already its blood was staining the sand.

Heart of Darkness, Joseph Conrad

Theme

The limits of human knowledge. One critic explains the mood of 1899, when this novella was first published as a three-part serial in *Blackwood's Magazine*: "The darkness of the title is the major theme of the book, but the meaning of that darkness is never clearly defined. On the whole it stands for the unknown and

the unknowable; it represents the opposite of the progress and enlightenment that dominated the nineteenth century. Not many years before, it had been widely believed that science was eventually going to cure the ills of the world; but by the end of the century a deeper pessimism had taken hold, and the darkness is Conrad's image for everything he most dreaded. Science had turned out to be a sham, at least as a route to human happiness—the world wasn't getting any better. Was the darkness something that was simply a part of the universe, something that could never be defeated? Or did it come from within human beings? The "heart of darkness" stands for many things—the interior of the jungle, the Inner Station, Kurtz's own black heart, perhaps the heart of every human being." — A Critic

In the frame story, Marlow is telling his tale to seamen aboard the sailing yacht Nellie, anchored in the Thames near Gravesend (England). The main story is set on the Congo River in the late nineteenth century:

"The brown current ran swiftly out of the heart of darkness, bearing us down towards the sea with twice the speed of our upward progress; and Kurtz's life was running swiftly, too, ebbing, ebbing out of his heart into the sea of inexorable time. The manager was very placid, he had no vital anxieties now, he took us both in with a comprehensive and satisfied glance: the 'affair' had come off as well as could be wished. I saw the time approaching when I would be left alone of the party of unsound method. The pilgrims looked upon me with disfavour. I was, so to speak, numbered with the dead. It is strange how I accepted this unforeseen partnership, this choice of nightmares forced upon me in the tenebrous land invaded by these mean and greedy phantoms.

"Kurtz discoursed. A voice! a voice! It rang deep to the very last. It survived his strength to hide in the magnificent folds of eloquence the barren darkness of his heart. Oh, he struggled! he struggled! The wastes of his weary brain were haunted by shadowy images now—images of wealth and fame revolving obsequiously round his unextinguishable gift of noble and lofty expression. My Intended, my station, my career, my ideas—these were the subjects for the occasional utterances of elevated sentiments. The shade of the original Kurtz frequented the bedside of the hollow sham, whose fate it was to be buried presently in the mould of primeval earth. But both the diabolic love and the unearthly hate of the mysteries it had penetrated fought for the possession of that soul satiated with primitive emotions, avid of lying fame, of sham distinction, of all the appearances of success and power.

"Sometimes he was contemptibly childish. He desired to have kings meet him at railway-stations on his return from some ghastly Nowhere, where he intended to accomplish great things. 'You show them you have in you something that is really profitable, and then there will be no limits to the recognition of your ability,' he would say. 'Of course you must take care of the motives—right motives—always.' The long reaches that were like one and the same reach, monotonous bends that were exactly alike, slipped past the steamer with their multitude of secular trees looking patiently after this grimy fragment of another world, the forerunner of change, of conquest, of trade, of massacres, of blessings. I looked ahead—piloting. 'Close the shutter,' said Kurtz suddenly one day; 'I can't bear to look at this.' I did so. There was a silence. 'Oh, but I will wring your heart yet!' he cried at the invisible wilderness.

"We broke down—as I had expected—and had to lie up for repairs at the head of an island. This delay was the first thing that shook Kurtz's confidence.

One morning he gave me a packet of papers and a photograph—the lot tied together with a shoe-string. 'Keep this for me,' he said. 'This noxious fool' (meaning the manager) 'is capable of prying into my boxes when I am not looking.' In the afternoon I saw him. He was lying on his back with closed eyes, and I withdrew quietly, but I heard him mutter, 'Live rightly, die, die . . .' I listened. There was nothing more. Was he rehearsing some speech in his sleep, or was it a fragment of a phrase from some newspaper article? He had been writing for the papers and meant to do so again, 'for the furthering of my ideas. It's a duty.'

"His was an impenetrable darkness. I looked at him as you peer down at a man who is lying at the bottom of a precipice where the sun never shines. But I had not much time to give him, because I was helping the engine-driver to take to pieces the leaky cylinders, to straighten a bent connecting-rod, and in other such matters. I lived in an infernal mess of rust, filings, nuts, bolts, spanners, hammers, ratchet-drills—things I abominate, because I don't get on with them. I tended the little forge we fortunately had aboard; I toiled wearily in a wretched scrap-heap—unless I had the shakes too bad to stand.

"One evening coming in with a candle I was startled to hear him say a little tremulously, 'I am lying here in the dark waiting for death.' The light was within a foot of his eyes. I forced myself to murmur, 'Oh, nonsense!' and stood over him as if transfixed.

"Anything approaching the change that came over his features I have never seen before, and hope never to see again. Oh, I wasn't touched. I was fascinated. It was as though a veil had been rent. I saw on that ivory face the expression of sombre pride, of ruthless power, of craven terror—of an intense and hopeless despair. Did he live his life again in every detail of desire, temptation, and surrender during that supreme moment of complete knowledge? He cried in a whisper at some image, at some vision—he cried out twice, a cry that was no more than a breath:

"'The horror! The horror!'

"I blew the candle out and left the cabin. The pilgrims were dining in the mess-room, and I took my place opposite the manager, who lifted his eyes to give me a questioning glance, which I successfully ignored. He leaned back, serene, with that peculiar smile of his sealing the unexpressed depths of his meanness. A continuous shower of small flies streamed upon the lamp, upon the cloth, upon our hands and faces. Suddenly the manager's boy put his insolent black head in the doorway, and said in a tone of scathing contempt:

"'Mithra Kurtz—he dead.'"

Comments on Heart of Darkness

[Marlow's perspective] can be summarized along the following lines: the physical universe began in darkness, and will end in it, the same holds for the world of human history, which is dark in the sense of being obscure, amoral, and without purpose; and so, essentially, is man. Through some fortuitous and inexplicable development, however, men have occasionally been able to bring light to this darkness in the form of civilization—a structure of behavior and belief which can sometimes keep the darkness at bay. But this containing action is highly precarious, because the operations of darkness are much more active, numerous, and omnipresent, both in society and in the individual, than civilized people usually suppose. They must learn that light is not only a lesser force than  darkness in power, magnitude, and duration, but is in some way subordinate to it, or included within it: in short, that the darkness which Marlow discovers in the wilderness, in Kurtz and in himself, is the primary and all-encompassing reality of the universe. . . . In any case, neither Conrad nor Marlow stands for the position that darkness is irresistible; their attitude, rather, is to enjoin us to defend ourselves in full knowledge of the difficulties to which we have been blinded by the illusions of civilisation. —Ian Watt

The Emperor Jones, by Eugene O'Neill

Theme

The tragedy of unforgiveness. Brutus Jones has lost his harmony and is trying to make peace with himself and his world. The Emperor Jones is haunted by unforgiveness that has been visited on him by others for his past sins. Tragically, he is destroyed by that unforgiveness even as he begs to be forgiven.

The Drama

The play is divided into eight scenes. Scenes 2 through 7 are from the point of view of Jones, and no other character speaks. This is a masterful use of stream of consciousness. The first and last scenes feature a character named Smithers, a white trader who appears to be part of illegal activities. He is the perfect foil. In the first scene, Smithers is told about the rebellion by an old woman, and then he has a lengthy conversation with Jones, through which O'Neill effectively develops Brutus Jones. In the last scene, Smithers has a conversation with Lem, the leader of the rebellion. Smithers is the only character in the play who has any sympathy for Jones. During this last scene, Jones is killed by a silver bullet, which was the only way that the rebels believed Jones could be killed, and the way in which Jones planned to kill himself if he was captured.

Scene 7

The foot of a gigantic tree is by the edge of a great river. A rough structure of boulders, like an altar, is by the tree. The raised river bank is in the nearer background. Beyond this the surface of the river spreads out, brilliant and unruffled in the moonlight, blotted out and merged into a veil of bluish mist in the distance. Jones' voice is heard from the left rising and falling in the long, despairing wail of the chained slaves, to the rhythmic beat of the tom-tom. As his voice sinks into silence, he enters the open space. The expression on his face is fixed and stony, his eyes have an obsessed glare, he moves with a strange deliberation like a sleepwalker or one in a trance. He looks around at the tree, the rough stone altar, the moonlit  *surface of the river beyond, and passes his hand over his head with a vague gesture of puzzled bewilderment. Then, as if in obedience to some obscure impulse, he sinks into a kneeling, devotional posture before the altar. Then he seems to come to himself partly, to have an uncertain realization of what he is doing, for he straightens up and stares about him horrifiedly — in an incoherent mumble.*

What—what is I doin? What is—dis place? Seems like—seems like I know dat tree—an' dem stones—an' de river. I remember—seems like I been heah befo'. (*tremblingly*) Oh, Gorry, I'se skeered in dis place! I'se skeered! Oh, Lawd, pertect dis sinner!

(Crawling away from the altar, he cowers close to the ground, his face hidden, his shoulders heaving with sobs of hysterical fright. From behind the trunk of the tree, as if he had sprung out of it, the figure of the Congo witch-doctor appears. He is wizened and old, naked except for the fur of some small animal tied about his waist, its bushy tail hanging down in front. His body is stained all over a bright red. Antelope horns are on each side of his head, branching upward. In one hand he carries a bone rattle, in the other a charm stick with a bunch of white cockatoo feathers tied to the end. A great number of glass beads and bone ornaments are about his neck, ears, wrists, and ankles. He struts noiselessly with a queer prancing step to a position in the clear ground between Jones and the altar. Then with a preliminary, summoning stamp of his foot on the earth, he begins to dance and to chant. As if in response to his summons the beating of the tom-tom grows to a fierce, exultant boom whose throbs seem to fill the air with vibrating rhythm. Jones looks up, starts to spring to his feet, reaches a half kneeling, half-squatting position and remains rigidly fixed there, paralyzed with awed fascination by this new apparition. The witch-doctor sways, stamping with his foot, his bone rattle clicking the time. His voice rises and falls in a weird, monotonous croon, without articulate word divisions. Gradually his dance becomes clearly one of a narrative in pantomime, his croon is an incantation, a charm to allay the fierceness of some implacable deity demanding sacrifice. He flees, he is pursued by devils, he hides, he flees again. Ever wilder and wilder becomes his flight, nearer and nearer draws the pursuing evil, more and more the spirit of terror gains possession of him. His croon, rising to intensity, is punctuated by shrill cries. Jones has become completely hypnotized. His voice joins in the incantation, in the cries, he beats time with his hands and sways his body to and fro from the waist. The whole spirit and meaning of the dance has entered into him, has become his spirit. Finally the theme of the pantomime halts on a howl of despair, and is taken up again in a note of savage hope. There is a salvation. The forces of evil demand sacrifice. They must be appeased. The witch-doctor points with his wand to the sacred tree, to the river beyond, to the altar, and finally to Jones with a ferocious command. Jones seems to sense the meaning of this. It is he who must offer himself for sacrifice. He beats his forehead abjectly to the ground, moaning hysterically.)

Mercy, Oh Lawd! Mercy! Mercy on dis po' sinner.

(The witch-doctor springs to the river bank. He stretches out his arms and calls to some God within its depths. Then he starts backward slowly, his arms remaining out. A huge head of a crocodile appears over the bank and its eyes, glittering greenly, fasten upon Jones. He stares into them fascinatedly. The witch-doctor prances up to him,

touches him with his wand, motions with hideous command toward the waiting monster. Jones squirms on his belly nearer and nearer, moaning continually.)

Mercy, Lawd! Mercy!

(The crocodile heaves more of his enormous hulk onto the land. Jones squirms toward him. The witch-doctor's voice shrills out in furious exultation, the tom-tom beats madly. Jones cries out in a fierce, exhausted spasm of anguished pleading.)

Lawd, save me! Lawd Jesus, hear my prayer!

(Immediately, in answer to his prayer, comes the thought of the one bullet left him. He snatches at his hip, shouting defiantly.)

De silver bullet! You don't git me yit!

(He fires at the green eyes in front of him. The head of the crocodile sinks back behind the river bank, the witch-doctor springs behind the sacred tree and disappears. Jones lies with his face to the ground, his arms outstretched, whimpering with fear as the throb of the tom-tom fills the silence about him with a somber pulsation, a baffled but revengeful power.)

Comment on The Emperor Jones

The Emperor Jones is haunted by unforgiveness that has been visited on him by others. Tragically, he is destroyed by others' unforgivingness, their refusal to forgive him.

Twenty years after World War II, a psychologist conducted a study of survivors of the Nazi concentration camps and their guards. To his horror, he discovered that the survivors had a higher divorce rate, suicide rate, and even higher rate of death by cancer than the concentration camp guards. In spite of the fact that the guards were guilty of heinous crimes, and the former inmates were innocent victims, it was the innocent victims who fared much worse. The physical deprivations and mental agony took their toll. And who can blame inmates who struggled to forgive the Nazis? Yet harboring unforgiving attitudes may extend one's own suffering as well as add to the suffering of others.

Once Americans had dreams
and no technology to accomplish those dreams.

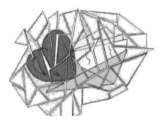

Now Americans have plenty of technology
but no dreams left to fulfill. — Harvey Cox

Father Goriot, by Honoré de Balzac

Themes: discipline; the individual in relation to the cosmos; Balzac's wit pierces avarice.

Old Goriot, or *Le Père Goriot* is an 1835 novel by French novelist and playwright Honoré de Balzac (1799–1850). Set in Paris in 1819, it portrays the intertwined lives of three characters: the elderly doting Goriot who has spoiled his daughters beyond recognition; a mysterious criminal-in-hiding named Vautrin; and a naive law student named Eugène de Rastignac. Balzac, like Mark Twain in The Adventures of Huckleberry Finn, uses minute details to create character and subtext. Also, like Alexei Karamazov in Fyodor Dostoevsky's

Brother Karamazov, de Balzac's characters consciously make realistic decisions in a moral universe. Notice the skillful way that de Balzac uses dialogue to reveal the inner thoughts, and feelings, of his characters.

"The world is basely ungrateful and ill-natured," said the Vicomtesse at last. "No sooner does a trouble befall you than a friend is ready to bring the tidings and to probe your heart with the point of a dagger while calling on you to admire the handle. Epigrams and sarcasms already! Ah! I will defend myself!"

She raised her head like the great lady that she was, and lightnings flashed from her proud eyes.

"Ah!" she said, as she saw Eugene, "are you there?"

"Still," he said piteously.

"Well, then, M. de Rastignac, deal with the world as it deserves. You are determined to succeed? I will help you. You shall sound the depths of corruption in woman; you shall measure the extent of man's pitiful vanity. Deeply as I am versed in such learning, there were pages in the book of life that I had not read. Now I know all. The more cold-blooded your calculations, the further you will go. Strike ruthlessly; you will be feared. Men and women for you must be nothing more than post-horses; take a fresh relay, and leave the last to drop by the roadside; in this way you will reach the goal of your ambition. You will be nothing here, you see, unless a woman interests herself in you; and she must be young and wealthy, and a woman of the world. Yet, if you have a heart, lock it carefully away like a treasure; do not let any one suspect it, or you will be lost; you would cease to be the executioner, you would take the victim's place. And if ever you should love, never let your secret escape you! Trust no one until you are very sure of the heart to which you open your heart. Learn to mistrust every one; take every precaution for the sake of the love which does not exist as yet. Listen, Miguel"—the name slipped from her so naturally that she did not notice her mistake—"there is something still more appalling than the ingratitude of daughters who have cast off their old father and wish that he were dead, and that is a rivalry between two sisters. Restaud comes of a good family, his wife has been received into their circle; she has been presented at court; and her sister, her wealthy sister, Mme. Delphine de Nucingen, the wife of a great capitalist, is consumed with envy, and ready to die of spleen. There is gulf set between the sisters—indeed, they are sisters no longer—the two women who refuse to acknowledge their father do not acknowledge each other. So Mme. de Nucingen would lap up all the mud that lies between the Rue Saint-Lazare and the Rue de

Grenelle to gain admittance to my salon. She fancied that she should gain her end through de Marsay; she has made herself de Marsay's slave, and she bores him. De Marsay cares very little about her. If you will introduce her to me, you will be her darling, her Benjamin; she will idolize you. If, after that, you can love her, do so; if not, make her useful. I will ask her to come once or twice to one of my great crushes, but I will never receive her here in the morning. I will bow to her when I see her, and that will be quite sufficient. You have shut the Comtesse de Restaud's door against you by mentioning Father Goriot's name. Yes, my good friend, you may call at her house twenty times, and every time out of the twenty you will find that she is not at home. The servants have their orders, and will not admit you. Very well, then, now let Father Goriot gain the right of entry into her sister's house for you. The beautiful Mme. de Nucingen will give the signal for a battle. As soon as she singles you out, other women will begin to lose their heads about you, and her enemies and rivals and intimate friends will all try to take you from her. There are women who will fall in love with a man because another woman has chosen him; like the city madams, poor things, who copy our millinery, and hope thereby to acquire our manners. You will have a success, and in Paris success is everything; it is the key of power. If the women credit you with wit and talent, the men will follow suit so long as you do not undeceive them yourself.

The Individual and the Cosmos in the Bible

God's Speech to Job: Job 41

> "Can you pull in Leviathan with a fishhook
>   or tie down its tongue with a rope?
> Can you put a cord through its nose
>   or pierce its jaw with a hook?

Will it keep begging you for mercy?
  Will it speak to you with gentle words?
Will it make an agreement with you
  for you to take it as your slave for life?
Can you make a pet of it like a bird
  or put it on a leash for the young women in your house?
Will traders barter for it?
  Will they divide it up among the merchants?
Can you fill its hide with harpoons
  or its head with fishing spears?
If you lay a hand on it,
  you will remember the struggle and never do it again!
Any hope of subduing it is false;
  the mere sight of it is overpowering.
No one is fierce enough to rouse it.
  Who then is able to stand against me?
Who has a claim against me that I must pay?
  Everything under heaven belongs to me.
"I will not fail to speak of Leviathan's limbs,
  its strength and its graceful form.
Who can strip off its outer coat?
  Who can penetrate its double coat of armor?
Who dares open the doors of its mouth,
  ringed about with fearsome teeth?
Its back has rows of shields
  tightly sealed together;
each is so close to the next
  that no air can pass between.

They are joined fast to one another;
  they cling together and cannot be parted.
Its snorting throws out flashes of light;
  its eyes are like the rays of dawn.
Flames stream from its mouth;
  sparks of fire shoot out.
Smoke pours from its nostrils
  as from a boiling pot over burning reeds.
Its breath sets coals ablaze,

and flames dart from its mouth.
Strength resides in its neck;
    dismay goes before it.
The folds of its flesh are tightly joined;
    they are firm and immovable.
Its chest is hard as rock,
    hard as a lower millstone.
When it rises up, the mighty are terrified;
    they retreat before its thrashing.
The sword that reaches it has no effect,
    nor does the spear or the dart or the javelin.
Iron it treats like straw
    and bronze like rotten wood.
Arrows do not make it flee;
    slingstones are like chaff to it.
A club seems to it but a piece of straw;
    it laughs at the rattling of the lance.
Its undersides are jagged potsherds,
    leaving a trail in the mud like a threshing sledge.
It makes the depths churn like a boiling caldron
    and stirs up the sea like a pot of ointment.
It leaves a glistening wake behind it;
    one would think the deep had white hair.
Nothing on earth is its equal—
    a creature without fear.
It looks down on all that are haughty;
    it is king over all that are proud."

Comment on Leviathan, by Matthew Henry

The description here given of the leviathan, a very large, strong, formidable fish, or water-animal, is designed yet further to convince Job of his own impotency, and of God's omnipotence, that he might be humbled for his folly in making so bold with him as he had done.

To convince Job of his own weakness, he is here challenged to subdue and tame this leviathan if he can, and make himself master of him (Job 41:1–9), and, since he cannot do this, he must own himself utterly unable to stand before the great God, Job 41:10.

To convince Job of God's power and terrible majesty, several particular instances are here given of the strength and terror of the leviathan, which is no more than what God has given him, nor more than he has under his check (Job 41:11–12). The face of the leviathan is here described to be terrible (Job 41:12, 14), his scales close (Job 41:15–17), his breath and neesings [sneezing, snortings] sparkling (Job 41:18–21), his flesh firm (Job 41:22–24), his strength and spirit, when he is attacked, insuperable (Job 41:25–30).

Satire

Gulliver's Travels, by Jonathan Swift

Part 4, Chapter 5

The author, at his master's command, informs him of the state of England and causes of war among Europe's princes. The author begins to explain the English constitution.

The reader may please to observe, that the following extract of many conversations I had with my master, contains a summary of the most material points which were discoursed at several times for above two years; his honor often desiring fuller satisfaction, as I farther improved in the Houyhnhnm tongue. I laid before him, as well as I could, the whole state of Europe; I discoursed of trade and manufactures, of arts and sciences; and the answers I gave to all the questions he made, as they arose upon several subjects, were a fund of conversation not to be exhausted. But I shall here only set down the substance of what passed between us concerning my own country, reducing it in order as well as I can, without any regard to time or other circumstances, while I strictly adhere to truth. My only concern is, that I shall hardly be able to do justice to my master's arguments and expressions, which must needs suffer by my want of capacity, as well as by a translation into our barbarous English.

Gulliver interrogated by his master, a Houyhnhnm

In obedience, therefore, to his honour's commands, I related to him the Revolution under the Prince of Orange; the long war with France, entered into by the said prince, and renewed by his successor, the present queen, wherein the greatest powers of Christendom were engaged, and which still continued: I computed, at his request, "that about a million of Yahoos might have been killed in the whole progress of it; and perhaps a hundred or more cities taken, and five times as many ships burnt or sunk."

He asked me, "what were the usual causes or motives that made one country go to war with another?" I answered "they were innumerable; but I should only mention a few of the chief. Sometimes the ambition of princes, who never think they have land or people enough to govern; sometimes the corruption of ministers, who engage their master in a war, in order to stifle or divert the clamour of the subjects against their evil administration. Difference in opinions has cost many millions of lives: for instance, whether flesh be bread, or bread be flesh; whether the juice of a certain berry be blood or wine; whether whistling be a vice or a virtue; whether it be better to kiss a post, or throw it into the fire; what is the best color for a coat, whether black, white, red, or gray; and whether it should be long or short, narrow or wide, dirty or clean; with many more. Neither are any wars so furious and bloody, or of so long a continuance, as those occasioned by difference in opinion, especially if it be in things indifferent.

"Sometimes the quarrel between two princes is to decide which of them shall dispossess a third of his dominions, where neither of them pretend to any right. Sometimes one prince quarrels with another for fear the other should quarrel with him. Sometimes a war is entered upon, because the enemy is too strong; and sometimes, because he is too weak. Sometimes our neighbours want the things which we have, or have the things which we want, and we both fight, till they take ours, or give us theirs. It is a very justifiable cause of a war, to invade a country after the people have been wasted by famine, destroyed by pestilence, or embroiled by factions among themselves. It is justifiable to enter into war against our nearest ally, when one of his towns lies convenient for us, or a territory of land, that would render our dominions round and complete. If a prince sends forces into a nation, where the people are poor and ignorant, he may lawfully put half of them to death, and make slaves of the rest, in order to civilize and reduce them from their barbarous way of living. It is a very kingly, honorable, and frequent practice, when one prince desires the assistance of another, to secure him against an invasion, that the assistant, when he has driven out the invader, should seize on the dominions himself, and kill, imprison, or banish, the prince he came to relieve. Alliance by blood, or marriage, is a frequent cause of war between princes; and the nearer the kindred is, the greater their disposition to quarrel; poor nations are hungry, and rich nations are proud; and pride and hunger will ever be at variance. For these reasons, the trade of a soldier is held the most honorable of all others; because a soldier is a Yahoo hired to kill, in cold blood, as many of his own species, who have never offended him, as possibly he can.

"There is likewise a kind of beggarly princes in Europe, not able to make war by themselves, who hire out their troops to richer nations, for so much a day to each man; of which they keep three-fourths to themselves, and it is the best part of their maintenance: such are those in many northern parts of Europe."

"What you have told me," said my master, "upon the subject of war, does indeed discover most admirably the effects of that reason you pretend to: however, it is happy that the shame is greater than the danger; and that nature has left you utterly incapable of doing much mischief. For, your mouths lying flat with your faces, you can hardly bite each other to any purpose, unless by consent. Then as to the claws upon your feet before and behind, they are so short and tender, that one of our Yahoos would drive a dozen of yours before him. And therefore, in recounting the numbers of those who have been killed in battle, I cannot but think you have said the thing which is not."

I could not forbear shaking my head, and smiling a little at his ignorance. And being no stranger to the art of war, I gave him a description of cannons, culverins, muskets, carabines, pistols, bullets, powder, swords, bayonets, battles, sieges, retreats, attacks, undermines, countermines, bombardments, sea fights, ships sunk with a thousand men, twenty thousand killed on each side, dying groans, limbs flying in the air, smoke, noise, confusion, trampling to death under horses' feet, flight, pursuit, victory; fields strewed with carcases, left for food to dogs and wolves and birds of prey; plundering, stripping, ravishing, burning, and destroying. And to set forth the valour of my own dear countrymen, I assured him, "that I had seen them blow up a hundred enemies at once in a siege, and as many in a ship, and beheld the dead bodies drop down in pieces from the clouds, to the great diversion of the spectators."

I was going on to more particulars, when my master commanded me silence. He said, "whoever understood the nature of Yahoos, might easily believe it possible for so vile an animal to be capable of every action I had named, if their strength and cunning equalled their malice. But as my discourse had increased his abhorrence of the whole species, so he found it gave him a disturbance in his mind to which he was wholly a stranger before. He thought his ears, being used to such abominable words, might, by degrees, admit them with less detestation:

that although he hated the Yahoos of this country, yet he no more blamed them for their odious qualities, than he did a *gnnayh* (a bird of prey) for its cruelty, or a sharp stone for cutting his hoof. But when a creature pretending to reason could be capable of such enormities, he dreaded lest the corruption of that faculty might be worse than brutality itself. He seemed therefore confident, that, instead of reason we were only possessed of some quality fitted to increase our natural vices; as the reflection from a troubled stream returns the image of an ill-shapen body, not only larger but more distorted."

He added, "that he had heard too much upon the subject of war, both in this and some former discourses. There was another point, which a little perplexed him at present. I had informed him, that some of our crew left their country on account of being ruined by law; that I had already explained the meaning of the word; but he was at a loss how it should come to pass, that the law, which was intended for every man's preservation, should be any man's ruin. Therefore he desired to be further satisfied what I meant by law, and the dispensers thereof, according to the present practice in my own country; because he thought nature and reason were sufficient guides for a reasonable animal, as we pretended to be, in showing us what he ought to do, and what to avoid."

Gulliver tied down by Lilliputians

I assured his honor, "that the law was a science in which I had not much conversed, further than by employing advocates, in vain, upon some injustices that had been done me: however, I would give him all the satisfaction I was able."

I said, "there was a society of men among us, bred up from their youth in the art of proving, by words multiplied for the purpose, that white is black, and black is white, according as they are paid. To this society all the rest of the people are slaves.

For example, if my neighbor has a mind to my cow, he has a lawyer to prove that he ought to have my cow from me. I must then hire another to defend my right, it being against all rules of law that any man should be allowed to speak for himself. Now, in this case, I, who am the right owner, lie under two great disadvantages: first, my lawyer, being practised almost from his cradle in defending falsehood, is quite out of his element when he would be an advocate for justice, which is an unnatural office he always attempts with great awkwardness, if not with ill-will. The second disadvantage is, that my lawyer must proceed with great caution, or else he will be reprimanded by the judges, and abhorred by his brethren, as one that would lessen the practice of the law. And therefore I have but two methods to preserve my cow. The first is, to gain over my adversary's lawyer with a double fee, who will then betray his client by insinuating that he hath justice on his side. The second way is for my lawyer to make my cause appear as unjust as he can, by allowing the cow to belong to my adversary: and this, if it be skilfully done, will certainly bespeak the favour of the bench. Now your honor is to know, that these judges are persons appointed to decide all controversies of property, as well as for the trial of criminals, and picked out from the most dexterous lawyers, who are grown old or lazy; and having been biassed all their lives against truth and equity, lie under such a fatal necessity of favouring fraud, perjury, and oppression, that I have known some of them refuse a large bribe from the side where justice lay, rather than injure the faculty, by doing any thing unbecoming their nature or their office.

"It is a maxim among these lawyers that whatever has been done before, may legally be done again: and therefore they take special care to record all the decisions formerly made against common justice, and the general reason of mankind. These, under the name of precedents, they produce as authorities to justify the most iniquitous opinions; and the judges never fail of directing accordingly.

"In pleading, they studiously avoid entering into the merits of the cause; but are loud, violent, and tedious, in dwelling upon all circumstances which are not to the purpose. For instance, in the case already mentioned; they never desire to know what claim or title my adversary has to my cow; but whether the said cow were red or black; her horns long or short; whether the field I graze her in be round or square; whether she was milked at home or abroad; what diseases she is subject to, and the like; after which they consult precedents, adjourn the cause from time to time, and in ten, twenty, or thirty years, come to an issue.

"It is likewise to be observed, that this society has a peculiar cant and jargon of their own, that no other mortal can understand, and wherein all their laws are written, which they take special care to multiply; whereby they have wholly confounded the very essence of truth and falsehood, of right and wrong; so that it will take thirty years to decide, whether the field left me by my ancestors for six generations belongs to me, or to a stranger three hundred miles off.

"In the trial of persons accused for crimes against the state, the method is much more short and commendable: the judge first sends to sound the disposition of those in power, after which he can easily hang or save a criminal, strictly preserving all due forms of law."

Here my master interposing, said, "it was a pity, that creatures endowed with such prodigious abilities of mind, as these lawyers, by the description I gave of them, must certainly be, were not rather encouraged to be instructors of others in wisdom and knowledge." In answer to which I assured his honor, "that in all points out of their own trade, they were usually the most ignorant and stupid generation among us, the most despicable in common conversation, avowed enemies to all knowledge and learning, and equally disposed to pervert the general reason of mankind in every other subject of discourse as in that of their own profession."

Comments on Gulliver's Travels

The Yahoos are so startling and unforgettable that the term has stayed in our language. When someone today refers to a person as a Yahoo, he means that that person is a hick, somewhat less than civilized. To Swift, it meant something far more d---ing. The Yahoos in *Gulliver's Travels* embody the lowest traits in human nature. They are gluttonous, filthy, lascivious, thieving, violent brutes. Only physically do they resemble civilized people. They live in kennels and function as the Houyhnhnms' "horses." To Gulliver, they represent humankind, period. To Swift, they represent what humans must strive to overcome. Bear in mind that the Yahoos ended up on the Houyhnhnms' island by accident. A female and a male arrived and, stranded, never left. The original couple had children, so did their children, and so forth. Totally cut off from other humans, they degenerated to the level of beasts. It's possible that Swift is saying here that people need to be with other people to remain civilized. Swift, who has been attacked for misanthropy, is actually arguing against it here. — A Literary Critic

Animal rationale — *animal rationis capax*! Swift's somewhat scholastic distinction turns out, in the light of seventeenth century thought, to be by no means scholastic. It symbolizes, in fact, the chief intellectual battle of the age. Swift seems to have seen clearly enough that in assaulting man's pride in reason, he was attacking the new optimism at its very root. — T. O. Wedel

The Screwtape Letters, by C. S. Lewis

This work takes the form of a series of satirical letters from a senior demon, Screwtape, to his Nephew, a junior "tempter" named Wormwood. The letters advise Wormwood on methods for securing the damnation of a man known only as "the Patient." Accordingly, "Our Father Below" is the devil, and "the Enemy" is God. There is keen insight into how people are distracted from sincere faith in God and trust in Christ.

My Dear Wormwood,

I note what you say about guiding our patient's reading and taking care that he sees a good deal of his materialist friend. But are you not being a trifle naïf? It sounds as if you supposed that argument was the way to keep him out of the Enemy's clutches. That might have been so if he had lived a few centuries earlier. At that time the humans still knew pretty well when a thing was proved and when it was not; and if it was proved they really believed it. They still connected thinking with doing and were prepared to alter their way of life as the result of a chain of reasoning. But what with the weekly press and other such weapons we have largely altered that. Your man has been accustomed, ever since he was a boy, to have a dozen incompatible philosophies dancing about together inside his head. He doesn't think of doctrines as primarily "true" or "false," but as "academic" or "practical," "outworn" or "contemporary," "conventional" or "ruthless." Jargon, not argument, is your best ally in keeping him from the Church. Don't waste time trying to make him think that materialism is true! Make him think it is strong, or stark, or courageous — that it is the philosophy of the future. That's the sort of thing he cares about.

The trouble about argument is that it moves the whole struggle onto the Enemy's own ground. He can argue too; whereas in really practical propaganda of the kind I am suggesting He has been shown for centuries to be greatly the inferior of Our Father Below. By the very act of arguing, you awake the patient's reason; and once it is awake, who can foresee the result? Even if a particular train of thought can be twisted so as to end in our favour, you will find that you have been strengthening in your patient the fatal habit of attending to universal issues and withdrawing his attention from the stream of immediate sense experiences. Your business is to fix his attention on the stream. Teach him to call it "real life" and don't let him ask what he means by "real."

Remember, he is not, like you, a pure spirit. Never having been a human (Oh that abominable advantage of the Enemy's!) you don't realise how enslaved they are to the pressure of the ordinary. I once had a patient, a sound atheist, who used to read in the British Museum. One day, as he sat reading, I saw a train of thought in his mind beginning to go the wrong way. The Enemy, of course, was at his elbow in a moment. Before I knew where I was I saw my twenty years' work beginning to totter. If I had lost my head and begun to attempt a defense by argument I should have been undone. But I was not such a fool. I struck instantly at the part of the man which I had best under my control and suggested that it was just about time he had some lunch. The Enemy presumably made the counter-suggestion (you know how one can never quite overhear what He says to them?) that this was more important than lunch. At least I think that must have been His line for when I said "Quite. In fact much too important to tackle it the end of a morning," the patient brightened up considerably; and by the time I had added "Much better come back after lunch and go into it with a fresh mind," he was already half way to the door. Once he was in the street the battle was won. I showed him a newsboy shouting the midday paper, and a No. 73 bus going past, and before he reached the bottom of the steps I had got into him an unalterable conviction that, whatever odd ideas might come into a man's head when he was shut up alone with his books, a healthy dose of "real life" (by which he meant the bus and the newsboy) was enough to show him that all "that sort of thing" just couldn't be true. He knew he'd had a narrow escape and in later years was fond of talking about "that inarticulate sense for actuality which is our ultimate safeguard against the aberrations of mere logic." He is now safe in Our Father's house.

You begin to see the point? Thanks to processes which we set at work in them centuries ago, they find it all but impossible to believe in the unfamiliar while the familiar is before their eyes. Keep pressing home on him the ordinariness of things. Above all, do not attempt to use science (I mean, the real sciences) as a defense against Christianity. They will positively encourage him to think about realities he can't touch and see. There have been sad cases among the modern physicists. If he must dabble in science, keep him on economics and sociology; don't let him get away from that invaluable "real life." But the best of all is to let him read no science but to give him a grand general idea that he knows it all and that everything he happens to have picked up in casual talk and reading is "the results of modern investigation." Do remember you are there to fuddle him.

From the way some of you young fiends talk, anyone would suppose it was our job to teach!

Your affectionate uncle,

SCREWTAPE

My Dear Wormwood,

I note with grave displeasure that your patient has become a Christian. Do not indulge the hope that you will escape the usual penalties; indeed, in your better moments, I trust you would hardly even wish to do so. In the meantime we must make the best of the situation. There is no need to despair; hundreds of these adult converts have been reclaimed after a brief sojourn in the Enemy's camp and are now with us. All the habits of the patient, both mental and bodily, are still in our favour.

One of our great allies at present is the Church itself. Do not misunderstand me. I do not mean the Church as we see her spread but through all time and space and rooted in eternity, terrible as an army with banners. That, I confess, is a spectacle which makes our boldest tempters uneasy. But fortunately it is quite invisible to these humans. All your patient sees is the half-finished, sham Gothic erection on the new building estate. When he goes inside, he sees the local grocer with rather an oily expression on his face bustling up to offer him one shiny little book containing a liturgy which neither of them understands, and one shabby little book containing corrupt texts of a number of religious lyrics, mostly bad, and in very small print. When he gets to his pew and looks round him he sees just that selection of his neighbor whom he has hitherto avoided. You want to lean pretty heavily on those neighbors. Make his mind flit to and fro between an expression like "the body of Christ" and the actual faces in the

next pew. It matters very little, of course, what kind of people that next pew really contains. You may know one of them to be a great warrior on the Enemy's side. No matter. Your patient, thanks to Our Father Below, is a fool. Provided that any of those neighbors sing out of tune, or have boots that squeak, or double chins, or odd clothes, the patient will quite easily believe that their religion must therefore be somehow ridiculous. At his present stage, you see, he has an idea of "Christians" in his mind which he supposes to be spiritual but which, in fact, is largely pictorial. His mind is full of togas and sandals and armour and bare legs and the mere fact that the other people in church wear modern clothes is a real — though of course an unconscious — difficulty to him. Never let it come to the surface; never let him ask what he expected them to look like. Keep everything hazy in his mind now, and you will have all eternity wherein to amuse yourself by producing in him the peculiar kind of clarity which Hell affords.

Work hard, then, on the disappointment or anticlimax which is certainly coming to the patient during his first few weeks as a churchman. The Enemy allows this disappointment to occur on the threshold of every human endeavour.

It occurs when the boy who has been enchanted in the nursery by *Stories from the Odyssey* buckles down to really learning Greek. It occurs when lovers have got married and begin the real task of learning to live together. In every department of life it marks the transition from dreaming aspiration to laborious doing. The Enemy takes this risk because He has a curious fantasy of making all these disgusting little human vermin into what He calls His "free" lovers and servants — "sons" is the word He uses, with His inveterate love of degrading the whole spiritual world by unnatural liaisons with the two-legged animals. Desiring their freedom, He therefore refuses to carry them, by their mere affections and habits, to any of the goals which He sets before them: He leaves them to "do it on their own." And there lies our opportunity. But also, remember, there lies our danger. If once they get through this initial dryness successfully, they become much less dependent on emotion and therefore much harder to tempt.

I have been writing hitherto on the assumption that the people in the next pew afford no rational ground for disappointment. Of course if they do — if the patient knows that the woman with the absurd hat is a fanatical bridge-player or the man with squeaky boots a miser and an extortioner — then your task is so much the easier. All you then have to do is to keep out of his mind the question "If I, being what I am, can consider that I am in some sense a Christian, why should the different vices of those people in the next pew prove that their religion is mere hypocrisy and convention?" You may ask whether it is possible to keep such an obvious thought from occurring even to a human mind. It is, Wormwood, it is! Handle him properly and it simply won't come into his head. He has not been anything like long enough with the Enemy to have any real humility yet. What he says, even on his knees, about his own sinfulness is all parrot talk. At bottom, he still believes he has run up a very favorable credit-balance in the Enemy's ledger by allowing himself to be converted, and thinks that he is showing great humility and condescension in going to church with these "smug," commonplace neighbors at all. Keep him in that state of mind as long as you can.

Your affectionate uncle,

SCREWTAPE

Story with a Moral, a Lesson

A theme is not a moral. A theme is a statement of purpose of the piece. A moral is a lesson learned in the piece, as in the following story.

"The Brave Quail," a *Panchatantra* Indian Folktale (Adapted)

In a forest near Varanasi, there once lived some quails. The shady grove in which they nested was also the favorite grazing ground of a herd of elephants. The leader of the herd was a wise and just elephant, the Bodhisattva.

One day, one of the quails laid some eggs. "I hope my eggs will be safe till they are hatched," she said to the father quail.

"You will have to keep careful watch," replied the father quail. Soon after the

fledglings were hatched, the elephant herd arrived.

"What shall I do?" cried the mother. "I can only fall at their feet and beg for protection."

"As the leader came close to her nest, the mother quail cried out, "Oh mighty elephant, my little ones are in danger. If your herd enters the grove, they will be trampled to death."

"Do not fear little one," said the elephant leader, "Your fledglings will not be harmed."

The kind elephant stood over the nest as the herd grazed. When the herd was leaving, the leader cautioned, "There is a rogue elephant who is wild and dangerous. He might soon be coming this way."

"What shall I do, I am so small and weak," said the helpless quail.

"All you can do is appeal to him for mercy," advised the good elephant and departed. Before long the rogue elephant arrived. The mother wasted no time and ran to the rogue elephant, begging,

"Oh powerful one! I beg of you, spare my young ones!"

"How dare you come in my way?" the rogue elephant replied and in no time destroyed the nest and killed the father.

"There! That is the end of your silly brood," the rogue elephant sneered.

The mother quail grieved over her family for a long time. She vowed to teach the rogue elephant a lesson. She thought long and hard and finally came up with a plan.

She went to her friend crow and narrated her sad tale. The crow was very sympathetic. "The rogue must not go unpunished," the crow proclaimed and agreed to the mother quail's plan.

The quail then went to her friend, the ant and sought her help.

"I heard about your babies," the ant said. "I am deeply grieved. What can I do?"

The quail told the ant her plan and the ant readily agreed.

The quail then went to the frog, her longtime friend, and narrated what happened. "I am trying to get my friends—the crow, the ant, and you—to help me punish the spiteful elephant who killed my babies."

"You can count on me," said the frog and followed the quail.

The three friends then implemented the quail's plan. First, the crow darted at the elephant and plucked out the elephant's eyes. Then the ant quickly went and laid her eggs in the eye sockets. As the eggs hatched and the baby ants began biting, the elephant could not bear the pain anymore and desperately searched for water to wash his eyes. As the elephant dashed around in pain, the frog croaked close to a steep precipice.

The blind elephant followed the sound of the frog's croaking, thinking that water would be nearby.

Soon the elephant hurtled down to his death.

The three friends came together near the pond. "Thank you all for helping me to carry out my plan," the mother quail said. "Let this be a lesson to all that even the small and weak can join together to correct an injustice."

Motif

A motif is any recurring image that has symbolic significance in a story. Through its repetition, a motif affects other narrative aspects such as theme or mood.

"While the term "motif" may appear to be interchangeable with the related concept 'theme,' it does differ somewhat in usage. Any number of narrative elements with symbolic significance can be classified as motifs, whether they are images, spoken or written phrases, structural or stylistic devices, or other elements like sound, physical movement, or visual components in narratives. A motif is not necessarily a theme. A theme is usually defined as a message, statement, or idea; on the other hand, a motif is simply a detail repeated for larger symbolic meaning, whatever that meaning may be. In other words, a narrative motif—a detail repeated in a pattern of meaning—can produce a theme; but it can also create other narrative aspects distinct from theme." —An Critic via Internet

The Great Gatsby, by F. Scott Fitzgerald

Background

Nick Carraway, the narrator, is a young Midwesterner who, having graduated from Yale in 1915 and fought in World War I ("The Great War"), has returned home to begin a career. Like others in his generation, he is restless and has decided to move East to New York and learn the bond business. The novel opens early in the summer of 1922 in West Egg, Long Island, where Nick has rented a house. Next to his place is a huge mansion complete with Gothic tower and marble swimming pool, which belongs to a Mr. Gatsby, whom Nick has not met. Directly across the bay from West Egg, where Tom and Daisy Buchanan live, Daisy is Nick's cousin; and Tom, a well-known football player at Yale, had been in the same senior society as Nick in New Haven. Like Nick, they are Midwesterners who have come East to be a part of the glamour and mystery of the New York City area. They invite Nick to Dinner at their mansion, and here

Nick meets a young woman golfer named Jordan Baker, a friend of Daisy's from Louisville, whom Daisy wants Nick to become interested in. — *Barron's Booknotes*

Chapter 1

In my younger and more vulnerable years my father gave me some advice that I've been turning over in my mind ever since.

"Whenever you feel like criticizing any one," he told me, "just remember that all the people in this world haven't had the advantages that you've had."

He didn't say any more, but we've always been unusually communicative in a reserved way, and I understood that he meant a great deal more than that. In consequence, I'm inclined to reserve all judgments, a habit that has opened up many curious natures to me and also made me the victim of not a few veteran bores. The abnormal mind is quick to detect and attach itself to this quality when it appears in a normal person, and so it came about that in college I was unjustly accused of being a politician, because I was privy to the secret griefs of wild, unknown men. Most of the confidences were unsought — frequently I have feigned sleep, preoccupation, or a hostile levity when I realized by some unmistakable sign that an intimate revelation was quivering on the horizon; for the intimate revelations of young men, or at least the terms in which they express them, are usually plagiaristic and marred by obvious suppressions. Reserving judgments is a matter of infinite hope. I am still a little afraid of missing something if I forget that, as my father snobbishly suggested, I snobbishly repeat, a sense of the fundamental decencies is parceled out unequally at birth.

And, after boasting this way of my tolerance, I come to the admission that it has a limit. Conduct may be founded on the hard rock or the wet marshes, but after a certain point I don't care what it's founded on. When I came back from the East last autumn I felt that I wanted the world to be in uniform and at a sort of moral attention forever; I wanted no more riotous excursions with privileged glimpses into the human heart. Only Gatsby, the man who gives his name to this book, was exempt from my reaction — Gatsby, who represented everything for which I have an unaffected scorn. If personality is an unbroken series of successful gestures, then there was something gorgeous about him, some heightened sensitivity to the promises of life, as if he were related to one of those intricate machines that register earthquakes ten thousand miles away. This responsiveness had nothing to do with that flabby impressionability which is dignified under the name of the "creative temperament" — it was an extraordinary gift for hope, a romantic readiness such as I have never found in any other person and which it is not likely I shall ever find again. No—Gatsby turned out all right at the end; it is what preyed on Gatsby, what foul dust floated in the wake of his dreams that temporarily closed out my interest in the abortive sorrows and short-winded elations of men.

My family has been prominent, well-to-do people in this Middle Western city for three generations. The Carraways are something of a clan, and we have a  tradition that we're descended from the Dukes of Buccleuch, but the actual founder of my line was my grandfather's brother, who came here in fifty-one, sent a substitute to the Civil War, and started the wholesale hardware business that my father carries on to-day.

I never saw this great-uncle, but I'm supposed to look like him—with special reference to the rather hard-boiled painting that hangs in father's office. I graduated from New Haven in 1915, just a quarter of a century after my father, and a little later I participated in that delayed Teutonic migration known as the Great War. I enjoyed the counter-raid so thoroughly that I came back restless. Instead of being the warm centre of the world, the Middle West now seemed like the ragged edge of the universe—so I decided to go East and learn the bond business. Everybody I knew was in the bond business, so I supposed it could support one more single man. All my aunts and uncles talked it over as if they were choosing a prep school for me, and finally said, "Why—ye—es," with very grave, hesitant faces. Father agreed to finance me for a year, and after various delays I came East, permanently, I thought, in the spring of twenty-two.

The practical thing was to find rooms in the city, but it was a warm season, and I had just left a country of wide lawns and friendly trees, so when a young man at the office suggested that we take a house together in a commuting town, it sounded like a great idea. He found the house, a weather-beaten cardboard bungalow at eighty a month, but at the last minute the firm ordered him to Washington, and I went out to the country alone. I had a dog—at least I had him for a few days until he ran away—and an old Dodge and a Finnish woman, who made my bed and cooked breakfast and muttered Finnish wisdom to herself over the electric stove.

It was lonely for a day or so until one morning some man, more recently arrived than I, stopped me on the road.

"How do you get to West Egg village?" he asked helplessly.

I told him. And as I walked on I was lonely no longer. I was a guide, a pathfinder, an original settler. He had casually conferred on me the freedom of the neighborhood.

And so with the sunshine and the great bursts of leaves growing on the trees, just as things grow in fast movies, I had that familiar conviction that life was beginning over again with the summer.

There was so much to read, for one thing, and so much fine health to be pulled down out of the young breath-giving air. I bought a dozen volumes on banking and credit and investment securities, and they stood on my shelf in red and gold like new money from the mint, promising to unfold the shining secrets that only Midas and Morgan and Maecenas knew. And I had the high intention of reading many other books besides. I was rather literary in college—one year I wrote a series of very solemn and obvious editorials for the "Yale News"—and now I was going to bring back all such things into my life and become again that most limited of all specialists, the "well-rounded man." This isn't just an epigram—life is much more successfully looked at from a single window, after all.

It was a matter of chance that I should have rented a house in one of the strangest communities in North America. It was on that slender riotous island which extends itself due east of New York—and where there are, among other natural curiosities, two unusual formations of land. Twenty miles from the city a pair of enormous eggs, identical in contour and separated only by a courtesy bay, jut out into the most domesticated body of salt water in the Western hemisphere, the great wet barnyard of Long Island Sound. They are not perfect ovals—like the egg in the Columbus story, they are both crushed flat at the contact end—but their physical resemblance must be a source of perpetual confusion to the gulls that fly overhead. To the wingless a more arresting phenomenon is their dissimilarity in every particular except shape and size.

I lived at West Egg, the—well, the less fashionable of the two, though this is a most superficial tag to express the bizarre and not a little sinister contrast between them. My house was at the very tip of the egg, only fifty yards from the Sound, and squeezed between two huge places that rented for twelve or fifteen thousand a season. The one on my right was a colossal affair by any standard—it was a factual imitation of some Hotel de Ville in Normandy, with a tower on one side, spanking new under a thin beard of raw ivy, and a marble swimming pool, and more than forty acres of lawn and garden. It was Gatsby's mansion. Or, rather, as I didn't know Mr. Gatsby, it was a mansion inhabited by a gentleman of that name. My own house was an eyesore, but it was a small eyesore, and it had been overlooked, so I had a view of the water, a partial view of my neighbor's lawn, and the consoling proximity of millionaires—all for eighty dollars a month.

Across the courtesy bay the white palaces of fashionable East Egg glittered along the water, and the history of the summer really begins on the evening I drove over there to have dinner with the Tom Buchanans. Daisy was my second cousin once removed, and I'd known Tom in college. And just after the war I spent two days with them in Chicago.

Her husband, among various physical accomplishments, had been one of the most powerful ends that ever played football at New Haven—a national figure in a way, one of those men who reach such an acute limited excellence at twenty-one that everything afterward savors of anti-climax. His family were enormously wealthy—even in college his freedom with money was a matter for reproach—

but now he'd left Chicago and come East in a fashion that rather took your breath away: for instance, he'd brought down a string of polo ponies from Lake Forest. It was hard to realize that a man in my own generation was wealthy enough to do that.

Why they came East I don't know. They had spent a year in France for no particular reason, and then drifted here and there unrestfully wherever people played polo and were rich together. This was a permanent move, said Daisy over the telephone, but I didn't believe it—I had no sight into Daisy's heart, but I felt that Tom would drift on forever seeking, a little wistfully, for the dramatic turbulence of some irrecoverable football game.

And so it happened that on a warm windy evening I drove over to East Egg to see two old friends whom I scarcely knew at all. Their house was even more elaborate than I expected, a cheerful red-and-white Georgian Colonial mansion, overlooking the bay. The lawn started at the beach and ran toward the front door for a quarter of a mile, jumping over sun-dials and brick walks and burning gardens—finally when it reached the house drifting up the side in bright vines as though from the momentum of its run. The front was broken by a line of French windows, glowing now with reflected gold and wide open to the warm windy afternoon, and Tom Buchanan in riding clothes was standing with his legs apart on the front porch.

He had changed since his New Haven years. Now he was a sturdy straw-haired man of thirty with a rather hard mouth and a supercilious manner. Two shining arrogant eyes had established dominance over his face and gave him the appearance of always leaning aggressively forward. Not even the effeminate swank of his riding clothes could hide the enormous power of that body—he seemed to fill those glistening boots until he strained the top lacing, and you could see a great pack of muscle shifting when his shoulder moved under his thin coat. It was a body capable of enormous leverage—a cruel body.

His speaking voice, a gruff husky tenor, added to the impression of fractiousness he conveyed. There was a touch of paternal contempt in it, even toward people he liked—and there were men at New Haven who had hated his guts.

"Now, don't think my opinion on these matters is final," he seemed to say, "just because I'm stronger and more of a man than you are." We were in the same senior society, and while we were never intimate I always had the impression that he approved of me and wanted me to like him with some harsh, defiant wistfulness of his own.

We talked for a few minutes on the sunny porch.

"I've got a nice place here," he said, his eyes flashing about restlessly.

Turning me around by one arm, he moved a broad flat hand along the front vista, including in its sweep a sunken Italian garden, a half acre of  deep, pungent roses, and a snub-nosed motor-boat that bumped the tide offshore.

"It belonged to Demaine, the oil man." He turned me around again, politely and abruptly. "We'll go inside."

We walked through a high hallway into a bright rosy-colored space, fragilely bound into the house by French windows at either end. The windows were ajar and gleaming white against the fresh grass outside that seemed to grow a little way into the house. A breeze blew through the room, blew curtains in at one end and out the other like pale flags, twisting them up toward the frosted wedding-cake of the ceiling, and then rippled over the wine-colored rug, making a shadow on it as wind does on the sea.

The only completely stationary object in the room was an enormous couch on which two young women were buoyed up as though upon an anchored balloon. They were both in white, and their dresses were rippling and fluttering as if they had just been blown back in after a short flight around the house. I must have stood for a few moments listening to the whip and snap of the curtains and the groan of a picture on the wall. Then there was a boom as Tom Buchanan shut the rear windows and the caught wind died out about the room, and the curtains and the rugs and the two young women ballooned slowly to the floor.

The younger of the two was a stranger to me. She was extended full length at her end of the divan, completely motionless, and with her chin raised a little, as if she were balancing something on it which was quite likely to fall. If she saw me out of the corner of her eyes she gave no hint of it—indeed, I was almost surprised into murmuring an apology for having disturbed her by coming in.

The other girl, Daisy, made an attempt to rise—she leaned slightly forward with a conscientious expression—then she laughed, an absurd, charming little laugh, and I laughed too and came forward into the room.

"I'm p-paralyzed with happiness." She laughed again, as if she said something very witty, and held my hand for a moment, looking up into my face, promising that there was no one in the world she so much wanted to see. That was a way she had. She hinted in a murmur that the surname of the balancing girl was Baker. (I've heard it said that Daisy's murmur was only to make people lean toward her; an irrelevant criticism that made it no less charming.)

At any rate, Miss Baker's lips fluttered, she nodded at me almost imperceptibly, and then quickly tipped her head back again—the object she was balancing had obviously tottered a little and given her something of a fright. Again a sort of apology arose to my lips. Almost any exhibition of complete self-sufficiency draws a stunned tribute from me.

I looked back at my cousin, who began to ask me questions in her low, thrilling voice. It was the kind of voice that the ear follows up and down, as if each speech is an arrangement of notes that will never be played again. Her face was sad and lovely with bright things in it, bright eyes and a bright passionate mouth, but there was an excitement in her voice that men who had cared for her found difficult to forget: a singing compulsion, a whispered "Listen," a promise that she had done gay, exciting things just a while since and that there were gay, exciting things hovering in the next hour.

I told her how I had stopped off in Chicago for a day on my way East, and how a dozen people had sent their love through me.

"Do they miss me?" she cried ecstatically.

"The whole town is desolate. All the cars have the left rear wheel painted black as a mourning wreath, and there's a persistent wail all night along the north shore."

"How gorgeous! Let's go back, Tom. To-morrow!" Then she added irrelevantly: "You ought to see the baby."

"I'd like to."

"She's asleep. She's three years old. Haven't you ever seen her?"

"Never."

"Well, you ought to see her. She's—"

Tom Buchanan, who had been hovering restlessly about the room, stopped and rested his hand on my shoulder.

"What you doing, Nick?"

"I'm a bond man."

"Who with?"

I told him.

"Never heard of them," he remarked decisively.

This annoyed me.

"You will," I answered shortly. "You will if you stay in the East."

"Oh, I'll stay in the East, don't you worry," he said, glancing at Daisy and then back at me, as if he were alert for something more. "I'd be a God d----d fool to live anywhere else."

At this point Miss Baker said: "Absolutely!" with such suddenness that I started—it was the first word she uttered since I came into the room. Evidently it surprised her as much as it did me, for she yawned and with a series of rapid, deft movements stood up into the room.

"I'm stiff," she complained, "I've been lying on that sofa for as long as I can remember."

"Don't look at me," Daisy retorted, "I've been trying to get you to New York all afternoon."

"No, thanks," said Miss Baker to the four cocktails just in from the pantry, "I'm absolutely in training."

Her host looked at her incredulously.

"You are!" He took down his drink as if it were a drop in the bottom of a glass. "How you ever get anything done is beyond me."

I looked at Miss Baker, wondering what it was she "got done." I enjoyed looking at her. She was a slender, small-breasted girl, with an erect carriage, which she accentuated by throwing her body backward at the shoulders like a young cadet. Her gray sun-strained eyes looked back at me with polite reciprocal curiosity out of a wan, charming, discontented face. It occurred to me now that I had seen her, or a picture of her, somewhere before.

"You live in West Egg," she remarked contemptuously. "I know somebody there."

"I don't know a single—"

"You must know Gatsby."

"Gatsby?" demanded Daisy. "What Gatsby?"

Before I could reply that he was my neighbor dinner was announced; wedging his tense arm imperatively under mine, Tom Buchanan compelled me from the room as though he were moving a checker to another square.

Slenderly, languidly, their hands set lightly on their hips, the two young women preceded us out onto a rosy-colored porch, open toward the sunset, where four candles flickered on the table in the diminished wind.

"Why *candles*?" objected Daisy, frowning. She snapped them out with her fingers. "In two weeks it'll be the longest day in the year." She looked at us all radiantly. "Do you always watch for the longest day of the year and then miss it? I always watch for the longest day in the year and then miss it."

"We ought to plan something," yawned Miss Baker, sitting down at the table as if she were getting into bed.

"All right," said Daisy. "What'll we plan?" She turned to me helplessly: "What do people plan?"

Before I could answer her eyes fastened with an awed expression on her little finger.

"Look!" she complained; "I hurt it."

We all looked—the knuckle was black and blue.

"You did it, Tom," she said accusingly. "I know you didn't mean to, but you *did* do it. That's what I get for marrying a brute of a man, a great, big, hulking physical specimen of a—"

"I hate that word hulking," objected Tom crossly, "even in kidding."

"Hulking," insisted Daisy.

Sometimes she and Miss Baker talked at once, unobtrusively and with a bantering inconsequence that was never quite chatter, that was as cool as their white dresses and their impersonal eyes in the absence of all desire. They were here, and they accepted Tom and me, making only a polite pleasant effort to entertain or to be entertained. They knew that presently dinner would be over and a little later the evening too would be over and casually put away. It was sharply different from the West, where an evening was hurried from phase to phase toward its close, in a continually disappointed anticipation or else in sheer nervous dread of the moment itself.

"You make me feel uncivilized, Daisy," I confessed on my second glass of corky but rather impressive claret. "Can't you talk about crops or something?"

I meant nothing in particular by this remark, but it was taken up in an unexpected way.

"Civilization's going to pieces," broke out Tom violently. "I've gotten to be a terrible pessimist about things. Have you read *The Rise of the Colored Empires* by this man Goddard?"

"Why, no," I answered, rather surprised by his tone.

"Well, it's a fine book, and everybody ought to read it. The idea is if we don't look out the white race will be — will be utterly submerged. It's all scientific stuff; it's been proved."

"Tom's getting very profound," said Daisy, with an expression of unthoughtful sadness. "He reads deep books with long words in them. What was that word we —"

"Well, these books are all scientific," insisted Tom, glancing at her impatiently. "This fellow has worked out the whole thing. It's up to us, who are the dominant race, to watch out or these other races will have control of things."

"We've got to beat them down," whispered Daisy, winking ferociously toward the fervent sun.

"You ought to live in California —" began Miss Baker, but Tom interrupted her by shifting heavily in his chair.

"This idea is that we're Nordics. I am, and you are, and you are, and —" After an infinitesimal hesitation he included Daisy with a slight nod, and she winked at me again. " — And we've produced all the things that go to make civilization — oh, science and art, and all that. Do you see?"

There was something pathetic in his concentration, as if his complacency, more acute than of old, was not enough to him any more. When, almost immediately, the telephone rang inside and the butler left the porch Daisy seized upon the momentary interruption and leaned toward me.

"I'll tell you a family secret," she whispered enthusiastically. "It's about the butler's nose. Do you want to hear about the butler's nose?"

"That's why I came over to-night."

"Well, he wasn't always a butler; he used to be the silver polisher for some people in New York that had a silver service for two hundred people. He had to polish it from morning till night, until finally it began to affect his nose—"

"Things went from bad to worse," suggested Miss Baker.

"Yes. Things went from bad to worse, until finally he had to give up his position."

For a moment the last sunshine fell with romantic affection upon her glowing face; her voice compelled me forward breathlessly as I listened—then the glow faded, each light deserting her with lingering regret, like children leaving a pleasant street at dusk.

The butler came back and murmured something close to Tom's ear, whereupon Tom frowned, pushed back his chair, and without a word went inside. As if his absence quickened something within her, Daisy leaned forward again, her voice glowing and singing.

"I love to see you at my table, Nick. You remind me of a—of a rose, an absolute rose. Doesn't he?" She turned to Miss Baker for confirmation: "An absolute rose?"

This was untrue. I am not even faintly like a rose. She was only extemporizing, but a stirring warmth flowed from her, as if her heart was trying to come out to you concealed in one of those breathless, thrilling words. Then suddenly she threw her napkin on the table and excused herself and went into the house.

Miss Baker and I exchanged a short glance consciously devoid of meaning. I was about to speak when she sat up alertly and said "Sh!" in a warning voice. A subdued impassioned murmur was audible in the room beyond, and Miss Baker leaned forward unashamed, trying to hear. The murmur trembled on the verge of coherence, sank down, mounted excitedly, and then ceased altogether.

"This Mr. Gatsby you spoke of is my neighbor—" I said.

"Don't talk. I want to hear what happens."

"Is something happening?" I inquired innocently.

"You mean to say you don't know?" said Miss Baker, honestly

surprised. "I thought everybody knew."

"I don't."

"Why —" she said hesitantly, "Tom's got some woman in New York."

"Got some woman?" I repeated blankly.

Miss Baker nodded.

"She might have the decency not to telephone him at dinner time. Don't you think?"

Almost before I had grasped her meaning there was the flutter of a dress and the crunch of leather boots, and Tom and Daisy were back at the table.

"It couldn't be helped!" cried Daisy with tense gaiety.

She sat down, glanced searchingly at Miss Baker and then at me, and continued: "I looked outdoors for a minute, and it's very romantic outdoors. There's a bird on the lawn that I think must be a nightingale come over on the Cunard or White Star Line. He's singing away —" Her voice sang: "It's romantic, isn't it, Tom?"

"Very romantic," he said, and then miserably to me: "If it's light enough after dinner, I want to take you down to the stables."

The telephone rang inside, startlingly, and as Daisy shook her head decisively at Tom the subject of the stables, in fact all subjects, vanished into air. Among the broken fragments of the last five minutes at table I remember the candles being lit again, pointlessly, and I was conscious of wanting to look squarely at every one, and yet to avoid all eyes. I couldn't guess what Daisy and Tom were thinking, but I doubt if even Miss Baker, who seemed to have mastered a certain hardy scepticism, was able utterly to put this fifth guest's shrill metallic urgency out of mind. To a certain temperament the situation might have seemed intriguing — my own instinct was to telephone immediately for the police.

The horses, needless to say, were not mentioned again. Tom and Miss Baker, with several feet of twilight between them, strolled back into the library, as if to a vigil beside a perfectly tangible body, while, trying to look pleasantly interested and a little deaf, I followed Daisy around a chain of connecting verandas to the porch in front. In its deep gloom we sat down side by side on a wicker settee.

Daisy took her face in her hands as if feeling its lovely shape, and her eyes moved gradually out into the velvet dusk. I saw that turbulent emotions possessed her, so I asked what I thought would be some sedative questions about her little girl.

"We don't know each other very well, Nick," she said suddenly. "Even if we are cousins. You didn't come to my wedding."

"I wasn't back from the war."

"That's true." She hesitated. "Well, I've had a very bad time, Nick, and I'm pretty cynical about everything."

Evidently she had reason to be. I waited but she didn't say any more, and after a moment I returned rather feebly to the subject of her daughter.

"I suppose she talks, and — eats, and everything."

"Oh, yes." She looked at me absently. "Listen, Nick; let me tell you what I said when she was born. Would you like to hear?"

"Very much."

"It'll show you how I've gotten to feel about — things. Well, she was less than an hour old and Tom was God knows where. I woke up out of the ether with an utterly abandoned feeling, and asked the nurse right away if it was a boy or a girl. She told me it was a girl, and so I turned my head away and wept. 'All right,' I said, 'I'm glad it's a girl. And I hope she'll be a fool — that's the best thing a girl can be in this world, a beautiful little fool.'

"You see I think everything's terrible anyhow," she went on in a convinced way. "Everybody thinks so — the most advanced people. And I *know*. I've been everywhere and seen everything and done everything." Her eyes flashed around her in a defiant way, rather like Tom's, and she laughed with thrilling scorn. "Sophisticated — God, I'm sophisticated!"

The instant her voice broke off, ceasing to compel my attention, my belief, I felt the basic insincerity of what she had said. It made me uneasy, as though the whole evening had been a trick of some sort to exact a contributory emotion from me. I waited, and sure enough, in a moment she looked at me with an absolute smirk on her lovely face, as if she had asserted her membership in a rather distinguished secret society to which she and Tom belonged.

Inside, the crimson room bloomed with light.

Tom and Miss Baker sat at either end of the long couch and she read aloud to him from the *Saturday Evening Post* — the words, murmurous and uninflected, running together in a soothing tune. The lamp-light, bright on his boots and dull on the autumn-leaf yellow of her hair, glinted along the paper as she turned a page with a flutter of slender muscles in her arms.

When we came in she held us silent for a moment with a lifted hand.

"To be continued," she said, tossing the magazine on the table, "in our very next issue."

Her body asserted itself with a restless movement of her knee, and she stood up.

"Ten o'clock," she remarked, apparently finding the time on the ceiling. "Time for this good girl to go to bed."

"Jordan's going to play in the tournament to-morrow," explained Daisy, "over at Westchester."

"Oh—you're Jordan *Baker*."

I knew now why her face was familiar—its pleasing contemptuous expression had looked out at me from many rotogravure pictures of the sporting life at Asheville and Hot Springs and Palm Beach. I had heard some story of her too, a critical, unpleasant story, but what it was I had forgotten long ago.

"Good night," she said softly. "Wake me at eight, won't you?"

"If you'll get up."

"I will. Good night, Mr. Carraway. See you anon."

"Of course you will," confirmed Daisy. "In fact I think I'll arrange a marriage. Come over often, Nick, and I'll sort of—oh—fling you together. You know—lock you up accidentally in linen closets and push you out to sea in a boat, and all that sort of thing—"

"Good night," called Miss Baker from the stairs. "I haven't heard a word."

"She's a nice girl," said Tom after a moment. "They oughtn't to let her run around the country this way."

"Who oughtn't to?" inquired Daisy coldly.

"Her family."

"Her family is one aunt about a thousand years old. Besides, Nick's going to look after her, aren't you, Nick? She's going to spend lots of week-ends out here this summer. I think the home influence will be very good for her."

Daisy and Tom looked at each other for a moment in silence.

"Is she from New York?" I asked quickly.

"From Louisville. Our white girlhood was passed together there. Our beautiful white—"

"Did you give Nick a little heart to heart talk on the veranda?" demanded Tom suddenly.

"Did I?" She looked at me. "I can't seem to remember, but I think we talked about the Nordic race. Yes, I'm sure we did. It sort of crept up on us and first thing you know—"

"Don't believe everything you hear, Nick," he advised me.

I said lightly that I had heard nothing at all, and a few minutes later I got up to go home. They came to the door with me and stood side by side in a cheerful square of light. As I started my motor Daisy peremptorily called: "Wait!"

"I forgot to ask you something, and it's important. We heard you were engaged to a girl out West."

"That's right," corroborated Tom kindly. "We heard that you were engaged."

"It's libel. I'm too poor."

"But we heard it," insisted Daisy, surprising me by opening up again in a flower-like way. "We heard it from three people, so it must be true."

Of course I knew what they were referring to, but I wasn't even vaguely engaged. The fact that gossip had published the banns was one of the reasons I had come East. You can't stop going with an old friend on account of rumors, and on the other hand I had no intention of being rumored into marriage.

Their interest rather touched me and made them less remotely rich — nevertheless, I was confused and a little disgusted as I drove away. It seemed to me that the thing for Daisy to do was to rush out of the house, child in arms — but

apparently there were no such intentions in her head. As for Tom, the fact that he "had some woman in New York" was really less surprising than that he had been depressed by a book. Something was making him nibble at the edge of stale ideas as if his sturdy physical egotism no longer nourished his peremptory heart.

Already it was deep summer on roadhouse roofs and in front of wayside garages, where new red gas-pumps sat out in pools of light, and when I reached my estate at West Egg I ran the car under its shed and sat for a while on an abandoned grass roller in the yard. The wind had blown off, leaving a loud, bright night, with wings beating in the trees and a persistent organ sound as the full bellows of the earth blew the frogs full of life. The silhouette of a moving cat wavered across the moonlight, and turning my head to watch it, I saw that I was not alone — fifty feet away a figure had emerged from the shadow of my neighbor's mansion and was standing with his hands in his pockets regarding the silver pepper of the stars. Something in his leisurely movements and the secure position of his feet upon the lawn suggested that it was Mr. Gatsby himself, come out to determine what share was his of our local heavens.

I decided to call to him. Miss Baker had mentioned him at dinner, and that would do for an introduction. But I didn't call to him, for he gave a sudden intimation that he was content to be alone — he stretched out his arms toward the dark water in a curious way, and, far as I was from him, I could have sworn he was trembling. Involuntarily I glanced seaward — and distinguished nothing except a single green light, minute and far away, that might have been the end of a dock. When I looked once more for Gatsby he had vanished, and I was alone again in the unquiet darkness. [emphasis added]

From Chapter 3

On week-ends his Rolls-Royce became an omnibus, bearing parties to and from the city between nine in the morning and long past midnight. . . .

I believe that on the first night I went to Gatsby's house I was one of the few guests who had actually been invited. People were not invited — they went there. They got into automobiles which bore them out to Long Island, and somehow they ended up at Gatsby's door. . . .

"I'm Gatsby," he said suddenly.

"What!" I exclaimed. "Oh, I beg your pardon."

"I thought you knew, old sport. I'm afraid I'm not a very good host."

The yellow 1928 Rolls Royce from the Great Gatsby

He smiled understandingly — much more than understandingly. It was one of those rare smiles with a quality of eternal reassurance in it, that you may come across four or five times in life. It faced — or seemed to face — the whole external world for an instant, and then concentrated on you with an irresistible prejudice in your favor. It understood you just so far as you wanted to be understood, believed in you as you would like to believe in yourself, and assured you that it had precisely the impression of you that, at your best, you hoped to convey. Precisely at that point it vanished — and I was looking at an elegant young rough-neck, a year or two over thirty, whose elaborate formality of speech just missed being absurd. Some time before he introduced himself I'd got a strong impression that he was picking his words with care.

The Ending of The Great Gatsby

On the last night, with my trunk packed and my car sold to the grocer, I went over and looked at that huge incoherent failure of a house once more. On the white steps an obscene word, scrawled by some boy with a piece of brick, stood out clearly in the moonlight, and I erased it, drawing my shoe raspingly along the stone. Then I wandered down to the beach and sprawled out on the sand.

Most of the big shore places were closed now and there were hardly any lights except the shadowy, moving glow of a ferryboat across the Sound. And as the moon rose higher the inessential houses began to melt away until gradually I became aware of the old island here that flowered once for Dutch sailors' eyes — a fresh, green breast of the new world. Its vanished trees, the trees that had made way for Gatsby's house, had once pandered in whispers to the last and greatest of all human dreams; for a transitory enchanted moment man must have held his breath in the presence of this continent, compelled into an aesthetic contemplation he neither understood nor desired, face to face for the last time in history with something commensurate to his capacity for wonder.

And as I sat there brooding on the old, unknown world, I thought of Gatsby's wonder when he first picked out *the green light* at the end of Daisy's dock. He had come a long way to this blue lawn, and his dream must have seemed so close that he could hardly fail to grasp it. He did not know that it was already behind him, somewhere back in that vast obscurity beyond the city, where the dark fields of the republic rolled on under the night. [emphasis added]

Gatsby believed in *the green light*, the orgastic future that year by year recedes before us. It eluded us then, but that's no matter — to-morrow we will run faster, stretch out our arms farther. . . . And one fine morning — [emphasis added]

So we beat on, boats against the current, borne back ceaselessly into the past.

Comments on The Great Gatsby

Motif of the "Green Light"

[At the end of chap. 1] is the first use of one of the novel's central motif, *the green light* at the end of Daisy's dock. What Fitzgerald seems to be doing is merely introducing a symbol that will gain in meaning as the story progresses. At this point, we don't even know that the light is on Daisy's dock, and we have no reason to associate Gatsby with Daisy. What we do know — and this is very important — is that Nick admires Gatsby because of his dream and this dream is somehow associated with the green light. The color green is a traditional symbol of spring and hope and youth. As long as Gatsby gazes at the green light, his dream lives. —A Critic

White Daisy

The white Daisy embodies the vision which Gatsby (who, like Lord Jim, usually wears white suits) seeks to embrace—but which Nick, who discovers the corrupt admixture of dream and reality, rejects in rejecting Jordan. For, except in Gatsby's extravagant imagination, the white does not exist pure: it is invariably stained by the money, the yellow. Daisy is the white flower—with the golden center. If in her virginal beauty she "dressed in white and had a little white roadster," she is, Nick realizes, "high in a white palace the king's daughter, the golden girl." "Her voice is like money"; she carries a "little gold pencil"; when she visits Gatsby there are "two rows of brass buttons on her dress." —Daniel J. Schneider

The Narrator's Lack of Fiber

Carraway's distinctiveness as a character is that he fails to learn anything from his story, that he can continue to blind himself even after his privileged overview of Gatsby's fate. . . . He refuses to admit that his alliance with Gatsby, his admiration for the man, results from their sharing the same weakness. . . . He  has learned nothing. His failure to come to any self-knowledge makes him like the person who blames the stone for stubbing his toe. It seems inevitable that he will repeat the same mistakes as soon as the feeling that "temporarily closed out my interest in the abortive sorrows and short-winded elations of men" has departed. . . . Had Carraway been defeated by the impersonal forces of an evil world in which he was an ineffectual innocent, his very existence—temporary or not—would lighten the picture. But his defeat is caused by something that lies within himself: his own lack of fiber, his own willingness to deny reality, his own substitution of dreams for knowledge of self and the world, his own sharing in the very vices of which his fellow men stand accused. —Gary J. Scrimgeour

Illusions and Reality

The Great Gatsby is an exploration of the American dream as it exists in a corrupt period, and it is an attempt to determine that concealed boundary that divides the reality from the illusions. The illusions seem more real than the reality itself. Embodied in the subordinate characters in the novel, they threaten to invade the whole of the picture. On the other hand, the reality is embodied in Gatsby; and as opposed to the hard, tangible illusions, the reality is a thing of the spirit, a promise rather than the possession of a vision, a faith in the half-glimpsed, but hardly understood possibilities of life. — Marius Bewley

Worldview in Literature

A significant part of a literary theme is the worldview of the author. What is a "worldview"? Worldview is the way a person or group understands, relates to, and responds from a philosophical position that is embraced for oneself. Worldview is a framework that ties everything together, that allows us to understand society, the world, and our place in it.

A worldview helps us make the critical decisions that will shape our future. A worldview colors all our decisions and all our artistic creations. In the first *Star Wars* movie (1977), for instance, Luke Skywalker clearly values a Judeo-Christian code of ethics. That does not mean that he is a believing Christian—indeed he is not—but he does uphold and fight for a moral world. Darth Vader, on the other hand, represents chaos and

amoral behavior. He does whatever it takes to advance the Emperor's agenda, regardless of who he hurts or what rule he breaks. It is important that we articulate our own worldview so that we will be ready to discern other worldviews later.

There are basically two worldview roots: One originated with Aristotle, who argued that the empirical world is primary. Thus, if one wants to advance knowledge, one has to learn more about the world. Another root originated with Plato, who argued that the unseen world is primary. In Plato's case, that means that one who wishes to understand the world must study the gods. In our case, we agree with Plato to the extent that we believe that God—who cannot be seen or measured—is in fact more real than the world.

Both Plato and Aristotle were impacted by *Socrates*, one of the most influential but mysterious figures in Western philosophy. As far as we know,

Socrates wrote nothing, yet he had a profound influence on someone who did: Plato carefully recorded most of Socrates' dialogues.

Unlike earlier philosophers, Socrates' main concern was with ethics. There was nothing remotely pragmatic about Socrates, who was the consummate idealist. Until his day, philosophers invested most of their time explaining the natural world. In fact, the natural world often intruded into the abstract world of ideas and reality. Socrates kept both worlds completely separate.

To Socrates, natural laws governing the rotation of the earth were merely uninteresting speculation of no earthly good. Socrates was more interested in such meaty concepts as "virtue" and "justice."

Taking issue with the Sophists, Socrates believed that ethics, specifically virtue, must be learned and practiced like any trade. One was not born virtuous; one developed virtue as he would a good habit. It could be practiced only by experts. There was, then, nothing pragmatic about the pursuit of virtue. It was systematic; it was intentional. Virtue was acquired and maintained by open and free dialogue. For the first time, the importance of human language was advanced by a philosopher (to reappear at the end of the twentieth century in postmodern philosophy).

There was no more important philosopher in Western culture than Socrates' disciple Plato. Like Socrates, Plato regarded ethics as the highest branch of knowledge. He stressed the intellectual basis of virtue, identifying virtue with wisdom. Plato believed that the world was made of forms (such as a rock) and ideas (such as virtue).

The ability of human beings to appreciate forms made a person virtuous. Knowledge came from the gods; opinion was from man. Virtuous activity, then, was dependent upon knowledge of the forms.

To Plato, knowledge and virtue were inseparable. To Aristotle, they were unconnected. Aristotle was not on a search for absolute truth. He was not even certain it existed. Truth, beauty, and goodness were to be observed and quantified from human behavior and the senses, but they were not the legal tender of the land. Goodness in particular was not an absolute, and in Aristotle's opinion it was much abused. Goodness was an average between two absolutes. Aristotle said that humankind should strike a balance between passion and temperance, between extremes of all sorts. He said that good people should seek the "golden mean" defined as a course of life that was never extreme.

Finally, while Plato argued that reality lay in knowledge of the gods, Aristotle argued that reality lay in empirical, measurable knowledge. To Aristotle, reality was tied to purpose and to action. For these reasons, Aristotle became known as the father of modern science. Aristotle's most enduring impact occurred in the area of *metaphysics* — philosophical speculation about the nature, substance, and structure of reality. It is not physics, which is concerned with the visible or natural world. Metaphysics is concerned with explaining the nonphysical world, that which is behind, beyond, and transcending the physical. It seeks to understand the fundamental nature of reality and being.

Aristotle, then, advanced the discussion about God, the human soul, and the nature of space and time. What makes this particularly interesting is Aristotle's penchant for delving into the metaphysical by talking about the gods in human terms.

Aristotle said, "All men by nature desire to know," and it is by the senses that the gods were known — or not. Faith had nothing to do with it. In other words, Aristotle, for the first time, discussed the gods as if they were quantified entities. He spoke about them as if they were not present. The Hebrews had done this earlier (Genesis 3), but Aristotle was probably not aware of Moses' text.

While some Christian thinkers such as Augustine and Aquinas employed Aristotelian logic in their discussions about God, they never speculated about God's existence as Aristotle did. They used Aristotle's techniques only to understand more about God.

— James P. Stobaugh, *World Literature* (Green Forest, AR: New Leaf Press, 2012)

Foundations of Major Worldviews

From the contrast of Aristotle versus Plato, a panoply of worldviews evolved in four main epochs. The following are characteristics of each epoch:

Classical Pagan Theism: Ancient Times to Augustine — Pernicious and fickle gods meddling in human affairs

Christian Theism: Augustine to Goethe — Loving Creator God intimately involved in all human affairs and in his universe

Modernism: Goethe to Camus — Faith in science, in human knowledge, displacing faith in God or gods

Postmodernism: Camus to Present Authors — Faith in experience (relativism); suspicious of science

Within these epochs are the following worldviews:
- ❶ Theism
- ❷ Deism
- ❸ Romanticism
- ❹ Naturalism
- ❺ Realism
- ❻ Existentialism
- ❼ Absurdism

Seven Major Worldviews

Here is a short sketch of these seven major worldviews, with examples:

❶ *Theism*

God, as portrayed in Scripture, is personally involved with humankind. Biblical theism argues that the universe is a purposive, divinely created entity. It insists that all human life is sacred and all persons are of equal dignity. They are, in other words, created in the image of God. History is linear and moves toward a final goal. Nature is controlled by God and is an orderly system. Humanity is neither the center of nature nor the universe, but is the steward of creation. Righteousness will triumph in a decisive conquest of evil. Earthly life does not exhaust human existence but looks ahead to the resurrection of the dead and to a final, comprehensive judgment of humanity (adapted from Carl F. H. Henry, *Toward a Recovery of Christian Belief*). This is the only viable worldview until the Renaissance.

Examples: Homer, Virgil, C. S. Lewis, A. J. Cronin, Tolkien.

❷ Deism

God *was* present but is no longer present. The world is like a clock wound up by God many years ago, but God is now absent. The clock (i.e., the world) is present; God is absent. Still, though, Deism embraces a Judeo-Christian morality. God's absence, for instance, in no way mitigates his importance to original creation. He is also omnipotent, but not omniscient. His absence is his decision. God is in no way forced to be absent from the world. He chooses to assume that role so that Socratic empiricism and rationalism can reign as sovereign king. Speculative Theism replaces revelatory Biblical Theism. Once the Living God is abandoned, Jesus Christ and the Bible become cognitive orphans (Carl F. H. Henry).

Examples: Ben Franklin, Thomas Jefferson.

❸ Romanticism

Once Americans distance themselves from the self-revealing God of the Old and New Testaments, they cannot resist making further concessions to subjectivity. Romanticism, and its American version, Transcendentalism, posits that God is Nature and that "It" is good. The more natural things are, the better. Nature is inherently good. Nature alone is the ultimate reality. In other words, Nature is the Romantic god. Man is essentially a complex animal, too complex to be controlled by absolute, codified truth (as one would find in the Bible). Human intuition replaces the Holy Spirit. Depending upon the demands on individual lives, truth and good are relative and changing. Yet Romanticism, like Deism, has not completely abandoned Judeo-Christian morality. Truth and the good, although changing, are nonetheless relatively durable.

Examples: James Fenimore Cooper, Ralph Waldo Emerson, Goethe.

❹ Naturalism

If God exists, he is rather wimpish. Only the laws of nature have any force. God is either uninterested or downright mean. All reality is reducible to impersonal processes and energy events (Carl F. H. Henry). All life, including human life, is transient. Its final destination is death. Truth and good, therefore, are also transient. The human race has projected culture-conditioned distinctions upon the cosmos and upon history (Carl F. H. Henry). This maturation, as it were, of the human race necessitated a deliberate rejection of all transcendentally final authority.

Examples: Joseph Conrad, Stephen Crane.

❺ Realism

Akin to Naturalism is Realism. Reality is, to a Realist, a world with no purpose, no meaning, no order. Realism insists that personality has no ultimate status in the universe, but is logically inconsistent when it affirms an ethically imperative social agenda congruent with universal human rights and dignity. Realism, then, throws around terms like "dignity" and "human rights" and "power." What Realists mean, however, is that these concepts are real when they fulfill a social agenda that enhances human dominance over the universal. Thus Realism believes in a world where bad things happen all the time to good people. Why not? There is no God, no ontological controlling force for good. The world is a place where the only reality is that which we can experience, but it must be experience that we can measure or replicate. Certainly pain and misery fit that category. If an experience is a unique occurrence (such as a miracle), it is not real.

Examples: Ernest Hemingway, F. Scott Fitzgerald.

❻ Existentialism

The submergence of God in immediate experience and overwhelming data is the first step toward putting God out to die. Truth is open to debate: everything is relative. Some of these themes are picked up in postmodernism, especially with its relativistic view of reality. Existentialism is quite pessimistic.

Examples: Albert Camus, Franz Kafka, and Jean Paul Sartre.

❼ Absurdism

A modern movement where there is neither a god nor any reason to have one. Everything is disorganized; anarchy rules. There is a compete abandonment of explaining the cosmos and therefore an abandonment of being in relationship with the Deity. It is not that Absurdists are unsure about who creates everything or who/what is in control of everything. Absurdists simply do not care one way or the other.

Examples: John Barth, Kurt Vonnegut Jr.

Now we will examine samples of literature illustrating these major worldviews, following the sequence in which they are identified above.

Iliad, by Homer

Background for Nonbiblical Theism

The gods and goddesses on Olympus, all-powerful and often ridiculous, are contrasted to the mortals, so seriously engaged on earth. The immortals are gigantic; they live forever and have nothing to fear. Beside them, humanity seems small, yet at the same time it gains tragic stature. Though the mortals are puny in comparison, there is something ennobling about their struggle to find value and moral meaning in their lives, and something heroic in the wholehearted way they engage in their pursuit. These men, whose lives are so clearly bounded by time and the fates, play out their destiny with fervor and depth of feeling. It is the gods, in fact, who often seem casual [fickle] and small-minded. The *Iliad* shows us a human world filled with struggle and brutality, a world nevertheless in which mortals exercise will in the face of divine intervention—to create their lives according to their own terms of value, to suffer existence and discover its possible meaning. —*Barron's Booknotes*

Tell me now, Muses, dwelling on Olympus,
as you are heavenly, and are everywhere,
and everything is known to you—
while we can only hear the tales and never know—
who were the Danaan lords and officers?
The rank and file I shall not name;
I could not, if I were gifted
with ten tongues and voices unfaltering,
and a brazen heart within me,
unless the Muses, daughters of Olympian Zeus
beyond the storm cloud, could recall
all those who sailed for the campaign at Troy.
Let me name only the captains of contingents
and number all the ships.

Combat between Menelaus & Hector (in the Iliad)

The Life and Morals of Jesus of Nazareth, by Jefferson

Background

This harmonizing paraphrase of the Gospels is called the Jefferson Bible. In it

Thomas Jefferson as a Deist rejects all supernatural aspects and believes that although God once was active among humankind, he is no longer active. Thus it is up to humans to govern themselves, to determine their own fate.

In an 1803 letter, Thomas Jefferson states that he conceived the idea of writing his view of the "Christian System" in a conversation with Dr. Benjamin Rush during 1798–99. He proposes beginning with a review of the morals of the ancient philosophers, moving on to the "deism and ethics of the Jews," and concluding with the "principles of a pure deism" taught by Jesus, "omitting the question of his deity."

(Sources identified within brackets and punctuation adjusted.)

[Matthew 27:15-31] Now at the feast the governor was wont to release unto the people a prisoner, whom they would. And they had then a notable prisoner, called Barabbas. Therefore when they were gathered together, Pilate said unto them, "Whom will ye that I release unto you? Barabbas, or Jesus which is called Christ?" For he knew that for envy they had delivered him.

Moreover, while he was set down on the judgment seat, his wife sent unto him, saying, "Have thou nothing to do with that just man: for I have suffered many things this day in a dream because of him."

But the chief priests and elders persuaded the multitude that they should ask for Barabbas, and destroy Jesus. The governor answered and said unto them, "Whether of the twain will ye that I release unto you?" They said, "Barabbas."

Pilate saith unto them, "What shall I do then with Jesus which is called Christ?" They all say unto him, "Let him be crucified." And the governor said, "Why, what evil hath he done?" But they cried out the more, saying, "Let him be crucified."

Then released he Barabbas unto them: and when he had scourged Jesus, he delivered him to be crucified. Then the soldiers of the governor took Jesus into the Praetorium, and gathered unto him the whole band of soldiers. And when they had platted a crown of thorns, they put it upon his head, and a reed in his right hand: and they bowed the knee before him, and mocked him, saying, "Hail, King of the Jews!" And they spit upon him, and took the reed, and smote him on the head. And after that they had mocked him, they took the robe off from him, and put his own raiment on him, and led him away to crucify him.

[Matthew 27:3–8] Then Judas, which had betrayed him, when he saw that he was condemned, repented himself, and brought again the thirty pieces of silver to the chief priests and elders, saying, "I have sinned in that I have betrayed innocent blood." And they said, "What is that to us? See thou to that." And he cast down the pieces of silver in the temple, and departed, and went and hanged himself. And the chief priests took the silver pieces, and said, "It is not lawful for to put them into the treasury, because it is the price of blood." And they took counsel, and bought with them the potter's field, to bury strangers in. Wherefore that field is called, The Field of Blood, unto this day.

[Luke 23:26–32] And as they led him away, they laid hold upon one Simon of Cyrene, coming out of the country, and on him they laid the cross, that he might bear it after Jesus. And there followed him a great company of people, and of women, which bewailed and lamented him. But Jesus turning unto them said, "Daughters of Jerusalem, weep not for me, but weep for yourselves, and for your children. For, behold, the days are coming, in the which they shall say, 'Blessed are the barren, and the wombs that never bare, and the paps which never gave suck.' Then shall they begin to say to the mountains, 'Fall on us; and to the hills, Cover us.' For if they do these things in a green tree, what shall be done in the dry? And there were also two other, malefactors, led with him to be put to death.

[John 19:17–24] And he bearing his cross went forth into a place called the place of a skull, which is called in the Hebrew Golgotha: There they crucified him, and two other with him, on either side one, and Jesus in the midst. And Pilate wrote a title, and put it on the cross. And the writing was JESUS OF NAZARETH THE KING OF THE JEWS. This title then read many of the Jews: for the place where Jesus was crucified was nigh to the city; and it was written in Hebrew, and Latin, and Greek. Then said the chief priests of the Jews to Pilate,

"Write not, 'The King of the Jews'; but, 'This man said, "I am King of the Jews."'" Pilate answered, "What I have written I have written."

Then the soldiers, when they had crucified Jesus, took his garments, and made four parts, to every soldier a part; and also his undergarment: now the undergarment was without seam, woven from the top to the bottom. They said therefore among themselves, "Let us not rend it, but cast lots for it, in order to determine whose it shall be."

[Matthew 27:39–43] And they that passed by reviled him, wagging their heads, and saying, "Thou that destroyest the temple, and buildest it in three days, save thyself. If thou be the Son of God, come down from the cross." Likewise also the chief priests mocking him, with the scribes and elders, said, "He saved others; himself he cannot save. If he be the King of Israel, let him now come down from the cross, and we will believe in him. He trusted in God; let him deliver him now, if he will have him: for he said, 'I am the Son of God.'"

[Luke 23:39–41, 34] And one of the malefactors which were hanged railed on him, saying, "Art thou not the Christ? Save thyself and us!" But the other answering rebuked him, saying, "Dost not thou fear God, seeing thou art in the same condemnation? And we indeed justly; for we receive the due reward of our deeds: but this man hath done nothing amiss." Then said Jesus, "Father, forgive them; for they know not what they do."

[John 19:25–27] Now there stood by the cross of Jesus his mother, and his mother's sister, Mary the wife of Cleophas, and Mary Magdalene. When Jesus therefore saw his mother, and the disciple standing by, whom he loved, he saith unto his mother, "Woman, behold thy son!" Then saith he to the disciple, "Behold thy mother!" And from that hour that disciple took her unto his own home.

[Matthew 27:46–50] And about the ninth hour Jesus cried with a loud voice, saying, "Eli, Eli, lama sabachthani?" that is to say, "My God, my God, why hast thou forsaken me?" Some of them that stood there, when they heard that, said, "This man calleth for Elijah." And straightway one of them ran, and took a sponge, and filled it with vinegar, and put it on a reed, and gave him to drink. The rest said, "Let be, let us see whether Elijah will come to save him." Jesus, when he had cried out again with a loud voice, yielded up the ghost.

[Matthew 27:55–56] And many women were there beholding afar off, which followed Jesus from Galilee, ministering unto him: Among which was Mary Magdalene, and Mary the mother of James and Joseph, and the mother of Zebedee's sons.

[John 19:31–34] The Jews therefore, because it was the day of preparation, that the bodies should not remain upon the cross on the sabbath, (for that sabbath was an high day,) besought Pilate that their legs might be broken, and that they might be taken away. Then came the soldiers, and brake the legs of the first, and of the other which was crucified with him. But when they came to Jesus, and saw that he was dead already, they brake not his legs: But one of the soldiers with a spear pierced his side, and forthwith came there out blood and water.

[John 19:38–42; Matthew 27:60] And after this Joseph of Arimathaea, being a disciple of Jesus, but secretly for fear of the Jews, besought Pilate that he might take away the body of Jesus: and Pilate gave him leave. He came therefore, and took the body of Jesus. And there came also Nicodemus, which at the first came to Jesus by night, and brought a mixture of myrrh and aloes, about an hundred pound weight. Then took they the body of Jesus, and wound it in linen cloths with the spices, as the manner of the Jews is to bury. Now in the place where he was crucified there was a garden; and in the garden a new sepulchre, wherein was never man yet laid. There laid they Jesus, and rolled a great stone to the door of the sepulchre, and departed.

Romanticism

Faust, by Johann Wolfgang von Goethe

Faust's Study, Night. In a high-vaulted, narrow Gothic chamber. FAUST, restless in his chair by his desk.

I've studied now Philosophy
And Jurisprudence, Medicine,—
And even, alas! Theology,—
From end to end, with labor keen;
And here, poor fool! with all my lore
I stand, no wiser than before:

I'm Magister — yea, Doctor — hight,
And straight or cross-wise, wrong or right,
These ten years long, with many woes,
I've led my scholars by the nose, —
And see, that nothing can be known!
That knowledge cuts me to the bone.
 I'm cleverer, true, than those fops of teachers,
Doctors and Magisters, Scribes and Preachers;
Neither scruples nor doubts come now to smite me,
Nor Hell nor Devil can longer affright me.
For this, all pleasure am I foregoing;
I do not pretend to aught worth knowing,
I do not pretend I could be a teacher
To help or convert a fellow-creature.
Then, too, I've neither lands nor gold,
Nor the world's least pomp or honor hold —
No dog would endure such a curst existence!
Wherefore, from Magic I seek assistance,

That many a secret perchance I reach
Through spirit-power and spirit-speech,
And thus the bitter task forego
Of saying the things I do not know, —
That I may detect the inmost force
Which binds the world, and guides its course;
Its germs, productive powers explore,
And rummage in empty words no more!
O full and splendid Moon, whom I
Have, from this desk, seen climb the sky
So many a midnight, — would thy glow
For the last time beheld my woe!
Ever thine eye, most mournful friend,
O'er books and papers saw me bend;
But would that I, on mountains grand,
Amid thy blessed light could stand,
With spirits through mountain-caverns hover,
Float in thy twilight the meadows over,
And, freed from the fumes of lore that swathe me,

To health in thy dewy fountains bathe me!
Ah, me! this dungeon still I see.
This drear, accursed masonry,
Where even the welcome daylight strains
But duskly through the painted panes.
Hemmed in by many a toppling heap
Of books worm-eaten, gray with dust,
Which to the vaulted ceiling creep,
Against the smoky paper thrust,—
With glasses, boxes, round me stacked,
And instruments together hurled,
Ancestral lumber, stuffed and packed—
Such is my world: and what a world!
And do I ask, wherefore my heart
Falters, oppressed with unknown needs?
Why some inexplicable smart
All movement of my life impedes?

Alas! in living Nature's stead,
Where God his human creature set,
In smoke and mould the fleshless dead
And bones of beasts surround me yet!
Fly! Up, and seek the broad, free land!
And this one Book of Mystery
From Nostradamus' very hand,
Is't not sufficient company?
When I the starry courses know,
And Nature's wise instruction seek,
With light of power my soul shall glow,
As when to spirits speak.
'Tis vain, this empty brooding here,
Though guessed the holy symbols be:
Ye, Spirits, come—ye hover near—
Oh, if you hear me, answer me!
"The spirit-world no closures fasten;
Thy sense is shut, thy heart is dead:
Disciple, up! untiring, hasten
To bathe thy breast in morning-red!"

(He contemplates the sign.)

How each the Whole its substance gives,
Each in the other works and lives!
Like heavenly forces rising and descending,
Their golden urns reciprocally lending,
With wings that winnow blessing
From Heaven through Earth I see them pressing,
Filling the All with harmony unceasing!
How grand a show! but, ah! a show alone.

(He opens the Book, and perceives the sign of the Macrocosm.)

 Ha! what a sudden rapture leaps from this
I view, through all my senses swiftly flowing!
I feel a youthful, holy, vital bliss
In every vein and fiber newly glowing.
Was it a God, who traced this sign,
With calm across my tumult stealing,
My troubled heart to joy unsealing,
With impulse, mystic and divine,
The powers of Nature here, around my path, revealing?
Am I a God? — so clear mine eyes!
In these pure features I behold
Creative Nature to my soul unfold.
What says the sage, now first I recognize:

Thee, boundless Nature, how make thee my own?
Where you, ye beasts? Founts of all Being, shining,
Whereon hang Heaven's and Earth's desire,
Whereto our withered hearts aspire, —
Ye flow, ye feed: and am I vainly pining?

(He turns the leaves hastily till he perceives the sign of the Earth- Spirit.)

How otherwise upon me works this sign!
Thou, Spirit of the Earth, art nearer:
Even now my powers are loftier, clearer;
I glow, as drunk with new-made wine:
New strength and heart to meet the world incite me,
The woe of earth, the bliss of earth, invite me,
And though the shock of storms may smite me,

No crash of shipwreck shall have power to fright me!
Clouds gather over me—
The moon conceals her light—
The lamp's extinguished!—
Mists rise,—red, angry rays are darting
Around my head!—There falls
A horror from the vaulted roof,
And seizes me!
I feel thy presence, Spirit I invoke!
Reveal thyself!
Ha! in my heart what rending stroke!
With new impulsion
My senses heave in this convulsion!
I feel thee draw my heart, absorb, exhaust me:
Thou must! thou must! and though my life it cost me!

*(He seizes the book, and mysteriously pronounces the sign of the Spirit.
A ruddy flame flashes: the Spirit appears in the flame.)*

Comments on *Faust*

After all it is a poem and not just a moral discourse—a poem which, more boldly perhaps than any in the modern era, attempts to convey what life is like, not, to be sure, in all its characteristics, but in some of them, as they appeared at a great moment in history. It so happens that Goethe [1749–1832] came at a time in Europe when there was a great upsurge of life. European society after a period of premature stability broke its bounds, emotionally, intellectually, and politically, and underwent a great expansion, the consequences of which we are still discovering. It was the spirit of this expansion, and the sense of energy and initiative that accompanied it in its first stages, that Goethe's Faust managed to capture and to set down in imperishable language. The result is a poem unlike all other great poems in its confidence in man, man's self-reliance, his capacity for growth, his future. It is true that Faust has his mistakes, his exasperations, his despairs. But these are incidental and subordinate to the poem's unquenchable optimism. What has appealed to past generations in this poem is its resonance, its potential, its affirmation of life, and this is what will appeal again to generations to come. —Barker Fairley

In the original Faust stories, Faust is dragged off to Hell at the end as Mephistopheles claims his soul. These stories warned Christians not to strive for more knowledge than a man should have. The gaping Hell mouth and the devils with pitchforks were designed to frighten the spectators into following the church's teaching. But Goethe's Faust does not convey a Christian moral. Mephistopheles does not win Faust's "immortal essence," because Faust was never so satisfied with the results of his striving that he wanted time to stand still. Mephistopheles can only seize Faust's soul by a trick, since he never turned Faust away from the "right way." Therefore, by appealing to God's "Romantic" side, Faust escapes Hell. The notion that a person is able to go to Heaven without the benefit of salvation through Christ is novel and troubling. It presages all sorts of problems for humankind. —James P. Stobaugh

Naturalism

"The Open Boat," by Stephen Crane

In a naturalistic world, characters often do not have names, do not have pasts, do not have futures. They are merely types, nameless characters. Impersonal animals (e.g., seagulls) populate the naturalist world. The implication is that they are not much different from human beings, only a different species.

As the story progresses, it becomes clear that they are survivors from a shipwreck off the Atlantic coast of Florida.

None of them knew the color of the sky. Their eyes glanced level, and were fastened upon the waves that swept toward them. These waves were of the hue of slate, save for the tops, which were of foaming white, and all of the men knew the colors of the sea. The horizon narrowed and widened, and dipped and rose, and at all times its edge was jagged with waves that seemed thrust up in points like rocks. Many a man ought to have a bath-tub larger than the boat which here rode upon the sea. These waves were most wrongfully and barbarously abrupt and tall, and each froth-top was a problem in small-boat navigation.

The cook squatted in the bottom and looked with both eyes at the six inches of gunwale which separated him from the ocean. His sleeves were rolled over his fat forearms, and the two flaps of his unbuttoned vest dangled as he bent to bail out the boat. Often he said: "Gawd! That was a narrow clip." As he remarked it he invariably gazed eastward over the broken sea.

The oiler, steering with one of the two oars in the boat, sometimes raised himself suddenly to keep clear of water that swirled in over the stern. It was a thin little oar and it seemed often ready to snap.

The correspondent, pulling at the other oar, watched the waves and wondered why he was there.

The injured captain, lying in the bow, was at this time buried in that profound dejection and indifference which comes, temporarily at least, to even the bravest and most enduring when, willy-nilly, the firm fails, the army loses, the ship goes down. The mind of the master of a vessel is rooted deep in the timbers of her, though he commanded for a day or a decade, and this captain had on him the stern impression of a scene in the grey of dawn of seven turned faces, and later a stump of a top-mast with a white ball on it that slashed to and fro at the waves, went low and lower, and down. Thereafter there was something strange in his voice. Although steady, it was, deep with mourning, and of a quality beyond oration or tears.

"Keep 'er a little more south, Billie," said he.

"'A little more south,' sir," said the oiler in the stern.

A seat in this boat was not unlike a seat upon a bucking bronco, and by the same token, a bronco is not much smaller. The craft pranced and reared, and plunged like an animal. As each wave came, and she rose for it, she seemed like a horse making at a fence outrageously high. The manner of her scramble over these walls of water is a mystic thing, and, moreover, at the top of them were ordinarily these problems in white water, the foam racing down from the summit of each wave, requiring a new leap, and a leap from the air. Then, after scornfully bumping a crest, she would slide, and race, and splash down a long incline, and arrive bobbing and nodding in front of the next menace.

A singular disadvantage of the sea lies in the fact that after successfully surmounting one wave you discover that there is another behind it just as important and just as nervously anxious to do something effective in the way of swamping boats. In a ten-foot dingey one can get an idea of the resources of the sea in the line of waves that is not probable to the average experience which is never at sea in a dingey.

As each slatey wall of water approached, it shut all else from the view of the men in the boat, and it was not difficult to imagine that this particular wave was the final outburst of the ocean, the last effort of the grim water. There was a terrible grace in the move of the waves, and they came in silence, save for the snarling of the crests.

In the wan light, the faces of the men must have been grey. Their eyes must have glinted in strange ways as they gazed steadily astern. Viewed from a balcony, the whole thing would doubtless have been weirdly picturesque. But the men in the boat had no time to see it, and if they had had leisure there were other things to occupy their minds. The sun swung steadily up the sky, and they knew it was broad day because the color of the sea changed from slate to emerald-green, streaked with amber lights, and the foam was like tumbling snow. The process of the breaking day was unknown to them. They were aware only of this effect upon the color of the waves that rolled toward them.

In disjointed sentences the cook and the correspondent argued as to the difference between a life-saving station and a house of refuge. The cook had said: "There's a house of refuge just north of the Mosquito Inlet Light, and as soon as they see us, they'll come off in their boat and pick us up."

"As soon as who see us?" said the correspondent. "The crew," said the cook.

"Houses of refuge don't have crews," said the correspondent. "As I understand them, they are only places where clothes and grub are stored for the benefit of ship-wrecked people. They don't carry crews."

"Oh, yes, they do," said the cook.

"No, they don't," said the correspondent.

"Well, we're not there yet, anyhow," said the oiler, in the stern.

"Well," said the cook, "perhaps it's not a house of refuge that I'm thinking of as being near Mosquito Inlet Light. Perhaps it's a life- saving station."

"We're not there yet," said the oiler, in the stern.

As the boat bounced from the top of each wave, the wind tore through the hair of the hatless men, and as the craft plopped her stern down again the spray splashed past them. The crest of each of these waves was a hill, from the top of which the men surveyed, for a moment, a broad tumultuous expanse, shining and wind-riven. It was probably splendid. It was probably glorious, this play of the free sea, wild with lights of emerald and white and amber.

"Bully good thing it's an on-shore wind," said the cook. "If not, where would we be? Wouldn't have a show."

"That's right," said the correspondent. The busy oiler nodded his assent.

Then the captain, in the bow, chuckled in a way that expressed humor, contempt, tragedy, all in one. "Do you think we've got much of a show now, boys?" said he.

Whereupon the three were silent, save for a trifle of hemming and hawing. To express any particular optimism at this time they felt to be childish and stupid, but they all doubtless possessed this sense of the situation in their mind. A young man thinks doggedly at such times. On the other hand, the ethics of their condition was decidedly against any open suggestion of hopelessness. So they were silent.

"Oh, well," said the captain, soothing his children, "we'll get ashore all right."

But there was that in his tone which made them think, so the oiler quoth: "Yes! If this wind holds!"

The cook was bailing: "Yes! If we don't catch hell in the surf."

Canton flannel gulls flew near and far. Sometimes they sat down on the sea, near patches of brown sea-weed that rolled on the waves with a movement like carpets on a line in a gale. The birds sat comfortably in groups, and they were envied by some in the dingey, for the wrath of the sea was no more to them than it was to a covey of prairie chickens a thousand miles inland. Often they came very close and stared at the men with black bead-like eyes. At these times they were uncanny and sinister in their unblinking scrutiny, and the men hooted angrily at them, telling them to be gone. One came, and evidently decided to alight on the top of the captain's head. The bird flew parallel to the boat and did not circle, but made short sidelong jumps in the air in chicken-fashion. His black eyes were wistfully fixed upon the captain's head. "Ugly brute," said the oiler to the bird. "You look as if you were made with a jack-knife." The cook and the correspondent swore darkly at the creature. The captain naturally wished to knock it away with the end of the heavy painter; but he did not dare do it, because anything resembling an emphatic gesture would have capsized this freighted boat, and so with his open hand, the captain gently and carefully waved the gull away. After it had been discouraged from the pursuit the captain breathed easier on account of his hair, and others breathed easier because the bird struck their minds at this time as being somehow gruesome and ominous.

In the meantime the oiler and the correspondent rowed.

They sat together in the same seat, and each rowed an oar. Then the oiler took both oars; then the correspondent took both oars; then the oiler; then the correspondent. They rowed and they rowed. The very ticklish part of the business was when the time came for the reclining one in the stern to take his turn at the oars. By the very last star of truth, it is easier to steal eggs from under a hen than it was to change seats in the dingey. First the man in the stern slid his hand along the thwart and moved with care, as if he were of Sèvres. Then the man in the rowing seat slid his hand along the other thwart. It was all done with most extraordinary care. As the two sidled past each other, the whole party kept watchful eyes on the coming wave, and the captain cried: "Look out now! Steady there!"

The brown mats of sea-weed that appeared from time to time were like islands, bits of earth. They were traveling, apparently, neither one way nor the other. They were, to all intents, stationary. They informed the men in the boat that it was making progress slowly toward the land.

The captain, rearing cautiously in the bow, after the dingey soared on a great swell, said that he had seen the lighthouse at Mosquito Inlet. Presently the cook remarked that he had seen it. The correspondent was at the oars then, and for some reason he too wished to look at the lighthouse, but his back was toward the far shore and the waves were important, and for some time he could not seize an opportunity to turn his head. But at last there came a wave more gentle than the others, and when at the crest of it he swiftly scoured the western horizon.

"See it?" said the captain.

"No," said the correspondent slowly, "I didn't see anything."

"Look again," said the captain. He pointed. "It's exactly in that direction."

At the top of another wave, the correspondent did as he was bid, and this time his eyes chanced on a small still thing on the edge of the swaying horizon. It was precisely like the point of a pin. It took an anxious eye to find a lighthouse so tiny.

"Think we'll make it, captain?"

"If this wind holds and the boat don't swamp, we can't do much else," said the captain.

The little boat, lifted by each towering sea, and splashed viciously by the crests, made progress that in the absence of sea-weed was not apparent to those in her. She seemed just a wee thing wallowing, miraculously top-up, at the mercy of five oceans. Occasionally, a great spread of water, like white flames, swarmed into her.

"Bail her, cook," said the captain serenely.

"All right, captain," said the cheerful cook.

It would be difficult to describe the subtle brotherhood of men that was here established on the seas. No one said that it was so. No one mentioned it. But it dwelt in the boat, and each man felt it warm him. They were a captain, an oiler, a cook, and a correspondent, and they were friends, friends in a more curiously iron-bound degree than may be common. The hurt captain, lying against the water-jar in the bow, spoke always in a low voice and calmly, but he could never command a more ready and swiftly obedient crew than the motley three of the dingey. It was more than a mere recognition of what was best for the common safety. There was surely in it a quality that was personal and heartfelt. And after this devotion to the commander of the boat there was this comradeship that the correspondent, for instance, who had been taught to be cynical of men, knew even at the time was the best experience of his life. But no one said that it was so. No one mentioned it.

"I wish we had a sail," remarked the captain. "We might try my overcoat on the end of an oar and give you two boys a chance to rest." So the cook and the correspondent held the mast and spread wide the overcoat. The oiler steered, and the little boat made good way with her new rig. Sometimes the oiler had to scull sharply to keep a sea from breaking into the boat, but otherwise sailing was a success.

Meanwhile the lighthouse had been growing slowly larger. It had now almost assumed color, and appeared like a little grey shadow on the sky. The man at the oars could not be prevented from turning his head rather often to try for a glimpse of this little grey shadow.

At last, from the top of each wave the men in the tossing boat could see land. Even as the lighthouse was an upright shadow on the sky, this land seemed but a long black shadow on the sea. It certainly was thinner than paper. "We must be about opposite New Smyrna," said the cook, who had coasted this shore often in schooners. "Captain, by the way, I believe they abandoned that life-saving station there about a year ago."

"Did they?" said the captain.

The wind slowly died away. The cook and the correspondent were not now obliged to slave in order to hold high the oar. But the waves continued their old impetuous swooping at the dingey, and the little craft, no longer under way, struggled woundily over them. The oiler or the correspondent took the oars again.

Shipwrecks are à propos of nothing. If men could only train for them and have them occur when the men had reached pink condition, there would be less drowning at sea. Of the four in the dingey none had slept any time worth mentioning for two days and two nights previous to embarking in the dingey, and in the excitement of clambering about the deck of a foundering ship they had also forgotten to eat heartily.

For these reasons, and for others, neither the oiler nor the correspondent was fond of rowing at this time. The correspondent wondered ingenuously how in the name of all that was sane could there be people who thought it amusing to row a boat. It was not an amusement; it was a diabolical punishment, and even a genius of mental aberrations could never conclude that it was anything but a horror to the muscles and a crime against the back. He mentioned to the boat in general how the amusement of rowing struck him, and the weary-faced oiler smiled in full sympathy. Previously to the foundering, by the way, the oiler had worked double-watch in the engine-room of the ship.

"Take her easy, now, boys," said the captain. "Don't spend yourselves. If we have to run a surf you'll need all your strength, because we'll sure have to swim for it. Take your time."

Slowly the land arose from the sea. From a black line it became a line of black and a line of white, trees and sand. Finally, the captain said that he could make out a house on the shore. "That's the house of refuge, sure," said the cook. "They'll see us before long, and come out after us."

The distant lighthouse reared high. "The keeper ought to be able to make us out now, if he's looking through a glass," said the captain. "He'll notify the life-saving people."

"None of those other boats could have got ashore to give word of the wreck," said the oiler, in a low voice. "Else the lifeboat would be out hunting us."

Slowly and beautifully the land loomed out of the sea. The wind came again. It had veered from the north-east to the south-east. Finally, a new sound struck the ears of the men in the boat. It was the low thunder of the surf on the shore. "We'll never be able to make the lighthouse now," said the captain. "Swing her head a little more north, Billie," said he.

"'A little more north,' sir," said the oiler.

Whereupon the little boat turned her nose once more down the wind, and all but the oarsman watched the shore grow. Under the influence of this expansion doubt and direful apprehension was leaving the minds of the men. The management of the boat was still most absorbing, but it could not prevent a quiet cheerfulness. In an hour, perhaps, they would be ashore.

Their backbones had become thoroughly used to balancing in the boat, and they now rode this wild colt of a dingey like circus men. The correspondent thought that he had been drenched to the skin, but happening to feel in the top pocket of his coat, he found therein eight cigars. Four of them were soaked with sea-water; four were perfectly scatheless. After a search, somebody produced three dry matches, and thereupon the four waifs rode impudently in their little boat, and with an assurance of an impending rescue shining in their eyes, puffed at the big cigars and judged well and ill of all men. Everybody took a drink of water.

"Cook," remarked the captain, "there don't seem to be any signs of life about your house of refuge."

"No," replied the cook. "Funny they don't see us!"

A broad stretch of lowly coast lay before the eyes of the men. It was of dunes topped with dark vegetation. The roar of the surf was plain, and sometimes they could see the white lip of a wave as it spun up the beach. A tiny house was blocked out black upon the sky. Southward, the slim lighthouse lifted its little grey length.

Tide, wind, and waves were swinging the dingey northward. "Funny they don't see us," said the men.

The surf's roar was here dulled, but its tone was, nevertheless, thunderous and mighty. As the boat swam over the great rollers, the men sat listening to this roar. "We'll swamp sure," said everybody.

It is fair to say here that there was not a life-saving station within twenty miles in either direction, but the men did not know this fact, and in consequence they made dark and opprobrious remarks concerning the eyesight of the nation's life-savers. Four scowling men sat in the dingey and surpassed records in the invention of epithets.

"Funny they don't see us."

The lightheartedness of a former time had completely faded. To their sharpened minds it was easy to conjure pictures of all kinds of incompetency and blindness and, indeed, cowardice. There was the shore of the populous land, and it was bitter and bitter to them that from it came no sign.

"Well," said the captain, ultimately, "I suppose we'll have to make a try for ourselves. If we stay out here too long, we'll none of us have strength left to swim after the boat swamps."

And so the oiler, who was at the oars, turned the boat straight for the shore. There was a sudden tightening of muscle. There was some thinking.

"If we don't all get ashore—" said the captain. "If we don't all get ashore, I suppose you fellows know where to send news of my finish?"

Reflections of rage in the face of Fate

They then briefly exchanged some addresses and admonitions. As for the reflections of the men, there was a great deal of rage in them. Perchance they might be formulated thus: "If I am going to be drowned—if I am going to be drowned—if I am going to be drowned, why, in the name of the seven mad gods who rule the sea, was I allowed to come thus far and contemplate sand and trees? Was I brought here merely to have my nose dragged away as I was about to nibble the sacred cheese of life? It is preposterous. If this old ninny-woman, Fate, cannot do better than this, she should be deprived of the management of men's fortunes. She is an old hen who knows not her intention. If she has decided to drown me, why did she not do it in the beginning and save me all this trouble? The whole affair is absurd. . . . But no, she cannot mean to drown me. She dare not drown me. She cannot drown me. Not after all this work." Afterward the man might have had an impulse to shake his fist at the clouds: "Just you drown me, now, and then hear what I call you!"

The billows that came at this time were more formidable. They seemed always just about to break and roll over the little boat in a turmoil of foam. There was a preparatory and long growl in the speech of them. No mind unused to the sea would have concluded that the dingey could ascend these sheer heights in time. The shore was

still afar. The oiler was a wily surfman. "Boys," he said swiftly, "she won't live three minutes more, and we're too far out to swim.

Shall I take her to sea again, captain?"

"Yes! Go ahead!" said the captain.

This oiler, by a series of quick miracles, and fast and steady oarsmanship, turned the boat in the middle of the surf and took her safely to sea again.

There was a considerable silence as the boat bumped over the furrowed sea to deeper water. Then somebody in gloom spoke. "Well, anyhow, they must have seen us from the shore by now."

The gulls went in slanting flight up the wind toward the grey desolate east. A squall, marked by dingy clouds, and clouds brick-red, like smoke from a burning building, appeared from the south-east.

"What do you think of those life-saving people? Ain't they peaches?"

"Funny they haven't seen us."

"Maybe they think we're out here for sport! Maybe they think we're fishin'. Maybe they think we're damned fools."

It was a long afternoon. A changed tide tried to force them southward, but the wind and wave said northward. Far ahead, where coast-line, sea, and sky formed their mighty angle, there were little dots which seemed to indicate a city on the shore.

"St. Augustine?"

The captain shook his head. "Too near Mosquito Inlet."

And the oiler rowed, and then the correspondent rowed. Then the oiler rowed. It was a weary business. The human back can become the seat of more aches and pains than are registered in books for the composite anatomy of a regiment. It is a limited area, but it can become the theatre of innumerable muscular conflicts, tangles, wrenches, knots, and other comforts.

"Did you ever like to row, Billie?" asked the correspondent.

"No," said the oiler. "Hang it!"

When one exchanged the rowing-seat for a place in the bottom of the boat, he suffered a bodily depression that caused him to be careless of everything save an obligation to wiggle one finger. There was cold sea-water swashing to and fro in the boat, and he lay in it. His head, pillowed on a thwart, was within an inch of the swirl of a wave crest, and sometimes a particularly obstreperous sea came in-board and drenched him once more. But these matters did not annoy him. It is almost certain that if the boat had capsized he would have tumbled comfortably out upon the ocean as if he felt sure that it was a great soft mattress.

"Look! There's a man on the shore!"

"Where?"

"There! See 'im? See 'im?"

"Yes, sure! He's walking along."

"Now he's stopped. Look! He's facing us!"

"He's waving at us!"

"So he is! By thunder!"

"Ah, now we're all right! Now we're all right! There'll be a boat out here for us in half-an-hour."

"He's going on. He's running. He's going up to that house there."

The people on shore are a tease, a world that these shipwrecked seamen may never reach again. The power that runs the naturalistic universe likes to tease its realm. Its inhabitants learn that bad things often happen to good people! Goodness and nobility are all irrelevant categories. Survival belongs to the fittest or the luckiest — not necessarily to the good.

The remote beach seemed lower than the sea, and it required a searching glance to discern the little black figure. The captain saw a floating stick and they rowed to it. A bath-towel was by some weird chance in the boat, and, tying this on the stick, the captain waved it. The oarsman did not dare turn his head, so he was obliged to ask questions.

"What's he doing now?"

"He's standing still again. He's looking, I think. . . . There he goes again. Toward the house. . . . Now he's stopped again."

"Is he waving at us?"

"No, not now! He was, though."

"Look! There comes another man!"

"He's running."

"Look at him go, would you."

"Why, he's on a bicycle. Now he's met the other man. They're both waving at us.

Look!"

"There comes something up the beach."

"What the devil is that thing?"

"Why, it looks like a boat."

"Why, certainly it's a boat."

"No, it's on wheels."

"Yes, so it is. Well, that must be the life-boat. They drag them along shore on a wagon."

"That's the life-boat, sure."

"No, by —, it's — it's an omnibus."

"I tell you it's a life-boat."

"It is not! It's an omnibus. I can see it plain. See? One of these big hotel omnibuses."

"By thunder, you're right. It's an omnibus, sure as fate. What do you suppose they are doing with an omnibus? Maybe they are going around collecting the life-crew, hey?"

"That's it, likely. Look! There's a fellow waving a little black flag. He's standing on the steps of the omnibus. There come those other two fellows. Now they're all talking together. Look at the fellow with the flag. Maybe he ain't waving it."

"That ain't a flag, is it? That's his coat. Why, certainly, that's his coat."

"So it is. It's his coat. He's taken it off and is waving it around his head. But would you look at him swing it."

Naturalistic authors prefer dialogue as a way to develop the plot and the characters. Using dialogue allows authors to remain aloof and uncommitted in their descriptions.

"Oh, say, there isn't any life-saving station there. That's just a winter resort hotel omnibus that has brought over some of the boarders to see us drown."

"What's that idiot with the coat mean? What's he signaling, anyhow?"

"It looks as if he were trying to tell us to go north. There must be a life-saving station up there."

"No! He thinks we're fishing. Just giving us a merry hand. See? Ah, there, Willie!"

"Well, I wish I could make something out of those signals. What do you suppose he means?"

"He don't mean anything. He's just playing."

"Well, if he'd just signal us to try the surf again, or to go to sea and wait, or go north, or go south, or go to Hell — there would be some reason in it. But look at him. He just stands there and keeps his coat revolving like a wheel. The ass!"

"There come more people."

"Now there's quite a mob. Look! Isn't that a boat?"

"Where? Oh, I see where you mean. No, that's no boat."

"That fellow is still waving his coat."

"He must think we like to see him do that. Why don't he quit it? It don't mean anything."

"I don't know. I think he is trying to make us go north. It must be that there's a life-saving station there somewhere."

"Say, he ain't tired yet. Look at 'im wave."

"Wonder how long he can keep that up. He's been revolving his coat ever since he caught sight of us. He's an idiot. Why aren't they getting men to bring a boat out? A fishing boat—one of those big yawls—could come out here all right. Why don't he do something?"

"Oh, it's all right, now."

"They'll have a boat out here for us in less than no time, now that they've seen us."

A faint yellow tone came into the sky over the low land. The shadows on the sea slowly deepened. The wind bore coldness with it, and the men began to shiver.

"Holy smoke!" said one, allowing his voice to express his impious mood, "if we keep on monkeying out here! If we've got to flounder out here all night!"

"Oh, we'll never have to stay here all night! Don't you worry. They've seen us now, and it won't be long before they'll come chasing out after us."

The shore grew dusky. The man waving a coat blended gradually into this gloom, and it swallowed in the same manner the omnibus and the group of people. The spray, when it dashed uproariously over the side, made the voyagers shrink and swear like men who were being branded.

"I'd like to catch the chump who waved the coat. I feel like soaking him one, just for luck."

"Why? What did he do?"

"Oh, nothing, but then he seemed so d----d cheerful."

In the meantime the oiler rowed, and then the correspondent rowed, and then the oiler rowed. Grey-faced and bowed forward, they mechanically, turn by turn, plied the leaden oars. The form of the lighthouse had vanished from the southern horizon, but finally a pale star appeared, just lifting from the sea. The streaked saffron in the west passed before the all-merging darkness, and the sea to the east was black. The land had vanished, and was expressed only by the low and drear thunder of the surf.

"If I am going to be drowned—if I am going to be drowned—if I am going to be drowned, why, in the name of the seven mad gods who rule the sea, was I allowed to come thus far and contemplate sand and trees? Was I brought here merely to have my nose dragged away as I was about to nibble the sacred cheese of life?"

The patient captain, drooped over the water-jar, was sometimes obliged to speak to the oarsman.

"Keep her head up! Keep her head up!"

"'Keep her head up,' sir." The voices were weary and low.

This was surely a quiet evening. All save the oarsman lay heavily and listlessly in the boat's bottom. As for him, his eyes were just capable of noting the tall black waves that swept forward in a most sinister silence, save for an occasional subdued growl of a crest.

The cook's head was on a thwart, and he looked without interest at the water under his nose. He was deep in other scenes. Finally he spoke. "Billie," he murmured, dreamfully, "what kind of pie do you like best?"

"Pie," said the oiler and the correspondent, agitatedly. "Don't talk about those things, blast you!"

"Well," said the cook, "I was just thinking about ham sandwiches, and —"

A night on the sea in an open boat is a long night. As darkness settled finally, the shine of the light, lifting from the sea in the south, changed to full gold. On the northern horizon a new light appeared, a small bluish gleam on the edge of the waters. These two lights were the furniture of the world. Otherwise there was nothing but waves.

Two men huddled in the stern, and distances were so magnificent in the dingey that the rower was enabled to keep his feet partly warmed by thrusting them under his companions. Their legs indeed extended far under the rowing-seat until they touched the feet of the captain forward. Sometimes, despite the efforts of the tired oarsman, a wave came piling into the boat, an icy wave of the night, and the chilling water soaked them anew. They would twist their bodies for a moment and groan, and sleep the dead sleep once more, while the water in the boat gurgled about them as the craft rocked.

The plan of the oiler and the correspondent was for one to row until he lost the ability, and then arouse the other from his sea-water couch in the bottom of the boat.

The oiler plied the oars until his head drooped forward, and the overpowering sleep blinded him. And he rowed yet afterward. Then he touched a man in the bottom of the boat, and called his name. "Will you spell me for a little while?" he said, meekly.

"Sure, Billie," said the correspondent, awakening and dragging himself to a sitting position. They exchanged places carefully, and the oiler, cuddling down in the sea-water at the cook's side, seemed to go to sleep instantly.

The particular violence of the sea had ceased. The waves came without snarling. The obligation of the man at the oars was to keep the boat headed so that the tilt of the rollers would not capsize her, and to preserve her from filling when the crests rushed past. The black waves were silent and hard to be seen in the darkness. Often one was almost upon the boat before the oarsman was aware.

In a low voice the correspondent addressed the captain. He was not sure that the captain was awake, although this iron man seemed to be always awake. "Captain, shall I keep her making for that light north, sir?"

The same steady voice answered him. "Yes. Keep it about two points off the port bow."

The cook had tied a life-belt around himself in order to get even the warmth which this clumsy cork contrivance could donate, and he seemed almost stove-like when a rower, whose teeth invariably chattered wildly as soon as he ceased his labor, dropped down to sleep.

The correspondent, as he rowed, looked down at the two men sleeping under foot. The cook's arm was around the oiler's shoulders, and, with their fragmentary clothing and haggard faces, they were the babes of the sea, a grotesque rendering of the old babes in the wood.

Later he must have grown stupid at his work, for suddenly there was a growling of water, and a crest came with a roar and a swash into the boat, and it was a wonder that it did not set the cook afloat in his life-belt. The cook continued to sleep, but the oiler sat up, blinking his eyes and shaking with the new cold.

"Oh, I'm awful sorry, Billie," said the correspondent contritely.

"That's all right, old boy," said the oiler, and lay down again and was asleep. Presently it seemed that even the captain dozed, and the correspondent thought that he was the one man afloat on all the oceans. The wind had a voice as it came over the waves, and it was sadder than the end.

There was a long, loud swishing astern of the boat, and a gleaming trail of phosphorescence, like blue flame, was furrowed on the black waters. It might have been made by a monstrous knife.

Then there came a stillness, while the correspondent breathed with the open mouth and looked at the sea.

Suddenly there was another swish and another long flash of bluish light, and this time it was alongside the boat, and might almost have been reached with an oar. The correspondent saw an enormous fin speed like a shadow through the water, hurling the crystalline spray and leaving the long glowing trail.

The shark — the ominous, dumb, but deadly shark — is an important foil that Crane uses to develop his action and characters.

The correspondent looked over his shoulder at the captain. His face was hidden, and he seemed to be asleep. He looked at the babes of the sea. They certainly were asleep. So, being bereft of sympathy, he leaned a little way to one side and swore softly into the sea.

But the thing did not then leave the vicinity of the boat. Ahead or astern, on one side or the other, at intervals long or short, fled the long sparkling streak, and there was to be heard the whirroo of the dark fin. The speed and power of the thing was greatly to be admired. It cut the water like a gigantic and keen projectile.

The presence of this biding thing did not affect the man with the same horror that it would if he had been a picnicker. He simply looked at the sea dully and swore in an undertone.

Nevertheless, it is true that he did not wish to be alone. He wished one of his companions to awaken by chance and keep him company with it. But the captain hung motionless over the water-jar, and the oiler and the cook in the bottom of the boat were plunged in slumber.

"If I am going to be drowned, why . . . was I allowed to come thus far?"

"If I am going to be drowned — if I am going to be drowned — if I am going to be drowned, why, in the name of the seven mad gods who rule the sea, was I allowed to come thus far and contemplate sand and trees?"

During this dismal night, it may be remarked that a man would conclude that it was really the intention of the seven mad gods to drown him, despite the abominable injustice of it. For it was certainly an abominable injustice to drown a man who had worked so hard, so hard. The man felt it would be a crime most unnatural. Other people had drowned at sea since galleys swarmed with painted sails, but still—

When it occurs to a man that nature does not regard him as important, and that she feels she would not maim the universe by disposing of him, he at first wishes to throw bricks at the temple, and he hates deeply the fact that there are no brick and no temples. Any visible expression of nature would surely be pelleted with his jeers.

Then, if there be no tangible thing to hoot he feels, perhaps, the desire to confront a personification and indulge in pleas, bowed to one knee, and with hands supplicant, saying: "Yes, but I love myself."

A high cold star on a winter's night is the word he feels that she says to him. Thereafter he knows the pathos of his situation.

The men in the dingey had not discussed these matters, but each had, no doubt, reflected upon them in silence and according to his mind. There was seldom any expression upon their faces save the general one of complete weariness. Speech was devoted to the business of the boat.

To chime the notes of his emotion, a verse mysteriously entered the correspondent's head. He had even forgotten that he had forgotten this verse, but it suddenly was in his mind.

> A soldier of the Legion lay dying in Algiers;
> There was a lack of woman's nursing, there was dearth of woman's tears;
> But a comrade stood beside him, and he took that comrade's hand,
> And he said: "I shall never see my own, my native land."

In his childhood, the correspondent had been made acquainted with the fact that a soldier of the Legion lay dying in Algiers, but he had never regarded the fact as important. Myriads of his school-fellows had informed him of the soldier's plight, but the dinning had naturally ended by making him perfectly indifferent. He had never consider it his affair that a soldier of the Legion lay dying in Algiers, nor had it appeared to him as a matter for sorrow. It was less to him than the breaking of a pencil's point.

Now, however, it quaintly came to him as a human, living thing. It was no longer merely a picture of a few throes in the breast of a poet, meanwhile drinking tea and warming his feet at the grate; it was an actuality—stern, mournful, and fine. The correspondent plainly saw the soldier. He lay on the sand with his feet out straight and still. While his pale left hand was upon his chest in an attempt to thwart the going of his life, the blood came between his fingers. In the far Algerian distance, a city of low square forms was set against a sky that was faint with the last sunset hues. The correspondent, plying the oars and dreaming of the slow and slower movements of the lips of the soldier, was moved by a profound and perfectly impersonal comprehension. He was sorry for the soldier of the Legion who lay dying in Algiers.

The thing which had followed the boat and waited, had evidently grown bored at the delay. There was no longer to be heard the slash of the cut-water, and there was no longer the flame of the long trail. The light in the north still glimmered, but it was apparently no nearer to the boat. Sometimes the boom of the surf rang in the correspondent's ears, and he turned the craft seaward then and rowed harder. Southward, someone had evidently built a watch-fire on the beach. It was too low and too far to be seen, but it made a shimmering, roseate reflection upon the bluff back of it, and this could be discerned from the boat. The wind came stronger, and sometimes a wave suddenly raged out like a mountain-cat, and there was to be seen the sheen and sparkle of a broken crest.

The captain, in the bow, moved on his water-jar and sat erect. "Pretty long night," he observed to the correspondent. He looked at the shore. "Those life-saving people take their time."

"Did you see that shark playing around?"

"Yes, I saw him. He was a big fellow, all right."

"Wish I had known you were awake."

Later the correspondent spoke into the bottom of the boat.

"Billie!" There was a slow and gradual disentanglement. "Billie, will you spell me?"

"Sure," said the oiler.

As soon as the correspondent touched the cold comfortable sea-water in the bottom of the boat, and had huddled close to the cook's life-belt he was deep in sleep, despite the fact that his teeth played all the popular airs. This sleep was so good to him that it was but a moment before he heard a voice call his name in a tone that demonstrated the last stages of exhaustion. "Will you spell me?"

"Sure, Billie."

The light in the north had mysteriously vanished, but the correspondent took his course from the wide-awake captain.

Later in the night they took the boat farther out to sea, and the captain directed the cook to take one oar at the stern and keep the boat facing the seas. He was to call out if he should hear the thunder of the surf. This plan enabled the oiler and the correspondent to get respite together. "We'll give those boys a chance to get into shape again," said the captain. They curled down and, after a few preliminary chatterings and trembles, slept once more the dead sleep. Neither knew they had bequeathed to the cook the company of another shark, or perhaps the same shark.

As the boat caroused on the waves, spray occasionally bumped over the side and gave them a fresh soaking, but this had no power to break their repose. The ominous slash of the wind and the water affected them as it would have affected mummies.

The rowing close to shore and then rowing out to sea again, before the boat is swamped – all this is a metaphor for the frustration that is so endemic to the naturalistic life.

"Boys," said the cook, with the notes of every reluctance in his voice, "she's drifted in pretty close. I guess one of you had better take her to sea again." The correspondent, aroused, heard the crash of the toppled crests.

As he was rowing, the captain gave him some whisky-and-water, and this steadied the chills out of him. "If I ever get ashore and anybody shows me even a photograph of an oar—"

At last there was a short conversation. "Billie. . . . Billie, will you spell me?"

"Sure," said the oiler.

When the correspondent again opened his eyes, the sea and the sky were each of the grey hue of the dawning. Later, carmine and gold was painted upon the waters. The morning appeared finally, in its splendor, with a sky of pure blue, and the sunlight flamed on the tips of the waves.

On the distant dunes were set many little black cottages, and a tall white windmill reared above them. No man, nor dog, nor bicycle appeared on the beach. The cottages might have formed a deserted village.

The voyagers scanned the shore. A conference was held in the boat. "Well," said the captain, "if no help is coming we might better try a run through the surf right away. If we stay out here much longer we will be too weak to do anything for ourselves at all." The others silently acquiesced in this reasoning. The boat was headed for the beach. The correspondent wondered if none ever ascended the tall wind-tower, and if then they never looked seaward. This tower was a giant, standing with its back to the plight of the ants. It represented in a degree, to the correspondent, the serenity of nature amid the struggles of the individual—nature in the wind, and nature in the vision of men. She did not seem cruel to him then, nor beneficent, nor treacherous, nor wise. But she was indifferent, flatly indifferent. It is, perhaps, plausible that a man in this situation, impressed with the unconcern of the universe, should see the innumerable flaws of his life, and have them taste wickedly in his mind and wish for another chance. A distinction between right and wrong seems absurdly clear to him, then, in this new ignorance of the grave-edge, and he understands that if he were given another opportunity he would mend his conduct and his words, and be better and brighter during an introduction or at a tea.

"Now, boys," said the captain, "she is going to swamp, sure. All we can do is to work her in as far as possible, and then when she swamps, pile out and scramble for the beach. Keep cool now, and don't jump until she swamps sure."

The oiler took the oars. Over his shoulders he scanned the surf. "Captain," he said, "I think I'd better bring her about, and keep her head-on to the seas and back her in."

"All right, Billie," said the captain. "Back her in." The oiler swung the boat then and, seated in the stern, the cook and the correspondent were obliged to look over their shoulders to contemplate the lonely and indifferent shore.

The monstrous in-shore rollers heaved the boat high until the men were again enabled to see the white sheets of water scudding up the slanted beach. "We won't get in very close," said the captain. Each time a man could wrest his attention from the rollers, he turned his glance toward the shore, and in the expression of the eyes during this contemplation there was a singular quality. The correspondent, observing the others, knew that they were not afraid, but the full meaning of their glances was shrouded.

As for himself, he was too tired to grapple fundamentally with the fact. He tried to coerce his mind into thinking of it, but the mind was dominated at this time by the muscles, and the muscles said they did not care. It merely occurred to him that if he should drown it would be a shame.

There were no hurried words, no pallor, no plain agitation. The men simply looked at the shore. "Now, remember to get well clear of the boat when you jump," said the captain.

Seaward the crest of a roller suddenly fell with a thunderous crash, and the long white comber came roaring down upon the boat.

"Steady now," said the captain. The men were silent. They turned their eyes from the shore to the comber and waited. The boat slid up the incline, leaped at the furious top, bounced over it, and swung down the long back of the wave. Some water had been shipped and the cook bailed it out.

But the next crest crashed also. The tumbling, boiling flood of white water caught the boat and whirled it almost perpendicular. Water swarmed in from all sides. The correspondent had his hands on the gunwale at this time, and when the water entered at that place he swiftly withdrew his fingers, as if he objected to wetting them.

The little boat, drunken with this weight of water, reeled and snuggled deeper into the sea.

"Bail her out, cook! Bail her out," said the captain.

"All right, captain," said the cook. "Now, boys, the next one will do for us, sure," said the oiler. "Mind to jump clear of the boat."

The third wave moved forward, huge, furious, implacable. It fairly swallowed the dingey, and almost simultaneously the men tumbled into the sea. A piece of life-belt had lain in the bottom of the boat, and as the correspondent went overboard he held this to his chest with his left hand. The January water was icy, and he reflected immediately that it was colder than he had expected to find it on the coast of Florida. This appeared to his dazed mind as a fact important enough to be noted at the time. The coldness of the water was sad; it was tragic. This fact was somehow so mixed and confused with his opinion of his own situation that it seemed almost a proper reason for tears. The water was cold.

When he came to the surface he was conscious of little but the noisy water. Afterward he saw his companions in the sea. The oiler was ahead in the race. He was swimming strongly and rapidly. Off to the correspondent's left, the cook's great white and corked back bulged out of the water, and in the rear the captain was hanging with his one good hand to the keel of the overturned dingey.

There is a certain immovable quality to a shore, and the correspondent wondered at it amid the confusion of the sea.

It seemed also very attractive, but the correspondent knew that it was a long journey, and he paddled leisurely. The piece of life-preserver lay under him, and sometimes he whirled down the incline of a wave as if he were on a hand-sled.

But finally he arrived at a place in the sea where travel was beset with difficulty. He did not pause swimming to inquire what manner of current had caught him, but there his progress ceased. The shore was set before him like a bit of scenery on a stage, and he looked at it and understood with his eyes each detail of it.

As the cook passed, much farther to the left, the captain was calling to him, "Turn over on your back, cook! Turn over on your back and use the oar."

"All right, sir." The cook turned on his back, and, paddling with an oar, went ahead as if he were a canoe.

Presently the boat also passed to the left of the correspondent with the captain clinging with one hand to the keel. He would have appeared like a man raising himself to look over a board fence, if it were not for the extraordinary gymnastics of the boat. The correspondent marvelled that the captain could still hold to it.

They passed on, nearer to shore—the oiler, the cook, the captain—and following them went the water-jar, bouncing gaily over the seas.

The correspondent remained in the grip of this strange new enemy—a current. The shore, with its white slope of sand and its green bluff, topped with little silent cottages, was spread like a picture before him. It was very near to him then, but he was impressed as one who in a gallery looks at a scene from Brittany or Holland.

He thought: "I am going to drown? Can it be possible? Can it be possible? Can it be possible?" Perhaps an individual must consider his own death to be the final phenomenon of nature.

But later a wave perhaps whirled him out of this small, deadly current, for he found suddenly that he could again make progress toward the shore. Later still, he was aware that the captain, clinging with one hand to the keel of the dingey, had his face turned away from the shore and toward him, and was calling his name. "Come to the boat! Come to the boat!"

In his struggle to reach the captain and the boat, he reflected that when one gets properly wearied, drowning must really be a comfortable arrangement, a cessation of hostilities accompanied by a large degree of relief, and he was glad of it, for the main thing in his mind for some months had been horror of the temporary agony. He did not wish to be hurt.

Presently he saw a man running along the shore. He was undressing with most remarkable speed. Coat, trousers, shirt, everything flew magically off him.

"Come to the boat," called the captain.

"All right, captain." As the correspondent paddled, he saw the captain let himself down to bottom and leave the boat. Then the correspondent performed his one little marvel of the voyage. A large wave caught him and flung him with ease and supreme speed completely over the boat and far beyond it. It struck him even then as an event in gymnastics, and a true miracle of the sea. An overturned boat in the surf is not a plaything to a swimming man.

The correspondent arrived in water that reached only to his waist, but his condition did not enable him to stand for more than a moment. Each wave knocked him into a heap, and the under-tow pulled at him.

Then he saw the man who had been running and undressing, and undressing and running, come bounding into the water. He dragged ashore the cook, and then waded towards the captain, but the captain waved him away, and sent him to the correspondent. He was naked, naked as a tree in winter, but a halo was about his head, and he shone like a saint. He gave a strong pull, and a long drag, and a bully heave at the correspondent's hand. The correspondent, schooled in the minor formulae, said: "Thanks, old man." But suddenly the man cried: "What's that?" He pointed a swift finger. The correspondent said: "Go."

In the shallows, face downward, lay the oiler. His forehead touched sand that was periodically, between each wave, clear of the sea.

The correspondent did not know all that transpired afterward. When he achieved safe ground he fell, striking the sand with each particular part of his body. It was as if he had dropped from a roof, but the thud was grateful to him.

Ironically the oiler, the good man, dies. Yet this is irrelevant in a world where there is no order, no justice, no larger purpose to life.

It seems that instantly the beach was populated with men with blankets, clothes, and flasks, and women with coffeepots and all the remedies sacred to their minds. The welcome of the land to the men from the sea was warm and generous, but a still and dripping shape was carried slowly up the beach, and the land's welcome for it could only be the different and sinister hospitality of the grave.

When it came night, the white waves paced to and fro in the moonlight, and the wind brought the sound of the great sea's voice to the men on shore, and they felt that they could then be interpreters.

Comments on Crane

Crane's magnum opus, *The Red Badge of Courage*, shows up the nature and value of courage. The heroic ideal is not what it has been claimed to be: so largely is it the product of instinctive responses to biological and traditional forces. But man does have will, and he has the ability to reflect, and though these do not guarantee that he can effect his own destiny, they do enable him to become responsible to some degree for the honesty of his personal vision. — Stanley B. Greenfield

Realism

The Old Man and the Sea, by Ernest Hemingway

The old man catches a huge fish. It will make him wealthy if he can get it back to shore, but he is too far out in the ocean. As he tugs it to shore, he tries to fight off a pack of sharks that eat the fish, all but the eighteen-foot skeleton. The irony of this situation is obvious.

He was an old man who fished alone in a skiff in the Gulf Stream and he had gone eighty-four days now without taking a fish. In the first forty days a boy had been with him. But after forty days without a fish the boy's parents had told him that the old man was now definitely and finally *salao*, which is the worst form of unlucky, and the boy had gone at their orders in another boat which caught three good fish the first week. It made the boy sad to see the old man come in each day with his skiff empty and he always went down to help him carry either the coiled lines or the gaff and harpoon and the sail that was furled around the mast. The sail was patched with flour sacks and, furled, it looked like the flag of permanent defeat.

The old man was thin and gaunt with deep wrinkles in the back of his neck. The brown blotches of the benevolent skin cancer the sun brings from its reflection on the tropic sea were on his cheeks. The blotches ran well down the sides of his face and his hands had the deep-creased scars from handling heavy fish on the cords. But none of these scars were fresh. They were as old as erosions in a fishless desert.

Everything about him was old except his eyes and they were the same color as the sea and were cheerful and undefeated.

. . .

I must not think nonsense, he thought. Luck is a thing that comes in many forms and who can recognize her? I would take some though in any form and pay what they asked. I wish I could see the glow from the lights, he thought. I wish too many things. But that is the thing I wish for now. He tried to settle more comfortably to steer and from his pain he knew he was not dead.

He saw the reflected glare of the lights of the city at what must have been around ten o'clock at night. They were only perceptible at first as the light is in the sky before the moon rises. Then they were steady to see across the ocean which was rough now with the increasing breeze. He steered inside of the glow and he thought that now, soon, he must hit the edge of the stream.

Now it is over, he thought. They will probably hit me again. But what can a man do against them in the dark without a weapon?

He was stiff and sore now and his wounds and all of the strained parts of his body hurt with the cold of the night. I hope I do not have to fight again, he thought. I hope so much I do not have to fight again.

But by midnight he fought and this time he knew the fight was useless. They came in a pack and he could only see the lines in the water that their fins made and their phosphorescence as they threw themselves on the fish. He clubbed at heads and heard the jaws chop and the shaking of the skiff as they took hold below. He clubbed desperately at what he could only feel and hear and he felt something seize the club and it was gone.

He jerked the tiller free from the rudder and beat and chopped with it, holding it in both hands and driving it down again and again. But they were up to the bow now and driving in one after the other and together, tearing off the pieces of meat that showed glowing below the sea as they turned to come once more.

One came, finally, against the head itself and he knew that it was over. He swung the tiller across the shark's head where the jaws were caught in the heaviness of the fish's head which would not tear. He swung it once and twice and again. He heard the tiller break and he lunged at the shark with the splintered butt. He felt it go in and knowing it was sharp he drove it in again. The shark let go and rolled away. That was the last shark of the pack that came. There was nothing more for them to eat.

The old man could hardly breathe now and he felt a strange taste in his mouth. It was coppery and sweet and he was afraid of it for a moment. But there was not much of it.

He spat into the ocean and said, "Eat that, *galanos* [shovel-nosed sharks]. And make a dream you've killed a man."

He knew he was beaten now finally and without remedy and he went back to the stern and found the jagged end of the tiller would fit in the slot of the rudder well enough for him to steer. He settled the sack around his shoulders and put the skiff on her course. He sailed lightly now and he had no thoughts nor any feelings of any kind. He was past everything now and he sailed the skiff to make his home port as well and as intelligently as he could. In the night sharks hit the carcass as someone might pick up crumbs from the table. The old man paid no attention to them and did not pay any attention to anything except steering. He only noticed how lightly and bow well the skiff sailed now there was no great weight beside her. . . .

A Doll's House, by Henrik Ibsen

It's Christmas Eve. Nora Helmer, a beautiful young wife, has been out doing some last-minute shopping. When she returns, her husband, Torvald, immediately comes to see what his "little squirrel" has bought. They playfully act out their rolls — Torvald as the big, strong husband; and Nora as the dependent, adoring wife. Before the end of the play, readers will meet the thoroughly realistic modern Nora!

Act 1

[SCENE. — A room furnished comfortably and tastefully, but not extravagantly. At the back, a door to the right leads to the entrance-hall, another to the left leads to Helmer's study. Between the doors stands a piano. In the middle of the left-hand wall is a door, and beyond it a window. Near the window are a round table, arm-chairs and a small sofa. In the right-hand wall, at the farther end, another door; and on the same side, nearer the footlights, a stove, two easy chairs and a rocking-chair; between the stove and the door, a small table. Engravings on the walls; a cabinet with china and other small objects; a small book-case with well-bound books. The floors are carpeted, and a fire burns in the stove.

It is winter. A bell rings in the hall; shortly afterwards the door is heard to open. Enter NORA, humming a tune and in high spirits. She is in outdoor dress and carries a number of parcels; these she lays on the table to the right. She leaves the outer door open after her, and through it is seen a PORTER who is carrying a Christmas Tree and a basket, which he gives to the MAID who has opened the door.]

NORA. Hide the Christmas Tree carefully, Helen. Be sure the children do not see it until this evening, when it is dressed. [*To the* PORTER, *taking out her purse.*] How much?

PORTER. Sixpence.

NORA. There is a shilling. No, keep the change. [The PORTER thanks her, and goes out. NORA shuts the door. She is laughing to herself, as she takes off her hat and coat. She takes a packet of macaroons from her pocket and eats one or two; then goes cautiously to her husband's door and listens.] Yes, he is in. [Still humming, she goes to the table on the right.]

HELMER [*calls out from his room*]. Is that my little lark twittering out there?

NORA [busy opening some of the parcels]. Yes, it is!

HELMER. Is it my little squirrel bustling about?

NORA. Yes!

HELMER. When did my squirrel come home?

NORA. Just now. [*Puts the bag of macaroons into her pocket and wipes her mouth.*] Come in here, Torvald, and see what I have bought.

Helmer. Don't disturb me. [*A little later, he opens the door and looks into the room, pen in hand.*] Bought, did you say? All these things? Has my little spendthrift been wasting money again?

NORA. Yes but, Torvald, this year we really can let ourselves go a little. This is the first Christmas that we have not needed to economise.

HELMER. Still, you know, we can't spend money recklessly.

NORA. Yes, Torvald, we may be a wee bit more reckless now, mayn't we? Just a tiny wee bit! You are going to have a big salary and earn lots and lots of money.

HELMER. Yes, after the New Year; but then it will be a whole quarter before the salary is due.

NORA. Pooh! We can borrow until then.

HELMER. Nora! [*Goes up to her and takes her playfully by the ear.*] The same little feather-head! Suppose, now, that I borrowed fifty pounds today, and you spent it all in the Christmas week, and then on New Year's Eve a slate fell on my head and killed me, and—

NORA [*putting her hands over his mouth*]. Oh! don't say such horrid things.

HELMER. Still, suppose that happened,—what then?

NORA. If that were to happen, I don't suppose I should care whether I owed money or not.

HELMER. Yes, but what about the people who had lent it?

NORA. They? Who would bother about them? I should not know who they were.

HELMER. That is like a woman! But seriously, Nora, you know what I think about that. No debt, no borrowing. There can be no freedom or beauty about a home life that depends on borrowing and debt. We two have kept bravely on the straight road so far, and we will go on the same way for the short time longer that there need be any struggle.

NORA [*moving towards the stove*]. As you please, Torvald.

HELMER [*following her*]. Come, come, my little skylark must not droop her wings. What is this! Is my little squirrel out of temper? [*Taking out his purse.*] Nora, what do you think I have got here?

NORA [turning round quickly]. Money!

HELMER. There you are. [*Gives her some money.*] Do you think I don't know what a lot is wanted for housekeeping at Christmas-time.

Comments on A Doll's House

A Doll's House almost irresistibly invites sweeping generalizations. It is the first Modern Tragedy, as Ibsen originally named it. The strong divorce play and the social drama are alike descended from it. *A Doll's House* stands in relation to modern drama as Queen Victoria to the royal families of Europe. It is not Ibsen's greatest play, but it is probably his most striking achievement, in the sense that it changed most decisively the course of literature. Its significance for contemporaries is quite distinct from its permanent significance or, again, from its place in the personal development of Ibsen as an artist. —M. C. Bradbrook

The Stranger, by Albert Camus

In this novel the protagonist is tried, convicted, and then executed for a murder that he commits. He has no remorse. To embrace any abstract concept like regret is to ignore one's existential being.

MOTHER died today. Or, maybe, yesterday; I can't be sure. The telegram from the Home says: YOUR MOTHER PASSED AWAY. FUNERAL TOMORROW. DEEP SYMPATHY. Which leaves the matter doubtful; it could have been yesterday.

The Home for Aged Persons is at Marengo, some fifty miles from Algiers. With the two o'clock bus I should get there well before nightfall. Then I can spend the night there, keeping the usual vigil beside the body, and be back here by tomorrow evening. I have fixed up with my employer for two days' leave; obviously, under the circumstances, he couldn't refuse. Still, I had an idea he looked annoyed, and I said, without thinking:

"Sorry, sir, but it's not my fault, you know."

Afterwards it struck me I needn't have said that. I had no reason to excuse myself; it was up to him to express his sympathy and so forth. Probably he will do so the day after tomorrow, when he sees me in black. For the present, it's almost as if Mother weren't really dead. The funeral will bring it home to me, put an official seal on it, so to speak.

I took the two-o'clock bus. It was a blazing hot afternoon. I'd lunched, as usual, at Céleste's restaurant. Everyone was most kind, and Céleste said to me, "There's no one like a mother." When I left they came with me to the door. It was something of a rush, getting away, as at the last moment I had to call in at Emmanuel's place to borrow his black tie and mourning band. He lost his uncle a few months ago.

I had to run to catch the bus. I suppose it was my hurrying like that, what with the glare off the road and from the sky, the reek of gasoline, and the jolts that made me feel so drowsy. Anyhow, I slept most of the way. When I woke I was leaning against a soldier; he grinned and asked me if I'd come from a long way off, and I just nodded, to cut things short. I wasn't in a mood for talking.

The Home is a little over a mile from the village. I went there on foot. I asked to be allowed to see Mother at once, but the doorkeeper told me I must see the warden first. He wasn't free, and I had to wait a bit. The doorkeeper chatted with me while I waited; then he led me to the office. The warden was a very small man, with gray hair, and a Legion of Honor rosette in his buttonhole. He gave me a long look with his watery blue eyes. Then we shook hands, and he held mine so long that I began to feel embarrassed. After that he consulted a register on his table, and said:

"Madame Meursault entered the Home three years ago. She had no private means and depended entirely on you." I had a feeling he was blaming me for something, and started to explain. But he cut me short.

"There's no need to excuse yourself, my boy. I've looked up the record and obviously you weren't in a position to see that she was properly cared for. She needed someone to be with her all the time, and young men in jobs like yours don't get too much pay. In any case, she was much happier in the Home."

I said, "Yes, sir; I'm sure of that."

Then he added: "She had good friends here, you know, old folks like herself, and one gets on better with people of one's own generation. You're much too young; you couldn't have been much of a companion to her."

That was so. When we lived together, Mother was always watching me, but we hardly ever talked. During her first few weeks at the Home she used to cry a good deal. But that was only because she hadn't settled down. After a month or two she'd have cried if she'd been told to leave the Home. Because this, too, would have been a wrench. That was why, during the last year, I seldom went to see her. Also, it would have meant losing my Sunday—not to mention the trouble of going to the bus, getting my ticket, and spending two hours on the journey each way.

The warden went on talking, but I didn't pay much attention. Finally he said:

"Now, I suppose you'd like to see your mother?"

I rose without replying, and he led the way to the door. As we were going down the stairs he explained:

"I've had the body moved to our little mortuary—so as not to upset the other old people, you understand. Every time there's a death here, they're in a nervous state for two or three days. Which means, of course, extra work and worry for our staff."

We crossed a courtyard where there were a number of old men, talking amongst themselves in little groups. They fell silent as we came up with them.

Then, behind our backs, the chattering began again. Their voices reminded me of parakeets in a cage, only the sound wasn't quite so shrill. The warden stopped outside the entrance of a small, low building.

"So here I leave you, Monsieur Meursault. If you want me for anything, you'll find me in my office. We propose to have the funeral tomorrow morning. That will enable you to spend the night beside your mother's coffin, as no doubt you would wish to do. Just one more thing; I gathered from your mother's friends that she wished to be buried with the rites of the Church. I've made arrangements for this; but I thought I should let you know."

I thanked him. So far as I knew, my mother, though not a professed atheist, had never given a thought to religion in her life.

I entered the mortuary. It was a bright, spotlessly clean room, with whitewashed walls and a big skylight. The furniture consisted of some chairs and trestles. Two of the latter stood open in the center of the room and the coffin rested on them. The lid was in place, but the screws had been given only a few turns and their nickeled heads stuck out above the wood, which was stained dark walnut. An Arab woman—a nurse, I supposed—was sitting beside the bier; she was wearing a blue smock and had a rather gaudy scarf wound round her hair.

Just then the keeper came up behind me. He'd evidently been running, as he was a little out of breath.

"We put the lid on, but I was told to unscrew it when you came, so that you could see her."

While he was going up to the coffin I told him not to trouble. "Eh? What's that?" he exclaimed. "You don't want me to . . . ?"

"No," I said.

He put back the screwdriver in his pocket and stared at me. I realized then that I shouldn't have said, "No," and it made me rather embarrassed. After eying me for some moments he asked:

"Why not?" But he didn't sound reproachful; he simply wanted to know.

"Well, really I couldn't say," I answered.

He began twiddling his white mustache; then, without looking at me, said gently: "I understand."

He was a pleasant-looking man, with blue eyes and ruddy cheeks. He drew up a chair for me near the coffin, and seated himself just behind. The nurse got up and moved toward the door. As she was going by, the keeper whispered in my ear:

"It's a tumor she has, poor thing."

I looked at her more carefully and I noticed that she had a bandage round her head, just below her eyes. It lay quite flat across the bridge of her nose, and one saw hardly anything of her face except that strip of whiteness.

As soon as she had gone, the keeper rose.

"Now I'll leave you to yourself."

I don't know whether I made some gesture, but instead of going he halted behind my chair. The sensation of someone posted at my back made me uncomfortable. The sun was getting low and the whole room was flooded with a pleasant, mellow light. Two hornets were buzzing overhead, against the skylight. I was so sleepy I could hardly keep my eyes open. Without looking round, I asked the keeper how long he'd been at the Home. "Five years." The answer came so pat that one could have thought he'd been expecting my question.

That started him off, and he became quite chatty. If anyone had told him ten years ago that he'd end his days as doorkeeper at a home at Marengo, he'd never have believed it. He was sixty-four, he said, and hailed from Paris.

When he said that, I broke in. "Ah, you don't come from here?"

I remembered then that, before taking me to the warden, he'd told me something about Mother. He had said she'd have to be buried mighty quickly because of the heat in these parts, especially down in the plain. "At Paris they keep the body for three days, sometimes four." After that he had mentioned that he'd spent the best part of his life in Paris, and could never manage to forget it. "Here," he had said, "things have to go with a rush, like. You've hardly time to get used to the idea that someone's dead, before you're hauled off to the funeral." "That's enough," his wife had put in. "You didn't ought to say such things to the poor young gentleman." The old fellow had blushed and begun to apologize. I told him it was quite all right. As a matter of fact, I found it rather interesting, what he'd been telling me; I hadn't thought of that before.

Comments on Camus

Society as Camus portrays it is as duplicitous, capricious, and lethal as fate, with one vital difference: fate makes no claim to rationality, while society does make one. Once Meursault has been labeled a "criminal," all of his previous actions that have seemed merely eccentric are brought against him as evidence of a heinous personality by the witnesses who gave no indication of judging him so harshly before his crime. There is implicit in *The Stranger* the theme that no matter how innocent a life one may have led, once he has been judged guilty of a crime, society sanctimoniously hastens to reinterpret all his past actions in a guilty light. It would be a mistake, however, to interpret the novel, as the jacket note of an American translation does, merely as the story of "an ordinary little man, . . . helpless in life's grip." Although Meursault does describe himself as being "just like everybody else," this represents a certain irony on Camus' part . . . for it is clear that Camus meant Meursault to be something more than a normal citizen whose minor eccentricities are turned against him because a freakish stroke of fate has caused him to commit a crime. Meursault is a social rebel. —Donald Lazere

The second part of the novel is concerned with the enigmatic problem of Meursault's act, a problem as puzzling to Meursault as to the reader. Of the usual interpretations, Camus makes short shrift, presenting them ironically in Meursault's semi-burlesque interviews with the prosecutor, magistrate, and lawyer, and in his account of the trial. The first-person narrative now establishes a strange dissociation between the facts and feelings Meursault had previously described, and the attempts made by others to interpret them coherently. A definite shift in perspective is introduced: the reader finds himself in the position of judge, jury, and privileged witness. He and Meursault alone know the facts. Camus has thereby put upon him the burden of an explanation Meursault is unable to furnish. Self-critical and self-correcting, the novel rapidly moves towards its end. —Germaine Bree

"You will never be happy if you continue to search for what happiness consists of. You will never live if you are looking for the meaning of life," says Albert Camus (1913–60). He was one of the earliest members of an artistic movement called Absurdism, which mainly centered on the idea that awareness of the certainty and finality of death makes life meaningless. In his journal Camus wrote: "There is only one case in which despair is true. It is that of a man sentenced to die." The post-World War II mood of disillusionment and skepticism was expressed in peculiar terms by a number of artists, most of whom lived in France. Camus was a member of this group. Although they did not consider themselves as belonging to a formal movement, they shared a belief that human life was essentially without meaning, purpose, and absolute morality. They therefore thought that valid communication in any form, artistic or otherwise, was no longer possible. They felt the human community had sunk to a state of absurdity ("the absurd" is a term coined by Albert Camus).

Camus was also an Existentialist. Absurdism is a literary movement; Existentialism is a philosophical movement. Existentialism rejects epistemology or the attempt to validate human knowledge as a basis for reality—a fundamental change in direction in Western philosophy. To Plato, ethical behavior was closely tied to knowledge. Plato argued that if one knew the right thing to do, one would do it. Existentialism argued that that was not so. People made decisions based on need and function rather than knowledge. People were quite capable of making an evil decision if it suited their purposes. Human beings were not solely or even primarily people who made decisions from a basis of knowledge; they merely desired, manipulated, and above all, chose and acted on their own selfish behalf. Thus Camus regarded objects not primarily as "things" for cognition, a derivative characteristic, but as tools for processing the world. Camus's characters are not detached observers of the world, but they are "in the world," participating in the chaotic events that we call everyday life. In short, Camus was more concerned with being rather than with knowing.

—James P. Stobaugh

Absurdism

'The Big Trip Up Yonder', by Kurt Vonnegut Jr.

GRAMPS FORD, his chin resting on his hands, his hands on the crook of his cane, was staring irascibly at the five-foot television screen that

133

dominated the room. On the screen, a news commentator was summarizing the day's happenings. Every thirty seconds or so, Gramps would jab the floor with his cane-tip and shout, "Hell, we did that a hundred years ago!"

Emerald and Lou, coming in from the balcony, where they had been seeking that 2185 A.D. rarity—privacy—were obliged to take seats in the back row, behind Lou's father and mother, brother and sister-in-law, son and daughter-in-law, grandson and wife, granddaughter and husband, great-grandson and wife, nephew and wife, grandnephew and wife, great-grandniece and husband, great-grandnephew and wife—and, of course, Gramps, who was in front of everybody. All save Gramps, who was somewhat withered and bent, seemed, by pre-anti-gerasone standards, to be about the same age—somewhere in their late twenties or early thirties. Gramps looked older because he had already reached 70 when anti-gerasone was invented. He had not aged in the 102 years since.

"Meanwhile," the commentator was saying, "Council Bluffs, Iowa, was still threatened by stark tragedy. But 200 weary rescue workers have refused to give up hope, and continue to dig in an effort to save Elbert Haggedorn, 183, who has been wedged for two days in a . . ."

"I wish he'd get something more cheerful," Emerald whispered to Lou. "SILENCE!" cried Gramps. "Next one shoots off his big bazoo while the TV's on is gonna find hisself cut off without a dollar—" his voice suddenly softened and sweetened—"when they wave that checkered flag at the Indianapolis Speedway, and old Gramps gets ready for the Big Trip Up Yonder."

He sniffed sentimentally, while his heirs concentrated desperately on not making the slightest sound. For them, the poignancy of the prospective Big Trip had been dulled somewhat, through having been mentioned by Gramps about once a day for fifty years.

"Dr. Brainard Keyes Bullard," continued the commentator, "President of Wyandotte College, said in an address tonight that most of the world's ills can be traced to the fact that Man's knowledge of himself has not kept pace with his knowledge of the physical world."

"H---!" snorted Gramps. "We said *that* a hundred years ago!"

"In Chicago tonight," the commentator went on, "a special celebration is taking place in the Chicago Lying-in Hospital. The guest of honor is Lowell W. Hitz, age zero. Hitz, born this morning, is the twenty-five-millionth child to be born in the hospital." The commentator faded, and was replaced on the screen by young Hitz, who squalled furiously.

"H---!" whispered Lou to Emerald. "We said that a hundred years ago."

"I heard that!" shouted Gramps. He snapped off the television set and his petrified descendants stared silently at the screen. "You, there, boy—"

"I didn't mean anything by it, sir," said Lou, aged 103.

"Get me my will. You know where it is. You kids *all* know where it is. Fetch, boy!" Gramps snapped his gnarled fingers sharply.

Lou nodded dully and found himself going down the hall, picking his way over bedding to Gramps' room, the only private room in the Ford apartment. The other rooms were the bathroom, the living room and the wide windowless hallway, which was originally intended to serve as a dining area, and which had a kitchenette in one end. Six mattresses and four sleeping bags were dispersed in the hallway and living room, and the daybed, in the living room, accommodated the eleventh couple, the favorites of the moment.

On Gramps' bureau was his will, smeared, dog-eared, perforated and blotched with hundreds of additions, deletions, accusations, conditions, warnings, advice and homely philosophy. The document was, Lou reflected, a fifty-year diary, all jammed onto two sheets—a garbled, illegible log of day after day of strife. This day, Lou would be disinherited for the eleventh time, and it would take him perhaps six months of impeccable behavior to regain the promise of a share in the estate. To say nothing of the daybed in the living room for Em and himself.

"Boy!" called Gramps.

"Coming, sir." Lou hurried back into the living room and handed Gramps the will.

"Pen!" said Gramps.

He was instantly offered eleven pens, one from each couple.

"Not *that* leaky thing," he said, brushing Lou's pen aside. "Ah, there's a nice one. Good boy, Willy." He accepted Willy's pen. That was the tip they had all been waiting for. Willy, then—Lou's father—was the new favorite.

Willy, who looked almost as young as Lou, though he was 142, did a poor job of concealing his pleasure. He glanced shyly at the daybed, which would become his, and from which Lou and Emerald would have to move back into the hall, back to the worst spot of all by the bathroom door.

Gramps missed none of the high drama he had authored and he gave his own familiar role everything he had. Frowning and running his finger along each line, as though he were seeing the will for the first time, he read aloud in a deep portentous monotone, like a bass note on a cathedral organ.

"I, Harold D. Ford, residing in Building 257 of Alden Village, New York City, Connecticut, do hereby make, publish and declare this to be my last Will and Testament, revoking any and all former wills and codicils by me at any time heretofore made." He blew his nose importantly and went on, not missing a word, and repeating many for emphasis—repeating in particular his ever-more-elaborate specifications for a funeral.

At the end of these specifications, Gramps was so choked with emotion that Lou thought he might have forgotten why he'd brought out the will in the first place. But Gramps heroically brought his powerful emotions under control and, after erasing for a full minute, began to write and speak at the same time. Lou could have spoken his lines for him, he had heard them so often.

"I have had many heartbreaks ere leaving this vale of tears for a better land," Gramps said and wrote. "But the deepest hurt of all has been dealt me by—" He looked around the group, trying to remember who the malefactor was.

Everyone looked helpfully at Lou, who held up his hand resignedly.

Gramps nodded, remembering, and completed the sentence—"my great-grandson, Louis J. Ford."

"Grandson, sir," said Lou.

"Don't quibble. You're in deep enough now, young man," said Gramps, but he made the change. And, from there, he went without a misstep through the phrasing of the disinheritance, causes for which were disrespectfulness and quibbling.

In the paragraph following, the paragraph that had belonged to everyone in the room at one time or another, Lou's name was scratched out and Willy's substituted as heir to the apartment and, the biggest plum of all, the double bed in the private bedroom.

"So!" said Gramps, beaming. He erased the date at the foot of the will and substituted a new one, including the time of day. "Well—time to watch the McGarvey Family." The McGarvey Family was a television serial that Gramps had been following since he was 60, or for a total of 112 years. "I can't wait to see what's going to happen next," he said.

Lou detached himself from the group and lay down on his bed of pain by the bathroom door. Wishing Em would join him, he wondered where she was.

He dozed for a few moments, until he was disturbed by someone stepping over him to get into the bathroom. A moment later, he heard a faint gurgling sound, as though something were being poured down the washbasin drain.

Suddenly, it entered his mind that Em had cracked up, that she was in there doing something drastic about Gramps.

"Em?" he whispered through the panel. There was no reply, and Lou pressed against the door. The worn lock, whose bolt barely engaged its socket, held for a second, then let the door swing inward.

"Morty!" gasped Lou.

Lou's great-grandnephew, Mortimer, who had just married and brought his wife home to the Ford ménage, looked at Lou with consternation and surprise. Morty kicked the door shut, but not before Lou had glimpsed what was in his hand—Gramps' enormous economy-size bottle of anti-gerasone, which had apparently been half-emptied, and which Morty was refilling with tap water.

A moment later, Morty came out, glared defiantly at Lou and brushed past him wordlessly to rejoin his pretty bride.

Shocked, Lou didn't know what to do. He couldn't let Gramps take the mousetrapped anti-gerasone—but, if he warned Gramps about it, Gramps would certainly make life in the apartment, which was merely insufferable now, harrowing.

Lou glanced into the living room and saw that the Fords, Emerald among them, were momentarily at rest, relishing the botches that the McGarveys had made of *their* lives. Stealthily, he went into the bathroom, locked the door as well as he could and began to pour the contents of Gramps' bottle down the drain. He was going to refill it with full-strength anti-gerasone from the 22 smaller bottles on the shelf.

The bottle contained a half-gallon, and its neck was small, so it seemed to Lou that the emptying would take forever. And the almost imperceptible smell of anti-gerasone, like Worcestershire sauce, now seemed to Lou, in his nervousness, to be pouring out into the rest of the apartment, through the keyhole and under the door.

The bottle gurgled monotonously. Suddenly, up came the sound of music from the living room and there were murmurs and the scraping of chair-legs on the floor. "Thus ends," said the television announcer, "the 29,121st chapter in the life of your neighbors and mine, the McGarveys." Footsteps were coming down the hall. There was a knock on the bathroom door.

"Just a sec," Lou cheerily called out. Desperately, he shook the big bottle, trying to speed up the flow. His palms slipped on the wet glass, and the heavy bottle smashed on the tile floor.

The door was pushed open, and Gramps, dumbfounded, stared at the incriminating mess.

Lou felt a hideous prickling sensation on his scalp and the back of his neck. He grinned engagingly through his nausea and, for want of anything remotely resembling a thought, waited for Gramps to speak.

"Well, boy," said Gramps at last, "looks like you've got a little tidying up to do." And that was all he said. He turned around, elbowed his way through the crowd and locked himself in his bedroom.

The Fords contemplated Lou in incredulous silence a moment longer, and then hurried back to the living room, as though some of his horrible guilt would taint them, too, if they looked too long. Morty stayed behind long enough to give Lou a quizzical, annoyed glance. Then he also went into the living room, leaving only Emerald standing in the doorway.

Tears streamed over her cheeks. "Oh, you poor lamb—*please* don't look so awful! It was my fault. I put you up to this with my nagging about Gramps."

"No," said Lou, finding his voice, "really you didn't. Honest, Em, I was just—"

"You don't have to explain anything to me, hon. I'm on your side, no matter what." She kissed him on one cheek and whispered in his ear, "It wouldn't have been murder, hon. It wouldn't have killed him. It wasn't such a terrible thing to do. It just would have fixed him up so he'd be able to go any time God decided He wanted him."

"What's going to happen next, Em?" said Lou hollowly. "What's he going to do?"

Lou and Emerald stayed fearfully awake almost all night, waiting to see what Gramps was going to do. But not a sound came from the sacred bedroom. Two hours before dawn, they finally dropped off to sleep.

At six o'clock, they arose again, for it was time for their generation to eat breakfast in the kitchenette. No one spoke to them. They had twenty minutes in which to eat, but their reflexes were so dulled by the bad night that they had hardly swallowed two mouthfuls of egg-type processed seaweed before it was time to surrender their places to their son's generation.

Then, as was the custom for whoever had been most recently disinherited, they began preparing Gramps' breakfast, which would presently be served to him in bed, on a tray. They tried to be cheerful about it. The toughest part of the job was having to handle the honest-to-God eggs and bacon and oleomargarine, on which Gramps spent so much of the income from his fortune.

"Well," said Emerald, "I'm not going to get all panicky until I'm sure there's something to be panicky about."

"Maybe he doesn't know what it was I busted," Lou said hopefully.

"Probably thinks it was your watch crystal," offered Eddie, their son, who was toying apathetically with his buckwheat-type processed sawdust cakes.

"Don't get sarcastic with your father," said Em, "and don't talk with your mouth full, either."

"I'd like to see anybody take a mouthful of this stuff and *not* say something," complained Eddie, who was 73. He glanced at the clock. "It's time to take Gramps his breakfast, you know."

"Yeah, it is, isn't it?" said Lou weakly. He shrugged. "Let's have the tray, Em."

"We'll both go."

Walking slowly, smiling bravely, they found a large semi-circle of long-faced Fords standing around the bedroom door.

Em knocked. "Gramps," she called brightly, "*break*-fast is *rea*-dy." There was no reply and she knocked again, harder.

The door swung open before her fist. In the middle of the room, the soft, deep, wide, canopied bed, the symbol of the sweet by-and-by to every Ford, was empty.

A sense of death, as unfamiliar to the Fords as Zoroastrianism or the causes of the Sepoy Mutiny, stilled every voice, slowed every heart. Awed, the heirs began to search gingerly, under the furniture and behind the drapes, for all that was mortal of Gramps, father of the clan.

But Gramps had left not his Earthly husk but a note, which Lou finally found on the dresser, under a paperweight which was a treasured souvenir from the World's Fair of 2000. Unsteadily, Lou read it aloud:

"'Somebody who I have sheltered and protected and taught the best I know how all these years last night turned on me like a mad dog and diluted my anti-gerasone, or tried to. I am no longer a young man. I can no longer bear the crushing burden of life as I once could. So, after last night's bitter experience, I say good-by. The cares of this world will soon drop away like a cloak of thorns and I shall know peace. By the time you find this, I will be gone.'"

"Gosh," said Willy brokenly, "he didn't even get to see how the 5000-mile Speedway Race was going to come out."

"Or the Solar Series," Eddie said, with large mournful eyes.

"Or whether Mrs. McGarvey got her eyesight back," added Morty.

"There's more," said Lou, and he began reading aloud again: "'I, Harold D. Ford, etc., do hereby make, publish and declare this to be my last Will and Testament, revoking any and all former wills and codicils by me at any time heretofore made.'"

"No!" cried Willy. "Not another one!"

"'I do stipulate,'" read Lou, "'that all of my property, of whatsoever kind and nature, not be divided, but do devise and bequeath it to be held in common by my issue, without regard for generation, equally, share and share alike.'"

"Issue?" said Emerald.

Lou included the multitude in a sweep of his hand. "It means we all own the whole damn shootin' match."

Each eye turned instantly to the bed. "Share and share alike?" asked Morty.

"Actually," said Willy, who was the oldest one present, "it's just like the old system, where the oldest people head up things with their headquarters in here and—"

"I like *that!*" exclaimed Em. "Lou owns as much of it as you do, and I say it ought to be for the oldest one who's still working. You can snooze around here all day, waiting for your pension check, while poor Lou stumbles in here after work, all tuckered out, and—"

"How about letting somebody who's never had *any* privacy get a little crack at it?" Eddie demanded hotly. "Hell, you old people had plenty of privacy back when you were kids. I was born and raised in the middle of that goddamn barracks in the hall! How about—"

"Yeah?" challenged Morty. "Sure, you've all had it pretty tough, and my heart bleeds for you. But try honeymooning in the hall for a real kick."

"*Silence!*" shouted Willy imperiously. "The next person who opens his mouth spends the next six months by the bathroom. Now clear out of my room. I want to think."

A vase shattered against the wall, inches above his head. In the next moment, a free-for-all was under way, with each couple battling to eject every other couple from the room. Fighting coalitions formed and dissolved with the lightning changes of the tactical situation. Em and Lou were thrown into the hall, where they organized others in the same situation, and stormed back into the room.

After two hours of struggle, with nothing like a decision in sight, the cops broke in, followed by television cameramen from mobile units.

For the next half-hour, patrol wagons and ambulances hauled away Fords, and then the apartment was still and spacious.

An hour later, films of the last stages of the riot were being televised to 500,000,000 delighted viewers on the Eastern Seaboard.

In the stillness of the three-room Ford apartment on the 76th floor of Building 257, the television set had been left on. Once more the air was filled with the cries and grunts and crashes of the fray, coming harmlessly now from the loudspeaker.

The battle also appeared on the screen of the television set in the police station, where the Fords and their captors watched with professional interest.

Em and Lou, in adjacent four-by-eight cells, were stretched out peacefully on their cots.

"Em," called Lou through the partition, "you got a washbasin all your own, too?"

"Sure. Washbasin, bed, light—the works. And we thought *Gramps'* room was something. How long has this been going on?" She held out her hand. "For the first time in forty years, hon, I haven't got the shakes—look at me!"

"Cross your fingers," said Lou. "The lawyer's going to try to get us a year."

"Gee!" Em said dreamily. "I wonder what kind of wires you'd have to pull to get put away in solitary?"

"All right, pipe down," said the turnkey, "or I'll toss the whole kit and caboodle of you right out. And first one who lets on to anybody outside how good jail is ain't never getting back in!"

The prisoners instantly fell silent.

The living room of the apartment darkened for a moment as the riot scenes faded on the television screen, and then the face of the announcer appeared, like  the Sun coming from behind a cloud. "And now, friends," he said, "I have a special message from the makers of anti-gerasone, a message for all you folks over 150. Are you hampered socially by wrinkles, by stiffness of joints and discoloration or loss of hair, all because these things came upon you before anti-gerasone was developed? Well, if you are, you need no longer suffer, need no longer feel different and out of things.

"After years of research, medical science has now developed *Super*-anti-gerasone! In weeks—yes, weeks—you can look, feel and act as young as your great-great-grandchildren! Wouldn't you pay $5,000 to be indistinguishable from everybody else? Well, you don't have to. Safe, tested *Super*-anti-gerasone costs you only a few dollars a day.

"Write now for your free trial carton. Just put your name and address on a dollar postcard, and mail it to '*Super*,' Box 500,000, Schenectady, N. Y. Have you got that? I'll repeat it. '*Super*,' Box 500,000 . . ."

Underlining the announcer's words was the scratching of Gramps' pen, the one Willy had given him the night before. He had come in, a few minutes earlier, from the Idle Hour Tavern, which commanded a view of Building 257 from across the square of asphalt known as the Alden Village Green. He had called a cleaning woman to come straighten the place up, then had hired the best lawyer in town to get his descendants a conviction, a genius who had never gotten a client less than a year and a day. Gramps had then moved the daybed before the television screen, so that he could watch from a reclining position. It was something he'd dreamed of doing for years.

"Schen-*ec*-ta-dy," murmured Gramps. "Got it!" His face had changed remarkably. His facial muscles seemed to have relaxed, revealing kindness and equanimity under what had been taut lines of bad temper. It was almost as though his trial package of *Super*-anti-gerasone had already arrived. When something amused him on television, he smiled easily, rather than barely managing to lengthen the thin line of his mouth a millimeter.

Life was good. He could hardly wait to see what was going to happen next.

Comments on Vonnegut

Vonnegut uses science fiction to open up the question of a purpose in the universe, the problem of man's morality in an amoral universe, and the adjunctive question of free will. The extraterrestrial domain in his novels shows what present scientific and social Earth trends may become, offers a detached perspective on Earth's condition as we look at it from the viewpoint of extraterrestrial beings, and suggests alternate modes of perception that might be opposed to our normal human view of ourselves. Vonnegut makes it very clear that space and technological invention are not escapes from Earth's problems. They magnify those problems rather than reducing them. — Robert A. Hipkiss

Vonnegut consciously chooses a stance of naïveté and wonder — the "child-like" — as well as sentiment and self-pity — the "childish." In many ways, he is sensitive and profound; in others, he remains a blurb-writer, still doing public relations work, but now for himself. — Clark Mayo

One thing is apparent from the start in reading Vonnegut: he is an enthusiast of sentimental detachment, a Pinball Wizard of cosmic cool who, through the charm of his style and the subtle challenge of his ideas, encourages us to adopt his interplanetary midwestern viewpoint and to believe once again in such radically updated values as love, compassion, humility, and conscience. He is a dervish of paradox as he suggests in his extended fables that we must learn to maintain happy illusions over villainous ones, that the best truth is a comforting lie, and that if there is any purpose to human history, it is best understood as a joke—at our expense. —James Lundquist

Not everyone likes Vonnegut. One reviewer dismissed Vonnegut's writing as "a series of narcissistic giggles," while others deplored his pacifism as being adolescent or downright un-American. But the majority of critical opinion was favorable, and it remains so today. Many critics claim that Vonnegut's most lasting contribution to American fiction is his innovative style, the "telegraphic-schizophrenic manner" of storytelling he developed in "The Trip Up Yonder." Others critics argue that he is more important as a satirist of American life, and they rank him with Sinclair Lewis and Mark Twain. What do you think?

—James P. Stobaugh

Student Essays

Themes in Anne of Green Gables

The setting and characters in Anne of Green Gables establish the unconditional love that the main character Anne Shirley bestows and receives.

Unconditional love and growing up are both themes that Lucy Maud Montgomery develops in *Anne of Green Gables*. They are developed through the plot, setting, and characterization. The small community of Avonlea and Anne's friends and neighbors establish and nurture the theme of unconditional love. As the plot progresses, Anne matures into a young woman. The foils in the story contribute to this development. The plot, setting, and characterization contribute to the themes of unconditional love and growing up.

The setting and characters in *Anne of Green Gables* establish the unconditional love that the main character, Anne Shirley, bestows and receives. The simple act of naming her surroundings in Avonlea expresses Anne's love for her community. She begins naming areas in chapter 2. "'They should call it—let me see—the White Way of Delight.'" ... "'That's Barry's pond,' said Matthew." "'Oh, I don't like that name either. I shall call it—let me see—the Lake of Shining Waters.'" Anne's love is expressed again in chapter 38, when she decides to give up her dream of going to college for the time being to stay with Marilla and keep Green Gables. "'Oh, Anne, I could get on real well if you were here, I know. But I can't let you sacrifice yourself so for me. It would be terrible.'" "'Nonsense!' Anne laughed merrily. 'There is no sacrifice. Nothing could be worse than giving up Green Gables—nothing could hurt me more. We must keep the dear old place. My mind is quite made up, Marilla.'" The foils in *Anne of Green Gables* not only receive Anne's love, but they also bestow their love to Anne. Throughout

the story, Anne's classmate Gilbert Blythe shows his love for Anne through both words and actions. His love does not falter, even though Anne dislikes him for a long time. In chapter 33, Gilbert's love is shown during a concert in which Anne will recite. "But suddenly, as her dilated, frightened eyes gazed out over the audience, she saw Gilbert Blythe away at the back of the room, bending forward with a smile on his face—a smile which seemed to Anne at once triumphant and taunting. In reality it was nothing of the kind. Gilbert was merely smiling with appreciation of the whole affair in general and of the effect produced by Anne's slender white form and spiritual face against a background of palms in particular." The theme of unconditional love in *Anne of Green Gables* is produced both by the love Anne gives and the love she receives.

The theme of growing up is developed through characterization as Anne matures into a young woman. The book begins with Anne as an imaginative and vivacious young girl. In chapter 3, Anne's personality is shown through how she views her name. "'But if you call me Anne please call me Anne spelled with an *e*.' 'What difference does it make how it's spelled?' asked Marilla with another rusty smile as she picked up the teapot. 'Oh, it makes such a difference. It looks so much nicer. When you hear a name pronounced can't you always see it in your mind, just as if it was printed out? I can; and A-n-n looks dreadful, but A-n-n-e looks so much more distinguished. If you'll only call me Anne spelled with an *e* I shall try to reconcile myself to not being called Cordelia.'"

The last sentence in *Anne of Green Gables* exemplifies how Anne has matured. "'God's in his heaven, all's right with the world,' whispered Anne softly." This sentence shows how Anne has progressed from being loquacious and verbose to someone who can state something significant with just a few words. Montgomery also illustrates Anne's maturation process through her reconciliation with Gilbert Blythe in chapter 38. "'Who was that came up the lane with you, Anne?' 'Gilbert Blythe,' answered Anne vexed to find herself blushing. 'I met him on Barry's hill.' 'I didn't think you and Gilbert Blythe were such good friends that you'd stand for half an hour at the gate talking to him,' said Marilla, with a dry smile. 'We haven't been—we've been good enemies. But we have decided that it will be much more sensible to be good friends in future.'" After a few years of hating Gilbert, Anne had matured enough to set aside her grudge and reconcile with Gilbert. It is through these progressions that the theme of growing up is apparent.

Through *Anne of Green Gable*'s plot, setting, and characterization, the themes of unconditional love and growing up become apparent. The theme of unconditional love is shown through the love Anne gives and receives. As Anne's character progresses through the story, the theme of growing up becomes evident.

The economy and directness of this essay is extraordinary. The student measures and evaluates every single word before using it. This essay thus is inviting, cogent, and informative.

The Theme of Alice in Wonderland

Throughout Alice in Wonderland, the trials Alice faces evolve her maturity. The characters of the book also can represent Victorian England's leaders and their lack of maturity.

The theme of *Alice in Wonderland*, by Lewis Carroll, is maturity. As defined by James Stobaugh in *Skills for Literary Analysis*, the theme is "the central idea of a literary piece, that enduring truth/opinion that transcends time and setting The many trials Alice faces in the course of this book aid her in becoming more mature. *Alice in Wonderland* can also be interpreted on a deeper level. In fact, Lewis Carroll is criticizing Victorian England as being immature.

The theme is developed through the trials Alice encounters while in Wonderland. Although the hardships could have hindered Alice, she was able to overcome them to become a more mature person. An example of this is in chapter 8, right after the Queen of Hearts has asked Alice a confusing, silly question:

"'How should I know?' said Alice, surprised at her own courage. 'It's no business of mine.' The queen turned crimson with fury and, after glaring at her for a moment like a wild beast, screamed 'Off with her head! Off—'

"'Nonsense!' said Alice, very loudly and decidedly, and the queen was silent."

Although Alice could have simply made up an answer, she stood her ground even when the queen threatened her by saying she would decapitate her. Alice did not give in and was then able to help others when they too were threatened by the queen. Another time Alice matures is in chapter 10, after the mock turtle and the Gryphon have just finished explaining the Lobster Quadrille. "'Thank you,' said Alice, 'it's very interesting. I never knew so much about a whiting before." Although their explanation was fairly confusing, Alice appreciated them for taking time to inform her about what a whiting was. This shows a growth of maturity in Alice. Previously in the book, Alice often questioned the other characters when they said something unusual to her. Trials are part of developing the theme of maturity in *Alice in Wonderland*.

Alice in Wonderland can also be read as a criticism of Victorian England, focusing on the country's lack of maturity. Many of the characters in this book represent actual figures of Victorian England. An example is the King of Hearts in chapter 11: "The judge, by the way, was the King; and as he wore his crown over the wig, . . . he did not look at all comfortable and it was certainly not becoming." One could understand this as Lewis Carroll's making fun of Prince Albert, Queen Victoria's husband. The author also seemed to be making fun of Queen Victoria. Many times the Queen of Hearts says, "Off with someone's head." Carroll gives the impression of making fun of Victorian England's servants in chapter 6:

> For a minute or two she stood looking at the house, and wondering what to do next, when suddenly a footman in livery came running out of the wood — (she considered him to be a footman because he was in livery: otherwise, judging by his face only, she would have called him a fish) — and rapped loudly at the door with his knuckles. It was opened by another footman in livery, with a round face, and large eyes like a frog; and both footmen, Alice noticed, had powdered hair that curled all over their heads. . . . The Fish-Footman began by producing from under his arm a great letter, nearly as large as himself, and this he handed over to the other, saying, in a solemn tone, "for the Duchess. An invitation from the Queen to play croquet." The Frog-Footman repeated, in the same solemn tone, only changing the order of the words a little, "From the Queen. An invitation for the Duchess to play croquet." Then they both bowed low, and their curls got entangled together.

This example stresses the footmen's clumsiness, stupidity, and formalness. Although Alice in Wonderland can be read at two different levels, the theme of the book remains the same.

Throughout *Alice in Wonderland*, the trials Alice faces mature her. The characters of the book also can represent Victorian England leaders and their lack of maturity.

Use of Songs to Set Up the Theme in *The Lord of the Rings*

J. R. R. Tolkien uses songs in his novels not only to describe the theme, but also to develop his characters.

The Lord of The Rings, J. R. R. Tolkien's wonderful masterpiece, is the tale of one Hobbit and a fellowship of men, elves, dwarfs, and wizards attempting to destroy an evil ring. As the characters, especially the Hobbits, experience hardships, struggles, and pains, they express their feelings through songs. Tolkien uses such songs to develop his characters, to create themes, as well as to describe the settings, as in this example (138):

Frodo was chilled to the marrow. After a while the song became clearer, and with dread in his heart he perceived that it had changed into an incantation:

> Cold be hand and heart and bone,
> and cold be sleep under stone:
> never to wake on stony bed,
> never, till the Sun fails and the Moon is dead.
> In the black wind the stars shall die,
> and still on gold here let them lie,
> till the dark lord lifts his hand
> over dead sea and withered land.

At this point in The Fellowship of the Ring, the first part of Tolkien's novel, the Hobbits are passing through some fog on the Barrow-Downs. Frodo is ahead of Merry, Pippin, and Sam and hears this song. It is one that does not offer assurance to these frightened Hobbits, and later songs scare the Hobbits further. Tolkien employs the above song in this instance to show the suspense of the fog and how the Hobbits passing through it are extremely terrified.

Another song offers a look into the Hobbits' character (138):

Ho! Tom Bombadil, Tom Bombadillo!
By water, wood and hill, by the reed and willow,
by fire, sun and moon, harken now and hear us!

Come, Tom Bombadil, for our need is near us!

After being spooked by the previous song, the Hobbits begin to sing for help. The reader can understand how these tiny, five-foot-tall creatures can be terrified even in the fog so much that they sing for help. Knowing this, the reader can truly appreciate the Hobbits' timidity.

After passing through the fog, the Hobbits reach the Prancing Pony Inn. Here, they are out of the darkness and are safe within the walls of a building. Frodo recalls a song (155):

> There is an inn, a merry old inn
> beneath an old grey hill,
> And there they brew a beer so brown
> that the Man in the Moon himself came down
> on night to drink his fill
> The Man in the Moon took another mug,
> and then rolled beneath his chair;
> And there he dozed and dreamed of ale,
> till in the sky the stars were pale,
> and dawn was in the air.

This song is a song of happiness and is used by Tolkien to demonstrate the Hobbits' relief as they reached their destination. While the song may not necessarily describe the Prancing-Pony Inn, it still is used by Tolkien both to describe the happiness at the inn and to illustrate the Hobbits' thankfulness at being safe.

J. R. R. Tolkien uses songs in his novels not only to present the theme, but also to develop his characters. In the three songs quoted here, the reader learns that the Hobbits are terrified in the fog, use song to call for help, and sing a song when safe at the inn. The reader can also realize that these Hobbits have emotions that can quickly change: one moment the Hobbits are frightened while another they are relieved.

Morals in Panchatantra

"The Foolish Friend," "The Gold-Giving Snake," "The Brahman's Wife," and the "Mongoose" all contain morals that reflect what ancient Indian (South Asian) culture views as important.

Probably the most famous Western fable writer who ever lived is the ancient Greek slave Aesop. He wrote numerous fables, primarily beast fables, which, to this day, are commonly quoted and referred to as sources of truth and wisdom.

When one considers how often phrases such as "slow and steady wins the race," "sour grapes," and "a wolf in sheep's clothing" are used, one begins to realize how much of an impact Aesop truly had on Western society. However, Aesop's fables are definitely not the only stories that left large ripples in a culture. An Eastern equivalent to Aesop's fables is the *Panchatantra*, an Indian collection of fables. This anthology, like the stories of Aesop, has been observed as a source of wisdom for ages. Since the *Panchatantra* was meant to be a collection of truths, the morals of the stories in the compilation may be easily identified.

One of these fables is "The Foolish Friend." Although not the primary moral, an important concept introduced in this fable is the danger of anger. The text states that the monkey was "blinded by anger" when he took out his sword, killed the bee, and accidentally killed the king in the same stroke. The monkey's anger was dangerous enough to cause him to lose control and split the king's head, and in the end, this anger was powerful enough to bring the monkey from being the most loved creature in the kingdom to being the most shunned animal in the area. As Buddha said, "Holding on to anger is like grasping a hot coal with the intent of throwing it at someone else; you are the one who gets burned." The primary moral of "The Foolish Friend," however, is found in the last two sentences of the fable. "Thus it is said, 'Do not choose a fool for a friend, for the king was killed by a monkey.' And I say, 'It is better to have a clever enemy than a foolish friend.'" The king did not exercise wisdom in giving the monkey all his trust, and this lack of wisdom eventually killed him. As J. Willard Marriott once said, "Choose your friends wisely; they will make or break you."

Another fable from the *Panchatantra* that also contains a two-sided moral is "The Gold-Giving Snake." The first and most obvious moral is the danger of greed. The Brahman's son was greedy to collect all the dinars that the snake appeared to possess in her hole, and so he attempted to kill the snake, but instead, "The snake, as fate willed it, escaped with her life. Filled with rage, she bit the boy with her sharp, poisoned teeth, and the boy fell dead at once." When the boy tried to satisfy his greed—for as Horace stated, "He who is greedy is always in want" — it was as if the boy had picked up the venomous snake by her tail. The boy's own dangerous greed killed him.

Yet another side to this idea that is not so obvious, however, is the power of greed, separate from its dangerous aspects. After the death of his son, the Brahman came back to the anthill where the snake lived and once again requested that the snake come forth. The snake asked, "How can you forget the pain and sorrow for your son?" The answer to this question is simply greed. Mahatma Gandhi once noted, "Earth provides enough to satisfy every man's need, but not every man's greed." The Brahman ended up actually cursing his dead son's lack of understanding because it meant that the Brahman could no longer continue to satisfy his ceaseless greed. Greed wields much power.

The fable "The Brahman's Wife and the Mongoose" repeats two morals previously discussed: the danger of anger presented in "The Foolish Friend," and the danger of greed mentioned in "The Gold-Giving Snake." The text reads, "Driven by anger and without further investigation, [the mother] threw the water-filled pitcher at the mongoose, killing him instantly." The mother had always (inaccurately) viewed this mongoose, one of her offspring, as a threat to her other children. Thus, when the mongoose succeeded in defending one of his brothers from a black snake and came to his mother without washing the blood off his face, the mother, in thoughtless angry haste, killed the very creature which had saved her child's life. Indeed, "Anger is never without a reason, but seldom with a good one" However, the mother's anger was not the only cause of this disaster. The Brahman, who was supposed to be staying in his house protecting his children while his wife was out, instead left to collect alms. It was during this time that the mongoose fought the snake. As the Brahman's wife said, "You greedy one! Because you let greed rule, . . . you now must taste the fruit of your own tree of sin." In his greed, the Brahman had not stayed behind. If nothing else, the Brahman would have been able to testify to the fact that the mongoose killed the snake, not the boy. The Brahman painfully experienced the truth of the Chinese proverb "Covetous men's chests are rich, not they."

"The Foolish Friend," "The Gold-Giving Snake," and "The Brahman's Wife" and the "Mongoose" all contain morals that reflect what ancient Indian culture viewed as important. Like Aesop's fables, the stories of the *Panchatantra* hold truths that have been echoed all the way to present times. "All fortune belongs to him who has a contented mind." "We tend to forget that happiness doesn't come as a result of getting something we don't have, but rather of recognizing and appreciating what we do have."

Earth provides enough to satisfy everyone's need, but not everyone's greed. — Mahatma Gandhi

Augustine's *Confessions* Compared with Virgil's *Aeneid*

Virgil (70–19 BCE) was a Roman poet who glorified the Roman Empire and Augustus, the first Roman emperor. Augustine (354–430 CE) was a prolific Christian author and bishop (396–430) of the Roman city Hippo, in North Africa.

A man is called by his God to make a long and tedious journey that will eventually bring him to his ultimate home. This motif describes Virgil's *Aeneid* and Augustine's *Confessions*. Even though these two famous works seem entirely different on the surface, there are several striking similarities between them.

The first similarity between the two books is that of the protagonist's calling. In the *Aeneid*, Aeneas's dead wife comes to him as a spirit and instructs him in what he must do after fleeing his burning hometown of Troy:

> High Olympus will(s) it.
> Long exile must be your lot,
> the vast expanse of sea be ploughed;
> and you shall see the Hesperian land,
> where Lydian Tiber flows with gentle course
> between the fertile fields where heroes dwell.
> Prosperity, a kingdom, and a spouse of royal rank
> are there obtained for you.

As the spirit of Creusa, Aeneas's wife, states, the gods have called Aeneas to marry again and found a great city, Rome. Aeneas was called by the gods to begin his journey. In the Confessions, Augustine, too, felt called by his God. "I call upon you, Lord, in my faith which you have given me, which you have inspired in me through the humanity of your son, and through the ministry of your preacher." The phrase "my faith which you have given me" shows that Augustine clearly felt that it was only because of God that he was able to undertake the amazing journey that eventually led him to become one of the greatest Christian leaders who ever lived.

Aeneas and Augustine start at the same point, but do their journeys actually remain parallel past the beginning? In the *Aeneid*, Aeneas faces many obstacles as he travels along what proves to be an extremely tedious journey. Aeneas faces

Cyclops, Harpies, evil spirits, and many other difficulties as he makes his way to his destination. On the other hand, as one critic wrote, "The *Confessions* are a history of the young Augustine's fierce struggle to overcome his profligate ways and achieve a life of spiritual grace." Much of the *Confessions* is a story of Augustine's wearisome journey from an "unsaved" immoral life to a "redeemed" Christian life. Like Aeneas, Augustine faced many impediments along his spiritual journey, two of the largest being peer pressure and the teachings of Manichaeism. Aeneas's and Augustine's journeys are indeed similar.

Finally, Aeneas's and Augustine's goals are parallel. Aeneas wishes to arrive at his ultimate home. To Aeneas, this ultimate home is the future location of Rome. Because he was called by the gods to found a great city, Aeneas's journey eventually leads him to where this great city should be founded. Augustine, too, wishes to arrive at his ultimate home. The primary difference between the two goals, however, lies in the two protagonists' views of "home." To Aeneas, home is merely an earthly location; but to Augustine, the ultimate dwelling place is in heaven. Augustine's whole life looks forward to this end goal. As Dr. Noble wrote, "He [Augustine] regarded salvation as the goal of life." Webster's *Dictionary* of 1828 defines salvation as "the redemption of [the hu]man from the bondage of sin and liability to eternal death, and the conferring on [that person] everlasting happiness." Therefore, Augustine's goal was indirectly heaven, which, according to assured Christian hope, is attained at death.

Aeneas's and Augustine's journeys presented in the *Aeneid* and the *Confessions* respectively are surprisingly parallel from beginning to end. Don Williams Jr. once stated, "The road of life twists and turns and no two directions are ever the same." However, the twists and turns of the road of life ultimately directed two travelers in the same direction, one down a physical road, and one down a spiritual road. In the case of Aeneas and Augustine, "two directions [were] ever the same."

Plato's Three Main Questions in the *Republic*

This choice between the philosophic and tyrannic lives explains the plot of the Republic. Socrates takes a young man [Glaucon] tempted by the tyrannic life and attempts to give him at least that modicum of awareness of philosophy which will cure him of the lust for tyranny. Any other exhortation would amount to empty

moralism. — Allan Bloom

The Roman orator Cicero once stated, "Justice is the crowning glory of the virtues." Indeed, many virtues may be seen as sprouting from the foundational idea of justice. Because justice is such a vital concept, many have mused on what exactly a perfectly just man and a perfectly just society would look like. One of the most famous of these musings is recorded in Plato's *Republic*. This Socratic dialogue presents one of the many views of justice. Plato's dialogue *Republic* is based on three main questions, which all revolve around the central theme of justice.

First, and most foundationally, what is justice to an *individual*? In the context of discussing justice, Plato exhorts, "One man should practice one thing only, the thing to which his nature was best adapted." Yet this raises the question "How does a person know to what one's "nature [is] best adapted?'" In the *Republic*, Socrates and his inquisitors converse on this concept extensively, eventually agreeing that justice may be more easily delineated within the context of a community divided according to a class system. In the end, it is decided that the classes of the utopian society discussed throughout much of the dialogue are equivalent to the parts of a person's soul, and that temperance, courage, and wisdom, if exhibited in the right proportions, will lead a man to be perfectly just.

Second, what does a perfectly just *society* look like? Plato does not include justice as a virtue within the city, suggesting that justice does not naturally exist within the human soul either, rather that it is a consequence of a "well-ordered" soul. Plato argues that there are three cardinal virtues: temperance, courage, and wisdom. He divides people into three classes: Producers, Warriors,  and Leaders. Each group exhibits an extra amount of one of the three cardinal virtues. Producers exhibit extra temperance, warriors exhibit extra courage, and leaders exhibit extra wisdom. If rulers are willing to create just laws, warriors willing to carry out these laws, and producers willing to obey these laws, then a society will be just.

Third, having defined justice, Plato addresses the next logical question: What are the *consequences and rewards* of just and unjust behavior? Glaucon asserts that if people had the power to do injustice without fear of punishment, they would never try be just to one another. Glaucon uses this argument to challenge Socrates to defend the position that the just life is better than the unjust life.

Adeimantus adds to Glaucon's speech the charge that men are only just for the results that justice brings, such as fortune, honor, and reputation. Adeimantus challenges Socrates to prove that being just is worth something in and of itself, not only as a means to an end.

Socrates answers these challenges by claiming that the types of pleasure obtained by those who seek for money (the producers) and by those who seek for honor (the warriors) are merely cessation from pain. Socrates claims that only those who seek after truth (the leaders) may obtain genuine happiness. "When the whole soul follows the philosophical principle, and there is no division, the several parts are just, and do each of them their own business, and enjoy severally the best and truest pleasures of which they are capable."

Plato discusses three main questions in his *Republic*. What is justice to an individual? What does a just society look like? And what are the benefits of just behavior? The first question is answered only insofar as the rules of the utopian society may be applied to the soul. The second question spans the majority of the dialogue and is answered by the famous three-class system that Plato promotes. The third and final question is answered by Plato's assertion that leaders (who seek after truth) are the most just of all the classes, and therefore find the most genuine happiness. These leaders are crowned not only with power, but also with glory, for as Cicero once stated, "Justice is the crowning glory of the virtues."

The Use of Language to Develop the Theme in *Their Eyes Were Watching God*, by Edith Hurston

Language is the thread that ties together the plot of Hurston's novel *Their Eyes Were Watching God*. Indeed, language defines the protagonist. Because of her freedom to speak (or lack of it), Janie leaves Joe Stark and clings to Tea Cake.

After leaving her first arranged marriage for a charismatic, promising man named Joe Stark, Janie discovers that, after the glow of the first few years dies off, he restricts her language and expression:

"You gettin' too moufy, Janie," Starks told her. "Go fetch me de checker board and de checkers. Sam Watson, you'se mah fish." . . . She [Janie] was a rut in the road. Plenty of life beneath the surface but it was kept beaten down by the wheels. (76–77)

Because her husband, Joe Stark, stifles both herself and her freedom to speak, Janie grows discontented and worn down—like a "rut in the road."

After enduring Stark and his almost autocratic suppression until his death, Janie meets (and eventually marries) a young man who prefers to be called "Tea Cake." Even though Tea Cake eventually dies from hydrophobia, Janie loves him because he engages her in conversation and treats her as an equal—not someone to be used:

Tea Cake wasn't strange. Seemed as if she had known him all her life. Look how she had been able to talk with him right off! He tipped his hat at the door and was off with the briefest good night. (99)

In this passage, the reader learns that Janie loves Tea Cake in part because "she had been able to talk with him right off." No longer does Janie view the material gifts of a suitor as paramount. Instead, she realizes that her freedom to talk and converse is one of the most important factors in her marriages.

In *Their Eyes Were Watching God*, the theme of language runs consistently throughout the entire book. Indeed, it is language that propels Janie through her marriages. It is language that drives here to despise Stark and cherish Tea Cake. The theme of language is pivotal to the plot in *Their Eyes Were Watching God*.

Themes in *Silas Marner*, by George Eliot

Several themes occur in Silas Marner. These themes develop throughout the entire book. The setting, plot, and characterization are used to further develop the themes. One of the most prominent themes is that humans do not need a religion to be happy in life. The author writes that religion is a burden, as the main character is relieved when he altogether rejects religion. This type of belief is called Absurdism, in which people believe that there is no God and no reason for a God. Throughout the book, the plot shows that the main character, Silas Marner, continually rejects religion. The author also writes that

Marner has no ties to religion. Ironically, this same character possesses many of the traits expected from a religious person. Through characterization, the author shows that Marner does not have any ties to religion. As Marner is in a secluded village, there is no religious group, resulting in Marner's being unable to participate in religion even if he wanted to do so.

George Eliot also attempted to show that life was better when it was secluded. After Marner was banished to the secluded village, his life was "better that it was before." In his old village, he was constantly being bombarded by friends. In the new village, there were almost no people at all. Silas Marner seems to have a better life in the village that he spent the entire book in.

These two themes occur throughout the book. One of the themes is used to advance the author's absurdist worldview. She believes that religion is unnecessary in life. This belief strongly affects her book. Despite this, the author incorporates religious traits into her main character.

Background

Tone is the way an author communicates a feeling or attitude toward the subject about which one is writing. Perhaps no literary feature is harder to discern, and more important to meaning than tone. Tone is created through diction (the use of words) and syntax (style). Poets, in particular, love to use alliteration to create tone (or mood): "Once upon a midnight dreary, / while I wondered weak and weary." Other authors create humor by using colloquial language:

> "You don't know about me without you have read a book by the name of *The Adventures of Tom Sawyer*; but that ain't no matter. That book was made by Mr. Mark Twain, and he told the truth, mainly. There was things which he stretched, but mainly he told the truth. That is nothing. I never seen anybody but lied one time or another, without it was Aunt Polly, or the widow, or maybe Mary. Aunt Polly—Tom's Aunt Polly, she is—and Mary, and the Widow Douglas is all told about in that book, which is mostly a true book, with some stretchers, as I said before."

Suggested Literary Works

Baum, Frank. *The Wonderful Wizard of Oz.*
Bronte, Charlotte. *Jane Eyre.*
Homer. *Iliad.*
Homer. *Odyssey.*
Henry, O. "The Ransom of Red Chief."
Stevenson, Robert L. *Treasure Island.*
Sophocles. *Oedipus Rex.*
Stowe, Harriet Beecher. *Uncle Tom's Cabin.*
Tolkien, J. R. R. *The Lord of the Rings* trilogy.
Twain, Mark. *The Adventures of Huckleberry Finn.*

Terms

Tone is the manner in which authors express an *attitude, emotion,* or *mood.* Various adjectives can describe tone, and the possibilities are nearly endless. Tone can change from chapter to chapter or even line to line. It is the result of allusion, diction (vocabulary usage), figurative language, imagery, irony, symbol, and syntax (style). The following is a list of possible tones, but the list is by no means exhaustive:

aggravated . . . aloof . . . angry . . . apathetic . . . appreciative . . . arrogant . . . calm . . . clandestine . . . condescending . . . contemplative . . . contradictory . . . cynical . . . dark . . . dejected . . . desperate . . . despondent . . . didactic . . . disappointed . . . disinterested . . . droll . . . earnest . . . elegiac . . . encouraging . . . excited . . . happy . . . hurt . . . intense . . . joyful . . . lackadaisical . . . languid . . . lighthearted . . . manipulative . . . nonchalant . . . paranoid . . . passive . . . persuasive . . . plaintive . . . playful . . . pleading . . . proud . . . romantic . . . sad . . . sardonic . . . superficial . . . uninterested . . . vibrant . . . wistful

Irony

Irony involves a difference between appearance and reality. As one critic explains, irony creates a contrast between the following pairs:

> What is and what seems to be
> What is and what ought to be
> What is and what one wishes to be

There are three common types of irony in literature:

Verbal irony occurs when characters say the opposite of what they mean. It is often used by authors while writing humor. This is perhaps the most common type of irony. There are two kinds of verbal irony:

> Understatement through minimization
> Overstatement through exaggeration

Situational irony occurs when the unexpected event occurs.

Dramatic irony occurs when characters state something that they believe to be true but that the reader knows is not true.

Verbal Irony

The Adventures of Huckleberry Finn, by Mark Twain

All modern American literature comes from one book by Mark Twain called Huckleberry Finn. If you read it you must stop where the N----- Jim is stolen from the boys. That is the real end. The rest is just cheating. But it's the best book we've had. All American writing comes from that. There was nothing before. There has been nothing as good since. — Ernest Hemingway

Chapter 2

We went tiptoeing along a path amongst the trees back towards the end of the widow's garden, stooping down so as the branches wouldn't scrape our heads. When we was passing by the kitchen I fell over a root and made a noise. We scrouched down and laid still. Miss Watson's big nigger, named Jim, was setting in the kitchen door; we could see him pretty clear, because there was a light behind him. He got up and stretched his neck out about a minute, listening. Then he says:

"Who dah?"

He listened some more; then he come tiptoeing down and stood right between us; we could a touched him, nearly. Well, likely it was minutes and minutes that there warn't a sound, and we all there so close together. There was a place on my ankle that got to itching, but I dasn't scratch it; and then my ear begun to itch; and next my back, right between my shoulders. Seemed like I'd die if I couldn't scratch. Well, I've noticed that thing plenty times since. If you are with the quality, or at a funeral, or trying to go to sleep when you ain't sleepy — if you are anywheres where it won't do for you to scratch, why you will itch all over in upwards of a thousand places. Pretty soon Jim says:

TOM SAWYER'S BAND OF ROBBERS.

"Say, who is you? Whar is you? Dog my cats ef I didn' hear sumf'n. Well, I know what I's gwyne to do: I's gwyne to set down here and listen tell I hears it agin."

So he set down on the ground betwixt me and Tom. He leaned his back up against a tree, and stretched his legs out till one of them most touched one of mine. My nose begun to itch. It itched till the tears come into my eyes. But I dasn't scratch. Then it begun to itch on the inside. Next I got to itching underneath. I didn't know how I was going to set still. This miserableness went on as much as six or seven minutes; but it seemed a sight longer than that. I was itching in eleven different places now. I reckoned I couldn't stand it more'n a minute longer, but I set my teeth hard and got ready to try. Just then Jim begun to breathe heavy; next he begun to snore—and then I was pretty soon comfortable again.

Tom he made a sign to me—kind of a little noise with his mouth—and we went creeping away on our hands and knees. When we was ten foot off Tom whispered to me, and wanted to tie Jim to the tree for fun. But I said no; he might wake and make a disturbance, and then they'd find out I warn't in. Then Tom said he hadn't got candles enough, and he would slip in the kitchen and get some more. I didn't want him to try.

I said Jim might wake up and come. But Tom wanted to resk it; so we slid in there and got three candles, and Tom laid five cents on the table for pay. Then we got out, and I was in a sweat to get away; but nothing would do Tom but he must crawl to where Jim was, on his hands and knees, and play something on him. I waited, and it seemed a good while, everything was so still and lonesome.

As soon as Tom was back we cut along the path, around the garden fence, and by and by fetched up on the steep top of the hill the other side of the house. Tom said he slipped Jim's hat off of his head and hung it on a limb right over him, and Jim stirred a little, but he didn't wake. Afterwards Jim said the witches bewitched him and put him in a trance, and rode him all over the State, and then set him under the trees again, and hung his hat on a limb to show who done it. And next time Jim told it he said they rode him down to New Orleans; and, after that, every time he told it he spread it more and more, till by and by he said they rode him all over the world, and tired him most to death, and his back was all over saddle-boils. Jim was monstrous proud about it, and he got so he wouldn't hardly notice the other niggers. Niggers would come miles to hear Jim tell about it, and he was more looked up to than any nigger in that country. Strange niggers would stand with their mouths open and look him all over, same as if he was a wonder. Niggers is always talking about witches in the dark by the kitchen fire; but whenever one was talking and letting on to know all about such things, Jim would happen in and say, "Hm! What you know 'bout witches?" and that nigger was corked up and had to take a back seat. Jim always kept that five-center piece round his neck with a string, and said it was a charm the devil give to him with his own hands, and told him he could cure anybody with it and fetch witches whenever he wanted to just by saying something to it; but he never told what it was he said to it. Niggers would come from all around there and give Jim anything they had, just for a sight of that five-center piece; but they wouldn't touch it, because the devil had had his hands on it. Jim was most ruined for a servant, because he got stuck up on account of having seen the devil and been rode by witches.

Well, when Tom and me got to the edge of the hilltop we looked away down into the village and could see three or four lights twinkling, where there was sick folks, maybe; and the stars over us was sparkling ever so fine; and down by the village was the river, a whole mile broad, and awful still and grand. We went down the hill and found Jo Harper and Ben Rogers, and two or three more of the boys, hid in the old tanyard. So we unhitched a skiff and pulled down the river two mile and a half, to the big scar on the hillside, and went ashore.

We went to a clump of bushes, and Tom made everybody swear to keep the secret, and then showed them a hole in the hill, right in the thickest part of the bushes. Then we lit the candles, and crawled in on our hands and knees. We went about two hundred yards, and then the cave opened up. Tom poked about amongst the passages, and pretty soon ducked under a wall where you wouldn't a noticed that there was a hole. We went along a narrow place and got into a kind of room, all damp and sweaty and cold, and there we stopped. Tom says:

"Now, we'll start this band of robbers and call it Tom Sawyer's Gang. Everybody that wants to join has got to take an oath, and write his name in blood."

Everybody was willing. So Tom got out a sheet of paper that he had wrote the oath on, and read it. It swore every boy to stick to the band, and never tell any of the secrets; and if anybody done anything to any boy in the band, whichever boy was ordered to kill that person and his family must do it, and he mustn't eat and he mustn't sleep till he had killed them and hacked a cross in their breasts, which was the sign of the band. And nobody that didn't belong to the band could use that mark, and if he did he must be sued; and if he done it again he must be killed. And if anybody that belonged to the band told the secrets, he must have his throat cut, and then have his carcass burnt up and the ashes scattered all around, and his name blotted off of the list with blood and never mentioned again by the gang, but have a curse put on it and be forgot forever.

Everybody said it was a real beautiful oath, and asked Tom if he got it out of his own head. He said, some of it, but the rest was out of pirate-books and robber-books, and every gang that was high-toned had it.

Some thought it would be good to kill the FAMILIES of boys that told the secrets. Tom said it was a good idea, so he took a pencil and wrote it in. Then Ben Rogers says:

"Here's Huck Finn, he hain't got no family; what you going to do 'bout him?"

"Well, hain't he got a father?" says Tom Sawyer.

"Yes, he's got a father, but you can't never find him these days. He used to lay drunk with the hogs in the tanyard, but he hain't been seen in these parts for a year or more."

They talked it over, and they was going to rule me out, because they said every boy must have a family or somebody to kill, or else it wouldn't be fair and square for the others. Well, nobody could think of anything to do—everybody was stumped, and set still. I was most ready to cry; but all at once I thought of a way, and so I offered them Miss Watson—they could kill her. Everybody said:

"Oh, she'll do. That's all right. Huck can come in."

Then they all stuck a pin in their fingers to get blood to sign with, and I made my mark on the paper.

"Now," says Ben Rogers, "what's the line of business of this Gang?"

"Nothing only robbery and murder," Tom said.

"But who are we going to rob?— houses, or cattle, or—"

"Stuff! stealing cattle and such things ain't robbery; it's burglary," says Tom Sawyer. "We ain't burglars. That ain't no sort of style. We are highwaymen. We stop stages and carriages on the road, with masks on, and kill the people and take their watches and money."

"Must we always kill the people?"

"Oh, certainly. It's best. Some authorities think different, but mostly it's considered best to kill them—except some that you bring to the cave here, and keep them till they're ransomed."

"Ransomed? What's that?"

"I don't know. But that's what they do. I've seen it in books; and so of course that's what we've got to do."

"But how can we do it if we don't know what it is?"

"Why, blame it all, we've GOT to do it. Don't I tell you it's in the books? Do you want to go to doing different from what's in the books, and get things all muddled up?"

"Oh, that's all very fine to SAY, Tom Sawyer, but how in the nation are these fellows going to be ransomed if we don't know how to do it to them? — that's the thing I want to get at. Now, what do you reckon it is?"

"Well, I don't know. But per'aps if we keep them till they're ransomed, it means that we keep them till they're dead."

"Now, that's something LIKE. That'll answer. Why couldn't you said that before? We'll keep them till they're ransomed to death; and a bothersome lot they'll be, too — eating up everything, and always trying to get loose."

"How you talk, Ben Rogers. How can they get loose when there's a guard over them, ready to shoot them down if they move a peg?"

"A guard! Well, that IS good. So somebody's got to set up all night and never get any sleep, just so as to watch them. I think that's foolishness. Why can't a body take a club and ransom them as soon as they get here?"

"Because it ain't in the books so — that's why. Now, Ben Rogers, do you want to do things regular, or don't you? — that's the idea. Don't you reckon that the people that made the books knows what's the correct thing to do? Do you reckon YOU can learn 'em anything? Not by a good deal. No, sir, we'll just go on and ransom them in the regular way."

"All right. I don't mind; but I say it's a fool way, anyhow. Say, do we kill the women, too?"

"Well, Ben Rogers, if I was as ignorant as you I wouldn't let on. Kill the women? No; nobody ever saw anything in the books like that. You fetch them to the cave, and you're always as polite as pie to them; and by and by they fall in love with you, and never want to go home any more."

"Well, if that's the way I'm agreed, but I don't take no stock in it. Mighty soon we'll have the cave so cluttered up with women, and fellows waiting to be ransomed, that there won't be no place for the robbers. But go ahead, I ain't got nothing to say."

Little Tommy Barnes was asleep now, and when they waked him up he was scared, and cried, and said he wanted to go home to his ma, and didn't want to be a robber any more.

So they all made fun of him, and called him crybaby, and that made him mad, and he said he would go straight and tell all the secrets. But Tom give him five cents to keep quiet, and said we would all go home and meet next week, and rob somebody and kill some people.

Mark Twain (Samuel L. Clemens)

Ben Rogers said he couldn't get out much, only Sundays, and so he wanted to begin next Sunday; but all the boys said it would be wicked to do it on Sunday, and that settled the thing. They agreed to get together and fix a day as soon as they could, and then we elected Tom Sawyer first captain and Jo Harper second captain of the Gang, and so started home.

I clumb up the shed and crept into my window just before day was breaking. My new clothes was all greased up and clayey, and I was dog-tired.

Comments on The Adventures of Huckleberry Finn

Tom is obviously smarter than most everyone in this novel, but not nearly as smart as he thinks he is. He has, in short, read too many cheap adventure novels that he takes quite literally as the truth! But he's the leader of this group because he is a natural leader. Huck doesn't understand how ridiculous Tom's statements are. He takes Tom's statements at face value: that is verbal irony and also very humorous! Twain doesn't expect the reader to be that naive. He expects readers to see the truth about Tom, even if the young narrator Huck Finn misses it. — James P. Stobaugh

The Adventures of Huckleberry Finn is one of those rare books which are at once acceptable to the intelligentsia and to that celebrated American phenomenon, the average citizen; it is a book which even anti-literary children read and enjoy. Even if the language of the book should eventually be lost or, worse still, replaced by convenient abridgements, the memory of Huck Finn would still survive among us like some old and indestructible god. —James M. Cox

Huck Finn is alone: there is no more solitary character in fiction. The fact that he has a father only emphasizes his loneliness; and he views his father with a terrifying detachment. So we come to see Huck himself in the end as one of the permanent symbolic figures of fiction; not unworthy to take a place with Ulysses, Faust, Don Quixote, Don Juan, Hamlet and other great discoveries that man has made about himself. —T. S. Eliot

[In the last chapters:] Before Huck can get back to the raft, Tom and Jim are brought home by the doctor and a crowd. Jim's hands are tied, and Tom is carried on a mattress. In explaining how he managed to recapture the runaway slave, the doctor asks that Jim be treated well, since he showed more interest in Tom's health than he did in his own escape. The farmers take the doctor's advice, and Huck tells us, "Every one of them promised, right out and hearty, that they wouldn't cuss him no more." He notes that they weren't moved enough to remove Jim's chains or give him some decent food, but he figures he should leave well enough alone.

What follows is a wrap-up of the plot, moving at breakneck speed and leaving no loose ends. Tom tells Aunt Sally how he and Huck engineered the escape. Tom's Aunt Polly arrives to tell Aunt Sally who her two guests really are. Tom announces that Jim has been a free man for two months. And Jim reveals that Huck's father is dead. This last bit of news means that Huck's $6,000 is still waiting for him at home. "Home," that is, as far as everyone is concerned, except Huck.

As much as they seem to care for him, Huck isn't at all sure he belongs with these people—or any other people, for that matter. He's had some good glimpses of civilization on his journey up and down the river, and most of what he's seen hasn't been very pretty. So the last thing he tells us is that he intends to "light out for the territory," that part of the country that hasn't yet been blessed with statehood, or with civilization. Huck has had it with civilization. "I been there before," he says, and it doesn't have much to offer him. Because Huck tells his story himself, the stylistic richness is immeasurably deepened by the rhythms, intonations, and choice of words of this magnificent child. —Frank Baldanza

Situational Irony

When John Hinckley tried to assassinate Ronald Reagan, all of his shots initially missed the President; however, a bullet ricocheted off the bullet-proof Presidential limousine and struck Reagan in the chest. Thus, a vehicle made to protect the President from gunfire was partially responsible for his being shot. This is situational irony! —Doug Linder

The Wonderful Wizard of Oz, by Frank Baum

Chapter 7, "The Journey to the Great Oz"

They were obliged to camp out that night under a large tree in the forest, for there were no houses near. The tree made a good, thick covering to protect them from the dew, and the Tin Woodman chopped a great pile of wood with his axe and Dorothy built a splendid fire that warmed her and made her feel less lonely. She and Toto ate the last of their bread, and now she did not know what they would do for breakfast.

"If you wish," said the Lion, "I will go into the forest and kill a deer for you. You can roast it by the fire, since your tastes are so peculiar that you prefer cooked food, and then you will have a very good breakfast."

"Don't! Please don't," begged the Tin Woodman. "I should certainly weep if you killed a poor deer, and then my jaws would rust again."

But the Lion went away into the forest and found his own supper, and no one ever knew what it was, for he didn't mention it. And the Scarecrow found a tree full of nuts and filled Dorothy's basket with them, so that she would not be hungry for a long time. She thought this was very kind and thoughtful of the Scarecrow, but she laughed heartily at the awkward way in which the poor creature picked up the nuts. His padded hands were so clumsy and the nuts were so small that he dropped almost as many as he put in the basket. But the Scarecrow did not mind how long it took him to fill the basket, for it enabled him to keep away from the fire, as he feared a spark might get into his straw and burn him up. So he kept a good distance away from the flames, and only came near to cover Dorothy with dry leaves when she lay down to sleep. These kept her very snug and warm, and she slept soundly until morning.

When it was daylight, the girl bathed her face in a little rippling brook, and soon after they all started toward the Emerald City.

This was to be an eventful day for the travelers. They had hardly been walking an hour when they saw before them a great ditch that crossed the road and divided the forest as far as they could see on either side. It was a very wide ditch, and when they crept up to the edge and looked into it they could see it was also very deep, and there were many big, jagged rocks at the bottom. The sides were so steep that none of them could climb down, and for a moment it seemed that their journey must end.

"What shall we do?" asked Dorothy despairingly.

"I haven't the faintest idea," said the Tin Woodman, and the Lion shook his shaggy mane and looked thoughtful.

But the Scarecrow said, "We cannot fly, that is certain. Neither can we climb down into this great ditch. Therefore, if we cannot jump over it, we must stop where we are."

"I think I could jump over it," said the Cowardly Lion, after measuring the distance carefully in his mind.

"Then we are all right," answered the Scarecrow, "for you can carry us all over on your back, one at a time."

"Well, I'll try it," said the Lion. "Who will go first?"

"I will," declared the Scarecrow, "for, if you found that you could not jump over the gulf, Dorothy would be killed, or the Tin Woodman badly dented on the rocks below. But if I am on your back it will not matter so much, for the fall would not hurt me at all."

"I am terribly afraid of falling, myself," said the Cowardly Lion, "but I suppose there is nothing to do but try it. So get on my back and we will make the attempt."

The Scarecrow sat upon the Lion's back, and the big beast walked to the edge of the gulf and crouched down.

"Why don't you run and jump?" asked the Scarecrow.

"Because that isn't the way we Lions do these things," he replied. Then giving a great spring, he shot through the air and landed safely on the other side. They were all greatly pleased to see how easily he did it, and after the Scarecrow had got down from his back the Lion sprang across the ditch again.

Dorothy thought she would go next; so she took Toto in her arms and climbed on the Lion's back, holding tightly to his mane with one hand. The next moment it seemed as if she were flying through the air; and then, before she had time to think about it, she was safe on the other side. The Lion went back a third time and got the Tin Woodman, and then they all sat down for a few moments to give the beast a chance to rest, for his great leaps had made his breath short, and he panted like a big dog that has been running too long.

They found the forest very thick on this side, and it looked dark and gloomy. After the Lion had rested they started along the road of yellow brick, silently wondering, each in his own mind, if ever they would come to the end of the woods and reach the bright sunshine again. To add to their discomfort, they soon heard strange noises in the depths of the forest, and the Lion whispered to them that it was in this part of the country that the Kalidahs lived.

"What are the Kalidahs?" asked the girl.

"They are monstrous beasts with bodies like bears and heads like tigers," replied the Lion, "and with claws so long and sharp that they could tear me in two as easily as I could kill Toto. I'm terribly afraid of the Kalidahs."

"I'm not surprised that you are," returned Dorothy. "They must be dreadful beasts."

The Lion was about to reply when suddenly they came to another gulf across the road. But this one was so broad and deep that the Lion knew at once he could not leap across it.

So they sat down to consider what they should do, and after serious thought the Scarecrow said:

"Here is a great tree, standing close to the ditch. If the Tin Woodman can chop it down, so that it will fall to the other side, we can walk across it easily."

"That is a first-rate idea," said the Lion. "One would almost suspect you had brains in your head, instead of straw."

The Woodman set to work at once, and so sharp was his axe that the tree was soon chopped nearly through. Then the Lion put his strong front legs against the tree and pushed with all his might, and slowly the big tree tipped and fell with a crash across the ditch, with its top branches on the other side.

They had just started to cross this queer bridge when a sharp growl made them all look up, and to their horror they saw running toward them two great beasts with bodies like bears and heads like tigers.

"They are the Kalidahs!" said the Cowardly Lion, beginning to tremble.

"Quick!" cried the Scarecrow. "Let us cross over."

So Dorothy went first, holding Toto in her arms, the Tin Woodman followed, and the Scarecrow came next. The Lion, although he was certainly afraid, turned to face the Kalidahs, and then he gave so loud and terrible a roar that Dorothy screamed and the Scarecrow fell over backward, while even the fierce beasts stopped short and looked at him in surprise.

But, seeing they were bigger than the Lion, and remembering that there were two of them and only one of him, the Kalidahs again rushed forward, and the Lion crossed over the tree and turned to see what they would do next. Without stopping an instant the fierce beasts also began to cross the tree. And the Lion said to Dorothy:

"We are lost, for they will surely tear us to pieces with their sharp claws. But stand close behind me, and I will fight them as long as I am alive."

"Wait a minute!" called the Scarecrow. He had been thinking what was best to be done, and now he asked the Woodman to chop away the end of the tree that rested on their side of the ditch. The Tin Woodman began to use his axe at once, and, just as the two Kalidahs were nearly across, the tree fell with a crash into the gulf, carrying the ugly, snarling brutes with it, and both were dashed to pieces on the sharp rocks at the bottom.

"Well," said the Cowardly Lion, drawing a long breath of relief, "I see we are going to live a little while longer, and I am glad of it, for it must be a very uncomfortable thing not to be alive. Those creatures frightened me so badly that my heart is beating yet."

"Ah," said the Tin Woodman sadly, "I wish I had a heart to beat."

This adventure made the travelers more anxious than ever to get out of the forest, and they walked so fast that Dorothy became tired, and had to ride on the Lion's back. To their great joy the trees became thinner the farther they advanced, and in the afternoon they suddenly came upon a broad river, flowing swiftly just before them. On the other side of the water they could see the road of yellow brick running through a beautiful country, with green meadows dotted with bright flowers and all the road bordered with trees hanging full of delicious fruits. They were greatly pleased to see this delightful country before them.

"How shall we cross the river?" asked Dorothy. "That is easily done," replied the Scarecrow.

"The Tin Woodman must build us a raft, so we can float to the other side."

So the Woodman took his axe and began to chop down small trees to make a raft, and while he was busy at this the Scarecrow found on the riverbank a tree full of fine fruit. This pleased Dorothy, who had eaten nothing but nuts all day, and she made a hearty meal of the ripe fruit.

But it takes time to make a raft, even when one is as industrious and untiring as the Tin Woodman, and when night came the work was not done. So they found a cozy place under the trees where they slept well until the morning; and Dorothy dreamed of the Emerald City, and of the good Wizard Oz, who would soon send her back to her own home again.

> We're off to see the Wizard,
> The Wonderful Wizard of Oz.
> You'll find he is a whiz of a Wiz!
> If ever a Wiz! there was.
> If ever oh ever a Wiz! there was,
> The Wizard of Oz is one because,
> Because, because, because, because, because,
> Because of the wonderful things he does.
> We're off to see the Wizard,
> The Wonderful Wizard of Oz.

Comments on The Wonderful Wizard of Oz

The Wonderful Wizard of Oz is a story whose plot revolves around situational irony. Dorothy travels to a wizard and fulfills her challenging demands to go home, before discovering she had the ability to go back home all the time. The Scarecrow longs for intelligence, only to discover he is already a genius, and the Tin Woodsman longs to be capable of love, only to discover he already has a heart. The Lion, who at first appears to be a whimpering coward, turns out to be bold and fearless. The people in Emerald City believed the Wizard to be a powerful deity, only to discover that he is a bumbling, eccentric old man with no special powers at all. —A Critic

The Scarlet Letter, by Nathaniel Hawthorne

Dramatic irony occurs when readers know more than the other characters, a condition that pushes audience attention into the future because it creates anticipation about what is going to happen when the truth comes out. In this passage readers know that the pastor, Dimmesdale, is the father of Hester Prynne's child. Readers also know

that Chillingworth is the husband of Hester. The people of Salem (Mass.) in the book are unaware of both facts.

Chapter 3: The Recognition

From this intense consciousness of being the object of severe and universal observation, the wearer of the scarlet letter was at length relieved, by discerning, on the outskirts of the crowd, a figure which irresistibly took possession of her thoughts. An Indian, in his native garb, was standing there; but the red men were not so infrequent visitors of the English settlements, that one of them would have attracted any notice from Hester Prynne, at such a time; much less would he have excluded all other objects and ideas from her mind. By the Indian's side, and evidently sustaining a companionship with him, stood a white man, clad in a strange disarray of civilized and savage costume.

He was small in stature, with a furrowed visage, which, as yet, could hardly be termed aged. There was a remarkable intelligence in his features, as of a person who had so cultivated his mental part that it could not fail to mould the physical to itself, and become manifest by unmistakable tokens. Although, by a seemingly careless arrangement of his heterogeneous garb, he had endeavored to conceal or abate the peculiarity, it was sufficiently evident to Hester Prynne, that one of this man's shoulders rose higher than the other. Again, at the first instant of perceiving that thin visage, and the slight deformity of the figure, she pressed her infant to her bosom with so convulsive a force that the poor babe uttered another cry of pain. But the mother did not seem to hear it.

At his arrival in the market-place, and some time before she saw him, the stranger had bent his eyes on Hester Prynne. It was carelessly, at first, like a man

Reverend Arthur Dimmesdale

chiefly accustomed to look inward, and to whom external matters are of little value and import, unless they bear relation to something within his mind. Very soon, however, his look became keen and penetrative. A writhing horror twisted itself across his features, like a snake gliding swiftly over them, and making one little pause, with all its wreathed intervolutions in open sight. His face darkened with some powerful emotion, which, nevertheless, he so instantaneously controlled by an effort of his will, that, save at a single moment, its expression might have passed for calmness. After a brief space, the convulsion grew almost imperceptible, and finally subsided into the depths of his nature. When he found the eyes of Hester Prynne fastened on his own, and saw that she appeared to recognize him, he slowly and calmly raised his finger, made a gesture with it in the air, and laid it on his lips. Then, touching the shoulder of a townsman who stood next to him, he addressed him, in a formal and courteous manner.

"I pray you, good Sir," said he, "who is this woman?—and wherefore is she here set up to public shame?"

"You must needs be a stranger in this region, friend," answered the townsman, looking curiously at the questioner and his savage companion, "else you would surely have heard of Mistress Hester Prynne, and her evil doings. She hath raised a great scandal, I promise you, in godly Master Dimmesdale's church."

"You say truly," replied the other. "I am a stranger, and have been a wanderer, sorely against my will. I have met with grievous mishaps by sea and land, and have been long held in bonds among the heathen-folk, to the southward; and am now brought hither by this Indian, to be redeemed out of my captivity. Will it please you, therefore, to tell me of Hester Prynne's,—have I her name rightly?—of this woman's offences, and what has brought her to yonder scaffold?"

"Truly, friend; and methinks it must gladden your heart, after your troubles and sojourn in the wilderness," said the townsman, "to find yourself, at length,

Hester Prynne

in a land where iniquity is searched out, and punished in the sight of rulers and people; as here in our godly New England. Yonder woman, Sir, you must know, was the wife of a certain learned man, English by birth, but who had long dwelt in Amsterdam, whence, some good time agone, he was minded to cross over and cast in his lot with us of the Massachusetts. To this purpose, he sent his wife before him, remaining himself to look after some necessary affairs. Marry, good Sir, in some two years, or less, that the woman has been a dweller here in Boston, no tidings have come of this learned gentleman, Master Prynne; and his young wife,   look you, being left to her own misguidance—"

"Ah!—aha!—I conceive you," said the stranger, with a bitter smile. "So learned a man as you speak of should have learned this too in his books. And who, by your favor, Sir, may be the father of yonder babe—it is some three or four months old, I should judge—which Mistress Prynne is holding in her arms?"

"Of a truth, friend, that matter remaineth a riddle; and the Daniel who shall expound it is yet a-wanting," answered the townsman. "Madam Hester absolutely refuseth to speak, and the magistrates have laid their heads together in vain. Peradventure the guilty one stands looking on at this sad spectacle, unknown of man, and forgetting that God sees him."

"The learned man," observed the stranger, with another smile, "should come himself, to look into the mystery."

"It behooves him well, if he be still in life," responded the townsman. "Now, good Sir, our Massachusetts magistracy, bethinking themselves that this woman is youthful and fair, and doubtless was strongly tempted to her fall,—and that, moreover, as is most likely, her husband may be at the bottom of the sea,—they have not been bold to put in force the extremity of our righteous law against her. The penalty thereof is death. But in their great mercy and tenderness of heart, they have doomed Mistress Prynne to stand only a space of three hours on the platform of the pillory, and then and thereafter, for the remainder of her natural life, to wear a mark of shame upon her bosom."

"A wise sentence!" remarked the stranger, gravely bowing his head. "Thus she will be a living sermon against sin, until the ignominious letter be engraved upon her tombstone. It irks me, nevertheless, that the partner of her iniquity should not, at least, stand on the scaffold by her side. But he will be known!—he will be known!—he will be known!"

He bowed courteously to the communicative townsman, and, whispering a few words to his Indian attendant, they both made their way through the crowd.

While this passed, Hester Prynne had been standing on her pedestal, still with a fixed gaze towards the stranger; so fixed a gaze, that, at moments of intense absorption, all other objects in the visible world seemed to vanish,  leaving only him and her. Such an interview, perhaps, would have been more terrible than even to meet him as she now did, with the hot, midday sun burning down upon her face, and lighting up its shame; with the scarlet token of infamy on her breast; with the sin-born infant in her arms; with a whole people, drawn forth as to a festival, staring at the features that should have been seen only in the quiet gleam of the fireside, in the happy shadow of a home, or beneath a matronly veil, at church. Dreadful as it was, she was conscious of a shelter in the presence of these thousand witnesses. It was better to stand thus, with so many betwixt him and her, than to greet him, face to face, they two alone. She fled for refuge, as it were, to the public exposure, and dreaded the moment when its protection should be withdrawn from her. Involved in these thoughts, she scarcely heard a voice behind her, until it had repeated her name more than once, in a loud and solemn tone, audible to the whole multitude.

"Hearken unto me, Hester Prynne!" said the voice.

It has already been noticed, that directly over the platform on which Hester Prynne stood was a kind of balcony, or open gallery, appended to the meeting-house. It was the place whence proclamations were wont to be made, amidst an assemblage of the magistracy, with all the ceremonial that attended such public observances in those days. Here, to witness the scene which we are describing, sat Governor Bellingham himself, with four sergeants about his chair, bearing halberds, as a guard of honor. He wore a dark feather in his hat, a border of embroidery on his cloak, and a black velvet tunic beneath; a gentleman advanced in years, with a hard experience written in his wrinkles. He was not ill fitted to be the head and representative of a community, which owed its origin and progress, and its present state of development, not to the impulses of youth, but to the stern and tempered energies of manhood, and the sombre sagacity of age;

accomplishing so much, precisely because it imagined and hoped so little. The other eminent characters, by whom the chief ruler was surrounded, were distinguished by a dignity of mien, belonging to a period when the forms of authority were felt to possess the sacredness of Divine institutions. They were, doubtless, good men, just and sage. But, out of the whole human family, it would not have been easy to select the same number of wise and virtuous persons, who should be less capable of sitting in judgment on an erring woman's heart, and disentangling its mesh of good and evil, than the sages of rigid aspect towards whom Hester Prynne now turned her face. She seemed conscious, indeed, that whatever sympathy she might expect lay in the larger and warmer heart of the multitude; for, as she lifted her eyes towards the balcony, the unhappy woman grew pale and trembled.

The voice which had called her attention was that of the reverend and famous John Wilson, the eldest clergyman of Boston, a great scholar, like most of his contemporaries in the profession, and withal a man of kind and genial spirit. This last attribute, however, had been less carefully developed than his

intellectual gifts, and was, in truth, rather a matter of shame than self-congratulation with him. There he stood, with a border of grizzled locks beneath his skull-cap; while his gray eyes, accustomed to the shaded light of his study, were winking, like those of Hester's infant, in the unadulterated sunshine. He looked like the darkly engraved portraits which we see prefixed to old volumes of sermons; and had no more right than one of those portraits would have, to step forth, as he now did, and meddle with a question

John Wilson

of human guilt, passion, and anguish.

"Hester Prynne," said the clergyman, "I have striven with my young brother here, under whose preaching of the word you have been privileged to sit,"—here Mr. Wilson laid his hand on the shoulder of a pale young man beside him,—"I have sought, I say, to persuade this godly youth, that he should deal with you, here in the face of Heaven, and before these wise and upright rulers, and in hearing of all the people, as touching the vileness and blackness of your sin. Knowing your natural temper better than I, he could the better judge what arguments to use, whether of tenderness or terror, such as might prevail over your hardness and obstinacy; insomuch that you should no longer hide the name of him who tempted you to this grievous fall. But he opposes to me (with a young man's over-softness, albeit wise beyond his years), that it were wronging the very nature of woman to force her to lay open her heart's secrets in such broad daylight, and in presence of so great a multitude. Truly, as I sought to convince him, the shame lay in the commission of the sin, and not in the showing of it forth. What say you to it, once again, Brother Dimmesdale? Must it be thou, or I, that shall deal with this poor sinner's soul?"

There was a murmur among the dignified and reverend occupants of the balcony; and Governor Bellingham gave expression to its purport, speaking in an authoritative voice, although tempered with respect towards the youthful clergyman whom he addressed.

"Good Master Dimmesdale," said he, "the responsibility of this woman's soul lies greatly with you. It behooves you, therefore, to exhort her to repentance, and to confession, as a proof and consequence thereof."

The directness of this appeal drew the eyes of the whole crowd upon the Reverend Mr. Dimmesdale—young clergyman, who had come from one of the great English universities, bringing all the learning of the age into our wild forest-land. His eloquence and religious fervor had already given the earnest of high eminence in his profession. He was a person of very striking aspect, with a white, lofty, and impending brow, large brown, melancholy eyes, and a mouth which, unless when he forcibly compressed it, was apt to be tremulous, expressing both nervous sensibility and a vast power of self-restraint. Notwithstanding his high native gifts and scholar-like attainments, there was an air about this young minister,—an apprehensive, a startled, a half-frightened look,—as of a being who felt himself quite astray and at a loss in the pathway of human existence, and could only be at ease in some seclusion of his own. Therefore, so far as his duties would permit, he trod in the shadowy by-paths, and thus kept himself simple and childlike; coming forth, when occasion was, with a freshness, and fragrance, and dewy purity of thought, which, as many people said, affected them like the speech of an angel.

Such was the young man whom the Reverend Mr. Wilson and the Governor had introduced so openly to the public notice, bidding him speak, in the hearing of all men, to that mystery of a woman's soul, so sacred even in its pollution. The trying nature of his position drove the blood from his cheek, and made his lips tremulous.

"Speak to the woman, my brother," said Mr. Wilson. "It is of moment to her soul, and therefore, as the worshipful Governor says, momentous to thine own, in whose charge hers is. Exhort her to confess the truth!"

The Reverend Mr. Dimmesdale bent his head, in silent prayer, as it seemed, and then came forward.

"Hester Prynne," said he, leaning over the balcony and looking down steadfastly into her eyes, "thou hearest what this good man says, and seest the accountability under which I labor. If thou feelest it to be for thy soul's peace, and that thy earthly punishment will thereby be made more effectual to salvation, I charge thee to speak out the name of thy fellow-sinner and fellow-sufferer! Be not silent from any mistaken pity and tenderness for him; for, believe me, Hester, though he were to step down from a high place, and stand there beside thee, on thy pedestal of shame, yet better were it so than to hide a guilty heart through life. What can thy silence do for him, except it tempt him — yea, compel him, as it were — to add hypocrisy to sin? Heaven hath granted thee an open ignominy, that thereby thou mayest work out an open triumph over the evil within thee, and the sorrow without. Take heed how thou deniest to him — who, perchance, hath not the courage to grasp it for himself — the bitter, but wholesome, cup that is now presented to thy lips!"

Dimmesdale's appeal to Hester is quieter than Wilson's and far less self-assured. His call for confession is conditional, leaving some freedom of choice: "If thou feelest it to be for thy soul's peace, . . . I charge thee to speak out the name of thy fellow sinner." Yet the appeal seems churlish and hypocritical since he himself is the father of Pearl, Hester's child.

The young pastor's voice was tremulously sweet, rich, deep, and broken. The feeling that it so evidently manifested, rather than the direct purport of the words, caused it to vibrate within all hearts, and brought the listeners into one accord of sympathy. Even the poor baby, at Hester's bosom, was affected by the same influence; for it directed its hitherto vacant gaze towards Mr. Dimmesdale, and held up its little arms, with a half-pleased, half-plaintive murmur. So powerful seemed the minister's appeal, that the people could not believe but that Hester Prynne would speak out the guilty name; or else that the guilty one himself, in whatever high or lowly place he stood, would be drawn forth by an inward and inevitable necessity, and compelled to ascend to the scaffold.

Hester shook her head.

"Woman, transgress not beyond the limits of Heaven's mercy!" cried the Reverend Mr. Wilson, more harshly than before.

"That little babe hath been gifted with a voice, to second and confirm the counsel which thou hast heard. Speak out the name! That, and thy repentance, may avail to take the scarlet letter off thy breast."

"Never!" replied Hester Prynne, looking, not at Mr. Wilson, but into the deep and troubled eyes of the younger clergyman. "It is too deeply branded. Ye cannot take it off. And would that I might endure his agony, as well as mine!"

"Speak, woman!" said another voice, coldly and sternly, proceeding from the crowd about the scaffold. "Speak; and give your child a father!"

"I will not speak!" answered Hester, turning pale as death, but responding to this voice, which she too surely recognized. "And my child must seek a heavenly Father; she shall never know an earthly one!"

"She will not speak!" murmured Mr. Dimmesdale, who, leaning over the balcony, with his hand upon his heart, had awaited the result of his appeal. He now drew back, with a long respiration. "Wondrous strength and generosity of a woman's heart! She will not speak!"

Discerning the impracticable state of the poor culprit's mind, the elder clergyman, who had carefully prepared himself for the occasion, addressed to the multitude a discourse on sin, in all its branches, but with continual reference to the ignominious letter. So forcibly did he dwell upon this symbol, for the hour or more during which his periods were rolling over the people's heads, that it assumed new terrors in their imagination, and seemed to derive its scarlet hue from the flames of the infernal pit. Hester Prynne, meanwhile, kept her place upon the pedestal of shame, with glazed eyes, and an air of weary indifference. She had borne, that morning, all that nature could endure; and as her temperament was not of the order that escapes from too intense suffering by a swoon, her spirit could only shelter itself beneath a stony crust of insensibility, while the faculties of animal life remained entire. In this state, the voice of the preacher thundered remorselessly, but unavailingly, upon her ears. The infant, during the latter portion of her ordeal, pierced the air with its wailings and screams; she strove to hush it, mechanically, but seemed scarcely to sympathize with its trouble. With the same hard demeanour, she was led back to prison, and vanished from the public gaze within its iron-clamped portal. It was whispered, by those who peered after her, that the scarlet letter threw a lurid gleam along the dark passage-way of the interior.

Chapter 5: Hester at Her Needle

Hester Prynne's term of confinement was now at an end. Her prison-door was thrown open, and she came forth into the sunshine, which, falling on all alike, seemed, to her sick and morbid heart, as if meant for no other purpose than to reveal the scarlet letter on her breast. Perhaps there was a more real torture in her first unattended footsteps from the threshold of the prison than even in the procession and spectacle that have been described, where she was made the common infamy, at which all mankind was summoned to point its finger. Then, she was supported by an unnatural tension of the nerves, and by all the combative energy of her character, which enabled her to convert the scene into a kind of lurid triumph. It was, moreover, a separate and insulated event, to occur but once in her lifetime, and to meet which, therefore, reckless of economy, she might call up the vital strength that would have sufficed for many quiet years. The very law that condemned her—a giant of stem featured but with vigour to support, as well as to annihilate, in his iron arm—had held her up through the terrible ordeal of her ignominy. But now, with this unattended walk from her prison door, began the daily custom; and she must either sustain and carry it forward by the ordinary resources of her nature, or sink beneath it. She could no longer borrow from the future to help her through the present grief. Tomorrow would bring its own trial with it; so would the next day, and so would the next: each its own trial, and yet the very same that was now so unutterably grievous to be borne. The days of the far-off future would toil onward, still with the same burden for her to take up, and bear along with her, but never to fling down; for the accumulating days and added years would pile up their misery upon the heap of shame. Throughout them all, giving up her individuality, she would become the general symbol at which the preacher and moralist might point, and in which they might vivify and embody their images of woman's frailty and sinful passion. Thus the young and pure would be taught to look at her, with the scarlet letter flaming on her breast—at her, the child of honourable parents—at her, the mother of a babe that would hereafter be a woman—at her, who had once been innocent—as the figure, the body, the reality of sin. And over her grave, the infamy that she must carry thither would be her only monument. . . .

Lonely as was Hester's situation, and without a friend on earth who dared to show himself, she, however, incurred no risk of want. She possessed an art that sufficed, even in a land that afforded comparatively little scope for its exercise, to supply food for her thriving infant and herself. It was the art, then, as now, almost the only one within a woman's grasp—of needle-work. She bore on her breast, in the curiously embroidered

letter, a specimen of her delicate and imaginative skill, of which the dames of a court might gladly have availed themselves, to add the richer and more spiritual adornment of human ingenuity to their fabrics of silk and gold. Here, indeed, in the sable simplicity that generally characterised the Puritanic modes of dress, there might be an infrequent call for the finer productions of her handiwork. Yet the taste of the age, demanding whatever was elaborate in compositions of this kind, did not fail to extend its influence over our stern progenitors, who had cast behind them so many fashions which it might seem harder to dispense with. . . .

Public ceremonies, such as ordinations, the installation of magistrates, and all that could give majesty to the forms in which a new government manifested itself to the people, were, as a matter of policy, marked by a stately and well-conducted ceremonial, and a sombre, but yet a studied magnificence. Deep ruffs, painfully wrought bands, and gorgeously embroidered gloves, were all deemed necessary to the official state of men assuming the reins of power, and were readily allowed to individuals dignified by rank or wealth, even while sumptuary laws forbade these and similar extravagances to the plebeian order. In the array of funerals, too—whether for the apparel of the dead body, or to typify, by manifold emblematic devices of sable cloth and snowy lawn, the sorrow of the survivors—there was a frequent and characteristic demand for such labour as Hester Prynne could supply. Baby-linen—for babies then wore robes of state—afforded still another possibility of toil and emolument.

By degrees, not very slowly, her handiwork became what would now be termed the fashion. Whether from commiseration for a woman of so miserable a destiny; or from the morbid curiosity that gives a fictitious value even to common or worthless things; or by whatever other intangible circumstance was then, as now, sufficient to bestow, on some persons, what others might seek in vain; or because Hester really filled a gap which must otherwise have remained vacant; it is certain that she had ready and fairly equited employment for as many hours as she saw fit to occupy with her needle. Vanity, it may be, chose to mortify itself, by putting on, for ceremonials of pomp and state, the garments that had been wrought by her sinful hands. Her needle-work was seen on the ruff of the Governor; military men wore it on their scarfs, and the minister on his band; it decked the baby's little cap; it was shut up, to be mildewed and moulder away, in the coffins of the dead. But it is not recorded that, in a single instance, her skill was called in to embroider the white veil which was to cover the pure blushes of a bride. The exception indicated the ever relentless vigour with which society frowned upon her sin. . . .

Comments on The Scarlet Letter

Above all it is Hester Prynne whose passion and beauty dominate every other person, and color each event. Hawthorne has conceived her as he has conceived his scene, in the full strength of his feeling for ancient New England. He is the

Homer of that New England, and Hester is its most heroic creature. Tall, with dark and abundant hair and deep black eyes, a rich complexion that makes modern women (says Hawthorne) pale and thin by comparison, and a dignity that throws into low relief the "delicate, evanescent, and indescribable grace" by which gentility in girls has since come to be known, from the very first—and we believe it— she is said to cast a spell over those who behold her. —Mark Van Doren

Chapter 23: Revelation of the
Scarlet Letter

Gothic Tone and Mood

The use of primitive, medieval, wild, or mysterious elements in Gothic literature offended eighteenth-century classical writers but appealed to the Romantic writers who followed them. Gothic novels feature writers who use places like mysterious castles where horrifying supernatural events take place.

"The Cask of Amontillado," by Edgar Allan Poe

The thousand injuries of Fortunato I had borne as I best could; but when he ventured upon insult, I vowed revenge. You, who so well know the nature of my soul, will not suppose, however, that I gave utterance to a threat. *At length* I would be avenged; this was a point definitively settled—but the very definitiveness with which it was resolved, precluded the idea of risk. I must not only punish, but punish with impunity. A wrong is unredressed when retribution overtakes its redresser. It is equally unredressed when the avenger fails to make himself felt as such to him who has done the wrong.

It must be understood, that neither by word nor deed had I given Fortunato cause to doubt my good will. I continued, as was my wont, to smile in his face, and he did not perceive that my smile *now* was at the thought of his immolation.

He had a weak point—this Fortunato—although in other regards he was a man to be respected and even feared. He prided himself on his connoisseurship in wine. Few Italians have the true virtuoso spirit. For the most part their enthusiasm is adopted to suit the time and opportunity—to practise imposture upon the British and Austrian *millionaires*. In painting and gemmary, Fortunato, like his countrymen, was a quack—but in the matter of old wines he was sincere. In this respect I did not differ from him materially: I was skilful in the Italian vintages myself, and bought largely whenever I could.

It was about dusk, one evening during the supreme madness of the carnival season, that I encountered my friend. He accosted me with excessive warmth, for he had been drinking much. The man wore motley. He had on a tight-fitting parti-striped dress, and his head was surmounted by the conical cap and bells. I was so pleased to see him, that I thought I should never have done wringing his hand.

I said to him—"My dear Fortunato, you are luckily met. How remarkably well you are looking to-day! But I have received a pipe of what passes for Amontillado, and I have my doubts."

"How?" said he. "Amontillado? A pipe? Impossible! And in the middle of the carnival!"

"I have my doubts," I replied; "and I was silly enough to pay the full Amontillado price without consulting you in the matter. You were not to be found, and I was fearful of losing a bargain."

"Amontillado!"

"I have my doubts."

"Amontillado!"

"And I must satisfy them."

"Amontillado!"

"As you are engaged, I am on my way to Luchesi. If any one has a critical turn, it is he. He will tell me —"

"Luchesi cannot tell Amontillado from Sherry."

"And yet some fools will have it that his taste is a match for your own."

"Come, let us go."

"Whither?"

"To your vaults."

"My friend, no; I will not impose upon your good nature. I perceive you have an engagement. Luchesi —"

"I have no engagement; — come."

"My friend, no. It is not the engagement, but the severe cold with which I perceive you are afflicted. The vaults are insufferably damp. They are encrusted with nitre."

"Let us go, nevertheless. The cold is merely nothing. Amontillado! You have been imposed upon. And as for Luchesi, he cannot distinguish Sherry from Amontillado."

Thus speaking, Fortunato possessed himself of my arm. Putting on a mask of black silk, and drawing a *roquelaire* closely about my person, I suffered him to hurry me to my palazzo.

There were no attendants at home; they had absconded to make merry in honor of the time. I had told them that I should not return until the morning, and had given them explicit orders not to stir from the house. These orders were sufficient, I well knew, to insure their immediate disappearance, one and all, as soon as my back was turned.

I took from their sconces two flambeaux, and giving one to Fortunato, bowed him through several suites of rooms to the archway that led into the vaults. I passed down a long and winding staircase, requesting him to be cautious as he followed. We came at length to the foot of the descent, and stood together on the damp ground of the catacombs of the Montresors.

The gait of my friend was unsteady, and the bells upon his cap jingled as he strode.

"The pipe," said he.

"It is farther on," said I; "but observe the white web-work which gleams from these cavern walls."

He turned towards me, and looked into my eyes with two filmy orbs that distilled the rheum of intoxication.

"Nitre?" he asked, at length.

"Nitre," I replied. "How long have you had that cough?"

"Ugh! ugh! ugh!—ugh! ugh! ugh!—ugh! ugh! ugh!—ugh! ugh! ugh!—ugh! ugh! ugh!" My poor friend found it impossible to reply for many minutes.

"It is nothing," he said, at last.

"Come," I said, with decision, "we will go back; your health is precious. You are rich, respected, admired, beloved; you are happy, as once I was. You are a man to be missed. For me it is no matter. We will go back; you will be ill, and I cannot be responsible. Besides, there is Luchesi—"

"Enough," he said; "the cough is a mere nothing; it will not kill me. I shall not die of a cough."

"True—true," I replied; "and, indeed, I had no intention of alarming you unnecessarily—but you should use all proper caution. A draught of this Medoc will defend us from the damps."

Here I knocked off the neck of a bottle which I drew from a long row of its fellows that lay upon the mould.

"Drink," I said, presenting him the wine.

He raised it to his lips with a leer. He paused and nodded to me familiarly, while his bells jingled.

"I drink," he said, "to the buried that repose around us."

"And I to your long life."

He again took my arm, and we proceeded.

"These vaults," he said, "are extensive."

"The Montresors," I replied, "were a great and numerous family."

"I forget your arms."

"A huge human foot d'or, in a field azure; the foot crushes a serpent rampant whose fangs are imbedded in the heel."

"And the motto?"

"Nemo me impune lacessit. [No one harms me with impunity.]"

"Good!" he said. The wine sparkled in his eyes and the bells jingled. My own fancy grew warm with the Medoc. We had passed through walls of piled bones, with casks and puncheons intermingling, into the inmost recesses of the catacombs. I paused again, and this time I made bold to seize Fortunato by an arm above the elbow.

"The nitre!" I said: "see, it increases. It hangs like moss upon the vaults. We are below the river's bed. The drops of moisture trickle among the bones. Come, we will go back ere it is too late. Your cough—"

"It is nothing," he said; "let us go on. But first, another draught of the Medoc."

I broke and reached him a flaçon [flagon] of De Grâve. He emptied it at a breath. His eyes flashed with a fierce light. He laughed and threw the bottle upwards with a gesticulation I did not understand.

I looked at him in surprise. He repeated the movement—a grotesque one.

"You do not comprehend?" he said.

"Not I," I replied.

"Then you are not of the brotherhood."

"How?"

"You are not of the masons."

"Yes, yes," I said, "yes, yes."

"You? Impossible! A mason?"

"A mason," I replied.

"A sign," he said.

"It is this," I answered, producing a trowel from beneath the folds of my *roquelaire*.

"You jest," he exclaimed, recoiling a few paces. "But let us proceed to the Amontillado."

"Be it so," I said, replacing the tool beneath the cloak, and again offering him my arm. He leaned upon it heavily. We continued our route in search of the Amontillado. We passed through a range of low arches, descended, passed on, and descending again, arrived at a deep crypt, in which the foulness of the air caused our flambeaux rather to glow than flame.

At the most remote end of the crypt there appeared another less spacious. Its walls had been lined with human remains, piled to the vault overhead, in the fashion of the great catacombs of Paris. Three sides of this interior crypt were still ornamented in this manner. From the fourth the bones had been thrown down, and lay promiscuously upon the earth, forming at one point a mound of some size. Within the wall thus exposed by the displacing of the bones, we perceived a still interior recess, in depth about four feet, in width three, in height six or seven. It seemed to have been constructed for no especial use in itself, but formed merely the interval between two of the colossal supports of the roof of the catacombs, and was backed by one of their circumscribing walls of solid granite.

It was in vain that Fortunato, uplifting his dull torch, endeavored to pry into the depths of the recess. Its termination the feeble light did not enable us to see.

"Proceed," I said; "herein is the Amontillado. As for Luchesi—"

"He is an ignoramus," interrupted my friend, as he stepped unsteadily forward, while I followed immediately at his heels. In an instant he had reached the extremity of the niche, and finding his progress arrested by the rock, stood

stupidly bewildered. A moment more and I had fettered him to the granite. In its surface were two iron staples, distant from each other about two feet, horizontally. From one of these depended a short chain, from the other a padlock. Throwing the links about his waist, it was but the work of a few seconds to secure it. He was too much astounded to resist. Withdrawing the key I stepped back from the recess.

"Pass your hand," I said, "over the wall; you cannot help feeling the nitre. Indeed it is very damp. Once more let me *implore* you to return. No? Then I must positively leave you. But I must first render you all the little attentions in my power."

"The Amontillado!" ejaculated my friend, not yet recovered from his astonishment. "True," I replied; "the Amontillado."

As I said these words I busied myself among the pile of bones of which I have before spoken. Throwing them aside, I soon uncovered a quantity of building stone and mortar. With these materials and with the aid of my trowel, I began vigorously to wall up the entrance of the niche.

I had scarcely laid the first tier of my masonry when I discovered that the intoxication of Fortunato had in a great measure worn off. The earliest indication I had of this was a low moaning cry from the depth of the recess. It was *not* the cry of a drunken man. There was then a long and obstinate silence. I laid the second tier, and the third, and the fourth; and then I heard the furious vibrations of the chain. The noise lasted for several minutes, during which, that I might hearken to it with the more satisfaction, I ceased my labors and sat down upon the bones. When at last the clanking subsided, I resumed the trowel, and finished without interruption the fifth, the sixth, and the seventh tier. The wall was now nearly upon a level with my breast. I again paused, and holding the flambeaux over the mason-work, threw a few feeble rays upon the figure within.

A succession of loud and shrill screams, bursting suddenly from the throat of the chained form, seemed to thrust me violently back. For a brief moment I hesitated—I trembled. Unsheathing my rapier, I began to grope with it about the recess: but the thought of an instant reassured me. I placed my hand upon the solid fabric of the catacombs, and felt satisfied. I re-approached the wall. I replied to the yells of him who clamored. I re-echoed—I aided—I surpassed them in volume and in strength. I did this, and the clamorer grew still.

It was now midnight, and my task was drawing to a close. I had completed the eighth, the ninth, and the tenth tier. I had finished a portion of the last and the eleventh; there remained but a single stone to be fitted and plastered in. I struggled with its weight; I placed it partially in its destined position. But now there came from out the niche a low laugh that erected the hairs upon my head. It was succeeded by a sad voice, which I had difficulty in recognising as that of the noble Fortunato. The voice said—

"Ha! ha! ha!—he! he!—a very good joke indeed—an excellent jest. We will have many a rich laugh about it at the palazzo—he! he! he!—over our wine—he! he! he!"

"The Amontillado!" I said.

"He! he! he!—he! he! he!—yes, the Amontillado. But is it not getting late? Will not they be awaiting us at the palazzo, the Lady Fortunato and the rest? Let us be gone."

"Yes," I said, "let us be gone."

"For the love of God, Montressor!"

"Yes," I said, "for the love of God!"

But to these words I hearkened in vain for a reply. I grew impatient. I called aloud—

"Fortunato!"

No answer. I called again—

"Fortunato!"

No answer still. I thrust a torch through the remaining aperture and let it fall within. There came forth in return only a jingling of the bells. My heart grew sick—on account of the dampness of the catacombs. I hastened to make an end of my labor. I forced the last stone into its position; I plastered it up. Against the new masonry I re-erected the old rampart of bones. For the half of a century no mortal has disturbed them. *In pace requiescat!*

Humor

"The Ransom of Red Chief," by O. Henry

A plot that normally spells tragedy ends in utter chaos for the two criminals.

It looked like a good thing: but wait till I tell you. We were down South, in Alabama—Bill Driscoll and myself—when this kidnapping idea struck us. It was, as Bill afterward expressed it, "during a moment of temporary mental apparition"; but we didn't find that out till later.

There was a town down there, as flat as a flannel-cake, and called Summit, of course. It contained inhabitants of as undeleterious and self-satisfied a class of peasantry as ever clustered around a Maypole.

Bill and me had a joint capital of about six hundred dollars, and we needed just two thousand dollars more to pull off a fraudulent town-lot scheme in Western Illinois with. We talked it over on the front steps of the hotel. Philoprogenitiveness, says we, is strong in semi-rural communities; therefore and for other reasons, a kidnapping project ought to do better there than in the radius of newspapers that send reporters out in plain clothes to stir up talk about such things. We knew that Summit couldn't get after us with anything stronger than constables and maybe some lackadaisical bloodhounds and a diatribe or two in the *Weekly Farmers' Budget*. So, it looked good.

We selected for our victim the only child of a prominent citizen named Ebenezer Dorset. The father was respectable and tight, a mortgage fancier and a stern, upright collection-plate passer and forecloser. The kid was a boy of ten, with bas-relief freckles, and hair the color of the cover of the magazine you buy at the news-stand when you want to catch a train. Bill and me figured that Ebenezer would melt down for a ransom of two thousand dollars to a cent. But wait till I tell you.

About two miles from Summit was a little mountain, covered with a dense cedar brake. On the rear elevation of this mountain was a cave. There we stored provisions. One evening after sundown, we drove in a buggy past old Dorset's house. The kid was in the street, throwing rocks at a kitten on the opposite fence.

"Hey, little boy!" says Bill, "would you like to have a bag of candy and a nice ride?"

The boy catches Bill neatly in the eye with a piece of brick.

"That will cost the old man an extra five hundred dollars," says Bill, climbing over the wheel.

That boy put up a fight like a welter-weight cinnamon bear; but, at last, we got him down in the bottom of the buggy and drove away. We took him up to the cave and I hitched the horse in the cedar brake. After dark I drove the buggy to the little village, three miles away, where we had hired it, and walked back to the mountain.

Bill was pasting court-plaster over the scratches and bruises on his features. There was a fire burning behind the big rock at the entrance of the cave, and the boy was watching a pot of boiling coffee, with two buzzard tail-feathers stuck in his red hair. He points a stick at me when I come up, and says:

"Ha! cursed paleface, do you dare to enter the camp of Red Chief, the terror of the plains?"

"He's all right now," says Bill, rolling up his trousers and examining some bruises on his shins. "We're playing Indian. We're making Buffalo Bill's show look like magic-lantern views of Palestine in the town hall. I'm Old Hank, the Trapper, Red Chief's captive, and I'm to be scalped at daybreak. By Geronimo! that kid can kick hard."

Yes, sir, that boy seemed to be having the time of his life. The fun of camping out in a cave had made him forget that he was a captive himself. He immediately christened me Snake-eye, the Spy, and announced that, when his braves returned from the warpath, I was to be broiled at the stake at the rising of the sun.

Then we had supper; and he filled his mouth full of bacon and bread and gravy, and began to talk. He made a during-dinner speech something like this:

"I like this fine. I never camped out before; but I had a pet 'possum once, and I was nine last birthday. I hate to go to school. Rats ate up sixteen of Jimmy Talbot's aunt's speckled hen's eggs. Are there any real Indians in these woods? I want some more gravy. Does the trees moving make the wind blow? We had five puppies. What makes your nose so red, Hank? My father has lots of money. Are the stars hot? I whipped Ed Walker twice, Saturday. I don't like girls. You dassent catch toads unless with a string. Do oxen make any noise? Why are oranges round? Have you got beds to sleep on in this cave? Amos Murray has got six toes. A parrot can talk, but a monkey or a fish can't. How many does it take to make twelve?"

Every few minutes he would remember that he was a pesky redskin, and pick up his stick rifle and tiptoe to the mouth of the cave to rubber for the scouts of the hated paleface. Now and then he would let out a war-whoop that made Old Hank the Trapper shiver. That boy had Bill terrorized from the start.

"Red Chief," says I to the kid, "would you like to go home?"

"Aw, what for?" says he. "I don't have any fun at home. I hate to go to school. I like to camp out. You won't take me back home again, Snake-eye, will you?"

"Not right away," says I. "We'll stay here in the cave a while."

"All right!" says he. "That'll be fine. I never had such fun in all my life."

We went to bed about eleven o'clock. We spread down some wide blankets and quilts and put Red Chief between us. We weren't afraid he'd run away. He kept us awake for three hours, jumping up and reaching for his rifle and screeching: "Hist! pard," in mine and Bill's ears, as the fancied crackle of a twig or the rustle of a leaf revealed to his young imagination the stealthy approach of the outlaw band. At last, I fell into a troubled sleep, and dreamed that I had been kidnapped and chained to a tree by a ferocious pirate with red hair.

Just at daybreak, I was awakened by a series of awful screams from Bill. They weren't yells, or howls, or shouts, or whoops, or yawps, such as you'd expect from a manly set of vocal organs—they were simply indecent, terrifying, humiliating screams, such as women emit when they see ghosts or caterpillars. It's an awful thing to hear a strong, desperate, fat man scream incontinently in a cave at daybreak.

I jumped up to see what the matter was. Red Chief was sitting on Bill's chest, with one hand twined in Bill's hair. In the other he had the sharp case-knife we used for slicing bacon; and he was industriously and realistically trying to take Bill's scalp, according to the sentence that had been pronounced upon him the evening before.

I got the knife away from the kid and made him lie down again. But, from that moment, Bill's spirit was broken. He laid down on his side of the bed, but he never closed an eye again in sleep as long as that boy was with us. I dozed off for a while, but along toward sun-up I remembered that Red Chief had said I was to be burned at the stake at the rising of the sun. I wasn't nervous or afraid; but I sat up and lit my pipe and leaned against a rock.

"What you getting up so soon for, Sam?" asked Bill.

"Me?" says I. "Oh, I got a kind of a pain in my shoulder. I thought sitting up would rest it."

"You're a liar!" says Bill. "You're afraid. You was to be burned at sunrise, and you was afraid he'd do it. And he would, too, if he could find a match. Ain't it awful, Sam? Do you think anybody will pay out money to get a little imp like that back home?"

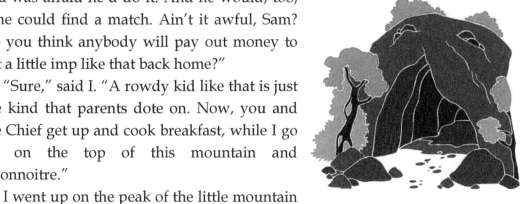

"Sure," said I. "A rowdy kid like that is just the kind that parents dote on. Now, you and the Chief get up and cook breakfast, while I go up on the top of this mountain and reconnoitre."

I went up on the peak of the little mountain and ran my eye over the contiguous vicinity. Over toward Summit I expected to see the sturdy yeomanry of the village armed with scythes and pitchforks beating the countryside for the dastardly kidnappers. But what I saw was a peaceful landscape dotted with one man ploughing with a dun mule. Nobody was dragging the creek; no couriers dashed hither and yon, bringing tidings of no news to the distracted parents. There was a sylvan attitude of somnolent sleepiness pervading that section of the external outward surface of Alabama that lay exposed to my view. "Perhaps," says I to myself, "it has not yet been discovered that the wolves have borne away the tender lambkin from the fold. Heaven help the wolves!" says I, and I went down the mountain to breakfast.

When I got to the cave I found Bill backed up against the side of it, breathing hard, and the boy threatening to smash him with a rock half as big as a cocoanut.

"He put a red-hot boiled potato down my back," explained Bill, "and then mashed it with his foot; and I boxed his ears. Have you got a gun about you, Sam?"

I took the rock away from the boy and kind of patched up the argument. "I'll fix you," says the kid to Bill. "No man ever yet struck the Red Chief but what he got paid for it. You better beware!"

After breakfast the kid takes a piece of leather with strings wrapped around it out of his pocket and goes outside the cave unwinding it.

"What's he up to now?" says Bill, anxiously. "You don't think he'll run away, do you, Sam?"

"No fear of it," says I. "He don't seem to be much of a home body. But we've got to fix up some plan about the ransom. There don't seem to be much excitement around Summit on account of his disappearance; but maybe they haven't realized yet that he's gone. His folks may think he's spending the night with Aunt Jane or one of the neighbours. Anyhow, he'll be missed to-day. To-night we must get a message to his father demanding the two thousand dollars for his return."

Just then we heard a kind of war-whoop, such as David might have emitted when he knocked out the champion Goliath. It was a sling that Red Chief had pulled out of his pocket, and he was whirling it around his head.

I dodged, and heard a heavy thud and a kind of a sigh from Bill, like a horse gives out when you take his saddle off. A niggerhead rock the size of an egg had caught Bill just behind his left ear. He loosened himself all over and fell in the fire across the frying pan of hot water for washing the dishes. I dragged him out and poured cold water on his head for half an hour.

By and by, Bill sits up and feels behind his ear and says: "Sam, do you know who my favourite Biblical character is?"

"Take it easy," says I. "You'll come to your senses presently."

"King Herod," says he. "You won't go away and leave me here alone, will you, Sam?"

I went out and caught that boy and shook him until his freckles rattled.

"If you don't behave," says I, "I'll take you straight home. Now, are you going to be good, or not?"

"I was only funning," says he sullenly. "I didn't mean to hurt Old Hank. But what did he hit me for? I'll behave, Snake-eye, if you won't send me home, and if you'll let me play the Black Scout to-day."

"I don't know the game," says I. "That's for you and Mr. Bill to decide. He's your playmate for the day. I'm going away for a while, on business. Now, you come in and make friends with him and say you are sorry for hurting him, or home you go, at once."

I made him and Bill shake hands, and then I took Bill aside and told him I was going to Poplar Cove, a little village three miles from the cave, and find out what I could about how the kidnapping had been regarded in Summit. Also, I thought it best to send a peremptory letter to old man Dorset that day, demanding the ransom and dictating how it should be paid.

"You know, Sam," says Bill, "I've stood by you without batting an eye in earthquakes, fire and flood—in poker games, dynamite outrages, police raids, train robberies and cyclones. I never lost my nerve yet till we kidnapped that two-legged skyrocket of a kid. He's got me going. You won't leave me long with him, will you, Sam?"

"I'll be back some time this afternoon," says I. "You must keep the boy amused and quiet till I return. And now we'll write the letter to old Dorset."

Bill and I got paper and pencil and worked on the letter while Red Chief, with a blanket wrapped around him, strutted up and down, guarding the mouth of the cave. Bill begged me tearfully to make the ransom fifteen hundred dollars instead of two thousand. "I ain't attempting," says he, "to decry the celebrated moral aspect of parental affection, but we're dealing with humans, and it ain't human for anybody to give up two thousand dollars for that forty-pound chunk of freckled wildcat. I'm willing to take a chance at fifteen hundred dollars. You can charge the difference up to me."

So, to relieve Bill, I acceded, and we collaborated a letter that ran this way:

Ebenezer Dorset, Esq.:

We have your boy concealed in a place far from Summit. It is useless for you or the most skilful detectives to attempt to find him. Absolutely, the only terms on which you can have him restored to you are these: We demand fifteen hundred dollars in large bills for his return; the money to be left at midnight to-night at the same spot and in the same box as your reply—as hereinafter described. If you agree to these terms, send your answer in writing by a solitary messenger to-night at half-past eight o'clock. After crossing Owl Creek, on the road to Poplar Cove, there are three large trees about a hundred yards apart, close to the fence of the wheat field on the right-hand side. At the bottom of the fence-post, opposite the third tree, will be found a small pasteboard box.

The messenger will place the answer in this box and return immediately to Summit. If you attempt any treachery or fail to comply with our demand as stated, you will never see your boy again. If you pay the money as demanded, he will be returned to you safe and well within three hours. These terms are final, and if you do not accede to them no further communication will be attempted.

TWO DESPERATE MEN.

I addressed this letter to Dorset, and put it in my pocket. As I was about to start, the kid comes up to me and says:

"Aw, Snake-eye, you said I could play the Black Scout while you was gone."

"Play it, of course," says I. "Mr. Bill will play with you. What kind of a game is it?"

"I'm the Black Scout," says Red Chief, "and I have to ride to the stockade to warn the settlers that the Indians are coming. I'm tired of playing Indian myself. I want to be the Black Scout."

"All right," says I. "It sounds harmless to me. I guess Mr. Bill will help you foil the pesky savages."

"What am I to do?" asks Bill, looking at the kid suspiciously.

"You are the hoss," says Black Scout. "Get down on your hands and knees. How can I ride to the stockade without a hoss?"

"You'd better keep him interested," said I, "till we get the scheme going. Loosen up."

Bill gets down on his all fours, and a look comes in his eye like a rabbit's when you catch it in a trap.

"How far is it to the stockade, kid?" he asks, in a husky manner of voice.

The Black Scout jumps on Bill's back and digs his heels in his side.

"Ninety miles," says the Black Scout. "And you have to hump yourself to get there on time. Whoa, now!"

"For Heaven's sake," says Bill, "hurry back, Sam, as soon as you can. I wish we hadn't made the ransom more than a thousand. Say, you quit kicking me or I'll get up and warm you good."

I walked over to Poplar Cove and sat around the post-office and store, talking with the chawbacons that came in to trade. One whiskerando says that he hears Summit is all upset on account of Elder Ebenezer Dorset's boy having been lost or stolen. That was all I wanted to know. I bought some smoking tobacco, referred casually to the price of black-eyed peas, posted my letter surreptitiously and came away. The postmaster said the mail-carrier would come by in an hour to take the mail on to Summit.

When I got back to the cave Bill and the boy were not to be found. I explored the vicinity of the cave, and risked a yodel or two, but there was no response.

So I lighted my pipe and sat down on a mossy bank to await developments.

In about half an hour I heard the bushes rustle, and Bill wabbled out into the little glade in front of the cave. Behind him was the kid, stepping softly like a scout, with a broad grin on his face. Bill stopped, took off his hat and wiped his face with a red handkerchief. The kid stopped about eight feet behind him.

"Sam," says Bill, "I suppose you'll think I'm a renegade, but I couldn't help it. I'm a grown person with masculine proclivities and habits of self-defense, but there is a time when all systems of egotism and predominance fail. The boy is gone. I have sent him home. All is off. There was martyrs in old times," goes on Bill, "that suffered death rather than give up the particular graft they enjoyed. None of 'em ever was subjugated to such supernatural tortures as I have been. I tried to be faithful to our articles of depredation; but there came a limit."

Exaggeration is stretching the truth or overstating something, often to show strong emotion or to emphasize a feeling or the quality of an event: "Sam," says Bill, "I suppose you'll think I'm a renegade, but I couldn't help it. . . . There was martyrs in old times. . . . None of 'em ever was subjugated to such supernatural tortures as I have been."

"What's the trouble, Bill?" I asks him.

"I was rode," says Bill, "the ninety miles to the stockade, not barring an inch. Then, when the settlers was rescued, I was given oats. Sand ain't a palatable substitute. And then, for an hour I had to try to explain to him why there was nothin' in holes, how a road can run both ways and what makes the grass green. I tell you, Sam, a human can only stand so much. I takes him by the neck of his clothes and drags him down the mountain. On the way he kicks my legs black-and-blue from the knees down; and I've got to have two or three bites on my thumb and hand cauterized.

"But he's gone" — continues Bill — "gone home. I showed him the road to Summit and kicked him about eight feet nearer there at one kick. I'm sorry we lose the ransom; but it was either that or Bill Driscoll to the madhouse."

Bill is puffing and blowing, but there is a look of ineffable peace and growing content on his rose-pink features.

"Bill," says I, "there isn't any heart disease in your family, is there?

"No," says Bill, "nothing chronic except malaria and accidents. Why?"

"Then you might turn around," says I, "and have a took behind you."

Bill turns and sees the boy, and loses his complexion and sits down plump on the ground and begins to pluck aimlessly at grass and little sticks. For an hour I was afraid for his mind. And then I told him that my scheme was to put the whole job through immediately and that we would get the ransom and be off with it by midnight if old Dorset fell in with our proposition. So Bill braced up enough to give the kid a weak sort of a smile and a promise to play the Russian in a Japanese war with him as soon as he felt a little better.

I had a scheme for collecting that ransom without danger of being caught by counterplots that ought to commend itself to professional kidnappers. The tree under which the answer was to be left—and the money later on—was close to the road fence with big, bare fields on all sides. If a gang of constables be watching for any one to come for the note they could see him a long way off crossing the fields or in the road. But no, sirree! At half-past eight I was up in that tree as well hidden as a tree toad, waiting for the messenger to arrive.

Exactly on time, a half-grown boy rides up the road on a bicycle, locates the pasteboard box at the foot of the fence-post, slips a folded piece of paper into it and pedals away again back toward Summit.

I waited an hour and then concluded the thing was square. I slid down the tree, got the note, slipped along the fence till I struck the woods, and was back at the cave in another half an hour. I opened the note, got near the lantern and read it to Bill. It was written with a pen in a crabbed hand, and the sum and substance of it was this:

Two Desperate Men.

Gentlemen: I received your letter to-day by post, in regard to the ransom you ask for the return of my son. I think you are a little high in your demands, and I hereby make you a counter-proposition, which I am inclined to believe you will accept. You bring Johnny home and pay me two hundred and fifty dollars in cash, and I agree to take him off your hands. You had better come at night, for the neighbors believe he is lost, and I couldn't be responsible for what they would do to anybody they saw bringing him back.

Very respectfully,

EBENEZER DORSET.

"Great pirates of Penzance!" says I; "of all the impudent—"

But I glanced at Bill, and hesitated. He had the most appealing look in his eyes I ever saw on the face of a dumb or a talking brute.

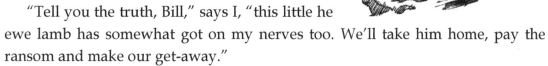

"Sam," says he, "what's two hundred and fifty dollars, after all? We've got the money. One more night of this kid will send me to a bed in Bedlam. Besides being a thorough gentleman, I think Mr. Dorset is a spendthrift for making us such a liberal offer. You ain't going to let the chance go, are you?"

"Tell you the truth, Bill," says I, "this little he ewe lamb has somewhat got on my nerves too. We'll take him home, pay the ransom and make our get-away."

We took him home that night. We got him to go by telling him that his father had bought a silver-mounted rifle and a pair of moccasins for him, and we were going to hunt bears the next day.

It was just twelve o'clock when we knocked at Ebenezer's front door. Just at the moment when I should have been abstracting the fifteen hundred dollars from the box under the tree, according to the original proposition, Bill was counting out two hundred and fifty dollars into Dorset's hand.

When the kid found out we were going to leave him at home he started up a howl like a calliope and fastened himself as tight as a leech to Bill's leg. His father peeled him away gradually, like a porous plaster.

"How long can you hold him?" asks Bill.

"I'm not as strong as I used to be," says old Dorset, "but I think I can promise you ten minutes."

"Enough," says Bill. "In ten minutes I shall cross the Central, Southern and Middle Western States, and be legging it trippingly for the Canadian border."

And, as dark as it was, and as fat as Bill was, and as good a runner as I am, he was a good mile and a half out of Summit before I could catch up with him.

Comments on O. Henry

In O. Henry American journalism and the Victorian tradition meet. His mind, quick to don the guise of modernity, was impervious to its spirit. The specifically modern movements, the scientific awakening, the religious upheaval and subsidence, the socialistic gospel, the enfranchisement of women—these never interfered with his artless and joyous pursuit of the old Romantic motives of love, hate, wealth, poverty, gentility, disguise, and crime. On two points a moral record which, in his literature, is everywhere sound and stainless, rises almost to nobility. In an age when sexual excitement had become available and permissible, this worshiper of stimulus never touched with so much as a fingertip that insidious and meretricious fruit. The second point is his feeling for underpaid working-girls. His passionate concern for this wrong derives a peculiar emphasis from the general refusal of his books to bestow countenance or notice of philanthropy in its collective forms. When, in his dream of Heaven, he is asked: "Are you one of the bunch?" (meaning one of the bunch of grasping and grinding employers), the response, through all its slang, is soul-stirring. "'Not on your immortality,' said I. 'I'm only the fellow that set fire to an orphan asylum and murdered a blind man for his pennies.'" The author of that retort may have some difficulty with the sentries that watch the entrance of Parnassus; he will have none with the gatekeeper of the New Jerusalem. —O. W. Firkins

Thriller

Thrillers are a genre of literature, film, video gaming, and television programming that use suspense, tension, and excitement as the main elements.

Odyssey, by Homer

Binding the wounds

In the final bloody scenes Odysseus kills all of Penelope's suitors. The violence disturbs the gods. Observing from Mount Olympus, Athena asks Zeus if this discord will go on forever. Zeus wants this quarrel to end. Odysseus' honor is satisfied. He will be king by a pact sworn forever, and the gods will blot out the memory of the slain sons and brothers. So Athena goes to the farmhouse to warn Odysseus. This builds suspense! As the citizens appear, Athena urges Laertes to throw his spear, killing Eupithes. Odysseus and his men attack, and more blood would have been spilled had Athena not stopped the fight. When she appears before them, the townspeople flee. Odysseus is about to pursue them when Zeus throws a thunderbolt: No more. Later a peace pact is sworn to by all parties, under the guidance of Athena.

From Book 23

Then thus Minerva in Laertes' ear:
"Son of Arcesius, reverend warrior, hear!
Jove and Jove's daughter first implore in prayer,
Then, whirling high, discharge thy lance in air."
She said, infusing courage with the word.
Jove and Jove's daughter then the chief implored,
And, whirling high, dismiss'd the lance in air.
Full at Eupithes drove the deathful spear:
The brass-cheek'd helmet opens to the wound;
He falls, earth thunders, and his arms resound.
Before the father and the conquering son

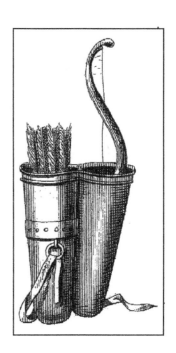

Heaps rush on heaps, they fight, they drop, they run;
Now by the sword, and now the javelin, fall
The rebel race, and death had swallow'd all;
But from on high the blue-eyed virgin cried;
Her awful voice detain'd the headlong tide:
"Forbear, ye nations, your mad hands forbear
From mutual slaughter; Peace descends to spare."
Fear shook the nations: at the voice divine
They drop their javelins, and their rage resign.
All scatter'd round their glittering weapons lie;
Some fall to earth, and some confusedly fly.

With dreadful shouts Ulysses pour'd along,
Swift as an eagle, as an eagle strong.
But Jove's red arm the burning thunder aims:
Before Minerva shot the livid flames;
Blazing they fell, and at her feet expired;

Then stopped the goddess, trembled and retired.
"Descended from the gods! Ulysses, cease;
Offend not Jove: obey, and give the peace."
So Pallas spoke: the mandate from above
The king obey'd. The virgin-seed of Jove,
In Mentor's form, confirm'd the full accord,
And willing nations knew their lawful lord.

Treasure Island, by Robert Louis Stevenson

Chapter 3

About noon I stopped at the captain's door with some cooling drinks and medicines. He was lying very much as we had left him, only a little higher, and he seemed both weak and excited.

"Jim," he said, "you're the only one here that's worth anything, and you know I've been always good to you. Never a month but I've given you a silver fourpenny for yourself. And now you see, mate, I'm pretty low, and deserted by all; and Jim, you'll bring me one noggin of rum, now, won't you, matey?"

"The doctor—" I began. But he broke in cursing the doctor, in a feeble voice but heartily. "Doctors is all swabs," he said; "and that doctor there, why, what do he know about seafaring men? I been in places hot as pitch, and mates dropping round with Yellow Jack, and the blessed land a-heaving like the sea with earthquakes—what does the doctor know of lands like that?—and I lived on rum, I tell you. It's been meat and drink, and man and wife, to me; and if I'm not to have my rum now I'm a poor old

Captain J. Flint

hulk on a lee shore, my blood'll be on you, Jim, and that doctor swab"; and he ran on again for a while with curses.

"Look, Jim, how my fingers fidges," he continued in the pleading tone. "I can't keep 'em still, not I. I haven't had a drop this blessed day. That doctor's a fool, I tell you. If I don't have a drain o' rum, Jim, I'll have the horrors; I seen some on 'em already. I seen old Flint in the corner there, behind you; as plain as print, I seen him; and if I get the horrors, I'm a man that has lived rough, and I'll raise Cain. Your doctor hisself said one glass wouldn't hurt me. I'll give you a golden guinea for a noggin, Jim."

He was growing more and more excited, and this alarmed me for my father, who was very low that day and needed quiet; besides, I was reassured by the doctor's words, now quoted to me, and rather offended by the offer of a bribe.

"I want none of your money," said I, "but what you owe my father. I'll get you one glass, and no more."

When I brought it to him, he seized it greedily and drank it out.

"Aye, aye," said he, "that's some better, sure enough. And now, matey, did that doctor say how long I was to lie here in this old berth?"

"A week at least," said I.

"Thunder!" he cried. "A week! I can't do that; they'd have the black spot on me by then. The lubbers is going about to get the wind of me this blessed moment; lubbers as couldn't keep what they got, and want to nail what is another's. Is that seamanly behaviour, now, I want to know? But I'm a saving soul. I never wasted good money of mine, nor lost it neither; and I'll trick 'em again. I'm not afraid on 'em. I'll shake out another reef, matey, and daddle 'em again."

As he was thus speaking, he had risen from bed with great difficulty, holding to my shoulder with a grip that almost made me cry out, and moving his legs like so much dead weight. His words, spirited as they were in meaning, contrasted sadly with the weakness of the voice in which they were uttered. He paused when he had got into a sitting position on the edge.

"That doctor's done me," he murmured. "My ears is singing. Lay me back."

Before I could do much to help him he had fallen back again to his former place, where he lay for a while silent.

"Jim," he said at length, "you saw that seafaring man today?"

"Black Dog?" I asked.

"Ah! Black Dog," says he. "*He's* a bad un; but there's worse that put him on. Now, if I can't get away nohow, and they tip me the black spot, mind you, it's my old sea-chest they're after; you get on a horse—you can, can't you? Well, then, you get on a horse, and go to—well, yes, I will!—to that eternal doctor swab, and tell him to pipe all hands—magistrates and sich—and he'll lay 'em aboard at the Admiral Benbow—all old Flint's crew, man and boy, all on 'em that's left. I was first mate, I was, old Flint's first mate, and I'm the on'y one as knows the place. He gave it me at Savannah, when he lay a-dying, like as if I was to now, you see. But you won't peach unless they get the black spot on me, or unless you see that Black Dog again or a seafaring man with one leg, Jim—him above all."

"But what is the black spot, captain?" I asked.

"That's a summons, mate. I'll tell you if they get that. But you keep your weather-eye open, Jim, and I'll share with you equals, upon my honor."

He wandered a little longer, his voice growing weaker; but soon after I had given him his medicine, which he took like a child, with the remark, "If ever a seaman wanted drugs, it's me," he fell at last into a heavy, swoon-like sleep, in which I left him. What I should have done had all gone well I do not know. Probably I should have told the whole story to the doctor, for I was in mortal fear lest the captain should repent of his confessions and make an end of me. But as things fell out, my poor father died quite suddenly that evening, which put all other matters on one side. Our natural distress, the visits of the neighbor, the arranging of the funeral, and all the work of the inn to be carried on in the meanwhile kept me so busy that I had scarcely time to think of the captain, far less to be afraid of him.

He got downstairs next morning, to be sure, and had his meals as usual, though he ate little and had more, I am afraid, than his usual supply of rum, for he helped himself out of the bar, scowling and blowing through his nose, and no one dared to cross him. On the night before the funeral he was as drunk as ever;

and it was shocking, in that house of mourning, to hear him singing away at his ugly old sea-song; but weak as he was, we were all in the fear of death for him, and the doctor was suddenly taken up with a case many miles away and was never near the house after my father's death. I have said the captain was weak, and indeed he seemed rather to grow weaker than regain his strength. He clambered up and down stairs, and went from the parlour to the bar and back again, and sometimes put his nose out of doors to smell the sea, holding on to the walls as he went for support and breathing hard and fast like a man on a steep mountain. He never particularly addressed me, and it is my belief he had as good as forgotten his confidences; but his temper was more flighty, and allowing for his bodily weakness, more violent than ever. He had an alarming way now when he was drunk of drawing his cutlass and laying it bare before him on the table. But with all that, he minded people less and seemed shut up in his own thoughts and rather wandering. Once, for instance, to our extreme wonder, he piped up to a different air, a kind of country love-song that he must have learned in his youth before he had begun to follow the sea.

So things passed until, the day after the funeral, and about three o'clock of a bitter, foggy, frosty afternoon, I was standing at the door for a moment, full of sad thoughts about my father, when I saw someone drawing slowly near along the road.

He was plainly blind, for he tapped before him with a stick and wore a great green shade over his eyes and nose; and he was hunched, as if with age or weakness, and wore a huge old tattered sea-cloak with a hood that made him appear positively deformed. I never saw in my life a more dreadful-looking figure. He stopped a little from the inn, and raising his voice in an odd sing-song, addressed the air in front of him, "Will any kind friend inform a poor blind man, who has lost the precious sight of his eyes in the gracious defense of his native country, England—and God bless King George!—where or in what part of this country he may now be?"

"You are at the Admiral Benbow, Black Hill Cove, my good man," said I.

"I hear a voice," said he, "a young voice. Will you give me your hand, my kind young friend, and lead me in?"

"Sir," said I, "upon my word I dare not."

"Oh," he sneered, "that's it! Take me in straight or I'll break your arm."

And he gave it, as he spoke, a wrench that made me cry out.

"Sir," said I, "it is for yourself I mean. The captain is not what he used to be. He sits with a drawn cutlass. Another gentleman—"

"Come, now, march," interrupted he; and I never heard a voice so cruel, and cold, and ugly as that blind man's. It cowed me more than the pain, and I began to obey him at once, walking straight in at the door and towards the parlour, where our sick old buccaneer was sitting, dazed with rum. The blind man clung close to me, holding me in one iron fist and leaning almost more of his weight on me than I could carry.

"Lead me straight up to him, and when I'm in view, cry out, 'Here's a friend for you, Bill.' If you don't, I'll do this," and with that he gave me a twitch that I thought would have made me faint. Between this and that, I was so utterly terrified of the blind beggar that I forgot my terror of the captain, and as I opened the parlour door, cried out the words he had ordered in a trembling voice.

The poor captain raised his eyes, and at one look the rum went out of him and left him staring sober. The expression of his face was not so much of terror as of mortal sickness. He made a movement to rise, but I do not believe he had enough force left in his body.

"Now, Bill, sit where you are," said the beggar. "If I can't see, I can hear a finger stirring. Business is business. Hold out your left hand. Boy, take his left hand by the wrist and bring it near to my right."

We both obeyed him to the letter, and I saw him pass something from the hollow of the hand that held his stick into the palm of the captain's, which closed upon it instantly.

And now that's done," said the blind man; and at the words he suddenly left hold of me, and with incredible accuracy and nimbleness, skipped out of the parlour and into the road, where, as I still stood motionless, I could hear his stick go tap-tap-tapping into the distance.

It was some time before either I or the captain seemed to gather our senses,

but at length, and about at the same moment, I released his wrist, which I was still holding, and he drew in his hand and looked sharply into the palm.

"Ten o'clock!" he cried. "Six hours. We'll do them yet," and he sprang to his feet.

Even as he did so, he reeled, put his hand to his throat, stood swaying for a moment, and then, with a peculiar sound, fell from his whole height face foremost to the floor.

I ran to him at once, calling to my mother. But haste was all in vain. The captain had been struck dead by thundering apoplexy. It is a curious thing to understand, for I had certainly never liked the man, though of late I had begun to pity him, but as soon as I saw that he was dead, I burst into a flood of tears. It was the second death I had known, and the sorrow of the first was still fresh in my heart.

Romance

In romances there can be several tones, such as anticipation, fear, hope, and disappointment. In *Jane Eyre*, all these exist!

Jane Eyre, by Charlotte Brontë

Chapter 37

The manor-house of Ferndean was a building of considerable antiquity, moderate size, and no architectural pretensions, deep buried in a wood. I had heard of it before. Mr. Rochester often spoke of it, and sometimes went there. His father had purchased the estate for the sake of the game covers. He would have let the house, but could find no tenant, in consequence of its ineligible and insalubrious site. Ferndean then remained uninhabited and unfurnished, with the exception of some two or three rooms fitted up for the accommodation of the squire when he went there in the season to shoot.

To this house I came just ere dark on an evening marked by the characteristics of sad sky, cold gale, and continued small penetrating rain. The  last mile I performed on foot, having dismissed the chaise and driver with the double remuneration I had promised. Even when within a very short distance of the manor-house, you could see nothing of it, so thick and dark grew the timber of the gloomy wood about it. Iron gates between granite pillars showed me where to enter, and passing through them, I found myself at once in the twilight of close-ranked trees. There was a grass-grown track descending the forest aisle between hoar and knotty shafts and under branched arches. I followed it, expecting soon to reach the dwelling; but it stretched on and on, it would far and farther: no sign of habitation or grounds was visible.

I thought I had taken a wrong direction and lost my way. The darkness of natural as well as of sylvan dusk gathered over me. I looked round in search of another road. There was none: all was interwoven stem, columnar trunk, dense summer foliage—no opening anywhere.

I proceeded: at last my way opened, the trees thinned a little; presently I beheld a railing, then the house—scarce, by this dim light, distinguishable from the trees; so dank and green were its decaying walls. Entering a portal, fastened only by a latch, I stood amidst a space of enclosed ground, from which the wood swept away in a semicircle. There were no flowers, no garden-beds; only a broad gravel-walk girdling a grass-plat, and this set in the heavy frame of the forest. The house presented two pointed gables in its front; the windows were latticed and narrow: the front door was narrow too, one step led up to it. The whole looked, as the host of the Rochester Arms had said, "quite a desolate spot." It was as still as a church on a week-day: the pattering rain on the forest leaves was the only sound audible in its vicinage.

"Can there be life here?" I asked.

Yes, life of some kind there was; for I heard a movement—that narrow front-door was unclosing, and some shape was about to issue from the grange.

It opened slowly: a figure came out into the twilight and stood on the step; a man without a hat: he stretched forth his hand as if to feel whether it rained. Dusk as it was, I had recognized him—it was my master, Edward Fairfax Rochester, and no other.

I stayed my step, almost my breath, and stood to watch him—to examine him, myself unseen, and alas! to him invisible. It was a sudden meeting, and one in which rapture was kept well in check by pain. I had no difficulty in restraining my voice from exclamation, my step from hasty advance.

His form was of the same strong and stalwart contour as ever: his port was still erect, his hair was still raven black; nor were his features altered or sunk: not in one year's space, by any sorrow, could his athletic strength be quelled or his vigorous prime blighted. But in his countenance I saw a change: that looked desperate and brooding—that reminded me of some wronged and fettered wild beast or bird, dangerous to approach in his sullen woe. The caged eagle, whose gold-ringed eyes cruelty has extinguished, might look as looked that sightless Samson.

And, reader, do you think I feared him in his blind ferocity? — if you do, you little know me. A soft hope blest with my sorrow that soon I should dare to drop a kiss on that brow of rock, and on those lips so sternly sealed beneath it: but not yet. I would not accost him yet.

He descended the one step, and advanced slowly and gropingly towards the grass-plat. Where was his daring stride now? Then he paused, as if he knew not which way to turn. He lifted his hand and opened his eyelids; gazed blank, and with a straining effort, on the sky, and toward the amphitheatre of trees: one saw that all to him was void darkness. He stretched his right hand (the left arm, the mutilated one, he kept hidden in his bosom); he seemed to wish by touch to gain an idea of what lay around him: he met but vacancy still; for the trees were some

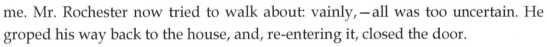

yards off where he stood. He relinquished the endeavour, folded his arms, and stood quiet and mute in the rain, now falling fast on his uncovered head. At this moment John approached him from some quarter.

"Will you take my arm, sir?" he said; "there is a heavy shower coming on: had you not better go in?"

"Let me alone," was the answer.

John withdrew without having observed me. Mr. Rochester now tried to walk about: vainly, — all was too uncertain. He groped his way back to the house, and, re-entering it, closed the door.

I now drew near and knocked: John's wife opened for me. "Mary," I said, "how are you?"

She started as if she had seen a ghost: I calmed her. To her hurried "Is it really you, miss, come at this late hour to this lonely place?" I answered by taking her hand; and then I followed her into the kitchen, where John now sat by a good fire. I explained to them, in few words, that I had heard all which had happened since I left Thornfield, and that I was come to see Mr. Rochester. I asked John to go down to the turn-pike-house, where I had dismissed the chaise, and bring my trunk, which I had left there: and then, while I removed my bonnet and shawl, I questioned Mary as to whether I could be accommodated at the Manor House for the night; and finding that arrangements to that effect, though difficult, would not be impossible, I informed her I should stay. Just at this moment the parlour-bell rang.

"When you go in," said I, "tell your master that a person wishes to speak to him, but do not give my name."

"I don't think he will see you," she answered; "he refuses everybody."

When she returned, I inquired what he had said. "You are to send in your name and your business," she replied. She then proceeded to fill a glass with water, and place it on a tray, together with candles.

"Is that what he rang for?" I asked.

"Yes: he always has candles brought in at dark, though he is blind."

"Give the tray to me; I will carry it in."

I took it from her hand: she pointed me out the parlour door. The tray shook as I held it; the water spilt from the glass; my heart struck my ribs loud and fast. Mary opened the door for me, and shut it behind me.

This parlour looked gloomy: a neglected handful of fire burnt low in the grate; and, leaning over it, with his head supported against the high, old-fashioned mantelpiece, appeared the blind tenant of the room. His old dog, Pilot, lay on one side, removed out of the way, and coiled up as if afraid of being inadvertently trodden upon. Pilot pricked up his ears when I came in: then he jumped up with a yelp and a whine, and bounded towards me: he almost knocked the tray from my hands. I set it on the table; then patted him, and said softly, "Lie down!" Mr. Rochester turned mechanically to see what the commotion was: but as he saw nothing, he returned and sighed. "Give me the water, Mary," he said.

I approached him with the now only half-filled glass; Pilot followed me, still excited.

"What is the matter?" he inquired.

"Down, Pilot!" I again said. He checked the water on its way to his lips, and seemed to listen: he drank, and put the glass down. "This is you, Mary, is it not?"

"Mary is in the kitchen," I answered.

He put out his hand with a quick gesture, but not seeing where I stood, he did not touch me. "Who is this? Who is this?" he demanded, trying, as it seemed, to *see* with those sightless eyes—unavailing and distressing attempt! "Answer me—speak again!" he ordered, imperiously and aloud.

"Will you have a little more water, sir? I spilt half of what was in the glass," I said.

"*Who* is it? *What* is it? Who speaks?"

"Pilot knows me, and John and Mary know I am here. I came only this evening," I answered.

"Great God!—what delusion has come over me? What sweet madness has seized me?"

"No delusion—no madness: your mind, sir, is too strong for delusion, your health too sound for frenzy."

"And where is the speaker? Is it only a voice? Oh! I cannot see, but I must feel, or my heart will stop and my brain burst. Whatever—whoever you are—be perceptible to the touch or I cannot live!"

He groped; I arrested his wandering hand, and prisoned it in both mine.

"Her very fingers!" he cried; "her small, slight fingers! If so there must be more of her."

The muscular hand broke from my custody; my arm was seized, my shoulder—neck—waist—I was entwined and gathered to him.

"Is it Jane? *What* is it? This is her shape—this is her size—"

"And this her voice," I added. "She is all here: her heart, too. God bless you, sir! I am glad to be so near you again."

"Jane Eyre!—Jane Eyre," was all he said.

"My dear master," I answered, "I am Jane Eyre: I have found you out—I am come back to you."

"In truth?—in the flesh? My living Jane?"

"What delusion has come over me? What sweet madness has seized me?"

"You touch me, sir,—you hold me, and fast enough: I am not cold like a corpse, nor vacant like air, am I?"

"My living darling! These are certainly her limbs, and these her features; but I cannot be so blest, after all my misery. It is a dream; such dreams as I have had at night when I have clasped her once more to my heart, as I do now; and kissed her, as thus—and felt that she loved me, and trusted that she would not leave me."

"Which I never will, sir, from this day."

"Never will, says the vision? But I always woke and found it an empty mockery; and I was desolate and abandoned—my life dark, lonely, hopeless—my soul athirst and forbidden to drink—my heart famished and never to be fed. Gentle, soft dream, nestling in my arms now, you will fly, too, as your sisters have all fled before you: but kiss me before you go—embrace me, Jane."

"There, sir—and there!"

I pressed my lips to his once brilliant and now rayless eyes—I swept his hair from his brow, and kissed that too. He suddenly seemed to arouse himself: the conviction of the reality of all this seized him.

"It is you—is it, Jane? You are come back to me then?"

"I am."

"And you do not lie dead in some ditch under some stream? And you are not a pining outcast amongst strangers?"

"No, sir! I am an independent woman now."

"Independent! What do you mean, Jane?"

"My uncle in Madeira is dead, and he left me five thousand pounds."

"Ah! this is practical—this is real!" he cried: "I should never dream that. Besides, there is that peculiar voice of hers, so animating and piquant, as well as soft: it cheers my withered heart; it puts life into it.—What, Jane! Are you an independent woman? A rich woman?"

"If you won't let me live with you, I can build a house of my own close up to your door, and you may come and sit in my parlour when you want company of an evening."

"But as you are rich, Jane, you have now, no doubt, friends who will look after you, and not suffer you to devote yourself to a blind lameter [lame person] like me?"

"I told you I am independent, sir, as well as rich: I am my own mistress."

"And you will stay with me?"

"Certainly—unless you object. I will be your neighbor, your nurse, your housekeeper. I find you lonely: I will be your companion—to read to you, to walk with you, to sit with you, to wait on you, to be eyes and hands to you. Cease to look so melancholy, my dear master; you shall not be left desolate, so long as I live."

He replied not: he seemed serious—abstracted; he sighed; he half-opened his lips as if to speak: he closed them again. I felt a little embarrassed. Perhaps I had too rashly over-leaped conventionalities; and he, like St. John, saw impropriety in my inconsiderateness. I had indeed made my proposal from the idea that he wished and would ask me to be his wife: an expectation, not the less certain because unexpressed, had buoyed me up, that he would claim me at once as his own. But no hint to that effect escaping him and his countenance becoming more overcast, I suddenly remembered that I might have been all wrong, and was perhaps playing the fool unwittingly; and I began gently to withdraw myself from his arms—but he eagerly snatched me closer.

"No—no—Jane; you must not go. No—I have touched you, heard you, felt the comfort of your presence—the sweetness of your consolation: I cannot give up these joys. I have little left in myself—I must have you. The world may laugh—may call me absurd, selfish—but it does not signify. My very soul demands you: it will be satisfied, or it will take deadly vengeance on its frame."

"Well, sir, I will stay with you: I have said so."

"Yes—but you understand one thing by staying with me; and I understand another. You, perhaps, could make up your mind to be about my hand and chair—to wait on me as a kind little nurse (for you have an affectionate heart and a generous spirit, which prompt you to make sacrifices for those you pity), and that ought to suffice for me no doubt. I suppose I should now entertain none but fatherly feelings for you: do you think so?"

"Come—tell me."

"I will think what you like, sir: I am content to be only your nurse, if you think it better."

"But you cannot always be my nurse, Jane, you are young—you must marry one day."

"I don't care about being married."

"You should care, Jane, if I were what I once was, I would try to make you care—but—a sightless block!"

He relapsed again into gloom. I, on the contrary, became more cheerful, and took fresh courage: these last words gave me an insight as to where the difficulty

lay; and as it was no difficulty with me, I felt quite relieved from my previous embarrassment. I resumed a livelier vein of conversation.

"It is time some one undertook to rehumanise you," said I, parting his thick and long uncut locks; "for I see you are being metamorphosed into a lion, or something of that sort. You have a 'faux air' of Nebuchadnezzar in the fields about you, that is certain: your hair reminds me of eagles' feathers; whether your nails are grown like birds' claws or not, I have not yet noticed."

"On this arm, I have neither hand nor nails," he said, drawing the mutilated limb from his breast, and showing it to me. "It is a mere stump—a ghastly sight! Don't you think so, Jane?"

"It is a pity to see it; and a pity to see your eyes—and the scar of fire on your forehead: and the worst of it is, one is in danger of loving you too well for all this; and making too much of you."

"I thought you would be revolted, Jane, when you saw my arm, and my cicatrised [scarred] visage."

"Did you? Don't tell me so—lest I should say something disparaging to your judgment. Now, let me leave you an instant, to make a better fire, and have the hearth swept up. Can you tell when there is a good fire?"

"Yes; with the right eye I see a glow—a ruddy haze."

"And you see the candles?"

"Very dimly—each is a luminous cloud."

"Can you see me?"

"No, my fairy: but I am only too thankful to hear and feel you."

"When do you take supper?"

"I never take supper."

"But you shall have some to-night. I am hungry: so are you, I daresay, only you forget."

Summoning Mary, I soon had the room in more cheerful order: I prepared him, likewise, a comfortable repast. My spirits were excited, and with pleasure and ease I talked to him during supper, and for a long time after. There was no harassing restraint, no repressing of glee and vivacity with him; for with him I was at perfect ease, because I knew I suited him; all I said or did seemed either to console or revive him. Delightful consciousness! It brought to life and light my whole nature: in his presence I thoroughly lived; and he lived in mine. Blind as he was, smiles played over his face, joy dawned on his forehead: his lineaments softened and warmed.

After supper, he began to ask me many questions, of where I had been, what I had been doing, how I had found him out; but I gave him only very partial replies: it was too late to enter into particulars that night. Besides, I wished to touch no deep-thrilling chord—to open no fresh well of emotion in his heart: my sole present aim was to cheer him. Cheered, as I have said, he was: and yet but by fits. If a moment's silence broke the conversation, he would turn restless, touch me, then say, "Jane."

"You are altogether a human being, Jane? You are certain of that?"

"I conscientiously believe so, Mr. Rochester."

"Yet how, on this dark and doleful evening, could you so suddenly rise on my lone hearth? I stretched my hand to take a glass of water from a hireling, and it was given me by you: I asked a question, expecting John's wife to answer me, and your voice spoke at my ear."

"Because I had come in, in Mary's stead, with the tray."

"And there is enchantment in the very hour I am now spending with you. Who can tell what a dark, dreary, hopeless life I have dragged on for months past? Doing nothing, expecting nothing; merging night in day; feeling but the sensation of cold when I let the fire go out, of hunger when I forgot to eat: and then a ceaseless sorrow, and, at times, a very delirium of desire to behold my Jane again. Yes: for her restoration I longed, far more than for that of my lost sight. How can it be that Jane is with me, and says she loves me? Will she not depart as suddenly as she came? To-morrow, I fear I shall find her no more."

A commonplace, practical reply, out of the train of his own disturbed ideas, was, I was sure, the best and most reassuring for him in this frame of mind. I passed my finger over his eyebrows, and remarked that they were scorched, and that I would apply something which would make them grow as broad and black as ever.

"Where is the use of doing me good in any way, beneficent spirit, when, at some fatal moment, you will again desert me — passing like a shadow, whither and how to me unknown, and for me remaining afterwards undiscoverable?

"Have you a pocket-comb about you, sir?"

"What for, Jane?"

"Just to comb out this shaggy black mane. I find you rather alarming, when I examine you close at hand: you talk of my being a fairy, but I am sure, you are more like a brownie."

"Am I hideous, Jane?"

"Very, sir: you always were, you know."

"Humph! The wickedness has not been taken out of you, wherever you have sojourned."

"Yet I have been with good people; far better than you: a hundred times better people; possessed of ideas and views you never entertained in your life: quite more refined and exalted."

"Who the deuce have you been with?"

"If you twist in that way you will make me pull the hair out of your head; and then I think you will cease to entertain doubts of my substantiality."

"Who have you been with, Jane?"

"You shall not get it out of me to-night, sir; you must wait till to-morrow; to leave my tale half told, will, you know, be a sort of security that I shall appear at your breakfast table to finish it. By the bye, I must mind not to rise on your hearth with only a glass of water then: I must bring an egg at the least, to say nothing of fried ham."

"You mocking changeling—fairy-born and human-bred! You make me feel as I have not felt these twelve months. If Saul could have had you for his David, the evil spirit would have been exorcised without the aid of the harp."

"There, sir, you are redd up and made decent. Now I'll leave you: I have been travelling these last three days, and I believe I am tired. Good night."

"Just one word, Jane: were there only ladies in the house where you have been?"

I laughed and made my escape, still laughing as I ran upstairs. "A good idea!" I thought with glee. "I see I have the means of fretting him out of his melancholy for some time to come."

Very early the next morning I heard him up and astir, wandering from one room to another. As soon as Mary came down I heard the question: "Is Miss Eyre here?" Then: "Which room did you put her into? Was it dry? Is she up? Go and ask if she wants anything; and when she will come down."

I came down as soon as I thought there was a prospect of breakfast. Entering the room very softly, I had a view of him before he discovered my presence. It was mournful, indeed, to witness the subjugation of that vigorous spirit to a corporeal infirmity. He sat in his chair—still, but not at rest: expectant evidently; the lines of now habitual sadness marking his strong features. His countenance reminded one of a lamp quenched, waiting to be relit—and alas! it was not himself that could now kindle the lustre of animated expression: he was dependent on another for that office! I had meant to be gay and careless, but the powerlessness of the strong man touched my heart to the quick: still I accosted him with what vivacity I could.

"It is a bright, sunny morning, sir," I said. "The rain is over and gone, and there is a tender shining after it: you shall have a walk soon."

I had wakened the glow: his features beamed.

"Oh, you are indeed there, my skylark! Come to me. You are not gone: not vanished? I heard one of your kind an hour ago, singing high over the wood: but its song had no music for me, any more than the rising sun had rays. All the melody on earth is concentrated in my Jane's tongue to my ear (I am glad it is not naturally a silent one): all the sunshine I can feel is in her presence."

The water stood in my eyes to hear this avowal of his dependence; just as if a royal eagle, chained to a perch, should be forced to entreat a sparrow to become its purveyor. But I would not be lachrymose: I dashed off the salt drops, and busied myself with preparing breakfast.

Most of the morning was spent in the open air. I led him out of the wet and wild wood into some cheerful fields: I described to him how brilliantly green they were; how the flowers and hedges looked refreshed; how sparklingly blue was the sky. I sought a seat for him in a hidden and lovely spot, a dry stump of a tree; nor did I refuse to let him, when seated, place me on his knee. Why should I, when both he and I were happier near than apart?

Pilot lay beside us: all was quiet. He broke out suddenly while clasping me in his arms—

"Cruel, cruel deserter! Oh, Jane, what did I feel when I discovered you had fled from Thornfield, and when I could nowhere find you; and, after examining your apartment, ascertained that you had taken no money, nor anything which could serve as an equivalent! A pearl necklace I had given you lay untouched in its little casket; your trunks were left corded and locked as they had been prepared for the bridal tour. What could my darling do, I asked, left destitute and penniless? And what did she do? Let me hear now."

Thus urged, I began the narrative of my experience for the last year. I softened considerably what related to the three days of wandering and starvation, because to have told him all would have been to inflict unnecessary pain: the little I did say lacerated his faithful heart deeper than I wished.

I should not have left him thus, he said, without any means of making my way: I should have told him my intention. I should have confided in him: he would never have forced me to be his mistress. Violent as he had seemed in his despair, he, in truth, loved me far too well and too tenderly to constitute himself my tyrant: he would have given me half his fortune, without demanding so much as a kiss in return, rather than I should have flung myself friendless on the wide world. I had endured, he was certain, more than I had confessed to him.

"Well, whatever my sufferings had been, they were very short," I answered and then I proceeded to tell him how I had been received at Moor House; how I had obtained the office of schoolmistress, &c. The accession of fortune, the discovery of my relations, followed in due order. Of course, St. John Rivers' name came in frequently in the progress of my tale. When I had done, that name was immediately taken up.

"This St. John, then, is your cousin?"

"Yes."

"You have spoken of him often: do you like him?"

"He was a very good man, sir; I could not help liking him."

"A good man. Does that mean a respectable well-conducted man of fifty? Or what does it mean?"

"St John was only twenty-nine, sir."

"'*Jeune encore*,' as the French say. Is he a person of low stature, phlegmatic, and plain? A person whose goodness consists rather in his guiltlessness of vice, than in his prowess in virtue?"

"He is untiringly active. Great and exalted deeds are what he lives to perform."

"But his brain? That is probably rather soft? He means well: but you shrug your shoulders to hear him talk?"

"He talks little, sir: what he does say is ever to the point. His brain is first-rate, I should think not impressible, but vigorous."

"Is he an able man, then?"

"Truly able."

"A thoroughly educated man?"

"St. John is an accomplished and profound scholar."

"His manners, I think, you said are not to your taste?—priggish and parsonic?"

"I never mentioned his manners; but, unless I had a very bad taste, they must suit it; they are polished, calm, and gentlemanlike."

"His appearance,—I forget what description you gave of his appearance;—a sort of raw curate, half strangled with his white neckcloth, and stilted up on his thick-soled high-lows, eh?"

"St. John dresses well. He is a handsome man: tall, fair, with blue eyes, and a Grecian profile."

(Aside.) "D--- him!" — (To me.) "Did you like him, Jane?"

"Yes, Mr. Rochester, I liked him: but you asked me that before."

I perceived, of course, the drift of my interlocutor. Jealousy had got hold of him: she stung him; but the sting was salutary: it gave him respite from the gnawing fang of melancholy. I would not, therefore, immediately charm the snake.

"Perhaps you would rather not sit any longer on my knee, Miss Eyre?" was the next somewhat unexpected observation.

"Why not, Mr. Rochester?"

"The picture you have just drawn is suggestive of a rather too overwhelming contrast. Your words have delineated very prettily a graceful Apollo: he is present to your imagination, — tall, fair, blue-eyed, and with a Grecian profile. Your eyes dwell on a Vulcan, — a real blacksmith, brown, broad-shouldered: and blind and lame into the bargain."

"I never thought of it, before; but you certainly are rather like Vulcan, sir."

"Well, you can leave me, ma'am: but before you go" (and he retained me by a firmer grasp than ever), "you will be pleased just to answer me a question or two." He paused.

"What questions, Mr. Rochester?"

Then followed this cross-examination.

"St. John made you schoolmistress of Morton before he knew you were his cousin?"

"Yes."

"You would often see him? He would visit the school sometimes?"

"Daily."

"He would approve of your plans, Jane? I know they would be clever, for you are a talented creature!"

"He approved of them — yes."

"He would discover many things in you he could not have expected to find? Some of your accomplishments are not ordinary."

"I don't know about that."

"You had a little cottage near the school, you say: did he ever come there to see you?"

"Now and then?"

"Of an evening?"

"Once or twice."

A pause.

"How long did you reside with him and his sisters after the cousinship was discovered?"

"Five months."

"Did Rivers spend much time with the ladies of his family?"

"Yes; the back parlour was both his study and ours: he sat near the window, and we by the table."

"Did he study much?"

"A good deal."

"What?"

"Hindostanee."

"And what did you do meantime?"

"I learnt German, at first."

"Did he teach you?"

"He did not understand German."

"Did he teach you nothing?"

"A little Hindostanee."

"Rivers taught you Hindostanee?"

"Yes, sir."

"And his sisters also?"

"No."

"Only you?"

"Only me."

"Did you ask to learn?"

"No."

"He wished to teach you?"

"Yes."

A second pause.

"Why did he wish it? Of what use could Hindostanee be to you?"

"He intended me to go with him to India."

"Ah! here I reach the root of the matter. He wanted you to marry him?"

"He asked me to marry him."

"That is a fiction—an impudent invention to vex me."

"I beg your pardon, it is the literal truth: he asked me more than once, and was as stiff about urging his point as ever you could be."

"Miss Eyre, I repeat it, you can leave me. How often am I to say the same thing? Why do you remain pertinaciously perched on my knee, when I have given you notice to quit?"

"Because I am comfortable there."

"No, Jane, you are not comfortable there, because your heart is not with me: it is with this cousin—this St. John. Oh, till this moment, I thought my little Jane was all mine! I had a belief she loved me even when she left me: that was an atom of sweet in much bitter. Long as we have been parted, hot tears as I have wept over our separation, I never thought that while I was mourning her, she was loving another! But it is useless grieving. Jane, leave me: go and marry Rivers."

"Shake me off, then, sir,—push me away, for I'll not leave you of my own accord."

"Jane, I ever like your tone of voice: it still renews hope, it sounds so truthful. When I hear it, it carries me back a year. I forget that you have formed a new tie. But I am not a fool—go—"

"Where must I go, sir?"

"Your own way—with the husband you have chosen."

"Who is that?"

"You know—this St. John Rivers."

"He is not my husband, nor ever will be. He does not love me: I do not love him. He loves (as he can love, and that is not as you love) a beautiful young lady called Rosamond. He wanted to marry me only because he thought I should make a suitable missionary's wife, which she would not have done. He is good and great, but severe; and, for me, cold as an iceberg. He is not like you, sir: I am not happy at his side, nor near him, nor with him. He has no indulgence for me—no fondness. He sees nothing attractive in me; not even youth—only a few useful mental points.—Then I must leave you, sir, to go to him?"

I shuddered involuntarily, and clung instinctively closer to my blind but beloved master. He smiled.

"What, Jane! Is this true? Is such really the state of matters between you and Rivers?"

"Absolutely, sir! Oh, you need not be jealous! I wanted to tease you a little to make you less sad: I thought anger would be better than grief. But if you wish me to love you, could you but see how much I do love you, you would be proud and content. All my heart is yours, sir: it belongs to you; and with you it would remain, were fate to exile the rest of me from your presence for ever."

Again, as he kissed me, painful thoughts darkened his aspect.

"My seared vision! My crippled strength!" he murmured regretfully.

I caressed, in order to soothe him. I knew of what he was thinking, and wanted to speak for him, but dared not. As he turned aside his face a minute, I saw a tear slide from under the sealed eyelid, and trickle down the manly cheek. My heart swelled.

"I am no better than the old lightning-struck chestnut-tree in Thornfield orchard," he remarked ere long. "And what right would that ruin have to bid a budding woodbine cover its decay with freshness?"

"You are no ruin, sir—no lightning-struck tree: you are green and vigorous. Plants will grow about your roots, whether you ask them or not, because they take delight in your bountiful shadow; and as they grow they will lean towards you, and wind round you, because your strength offers them so safe a prop."

Again he smiled: I gave him comfort. "You speak of friends, Jane?" he asked.

"Yes, of friends," I answered rather hesitatingly: for I knew I meant more than friends, but could not tell what other word to employ. He helped me.

"Ah! Jane. But I want a wife."

"Do you, sir?"

"Yes: is it news to you?"

"Of course: you said nothing about it before."

"Is it unwelcome news?"

"That depends on circumstances, sir—on your choice."

"Which you shall make for me, Jane. I will abide by your decision."

"Choose then, sir—her who loves you best."

"I will at least choose—her I love best. Jane, will you marry me?"

"Yes, sir."

"A poor blind man, whom you will have to lead about by the hand?"

"Yes, sir."

"A crippled man, twenty years older than you, whom you will have to wait on?"

"Yes, sir."

"Truly, Jane?"

"Most truly, sir."

"Oh! my darling! God bless you and reward you!"

"Mr. Rochester, if ever I did a good deed in my life—if ever I thought a good thought—if ever I prayed a sincere and blameless prayer—if ever I wished a righteous wish,—I am rewarded now. To be your wife is, for me, to be as happy as I can be on earth."

"Because you delight in sacrifice."

"Sacrifice! What do I sacrifice? Famine for food, expectation for content. To be privileged to put my arms round what I value—to press my lips to what I love—to repose on what I trust: is that to make a sacrifice? If so, then certainly I delight in sacrifice."

"And to bear with my infirmities, Jane: to overlook my deficiencies."

"Which are none, sir, to me. I love you better now, when I can really be useful to you, than I did in your state of proud independence, when you disdained every part but that of the giver and protector."

"Hitherto I have hated to be helped—to be led: henceforth, I feel I shall hate it no more. I did not like to put my hand into a hireling's, but it is pleasant to feel it circled by Jane's little fingers. I preferred utter loneliness to the constant attendance of servants; but Jane's soft ministry will be a perpetual joy. Jane suits me: do I suit her?"

"To the finest fiber of my nature, sir."

"The case being so, we have nothing in the world to wait for: we must be married instantly."

He looked and spoke with eagerness: his old impetuosity was rising.

"We must become one flesh without any delay, Jane: there is but the license to get—then we marry."

"Mr. Rochester, I have just discovered the sun is far declined from its meridian, and Pilot is actually gone home to his dinner. Let me look at your watch."

"Fasten it into your girdle, Janet, and keep it henceforward: I have no use for it."

"It is nearly four o'clock in the afternoon, sir. Don't you feel hungry?"

"The third day from this must be our wedding-day, Jane. Never mind fine clothes and jewels, now: all that is not worth a fillip."

"The sun has dried up all the rain-drops, sir. The breeze is still: it is quite hot."

"Do you know, Jane, I have your little pearl necklace at this moment fastened round my bronze scrag under my cravat? I have worn it since the day I lost my only treasure, as a memento of her."

"We will go home through the wood: that will be the shadiest way."
He pursued his own thoughts without heeding me.

"Jane! you think me, I daresay, an irreligious dog: but my heart swells with gratitude to the beneficent God of this earth just now. . . . I began to experience remorse, repentance; the wish for reconcilement to my Maker. I began sometimes to pray."

"Jane! you think me, I daresay, an irreligious dog: but my heart swells with gratitude to the beneficent God of this earth just now. He sees not as man sees, but far clearer: judges not as man judges, but far more wisely. I did wrong: I would have sullied my innocent flower—breathed guilt on its purity: the Omnipotent snatched it from me. I, in my stiff-necked rebellion, almost cursed the dispensation: instead of bending to the decree, I defied it. Divine justice pursued its course; disasters came thick on me: I was forced to pass through the valley of the shadow of death. His chastisements are mighty; and one smote me which has humbled me for ever. You know I was proud of my strength: but what is it now, when I must give it over to foreign guidance, as a child does its weakness? Of late, Jane—only—only of late—I began to see and acknowledge the hand of God in my doom. I began to experience remorse, repentance; the wish for reconcilement to my Maker. I began sometimes to pray: very brief prayers they were, but very sincere.

"Some days since: nay, I can number them—four; it was last Monday night, a singular mood came over me: one in which grief replaced frenzy—sorrow, sullenness. I had long had the impression that since I could nowhere find you, you must be dead. Late that night—perhaps it might be between eleven and twelve o'clock—ere I retired to my dreary rest, I supplicated God, that, if it seemed good to Him, I might soon be taken from this life, and admitted to that world to come, where there was still hope of rejoining Jane.

"That I merited all I endured, I acknowledged – that I could scarcely endure more, I pleaded; and the alpha and omega of my heart's wishes broke involuntarily from my lips in the words – 'Jane! Jane! Jane!'"

"I was in my own room, and sitting by the window, which was open: it soothed me to feel the balmy night-air; though I could see no stars and only by a vague, luminous haze, knew the presence of a moon. I longed for thee, Jane! Oh, I longed for thee both with soul and flesh! I asked of God, at once in anguish and humility, if I had not been long enough desolate, afflicted, tormented; and might not soon taste bliss and peace once more. That I merited all I endured, I acknowledged—that I could scarcely endure more, I pleaded; and the alpha and omega of my heart's wishes broke involuntarily from my lips in the words—'Jane! Jane! Jane!'"

"Did you speak these words aloud?"

"I did, Jane. If any listener had heard me, he would have thought me mad: I pronounced them with such frantic energy."

"And it was last Monday night, somewhere near midnight?"

"Yes; but the time is of no consequence: what followed is the strange point. You will think me superstitious,—some superstition I have in my blood, and always had: nevertheless, this is true—true at least it is that I heard what I now relate.

"As I exclaimed 'Jane! Jane! Jane!' a voice—I cannot tell whence the voice came, but I know whose voice it was—replied, 'I am coming: wait for me;' and a moment after, went whispering on the wind the words—'Where are you?'

"I'll tell you, if I can, the idea, the picture these words opened to my mind: yet it is difficult to express what I want to express. Ferndean is buried, as you see, in a heavy wood, where sound falls dull, and dies unreverberating. 'Where are you?' seemed spoken amongst mountains; for I heard a hill-sent echo repeat the words. Cooler and fresher at the moment the gale seemed to visit my brow: I could have deemed that in some wild, lone scene, I and Jane were meeting. In spirit, I believe we must have met. You no doubt were, at that hour, in unconscious sleep, Jane: perhaps your soul wandered from its cell to comfort mine; for those were your accents—as certain as I live—they were yours!"

Reader, it was on Monday night—near midnight—that I too had received the mysterious summons: those were the very words by which I replied to it. I listened to Mr. Rochester's narrative, but made no disclosure in return. The coincidence struck me as too awful and inexplicable to be communicated or discussed. If I told anything, my tale would be such as must necessarily make a 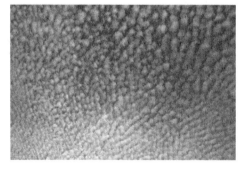 profound impression on the mind of my hearer: and that mind, yet from its sufferings too prone to gloom, needed not the deeper shade of the supernatural. I kept these things then, and pondered them in my heart.

"You cannot now wonder," continued my master, "that when you rose upon me so unexpectedly last night, I had difficulty in believing you any other than a mere voice and vision, something that would melt to silence and annihilation, as the midnight whisper and mountain echo had melted before. Now, I thank God! I know it to be otherwise. Yes, I thank God!"

He put me off his knee, rose, and reverently lifting his hat from his brow, and bending his sightless eyes to the earth, he stood in mute devotion. Only the last words of the worship were audible.

"I thank my Maker, that, in the midst of judgment, he has remembered mercy. I humbly entreat my Redeemer to give me strength to lead henceforth a purer life than I have done hitherto!"

Then he stretched his hand out to be led. I took that dear hand, held it a moment to my lips, then let it pass round my shoulder: being so much lower of stature than he, I served both for his prop and guide. We entered the wood, and wended homeward.

Comments on Jane Eyre

The writer has us by the hand, forces us along her road, makes us see what she sees, never leaves us for a moment or allows us to forget her. At the end we are steeped through and through with the genius, the vehemence, the indignation of Charlotte Brontë. Remarkable faces, figures of strong outline and gnarled feature have flashed upon us in passing; but it is through her eyes that we have seen them. —Virginia Woolf

Tone in the Bible

Sisera and Deborah: Judges 4

This story provides situational irony: Deborah, a supposedly powerless woman, leads the nation of Israel; and Jael, a supposedly powerless woman, does away with Sisera. It

also offers dramatic irony: Sisera's mother tragically waits for her son to return, but he is dead.

Again the Israelites did evil in the eyes of the LORD, now that Ehud was dead. So the LORD sold them into the hands of Jabin king of Canaan, who reigned in Hazor. Sisera, the commander of his army, was based in Harosheth Haggoyim. Because he had nine hundred chariots fitted with iron and had cruelly oppressed the Israelites for twenty years, they cried to the LORD for help.

Now Deborah, a prophet, the wife of Lappidoth, was leading Israel at that time. She held court under the Palm of Deborah between Ramah and Bethel in the hill country of Ephraim, and the Israelites went up to her to have their disputes decided. She sent for Barak son of Abinoam from Kedesh in Naphtali and said to him, "The LORD, the God of Israel, commands you: 'Go, take with you ten thousand men of Naphtali and Zebulun and lead them up to Mount Tabor. I will lead Sisera, the commander of Jabin's army, with his chariots and his troops to the Kishon River and give him into your hands.'"

Barak said to her, "If you go with me, I will go; but if you don't go with me, I won't go."

"Certainly I will go with you," said Deborah. "But because of the course you are taking, the honor will not be yours, for the LORD will deliver Sisera into the hands of a woman." So Deborah went with Barak to Kedesh. There Barak summoned Zebulun and Naphtali, and ten thousand men went up under his command. Deborah also went up with him.

Now Heber the Kenite had left the other Kenites, the descendants of Hobab, Moses' brother-in-law, and pitched his tent by the great tree in Zaanannim near Kedesh.

When they told Sisera that Barak son of Abinoam had gone up to Mount Tabor, Sisera summoned from Harosheth Haggoyim to the Kishon River all his men and his nine hundred chariots fitted with iron.

Then Deborah said to Barak, "Go! This is the day the LORD has given Sisera into your hands. Has not the LORD gone ahead of you?" So Barak went down Mount Tabor, with ten thousand men following him. At Barak's advance, the LORD routed Sisera and all his chariots and army by the sword, and Sisera got down from his chariot and fled on foot.

Barak pursued the chariots and army as far as Harosheth Haggoyim, and all Sisera's troops fell by the sword; not a man was left. Sisera, meanwhile, fled on foot to the tent of Jael, the wife of Heber the Kenite, because there was an alliance between Jabin king of Hazor and the family of Heber the Kenite.

Jael went out to meet Sisera and said to him, "Come, my lord, come right in. Don't be afraid." So he entered her tent, and she covered him with a blanket.

"I'm thirsty," he said. "Please give me some water." She opened a skin of milk, gave him a drink, and covered him up.

"Stand in the doorway of the tent," he told her. "If someone comes by and asks you, 'Is anyone in there?' say 'No.'"

But Jael, Heber's wife, picked up a tent peg and a hammer and went quietly to him while he lay fast asleep, exhausted. She drove the peg through his temple into the ground, and he died.

Just then Barak came by in pursuit of Sisera, and Jael went out to meet him. "Come," she said, "I will show you the man you're looking for." So he went in with her, and there lay Sisera with the tent peg through his temple—dead.

On that day God subdued Jabin king of Canaan before the Israelites. And the hand of the Israelites pressed harder and harder against Jabin king of Canaan until they destroyed him.

"The singers . . . recite the victories of the LORD." (Judges 5:10)

Legalism: Galatians 3

Paul is angry with the Galatians because they have rejected the freedom of the gospel and embraced a new form of legalism. This book is one of the most vitriolic in the Bible.

You foolish Galatians! Who has bewitched you? Before your very eyes Jesus Christ was clearly portrayed as crucified. I would like to learn just one thing from you: Did you receive the Spirit by the works of the law, or by believing what you heard? Are you so foolish? After beginning by means of the Spirit, are you now trying to finish by means of the flesh? Have you experienced so much in vain—if it really was in vain? So again I ask, does God give you his Spirit and work miracles among you by the works of the law, or by your believing what you heard? So also Abraham "believed God, and it was credited to him as righteousness."

Understand, then, that those who have faith are children of Abraham. Scripture foresaw that God would justify the Gentiles by faith, and announced the gospel in advance to Abraham: "All nations will be blessed through you." So those who rely on faith are blessed along with Abraham, the man of faith.

For all who rely on the works of the law are under a curse, as it is written: "Cursed is everyone who does not continue to do everything written in the Book of the Law." Clearly no one who relies on the law is justified before God, because "the righteous will live by faith." The law is not based on faith; on the contrary, it says, "The person who does these things will live by them." Christ redeemed us from the curse of the law by becoming a curse for us, for it is written: "Cursed is everyone who is hung on a pole." He redeemed us in order that the blessing given to Abraham might come to the Gentiles through Christ Jesus, so that by faith we might receive the promise of the Spirit.

Brothers and sisters, let me take an example from everyday life. Just as no one can set aside or add to a human covenant that has been duly established, so it is in this case. The promises were spoken to Abraham and to his seed. Scripture does not say "and to seeds," meaning many people, but "and to your seed," meaning one person, who is Christ. What I mean is this: The law, introduced 430 years later, does not set aside the covenant previously established by God and thus do away with the promise. For if the inheritance depends on the law, then it no longer depends on the promise; but God in his grace gave it to Abraham through a promise.

Why, then, was the law given at all? It was added because of transgressions until the Seed to whom the promise referred had come. The law was given through angels and entrusted to a mediator. A mediator, however, implies more than one party; but God is one.

The Ten Commandments, as in Exodus 20:1–17; 24:12

Is the law, therefore, opposed to the promises of God? Absolutely not! For if a law had been given that could impart life, then righteousness would certainly have come by the law. But Scripture has locked up everything under the control of sin, so that what was promised, being given through faith in Jesus Christ, might be given to those who believe.

Before the coming of this faith, we were held in custody under the law, locked up until the faith that was to come would be revealed. So the law was our guardian until Christ came that we might be justified by faith. Now that this faith has come, we are no longer under a guardian.

So in Christ Jesus you are all children of God through faith, for all of you who were baptized into Christ have clothed yourselves with Christ. There is neither Jew nor Gentile, neither slave nor free, nor is there male and female, for you are all one in Christ Jesus. If you belong to Christ, then you are Abraham's seed, and heirs according to the promise.

Love Song: Song of Solomon 1

She

> Let him kiss me with the kisses of his mouth —
>> for your love is more delightful than wine.
> Pleasing is the fragrance of your perfumes;
>> your name is like perfume poured out.
>> No wonder the young women love you!
> Take me away with you — let us hurry!
>> Let the king bring me into his chambers.

>> *Friends*
> We rejoice and delight in you;
>> we will praise your love more than wine.

She

> How right they are to adore you!
> Dark am I, yet lovely,
>> daughters of Jerusalem,
> dark like the tents of Kedar,
>> like the tent curtains of Solomon.
> Do not stare at me because I am dark,
>> because I am darkened by the sun.
> My mother's sons were angry with me
>> and made me take care of the vineyards;
>> my own vineyard I had to neglect.
> Tell me, you whom I love,

where you graze your flock
and where you rest your sheep at midday.
Why should I be like a veiled woman
beside the flocks of your friends?

Friends

If you do not know, most beautiful of women,
follow the tracks of the sheep
and graze your young goats
by the tents of the shepherds.

He

I liken you, my darling, to a mare
among Pharaoh's chariot horses.
Your cheeks are beautiful with earrings,
your neck with strings of jewels.
We will make you earrings of gold,
studded with silver.

She

While the king was at his table,
my perfume spread its fragrance.
My beloved is to me a sachet of myrrh
resting between my breasts.
My beloved is to me a cluster of henna blossoms
from the vineyards of En Gedi.

He

How beautiful you are, my darling!
Oh, how beautiful!
Your eyes are doves.

She

How handsome you are, my beloved!
Oh, how charming!
And our bed is verdant.

He

The beams of our house are cedars;
our rafters are firs.

Adoration and Praise: Psalm 150

Praise the LORD.

Praise God in his sanctuary;
    praise him in his mighty heavens.
Praise him for his acts of power;
    praise him for his surpassing greatness.
Praise him with the sounding of the trumpet,
    praise him with the harp and lyre,
praise him with timbrel and dancing,
    praise him with the strings and pipe,
praise him with the clash of cymbals,
    praise him with resounding cymbals.
Let everything that has breath praise the LORD.
Praise the LORD.

Drama

Unlike prose fiction (novels, short stories) and poetry, drama is to be performed, and the creation of a play performance is a joint work, involving input from producers, directors, actors, choreographers, and in some cases, such as Tennessee Williams's *The Glass Menagerie*, the audience. Even though a play has a written script, every performance of a play is different, involving a unique interpretation of the play text. Casting, set and costume design, the "blocking" or physical interaction of the actors, and the timing, phrasing, and tone of every speech affect the outcome. Prose fiction and poetry do not allow for such interpretative latitude.

Generally speaking drama has no point of view, no narrator. This is significantly different from prose fiction.  Description in drama is determined by stage directions, the set, characters, and props.

In prose fiction, exposition may occur in any number of different milieus, such as dialogue, narrative descriptions, plot action, and so forth. In drama, exposition generally emerges only through dialogue. In other words, the story, unless it is mime, is told by the characters to other characters.

A character is an imaginary person who takes part in the action of a play. Drama tends to simplify the personalities of characters, often relying on stereotypes quickly to reveal and draw contrasts among characters. A playwright does not have 400 pages to tell his story. He needs to identify and to develop all his literary elements with a few lines, or he will lose his audience.

In drama, plot is more important than it is in prose fiction. As one critic explains, the plot is "the invention, selection, and arrangement of action, unified by a sense of purpose that joins character, story line, and theme. Conflict shapes the dramatic structure of a play. In dramatic conflict, each of the opposing forces must at some point seem likely to triumph or be worthy of triumph.

Many plays have formal divisions, such as acts and scenes, that develop the plot. Many older plays, such as those by Shakespeare, have five acts, but modern plays tend to have two or three acts.

Most plays are structured to leave time for a break, or intermission, in the performance. In prose fiction this is not necessary. Time is controlled by the reader. Not so with drama. The audience is dependent upon the largesse of the playwright.

The Norton Anthology of Drama states, "There are many types of modern stages, including the traditional proscenium stage, the thrust stage (where an audience sits around three sides of the major acting area), and the arena stage (where an audience sits all the way around the acting area). Most plays are performed on proscenium stages. Older theatrical traditions made use of other kinds of stages, including the amphitheater of Greek theater, in which the audience sat in a raised semicircle around a circular orchestra and recessed stage area; and the stage of Shakespeare's age, which was something like a thrust stage. Before the modern period, plays were performed outdoors in the daylight and involved few pieces of scenery and little furniture or costume design."

Prose fiction has remained the same, more or less, since a Japanese concubine wrote the first novel two thousand years ago, and Homer wrote his long narrative poem, three thousand years ago. Theater has changed over time. In modern theater, sets and props may be realistic or bizarre (e.g., *Godspell*) and have no context at all in the plot.

The conventions of ancient Greek drama stipulated that playwrights adhere to the classical unities, or the unity of time, unity of place, and unity of action. Plays were supposed to represent a unified action that occurred over a short span of time (sometimes during the actual performance time) and in a single location. Modern plays often make use of multiple settings and jumps in time.

Gaps in time and changes in setting are often indicated by dialogue, scene breaks, changes in scenery, sound effects, stage directions, or notes in the program. Today most playwrights ignore convention and protocol. They write whatever they like; in fact, the more bizarre and sensational the set, the better. For instance, in the early part of the twenty-first century, Broadway offered *Spiderman*, whose special effects were extraordinary but whose plot and theme were weak indeed.

A play's tone is its style or manner of expression, which is a tricky thing to produce and to maintain. Actors and actresses must infer from the script how a line should be read and what tone of voice it demands. Directors help the characters in their interpretations. Tone can be affected by dramatic irony, in which a character's knowledge or expectation is contradicted by what the audience knows. Situational irony in drama, as in prose fiction, occurs when the outcome of the action contradicts the characters' and audience's expectations. Verbal irony occurs when speech and action don't match or the audience discerns a special meaning the actor doesn't realize.

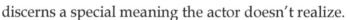

Monologues or soliloquies (discussed earlier) and lengthy speeches by one character often contain important images, metaphors, and other figures of speech. Actions, objects, and character names can hold symbolic significance. This is especially true in Richard Sheridan's masterpiece The Rivals.

Well-written plays often use props as metaphors, allowing objects to carry symbolic weight and convey key thematic points. For example, the dagger is a powerful metaphor in Shakespeare's *Macbeth*.

Theme more or less emerges the same way as it does in prose fiction. However, since theme is so dependent upon audience enlightenment and response, theme harvests can contain many mutated meanings.

Drama, like other genres of literature, has various subgenres, including pastoral plays, comedies, and satires.

Two of the oldest forms of drama are tragedy and comedy. In tragedy, values are universal and beyond human control. Tragedies tend to focus on a person of high rank with some sort of character flaw or limitation. For example, Oedipus is the victim of his hubris and fate. Tragedies end with the character's enlightenment and acceptance of punishment, often death.

In comedy, values are determined by the general opinion of society, an early manifestation of Kantian situational ethics, and therefore characters are defined primarily by their social roles. These social roles, of course, are valued differently by different generations. Hamlet's struggle concerning suicide seems entirely logical to a sixteenth-century audience but may seem silly to a narcissistic twenty-first-century audience.

Student Essays

Tone in Stephen Crane's *The Red Badge of Courage*

Stephen Crane's *The Red Badge of Courage*, with tone and style, highlights the pitilessness of the world that surrounds his characters. While his protagonist, Henry, is still in his unenlightened Romantic state, Crane utilizes surprisingly ordinary language to depict horrible scenes. However, when Henry turns to Naturalism, Crane's tone becomes much more precise and graphic as he details the thoughts of his newly enlightened protagonist.

When Henry tells his mother that he has enlisted, he expects his mother dramatically to beg her son not to leave and to acknowledge his bravery and sacrifice. Instead, she is surprisingly calm.

> Still, she had disappointed him by saying nothing whatever about returning with his shield or on it. He had privately primed himself for a beautiful scene. He had prepared certain sentences which he thought could be used with touching effect. But her words destroyed his plans. She had doggedly peeled potatoes and addressed him as follows: "You watch out, Henry, an' take good care of yerself in this here fighting business—you watch, an' take good care of yerself. Don't go a-thinkin' you can lick the hull rebel army at the start, because yeh can't. Yer jest one little feller amongst a hull lot of others, and yeh've got to keep quiet an' do what they tell yeh. I know how you are, Henry."

Crane paints the pathos of Henry's mother's grief with cold simplicity of style and rugged colloquial language. Instead of making her a classical heroine bravely saying good-bye to her "soldier boy," Crane depicts with rugged language and simplicity of style the pathos of the moment that Henry must say good-bye to his mother.

However, when Henry changes his views to that of a naturalist, Crane changes his tone and style. It progresses from cold, colloquial, and unfeeling to precise, educated, and emotional.

> It seemed to the youth that he saw everything. Each blade of the green grass was bold and clear. He thought that he was aware of every change in the thin, transparent vapor that floated idly in sheets. The brown or gray trunks of the trees showed each roughness of their surfaces. And the men of the regiment, with their starting eyes and sweating faces, running madly, or falling, as if thrown headlong, to queer, heaped-up corpses—all were comprehended. His mind took a mechanical but firm impression, so that afterward everything was pictured and explained to him, save why he himself was there.

As Henry gradually completes his transformation from Romantic to naturalist, Stephen Crane's writing style also undergoes transformation.

Henry Fleming, the protagonist of Stephen Crane's novel, transforms from a Romantic to a naturalist. Crane depicts this transformation by using his writing style, which progresses from cold, colloquial, and unfeeling to precise, educated, and emotional.

Feelings of Evil in Tolkien's *Lord of the Rings*

Wastelands have often been used in literature to indicate barren, evil souls. J. R. R. Tolkien uses this method to great effect in his novels of *The Lord of the Rings* trilogy. The realms of the two great evil lords, Sauron and Saruman, are barren wastes that are completely devoid of vegetation. There is no evil place in which anything green and good grows. This can be compared to an evil soul, in which no good fruit grows.

The land of Mordor, realm of the dark lord Sauron, the chief evil in Middle Earth, is a barren place. The ground is rocky, the air is poisonous, and the atmosphere is incredibly hot from the massive temperature of the volcano, Mount Doom. There is no possibility that anything other than evil could grow in Mordor. It is evil, and it breeds evil. Mordor is a massive, barren, wasteland.

The citadel of Isengard, realm of the evil wizard Saruman, used to be green and beautiful. But Saruman was corrupted by Sauron and became evil. He tore down all the trees in Isengard and used them to fuel his furnaces. He had to move his operations to nearby Fangorn Forest to collect wood, and all around Isengard there was a barren stretch of land. The evil of Isengard could not be contained by the stone walls that surrounded the citadel. Instead, it spread outward and consumed much of the land around it. Mordor and Isengard are two classic examples of wastelands being used to communicate evil, as the very appearance of them produces a feeling of evil. As evil conquered places in Middle Earth, they burned them, and destroyed everything green. As Legolas says in *The Two Towers*, "No other folk make such a trampling, it seems their delight to slash and beat down growing things that are not even in their way" (409). As one can see, in *The Lord of the Rings*, everything evil hated growing things because they were representative of good. Wherever evil people went, they laid waste to everything green and growing. Tolkien uses wastelands very well in *The Lord of the Rings* to create feelings of evil.

The Tone in Herman Melville's *Billy Budd*

In *Billy Budd*, Herman Melville writes, "The moral nature was seldom out of keeping with the physical make. Indeed, except as toned by the former, the comeliness and power, always attractive in masculine conjunction, hardly could have drawn the sort of honest homage the Handsome Sailor in some examples received from his less gifted associates." Billy Budd, the protagonist of Herman Melville's novel *Billy Budd*, is a Christlike figure.

First, Melville uses characterization to portray the innocuous virtue of his "Handsome Sailor," Billy Budd.

> Invariably a proficient in his perilous calling, he was also more or less of a mighty boxer or wrestler. It was strength and beauty. Tales of his prowess were recited. Ashore he was the champion; afloat the spokesman; on every suitable occasion always foremost. Close-reefing topsails in a gale, there he was, astride the weather yard-arm-end, foot in the Flemish horse as "stirrup," both hands tugging at the "earring" as at a bridle, in very much the attitude of young Alexander curbing the fiery Bucephalus. A superb figure, tossed up as by the horns of Taurus against the thunderous sky, cheerily hallooing to the strenuous file along the spar.

Budd here uses intricate description to confirm the combined strength and innocence in Billy Budd. Budd is capable and strong in body, but innocent and feeling in spirit. Melville uses the metaphor of Alexander's taming a horse, and employs the battle of Tartarus to describe the battle of Budd against the elements of nature. Budd conducts his duties with a carefree eye to danger. Next, Melville uses humor to solidify the character of his Billy Budd.

> To be sure, Billy's action was a terrible breach of naval decorum. But in that decorum he had never been instructed; in consideration of which the Lieutenant would hardly have been so energetic in reproof but for the concluding farewell to the ship. This he rather took as meant to convey a covert sally on the new recruit's part, a sly slur at impressments in general, and that of himself in especial. And yet, more likely, if satire it was in effect, it was hardly so by intention, for Billy,

tho' happily endowed with the gayety of high health, youth, and a free heart, was yet by no means of a satirical turn. The will to it and the sinister dexterity were alike wanting. To deal in double meanings and insinuations of any sort was quite foreign to his nature.

Here, Budd's gentle good humor, so perfectly free from any insinuation or wordplay, is highlighted by his exchange with the lieutenant. While Budd merely means his statement as a cheery farewell to his ship, the lieutenant interprets it as a sly double entendre: Billy just means to give a hearty and fond farewell to his dear ship.

Melville paints a picture of Christlike innocence in his character of Billy Budd. Through description and humor, Budd is understood to be an innocent, strong young man of great character, a great contrast to the setting around him.

"Days," by Ralph Waldo Emerson

"Daughters of Time, the hypocritic Days / muffled and dumb like barefoot dervishes." Emerson penned these opening lines of his poem "Days" in the early 1800s, during the birth of the Transcendental movement. "Days" reflects a penultimate transcendental worldview. Really? How? In "Days" Emerson laments the passing of a day full of the beauty of Nature, a day in which he had no part.

The opening lines of "Days" examine the character of the days that Nature brings:

> Daughters of Time, the hypocritic Days,
> Muffled and dumb like barefoot dervishes,
> And marching single in an endless file.

The days are merely actors in Emerson's poem. The days march through life, bringing their respective pleasures or pain. They are static, unseasonable creatures, marching in a single file. Emerson's extensive research into Middle Eastern philosophies is reflected by his comparison to the mythological Eastern dervishes, swathed in fabric, footsteps muffled.

Now that Emerson has established his characters, he must reveal their purpose within the scene that he has set:

> Bring diadems and fagots in their hands.
> To each they offer gifts after his will,
> Bread, kingdoms, stars, and sky that holds them all.

Here, Emerson examines what the days bring. He notes that the days bring great treasure of two kinds: mundane "bread," and royal "kingdoms, stars, and the sky that holds them all." All these gifts are gifts that Nature brings — to those who are willing to spend the day with Nature. Emerson moves on to note the consequences of what is done with the days.

As the narrator of the scene that he has set, Emerson makes his appearance in the second scene of the poem.

> I, in my pleachéd garden, watched the pomp,
> Forgot my morning wishes, hastily
> Took a few herbs and apples.

He watches from his garden as Nature's grandiose procession, full of bacchanalian joy, passes by him. Emerson forgets the duties of the day and instead focuses on joining Nature's procession. He brings herbs and apples, an offering to appease Nature for his vacillation. But — will he be refused?

The answer is revealed in the third and final scene of the poem:

> Took a few herbs and apples, and the Day
> Turned and departed silent. I, too late,
> Under her solemn fillet saw the scorn.

Emerson is too late for the blessings of nature. Instead, he feels emotionally ripped apart by her neglect of him.

Ralph Waldo Emerson constructed his poem "Days" in four scenes: first, he introduces the characters; second, he reveals their purpose; third, he makes his appearance; and fourth, the story's end. Emerson wished to enlighten his reader to the shortness of the days that Nature brings. He wishes to say that they must be used wisely — lest one reap the consequences.

Days
> Daughters of Time, the hypocritic Days,
> Muffled and dumb, like barefoot dervishes,
> And marching single in an endless file,
> Bring diadems and fagots in their hands.
> To each they offer gifts, after his will, —
> Bread, kingdoms, stars, or sky that holds them all.
> I, in my pleachéd garden, watched the pomp,

Forgot my morning wishes, hastily
Took a few herbs and apples, and the Day
Turned and departed silent. I, too late,
Under her solemn fillet saw the scorn.

Irony in "The Blue Hotel," by Stephen Crane

Crane did an excellent job on "The Blue Hotel." His use of setting, characters, and irony join together to bring to life this ironic story. Although well written, it bears a tone of pointlessness (irony, essentially). But this short story by Crane is an amazing example of Naturalism. I did not realize how clearly the writer's own beliefs will reflect through their work—and thus become so obvious to the reader.

The way Crane implements the setting is key. It is very naturalistic: the depictions of the "turmoil sea of snow" and the lengthy description of the surrounding landscape and the Blue Hotel itself—all are painting a clear picture in the reader's mind. This is not just a picture to imagine: the atmosphere and tone about the story reflect through Crane's writing as well.

There is an underlying feeling of dread, but it is masked in the mediocre characters and dreary ambiance. The reader intuitively knows something climatic is coming. Opening on a cold morning in a Midwestern small town, the reader is drawn to Scully, the proprietor of the Blue Hotel, who is trying to draw patrons into his establishment. After securing several men new to the town, Scully takes them in.

A severe blizzard sets in, stranding the characters in the hotel's front room, to amuse themselves in various ways. The mystery and tension build as the Swede displays sporadic attitudes of frantic fear or false security. All through the story,

little makes complete sense. It all seems incidental and ironic. The story leaves the reader feeling somewhat lost and not altogether sure exactly what moral or meaning Crane is trying to present.

The characters themselves are very ordinary: "a shaky, quick-eyed Swede, one was a tall bronzed cowboy, one was a little silent man from the East." None of the characters' descriptions or following conversations cause the reader's interest to increase greatly.

Irony is a much-used technique and is employed greatly in naturalistic writings. "The Blue Hotel" is no exception. It is ironical that a naive Easterner, the silent man, is mercilessly killed by a Westerner. The ground for the murder—cheating at cards—is hardly realistic and therefore has a certain ring of irony and even absurdness. Another example is the following excerpt: "The corpse of the Swede, alone in the saloon, had its eyes fixed upon a dreadful legend that dwelt atop of the cash-machine. 'This registers the amount of your purchase.'"

This in itself causes readers to roll their eyes at the irony of the poor man's fate. Also the ending comment made by the cowboy, "Well, I didn't do anythin', did I?" again displays irony on this character's part. The fact is that he fully observed the card cheating taking place, but he did not "stand up and be a man," and side with the Swede in the flight.

If the cowboy had joined the Swede, instead of leaving the poor man to fight alone, the Swede may not have died—causing such a climatic ending about such an unimportant issue.

Mood and Substance: A Comparison of Buddhism and Christianity

The religion Buddhism was founded during the seventh century BCE by a man named Buddha Shakyamuni. After living and meditating in the forest for six years, he became enlightened and was requested to teach an introduction to Buddhism. One of the main things that he taught was the four noble truths. These truths exhort and explain how a pious Buddhist is to live: (1) Life is suffering. (2) Suffering is caused by the ignorance of the nature of reality. (3) Suffering can be ended by overcoming ignorance and attachment. (4) Suffering is ended in the noble eightfold path, which consist of right views, right intention, right speech, right action, right livelihood, right effort, right-mindedness, and right contemplation. When these truths are thoroughly examined and compared to Christianity, many similarities and differenced are discovered.

The first truth: "Life is suffering," is just a fact, or reality, that Buddhists believe is part of their life. Because the world and the people in it are imperfect, suffering is inevitable. This means that a man will have to endure sickness, tiredness, pain, and sorrow. It also means that we know and acknowledge that happy moments will pass by, and we will one day pass away as well. This dismal view of life is counteracted by the Christian view of the apostle Paul when he writes, "Rejoice in the Lord always. I will say it again: Rejoice" (Philippians 4:4). And in 1 Peter 4:13 the apostle instructs, "But rejoice inasmuch as you participate in the sufferings of Christ, so that you may be overjoyed when his glory is revealed."

The second truth, "Suffering is caused by the ignorance of the nature of reality," explains that suffering has to do with everyone's being attached to vain earthly things yet being in ignorance about them. And because the loss of earthly things is inevitable, it follows that suffering is inevitable as well. The Buddha listed three forms of suffering: (1) craving for pleasure, (2) craving for existence, and (3) craving for nonexistence. In the sixth century, Bishop Gregory the Great

compiled a list of eight passions from the early monastic saints that can be compared to Buddhism's three forms of suffering. These are (1) gluttony, (2) lust, (3) covetousness, (4) anger, (5) dejection, (6) despondency, (7) vainglory, and (8) pride. Although these lists are written differently, the underlying message is the same in both.

The third truth, "Suffering can be ended by overcoming ignorance and attachment," expresses that through the Nirodha (the unmaking of cravings and attachments) suffering can be ended through dispassion. Once this dispassion has occurred, it ultimately results in the state called Nirvana. Nirvana is a state where one is free from worries, ideas, and passions. In Christianity overcoming passions is also a big part of our faith, but instead of its resulting in Nirvana, the outcome is peace with God, and ultimately eternal life.

In the fourth truth, "Suffering is ended in the noble eightfold path," right view, right intention, right speech, right action, right livelihood, right effort, right-mindfulness, and right concentration are necessary. This path can also lead to rebirth, which means that the path to end suffering will continue for several lifetimes as the state of Nirvana is being sought for. It is here that the biggest difference between Buddhism and Christianity arises. In Buddhism, the end goal is to be without suffering, but it cannot lead one beyond sickness and death. In Christianity, the end goal is to be with God. In Buddhism, Nirvana might take what they call lifetimes, but in Christianity, as David Withun said, "Almost 500 years after the Buddha's lifetime something remarkable happened, a key and essential ingredient was added, which the Buddha, because of his time and place, was unaware of: God became man. He was born, crucified, died, and resurrected—freeing us all from illness, from old age, and, ultimately, from death. We must continue to struggle with our passions, our craving, but there is a new dynamic: the grace of God."

So the biggest difference between Buddhism and Christianity in "the four truths of Buddhism" is not that the truths are incorrect, but rather that they are lacking. In the first truth they are lacking in joy, and in the third and fourth truths they are incomplete without grace. Acts 20:32, "'Now I commit you to God and to the word of his grace, which can build you up and give you an inheritance among all those who are sanctified.'" —James P. Stobaugh

Humor in *The Adventures of Tom Sawyer*, by Mark Twain

Humor is an important aspect in forming the characters of a story. It also creates the tone the reader feels while reading. There are three main types of humor: exaggeration, satire, and dramatic irony. Those types of humor work together to form the comedy in a story. Mark Twain uses humor in a clever way through the main character—a young boy named Tom—which makes his novel *Tom Sawyer* a true classic.

In Twain's *Tom Sawyer*, exaggeration is created through Tom. At one point in the story, Tom meets a boy whom he immediately dislikes. They began to argue and insult each other. Tom mentions that his "big brother" could beat up the other boy. Tom did not actually have a big brother and exaggerated to the other boy that someone imaginary could pound the other boy with one finger. The humor created through Tom's exaggeration is somewhat funny, but Tom exaggerates so often that it leads to his frequent lying.

> "You're a coward and a pup. I'll tell my big brother on you, and he can lam you with his little finger, and I'll make him do it to."
>
> "What do I care for your big brother? I've got a brother that's bigger than he is; and, what's more, he can throw him over that fence too."
> [Both brothers are imaginary.] (8)

Satire brings out other's faults, often through ridicule. In *Tom Sawyer*, Tom lives with his Aunt Polly and is repeatedly finding himself in trouble. At one point, he tricks his aunt to distract her and runs from their house, avoiding punishment. Aunt Polly starts laughing after this incident. Twain uses Tom to bring out some faults in his aunt, even though there is no direct ridicule of her. The reader sees that his aunt is easily fooled and never carries out her threats to punish Tom. With nothing but a talk from his Aunt Polly, Tom then just keeps getting into trouble. Satire in *Tom Sawyer* is commonly used when Tom is trying to avoid punishment and creates some humor that helps form the comedy in *Tom Sawyer*:

> The switch hovered in the air. The peril was desperate. "My! Look behind you, Aunt!"
>
> The old lady whirled around and snatched her skirts out of danger, and the lad fled; on the instant, scrambled up the high board fence, and disappeared over it. His Aunt Polly stood surprised for a moment, and then broke into a gentle laugh.
>
> "Hang the boy, can't I learn anything? Ain't he played me tricks enough like that for me to be looking out for him by this time? But old fools is the biggest fools there is. Can't learn any old dog new tricks, as the saying is. But, my goodness, he never plays them alike two days, and how is a body to know what's coming? he 'pears to know just how long he can torment me before I get my dander up, and he knows if he can make out to put me off for a minute, or make me laugh, it's all down

again, and I can't hit him a lick. I ain't doing my duty by that boy, and that's the Lord's truth, goodness knows." (2)

Dramatic irony is a technique used in some stories where the reader knows something the other characters do not. An example of dramatic irony in *Tom Sawyer* would be when Tom tricks the local boys into whitewashing his fence for him. Tom has the dreaded chore of whitewashing the fence around his house. When he sees some boys come along, he acts as if his chore is fun, and therefore the other boys want to do it as well because they see how much "fun" Tom is having. The reader knows that Tom is tricking the boys into doing his chore. The boys in the story do not know it is a trick. The technique of dramatic irony produces a humor that is more helpful in making one feel the hilarity in a story.

In the following humorous passage Tom Sawyer cons his friends into whitewashing the fence:

> Ben stopped nibbling his apple. Tom swept his brush daintily back and forth—stepped back to note the effect—added a touch here and there—criticized the effect again, Ben watching every move, and getting more an' more interested, more and more absorbed. Presently he said: "Say, Tom, let me whitewash a little."

The humor in Tom Sawyer creates a tone of adventure and mischief for the reader. The way Twain uses the types of humor causes them to tie together to form the comedic aspect of a story. The characters in Tom Sawyer are formed with the aid of humor, whether their own or another character's.

Awe in William Bradford's *Of Plimoth Plantation*

William Bradford regards nature with awe and wonder as a work of God's hands. However, in that awe there is a component of respect and fear. As North America was uncultivated and unsettled, the natural and biological aspects of the new world could not be anything less than terrifying to one just arrived in the land. Bradford, however, does not treat nature with a bitter and

resentful naturalistic eye, but instead turns to his God with a worshipful panegyric on his creation, beautiful and awe-inspiring in its wildness.

Bradford's fear of the untamedness of the new world is represented in his *Of Plimouth Plantation*. He describes his sentiments when first landing on the shores of North America as such:

> Besides, what could they see but a hideous and desolate wilderness, full of wild beasts and wild men? And what multitudes there might be of them they knew not. . . . Nether could they, as it were, go up to the top of Pisgah, to view from this wilderness a more goodly countries to feed their hopes; for which way soever they turned their eyes (save upward to the heavens) they could have little solace or content in respect of any outward objects. For summer being done, all things stand upon them with a weather-beaten face; and the whole countries, full of woods and thickets, represented a wild and savage hew.

It is obvious that Bradford is inspired with awe and fear when he first saw this spectacle. North America in winter was a rugged, untamed, and fearsome spectacle indeed to those who had come straight from the ready comforts and amenities of Great Britain and Leyden. However, this does not create in Bradford bitterness or resentfulness, nor does he look at his creator—the creator of this strange new country as well as of himself—and decry him as unjust, unmerciful, or pernicious.

To the contrary, Bradford turns to his maker with a worshipful gaze and gives thanks for the providence that carried them to this new world:

> Being thus arrived in a good harbor and brought safe to land, they fell upon their knees and blessed the God of heaven, who had brought them over the vast and furious ocean, and delivered them from all the perils and miseries thereof, again to set their feet on the firm and stable earth, their proper element. . . . May not and ought not the children of these fathers rightly say: "Our fathers were Englishmen which come over this great ocean, and were ready to perish in this wilderness; but they turned unto the Lord, and he heard their voice, and looked on their adversities," etc. "Let them therefore praise the Lord, because he is good, and his mercies endure forever."

Rather than turning a bitter naturalistic eye to God, Bradford worships his creator, and thanks him heartily for the good providences that brought them to this new land, the land that he had given them. Even though the wildness of the scene was terrifying to the metropolitan Bradford, he still finds occasion to stand in awe of what his creator has made.

When metropolitan pilgrim William Bradford stood on the shores of the new world, he had two choices before him. He could be bitter and disgusted with the land that he had hoped to be so fruitful, yet was so untamed, or he could thank his Creator for what he had given them. Two worldviews were at war for Bradford. Bradford fittingly chose to thank his creator for the providences he had given them: even in the wild ruggedness of his new situation, he saw the power and glory of his maker in his creation.

Comparison in Tone between Job and Plato's *Apology of Socrates*

Apology (or *The Trial and Death of Socrates* by Plato and the biblical book of Job are two accounts of men given in dialogue form, yet the tone and content of these dialogues are greatly different. Socrates defends himself in a trial, and Job deplores the loss of everything he has, condemns his birthday, but still praises God.

In the book of Job, chapter 3, Job condemns his birthday:

> "May the day of my birth perish,
>   and the night that said, 'A boy is conceived!'
> That day—may it turn to darkness;
>   may God above not care about it;
>   may no light shine on it." (Job 3:3-4)

After losing all his possessions, including his home, livestock, and children, Job wishes that he had never been born and that the day upon which he was born be looked down upon and forgotten. Socrates, on the other hand, never condemns his birthday or wishes he was never born. In fact, he says that he is just a victim of greed and jealousy. "I certainly have many enemies, and this is what will be my destruction if I am destroyed;—not [my accusers] . . . but the envy and detraction of the world, which has been the death of many good men, and will probably be the death of many more; there is no danger of my being the last of them" (Plato, 31). While the reader can feel that Job is depressed and downtrodden about his situation, at least in the beginning, the reader senses Job's regretting that he was born.

On the other hand, Socrates never regrets his life and fights for his life until the last moment. Job acknowledges that he is being tested by God while Socrates fights against his accusers down to the moment he is sentenced to die. "But I see clearly that to die and be released was better for me; and therefore the oracle gave no sign. For which reason, also, I am not angry with my accusers or my condemners; they have done me no harm, although neither of them meant to do me any good; and for this I may gently blame them" (44). Even after he has received his sentence and is condemned to die, Socrates is still blaming his accusers and arguing that they meant not to do any good to Socrates. Job has a different response to the Lord:

> "I am unworthy—how can I reply to you?
>> I put my hand over my mouth.
> I spoke once, but I have no answer—
>> twice, but I will say no more." (Job 40:3–5)

By the end of his trial, Job recognizes that God has allowed Satan to test Job and that all Job's losses were simply a test. Thus Job initially condemns his birth and wishes he had never been born, yet later he repents before God. On the other hand, Socrates never hints that he regrets being born, but instead acknowledges that he is neither going to be the first nor last victim of envy or petty criticism to die.

After the initial destruction in Job's life, and Socrates' sentencing to death, both men talk with their friends. Job's friends tell him that his situation is his fault and that he needs to repent. "If you are pure and upright, even now he will rouse himself on your behalf and restore you to your prosperous state" (Job 8:6). Neither Job nor his friends realize that Job is being tested by God, and the friends urge Job to repent since they feel his position is due to sin. On the contrary, Socrates' friends never urge him to repent of his alleged corruption of youth. Instead, they ask Socrates to let them help him escape his sentence. "Fear not. There are persons who at no great cost are willing to save you and bring you out of prison" (Plato, 49). Job's friends try to get Job to repent of his sins, while Socrates' friends offer to help him escape prison. Socrates' friends are probably more true and sincere then Job's friends since they try to help Socrates get out of prison, while Job's friends curse him and degrade him, claiming that he brought these events upon himself.

These are just a few of the similarities and differences between the dialogue in Job and *The Trial and Death of Socrates*. Job curses his birthday nearly immediately after he has lost everything; Socrates simply acknowledges that he is a victim of jealousy and petty accusations. Later, both men talk with their friends: Job's friends try to get him to repent, while Socrates' friends offer to help him escape from prison.

Background

Poetry is a literary genre in which authors use language for its artistic and evocative qualities in addition to its cognitive meaning. Poetry can stand alone, as solitary poems, or may occur as a song or other literary form (e.g., narrative). Poetry, like prose, has all the elements of literature: plot, theme, and so forth, but it also has sounds: meter and rhythm. Most scholars consider the *Gilgamesh Epic* to be the oldest extant poem. In fact, poetry is the oldest literary form. There was no novel until about 1000 CE. Poetry as an art form predates literacy. Examples of great narrative shaped in poetry are the Homeric epics, the *Odyssey* and the *Iliad*. "Poetry lifts the veil from the hidden beauty of the world, and makes familiar objects be as if they were not familiar" (Percy Shelley).

Suggested Literary Works

Bradstreet, Anne. "To My Dear and Loving Husband".

Bradstreet, Anne. "Verses upon the Burning of our House."

Chesterton, G. K. "Lepanto."

Crane, Stephen. "War Is Kind."

Emerson, Ralph Waldo. "A Psalm of Life."

Fields, James T. "The Owl Critic."

Frost, Robert. "After Apple Picking."

Frost, Robert. "Death of a Hired Hand."

Homer. Iliad.

Homer. Odyssey.

Housman, A. E. "Loveliest of Trees, the Cherry Now."

Longfellow, Henry Wadsworth. "The Midnight Ride of Paul Revere."

Mare, Walter de la. "Silver."

McCann, Paul. "Don't Delay Dawns Disarming Display."

McCrae, John. "In Flanders Fields."

Poe, Edgar Allan. "Bells."

Riley, James Whitcomb. "Thoughts Fer the Discuraged Farmer."

Sandburg, Carl. "Honky Tonk in Cleveland, Ohio."

Shakespeare, William. "Spring and Winter."

Tennyson, Alfred Lord. "Charge of the Light Brigade."

Thayer, E. L. "Casey at the Bat."

Yeats, William Butler. "The Second Coming."

Terms

Poetry is an imaginative awareness of experience expressed through meaning, sound, and rhythmic language choices so as to evoke an emotional or affective (spiritual) response. Scholars Norton and Gretton argue:

> The boundaries between poetry and prose are not final or definite. No one can say for sure where the shore ends and the sea begins, where prose ends and poetry begins. The difference between them is a matter of degree: poetry tends to be more compressed, to suggest and to imply more than does prose; it tends to place more emphasis on how something is said, and less on what is said; poetry tends to be more imaginative than prose, to use more comparisons, more surprises; poetry usually has a more regular rhythm than does prose, and an especially interesting shape of form.

Yet, while poetry shares some things with prose, it is different. In this section we will explore those differences.

Language: Denotation and Connotation

In poetry, language is everything. It is the tool by which poets convey their thoughts, dreams, and arguments. Words are not just words; they have hearts and souls and they create meaning. Therefore, readers must not only know the denotation of words; they must also know the connotations. *Denotation* refers to the literal meaning of a word, the "dictionary definition." *Connotation*, on the other hand, refers to the associations that are connected to a certain word or the emotional suggestions related to that word. For example, a few years ago I observed that one of my students was perspiring. I noted that she was "hot." My other students snickered. Clearly I did not grasp the connotation of the word *hot* (used in this context!).

"Loveliest of Trees, the Cherry Now," by A. E. Housman

The tree is beautiful but transitory. The blossoms denote beauty; they also denote inevitable death.

Loveliest of trees, the cherry now
Is hung with bloom along the bough,

253

And stands about the woodland ride
Wearing white for Eastertide.

Now, of my threescore years and ten,
Twenty will not come again,
And take from seventy springs a score,
It only leaves me fifty more.

And since to look at things in bloom
Fifty springs are little room,
About the woodlands I will go
To see the cherry hung with snow.

Theme

In poetry, as in prose, the theme is the purpose of a literary work. However, in poetry, there is more wriggle room for interpretation. What does the poet mean, and what impact does the poem have on the reader? Between these two questions lies the theme of a poem.

Very simply, a poem's theme is the statement it makes about its subject. Robert Frost discusses life and death. His central metaphor is apple picking. He is tired now, though, and with his task completed, he is looking forward to rest. Poems often have more than one theme, and such is the case here. On one level Frost writes a poem about apple picking. Period. On another level this is a much more profound and pensive poem.

"After Apple Picking," by Robert Frost

My long two-pointed ladder's sticking through a tree
Toward heaven still,
And there's a barrel that I didn't fill
Beside it, and there may be two or three
Apples I didn't pick upon some bough.
But I am done with apple-picking now.
Essence of winter sleep is on the night,

The scent of apples: I am drowsing off.
I cannot rub the strangeness from my sight
I got from looking through a pane of glass
I skimmed this morning from the drinking trough
And held against the world of hoary grass.
It melted, and I let it fall and break.
But I was well
Upon my way to sleep before it fell,
And I could tell
What form my dreaming was about to take.
Magnified apples appear and disappear,
Stem end and blossom end,
And every fleck of russet showing clear.
My instep arch not only keeps the ache,
It keeps the pressure of a ladder-round.
I feel the ladder sway as the boughs bend.
And I keep hearing from the cellar bin
The rumbling sound
Of load on load of apples coming in.
For I have had too much
Of apple-picking: I am overtired
Of the great harvest I myself desired.
There were ten thousand thousand fruit to touch,
Cherish in hand, lift down, and not let fall.
For all
That struck the earth,
No matter if not bruised or spiked with stubble,
Went surely to the cider-apple heap
As of no worth.
One can see what will trouble
This sleep of mine, whatever sleep it is.
Were he not gone,
The woodchuck could say whether it's like his
Long sleep, as I describe its coming on,
Or just some human sleep.

"To My Dear and Loving Husband," by Anne Bradstreet

If ever two were one, then surely we.
If ever man were lov'd by wife, then thee.
If ever wife was happy in a man,
Compare with me, ye women, if you can.

I prize thy love more than whole Mines of gold
Or all the riches that the East doth hold.
My love is such that Rivers cannot quench,
Nor ought but love from thee give recompense.

Thy love is such I can no way repay.
The heavens reward thee manifold, I pray.
Then while we live, in love let's so persevere
That when we live no more, we may live ever.

"Verses upon the Burning of Our House," by Anne Bradstreet

In silent night when rest I took,
For sorrow near I did not look,
I waken'd was with thund'ring noise
And piteous shrieks of dreadful voice.
That fearful sound of "fire" and "fire,"
Let no man know is my Desire.

I starting up, the light did spy,
And to my God my heart did cry
To straighten me in my Distress
And not to leave me succourless.
Then coming out, beheld a space,
The flame consume my dwelling place.

And, when I could no longer look,
I blest his grace that gave and took,
That laid my goods now in the dust.
Yea, so it was, and so 'twas just.
It was his own; it was not mine.

Far be it that I should repine.
He might of all justly bereft
But yet sufficient for us left.
When by the Ruins oft I past
My sorrowing eyes aside did cast
And here and there the places spy
Where oft I sate and long did lie.
Here stood that Trunk, and there that chest,
There lay that store I counted best,
My pleasant things in ashes lie
And them behold no more shall I.
Under the roof no guest shall sit,
Nor at thy Table eat a bit.

No pleasant talk shall 'ere be told
Nor things recounted done of old.
No Candle 'ere shall shine in Thee,
Nor bridegroom's voice ere heard shall be.
In silence ever shalt thou lie.
Adieu, Adieu, All's Vanity.
Then straight I 'gin my heart to chide:
And did thy wealth on earth abide,
Didst fix thy hope on mouldering dust,
The arm of flesh didst make thy trust?
Raise up thy thoughts above the sky
That dunghill mists away may fly.

Thou hast a house on high erect
Fram'd by that mighty Architect,
With glory richly furnished
Stands permanent, though this be fled.
It's purchased and paid for too
By him who hath enough to do.

A price so vast as is unknown,
Yet by his gift is made thine own.
There's wealth enough; I need no more.

Farewell, my Pelf; farewell, my Store.
The world no longer let me Love;
My hope and Treasure lies Above.

Comments on Anne Bradstreet

Anne Bradstreet was born in Northampton, England, in the year 1612, daughter of Thomas Dudley and Dorothy Yorke; both nonconformist Puritans. At the age of sixteen, Anne was married to Simon Bradstreet, a twenty-five-year-old assistant in the Massachusetts Bay Company and the son of a Puritan minister, who lived with Anne's parents after the death of his father. Anne and her family emigrated to America in 1630 on the *Arabella*, one of the first ships to bring Puritans to New England. Anne and Simon endured great hardships.

Simon had very responsible positions in his tenure in New England. Thomas Dudley and his friend John Winthrop made up the Boston settlement's government; Winthrop was governor, Dudley deputy governor, and Simon chief administrator.

The colonists' fight for survival had become daily routine, and the climate, lack of food, the birth of eight children, and primitive living arrangements made it very difficult for Anne to adapt. But she did. She found solace and strength in her God. Her faith and imagination guided her through the most difficult moments; the belief that God had not abandoned them helped her survive the hardships of the colony.

While Anne and her husband were very much in love, Simon's political duties kept him traveling to various colonies on diplomatic errands, so Anne would spend her lonely days and nights reading from her father's vast collection of books and educating her children. The reading would not only keep her from being lonely; she also learned a great deal about other subjects. In short, she was the quintessential, self-educated, and effective homeschool mom!

"The Death of a Hired Hand," by Robert Frost

Mary sat musing on the lamp-flame at the table
Waiting for Warren. When she heard his step,
She ran on tip-toe down the darkened passage
To meet him in the doorway with the news
And put him on his guard. "Silas is back."
She pushed him outward with her through the door
And shut it after her. "Be kind," she said.
She took the market things from Warren's arms
And set them on the porch, then drew him down
To sit beside her on the wooden steps.
"When was I ever anything but kind to him?
But I'll not have the fellow back," he said.

"I told him so last haying, didn't I?
'If he left then,' I said, 'that ended it.'
What good is he? Who else will harbour him
At his age for the little he can do?
What help he is there's no depending on.
Off he goes always when I need him most.
'He thinks he ought to earn a little pay,
Enough at least to buy tobacco with,
So he won't have to beg and be beholden.'
'All right,' I say, 'I can't afford to pay
Any fixed wages, though I wish I could.'
'Someone else can.' 'Then someone else will have to.'
I shouldn't mind his bettering himself
If that was what it was. You can be certain,
When he begins like that, there's someone at him
Trying to coax him off with pocket-money,—
In haying time, when any help is scarce.
In winter he comes back to us. I'm done."

"Sh! not so loud: he'll hear you," Mary said.

"I want him to: he'll have to soon or late."

"He's worn out. He's asleep beside the stove.
When I came up from Rowe's I found him here,
Huddled against the barn-door fast asleep,
A miserable sight, and frightening, too—
You needn't smile—I didn't recognise him—
I wasn't looking for him—and he's changed.
Wait till you see."

"Where did you say he'd been?"

"He didn't say. I dragged him to the house,
And gave him tea and tried to make him smoke.
I tried to make him talk about his travels.
Nothing would do: he just kept nodding off."

"What did he say? Did he say anything?"

"But little."

"Anything? Mary, confess
He said he'd come to ditch the meadow for me."

"Warren!"

"But did he? I just want to know."

"Of course he did. What would you have him say?
Surely you wouldn't grudge the poor old man
Some humble way to save his self-respect.
He added, if you really care to know,
He meant to clear the upper pasture, too.
That sounds like something you have heard before?
Warren, I wish you could have heard the way
He jumbled everything. I stopped to look

Two or three times—he made me feel so queer—
To see if he was talking in his sleep.
He ran on Harold Wilson—you remember—
The boy you had in haying four years since.
He's finished school, and teaching in his college.
Silas declares you'll have to get him back.
He says they two will make a team for work:
Between them they will lay this farm as smooth!
The way he mixed that in with other things.
He thinks young Wilson a likely lad, though daft
On education—you know how they fought
All through July under the blazing sun,
Silas up on the cart to build the load,
Harold along beside to pitch it on."

"Yes, I took care to keep well out of earshot."

"Well, those days trouble Silas like a dream.
You wouldn't think they would. How some things linger!
Harold's young college boy's assurance piqued him.
After so many years he still keeps finding
Good arguments he sees he might have used.
I sympathise. I know just how it feels
To think of the right thing to say too late.
Harold's associated in his mind with Latin.
He asked me what I thought of Harold's saying
He studied Latin like the violin
Because he liked it—that an argument!
He said he couldn't make the boy believe
He could find water with a hazel prong—
Which showed how much good school had ever done him.
He wanted to go over that. But most of all
He thinks if he could have another chance
To teach him how to build a load of hay—"

"I know, that's Silas' one accomplishment.
He bundles every forkful in its place,

And tags and numbers it for future reference,
So he can find and easily dislodge it
In the unloading. Silas does that well.
He takes it out in bunches like big birds' nests.
You never see him standing on the hay
He's trying to lift, straining to lift himself."

"He thinks if he could teach him that, he'd be
Some good perhaps to someone in the world.
He hates to see a boy the fool of books.
Poor Silas, so concerned for other folk,
And nothing to look backward to with pride,
And nothing to look forward to with hope,
So now and never any different."

Part of a moon was falling down the west,
Dragging the whole sky with it to the hills.
Its light poured softly in her lap. She saw
And spread her apron to it. She put out her hand
Among the harp-like morning-glory strings,
Taut with the dew from garden bed to eaves,
As if she played unheard the tenderness
That wrought on him beside her in the night.
"Warren," she said, "he has come home to die:
You needn't be afraid he'll leave you this time."

"Home," he mocked gently.

"Yes, what else but home?
It all depends on what you mean by home.
Of course he's nothing to us, any more
Than was the hound that came a stranger to us
Out of the woods, worn out upon the trail."

"Home is the place where, when you have to go there,
They have to take you in. "

"I should have called it
Something you somehow haven't to deserve."

Warren leaned out and took a step or two,
Picked up a little stick, and brought it back
And broke it in his hand and tossed it by.
"Silas has better claim on us you think
Than on his brother? Thirteen little miles
As the road winds would bring him to his door.
Silas has walked that far no doubt to-day.
Why didn't he go there? His brother's rich,
A somebody—director in the bank."

"He never told us that."

"We know it though."

"I think his brother ought to help, of course.
I'll see to that if there is need. He ought of right
To take him in, and might be willing to—
He may be better than appearances.
But have some pity on Silas. Do you think
If he'd had any pride in claiming kin
Or anything he looked for from his brother,
He'd keep so still about him all this time?"

"I wonder what's between them."

"I can tell you.
Silas is what he is—we wouldn't mind him—
But just the kind that kinsfolk can't abide.
He never did a thing so very bad.
He don't know why he isn't quite as good
As anyone. He won't be made ashamed
To please his brother, worthless though he is."

"*I* can't think Si ever hurt anyone."

"No, but he hurt my heart the way he lay
And rolled his old head on that sharp-edged chair-back.
He wouldn't let me put him on the lounge.
You must go in and see what you can do.
I made the bed up for him there to-night.
You'll be surprised at him—how much he's broken.
His working days are done; I'm sure of it."

"I'd not be in a hurry to say that."

"I haven't been. Go, look, see for yourself.
But, Warren, please remember how it is:
He's come to help you ditch the meadow.
He has a plan. You mustn't laugh at him.
He may not speak of it, and then he may.
I'll sit and see if that small sailing cloud
Will hit or miss the moon."

It hit the moon.
Then there were three there, making a dim row,
The moon, the little silver cloud, and she.

Warren returned—too soon, it seemed to her,
Slipped to her side, caught up her hand and waited.

"Warren," she questioned.
"Dead," was all he answered.

Epic Poems

Poetry existed a long time before prose. Homer's *Iliad* and the book of Job—two very ancient pieces of literature—were written in poetry. But a story, or narrative, whether it is in poetry or in prose, has the same literary elements: exposition, rising action, climax, falling action, denouement.

An epic story is a lengthy narrative poem, ordinarily concerning a serious subject containing details of heroic deeds and events significant to a culture. Whether it is the *Iliad* or "Casey at the Bat," there is always a hero, a crisis, a resolution. The theme inevitably is didactic.

The longest epic poem in the English language, *The Fairie Queen*, by Edmund Spenser, declares (in book 2):

> Yet gold all is not, that doth gold seem,
> Nor all good knights, that shake well spear and shield:
> The worth of all men by their end esteem,
> And then praise, or due reproach them yield.

Thus the poet is not merely entertaining: the epic poem is also teaching a lesson, which makes it a *didactic* poem. Like Achilles in Homer's *Iliad*, mighty Casey is overconfident to his own peril. It is hubris, or pride, that will cause Casey to fail, just as pride destroyed Achilles.

"Casey at the Bat," Ernest Lawrence Thayer

This popular American epic poem has been republished many times and given a wide number of alternative wordings. It is written in a varation of the ballad stanza — a rhyming, four-line, metrically regular stanza. Most lines have one iambic foot (de/DUM) plus three other feet, each with three unstressed syllables and then one stressed syllable (de/de/de/DUM), the quartus paeon type of tetrasyllable. (See "Sounds in Poetry," below.)

Here is the original version as it appeared in the San Francisco Examiner on June 3, 1888:

The outlook wasn't brilliant for the Mudville nine that day:
The score stood four to two with but one inning more to play;
And then when Cooney died at first, and Burrows did the same,
A sickly silence fell upon the patrons of the game.

A straggling few got up to go in deep despair. The rest
Clung to that hope which springs eternal in the human breast;
They thought if only Casey could get a whack at that —
We'd put up even money, with Casey at the bat.

But Flynn preceded Casey, as did also Jimmy Blake,
And the former was a lulu and the latter was a cake;
So upon that stricken multitude grim melancholy sat,
For there seemed but little chance of Casey's getting to the bat.

But Flynn let drive a single to the wonderment of all,
And Blake, the much despis-èd, tore the cover off the ball;
And when the dust had lifted, and the men saw what had occurred,
There was Johnnie [Jimmy] safe at second and Flynn a-hugging third.

Then from 5,000 throats and more there rose a lusty yell,
It rumbled through the valley, it rattled in the dell;
It knocked upon the mountain and recoiled upon on the flat;
For Casey, mighty Casey, was advancing to the bat.

There was ease in Casey's manner as he stepped into his place;
There was pride in Casey's bearing and a smile on Casey's face.
And when, responding to the cheers, he lightly doffed his hat,
No stranger in the crowd could doubt 'twas Casey at the bat.

Ten thousand eyes were on him as he rubbed his hands with dirt;
Five thousand tongues applauded when he wiped them on his shirt.
Then while the writhing pitcher ground the ball into his hip,
Defiance flashed in Casey's eye, a sneer curled Casey's lip.

And now the leather-covered sphere came hurtling through the air,
And Casey stood a-watching it in haughty grandeur there;
Close by the sturdy batsman the ball unheeded sped —
"That ain't my style," said Casey. "Strike one," the umpire said.

From the benches, black with people, there went up a muffled roar,
Like the beating of the storm-waves on a stern and distant shore
"Kill him! Kill the umpire!" shouted some one on the stand;
And it's likely they'd have killed him had not Casey raised his hand.

With a smile of Christian charity great Casey's visage shone;
He stilled the rising tumult; he bade the game go on;
He signaled to the pitcher, and once more the sphereoid flew;
But Casey still ignored it, and the umpire said, "Strike two."

"Fraud!" cried the maddened thousands, and the echo answered fraud;
But one scornful look from Casey and the audience was awed;
They saw his face grow stern and cold, they saw his muscles strain,
And they knew that Casey wouldn't let that ball go by again.

The sneer is gone from Casey's lip, his teeth are clenched with hate;
He pounds with cruel violence his bat upon the plate;
And now the pitcher holds the ball, and now he lets it go,
And now the air is shattered by the force of Casey's blow.

Oh, somewhere in this favored land the sun is shining bright,
The band is playing somewhere, and somewhere hearts are light,
And somewhere men are laughing, and somewhere children shout;
But there is no joy in Mudville — mighty Casey has struck out.

"The Charge of the Light Brigade," by Tennyson

This classic poem by Alfred Lord Tennyson honors the valor of the British Light Cavalry in carrying out their flawed orders on October 25, 1854, in the Crimean War. Due to miscommunication, they charged a well-defended Russian artillery battery in the Battle of Balaclava.

Half a league, half a league,
Half a league onward,
All in the valley of Death
Rode the six hundred.
"Forward, the Light Brigade!
"Charge for the guns!" he said:
Into the valley of Death

Rode the six hundred.

"Forward, the Light Brigade!"
Was there a man dismay'd?
Not tho' the soldier knew
Someone had blunder'd:
Theirs not to make reply,
Theirs not to reason why,
Theirs but to do and die:
Into the valley of Death
Rode the six hundred.
Cannon to right of them,
Cannon to left of them,
Cannon in front of them
Volley'd and thunder'd;
Storm'd at with shot and shell,
Boldly they rode and well,
Into the jaws of Death,
Into the mouth of Hell
Rode the six hundred.
Flash'd all their sabres bare,
Flash'd as they turn'd in air,
Sabring the gunners there,
Charging an army, while
All the world wonder'd:
Plunged in the battery-smoke
Right thro' the line they broke;
Cossack and Russian
Reel'd from the sabre stroke
Shatter'd and sunder'd.
Then they rode back, but not
Not the six hundred.
Cannon to right of them,
Cannon to left of them,
Cannon behind them
Volley'd and thunder'd;
Storm'd at with shot and shell,

THE CHARGE OF THE LIGHT BRIGADE

While horse and hero fell,
They that had fought so well
Came thro' the jaws of Death
Back from the mouth of Hell,
All that was left of them,
Left of six hundred.
When can their glory fade?
O the wild charge they made!
All the world wondered.
Honor the charge they made,
Honor the Light Brigade,
Noble six hundred.

Humorous Poems

"Thoughts fer the Discuraged Farmer,"

by James Whitcomb Riley

Riley uses colloquial language, slang, and corny metaphors to amuse his readers.

The summer winds is sniffin' round the bloomin' locus' trees;
And the clover in the pastur is a big day fer the bees,
And they been a-swiggin' honey, above board and on the sly,
Tel they stutter in theyr buzzin' and stagger as they fly.
The flicker on the fence-rail 'pears to jest spit on his wings
And roll up his feathers, by the sassy way he sings;
And the hoss-fly is a-whettin'-up his forelegs fer biz,
And the off-mare is a-switchin' all of her tale they is.

You can hear the blackbirds jawin' as they foller up the plow —
Oh, theyr bound to git theyr brekfast, and theyr not a-carin' how;
So they quarrel in the furries, and they quarrel on the wing —
But theyr peaceabler in pot-pies than any other thing:
And it's when I git my shotgun drawed up in stiddy rest,
She's as full of tribbelation as a yeller-jacket's nest;
And a few shots before dinner, when the sun's a-shinin' right,

Seems to kindo'-sorto' sharpen up a feller's appetite!

They's been a heap o' rain, but the sun's out to-day,
And the clouds of the wet spell is all cleared away,
And the woods is all the greener, and the grass is greener still;
It may rain again to-morry, but I don't think it will.
Some says the crops is ruined, and the corn's drownded out,
And propha-sy the wheat will be a failure, without doubt;
But the kind Providence that has never failed us yet,
Will be on hands onc't more at the 'leventh hour, I bet!

Does the medder-lark complane, as he swims high and dry
Through the waves of the wind and the blue of the sky?
Does the quail set up and whissel in a disappinted way,
Er hang his head in silunce, and sorrow all the day?
Is the chipmuck's health a-failin'? — Does he walk, er does he run?
Don't the buzzards ooze around up thare jest like they've allus done?
Is they anything the matter with the rooster's lungs er voice?
Ort a mortul be complanin' when dumb animals rejoice?

Then let us, one and all, be contentud with our lot;
The June is here this mornin', and the sun is shining hot.
Oh! let us fill our harts up with the glory of the day,
And banish ev'ry doubt and care and sorrow fur away!
Whatever be our station, with Providence fer guide,
Sich fine circumstances ort to make us satisfied;
Fer the world is full of roses, and the roses full of dew,
And the dew is full of heavenly love that drips fer me and you.

Fer the world is full of roses, and the roses full of dew,
And the dew is full of heavenly love that drips fer me and you.

"The Owl Critic," by James T. Fields

Fields is poking fun at educated people who lack common sense. He uses a silent but patient barber who "kept on shaving" as a refrain. Finally the owl itself, personified, speaks directly to the foolish customer.

"Who stuffed that white owl?" No one spoke in the shop,
The barber was busy, and he couldn't stop;

The customers, waiting their turns, were all reading
The "Daily," the "Herald," the "Post," little heeding
The young man who blurted out such a blunt question;
Not one raised a head, or even made a suggestion;
And the barber kept on shaving.

"Don't you see, Mr. Brown,"
Cried the youth, with a frown,
"How wrong the whole thing is,
How preposterous each wing is
How flattened the head is, how jammed down the neck is—
In short, the whole owl, what an ignorant wreck 'tis!
I make no apology;
I've learned owl-eology.

I've passed days and nights in a hundred collections,
And cannot be blinded to any deflections
Arising from unskilful fingers that fail
To stuff a bird right, from his beak to his tail.
Mister Brown! Mister Brown!
Do take that bird down,
Or you'll soon be the laughingstock all over town!"
And the barber kept on shaving.

"I've *studied* owls,
And other night-fowls,
And I tell you
What I know to be true;
An owl cannot roost
With his limbs so unloosed;
No owl in this world
Ever had his claws curled,
Ever had his legs slanted,
Ever had his bill canted,
Ever had his neck screwed
Into that attitude.
He can't *do* it, because

'Tis against all bird-laws.

Anatomy teaches,
Ornithology preaches,
An owl has a toe
That *can't* turn out so!
I've made the white owl my study for years,
And to see such a job almost moves me to tears!
Mr. Brown, I'm amazed
You should be so gone crazed
As to put up a bird
In that posture absurd!
To *look* at that owl really brings on a dizziness;
The man who *stuffed* him don't half know his business!"
And the barber kept on shaving.

"Examine those eyes.
I'm filled with surprise
Taxidermists should pass
Off on you such poor glass;
So unnatural they seem
They'd make Audubon scream,
And John Burroughs laugh
To encounter such chaff.
Do take that bird down;
Have him stuffed again, Brown!"
And the barber kept on shaving.

"With some sawdust and bark
I could stuff in the dark
An owl better than that.
I could make an old hat
Look more like an owl
Than that horrid fowl,
Stuck up there so stiff like a side of coarse leather.
In fact, about *him* there's not one natural feather."

Just then, with a wink and a sly normal lurch,
The owl, very gravely, got down from his perch,
Walked round, and regarded his fault-finding critic
(Who thought he was stuffed) with a glance analytic,
And then fairly hooted, as if he should say:
"Your learning's at fault *this* time, anyway;
Don't waste it again on a live bird, I pray.
I'm an owl; you're another. Sir Critic, good day!"
And the barber kept on shaving.

Imagery

"Spring and Winter," by William Shakespeare

Shakespeare uses imagery, images, and descriptions to convey the irony that spring can bring fear and the extreme cold of winter can bring cheer.

Part 1
WHEN daisies pied and violets blue,
And lady-smocks all silver-white,
And cuckoo-buds of yellow hue
Do paint the meadows with delight,
The cuckoo then, on every tree,
Mocks married men; for thus sings he,
　　Cuckoo!
Cuckoo, cuckoo! — O word of fear,
Unpleasing to a married ear!

When shepherds pipe on oaten straws,
And merry larks are ploughmen's clocks,
When turtles tread, and rooks, and daws,
And maidens bleach their summer smocks
The cuckoo then, on every tree,
Mocks married men; for thus sings he,
　　Cuckoo!
Cuckoo, cuckoo! — O word of fear,
Unpleasing to a married ear!

Part 2

WHEN icicles hang by the wall,
And Dick the shepherd blows his nail,
And Tom bears logs into the hall,
And milk comes frozen home in pail,
When blood is nipp'd, and ways be foul,
Then nightly sings the staring owl,
　To-whit!
To-who! — a merry note,
While greasy Joan doth keel the pot.

When all aloud the wind does blow,
And coughing drowns the parson's saw,
And birds sit brooding in the snow,
And Marian's nose looks red and raw,
When roasted crabs hiss in the bowl,
Then nightly sings the staring owl,
　To-whit!
To-who! — a merry note,
While greasy Joan doth keel the pot.

"Silver," by Walter de la Mare

Slowly, silently, now the moon
Walks the night in her silver shoon;
This way, and that, she peers, and sees
Silver fruit upon silver trees;
One by one the casements catch
Her beams beneath the silvery thatch;
Couched in his kennel, like a log,
With paws of silver sleeps the dog;
From their shadowy cote the white breasts peep
Of doves in silver feathered sleep;
A harvest mouse goes scampering by,
With silver claws, and silver eye;
And moveless fish in the water gleam,

By silver reeds in a silver stream.

"In Flanders Fields," by John McCrae

McCrae's "In Flanders Fields" is one of the most memorable war poems ever written. It is a legacy of the terrible battle in the Ypres salient in the spring of 1915, where the Canadian doctor Major John McCrae spent seventeen days treating injured men. It was impossible to get used to the suffering, the screams, and the blood. Later McCrae wrote, "Seventeen days of Hades! At the end of the first day if anyone had told us we had to spend seventeen days there, we would have folded our hands and said it could not have been done."

From The McCrae Museum of The Guelph [Ontario] Museum

The archaeologist Neil Asher Silberman reports: "For four hellish years during World War I, huge armies were bogged down here [at Ypres] in a bloody stalemate. . . . It was here that brutal trench warfare claimed the lives of nearly half a million British, Irish, Canadian, Australian, Indian, South African, New Zealand, German, French, and Belgian soldiers."

While sitting on the back of an ambulance parked near the dressing station beside the Canal de l'Yser, just a few hundred yards north of Ypres, McCrae vented his anguish by composing a poem. An observing young soldier reports that it was "an exact description of the scene. . . . The poppies actually were being blown that morning by a gentle east wind." McCrae was dissatisfied with the poem and tossed it away, but a fellow officer retrieved it and sent it to newspapers in England. London's Spectator rejected it, but Punch published it on December 8, 1915.

In Flanders fields the poppies blow
Between the crosses, row on row,
That mark our place; and in the sky

The larks, still bravely singing, fly
Scarce heard amid the guns below.

We are the Dead. Short days ago
We lived, felt dawn, saw sunset glow,
 Loved, and were loved, and now we lie,
 In Flanders fields.
Take up our quarrel with the foe:
To you from failing hands we throw
The torch; be yours to hold it high.
If ye break faith with us who die
We shall not sleep, though poppies grow
 In Flanders fields.

Metaphors and Related Figures of Speech

In a *metaphor*, a word or phrase denotes one kind of object or idea used in place of another to suggest a likeness or analogy between them: "The LORD lives! Praise be to my Rock!" (Psalm 18:46). "The LORD is my shepherd" (Psalm 23:1). "Life is but an empty dream!" (Longfellow).

A *simile* also compares things and is often introduced by *like* or *as*: "The kingdom of heaven is like a mustard seed" (Jesus, in Matthew 13:31). "O my Luve's like a red, red rose" (Robert Burns). "And our hearts, . . . like muffled drums, are beating" (Longfellow). "Be not like dumb, driven cattle!" (Longfellow). "The sight of them was as welcome to the Trojan host as a fair wind" (Homer).

In *personification* an inanimate object or concept is compared with a person: "Out in the open Wisdom calls aloud, she raises her voice in the public square" (Proverbs 1:20). "Let the dead Past bury its dead!" (Longfellow). "Bid Time and Nature gently spare / The shaft we raise to them and thee" (Emerson).

Hyperbole makes an extravagant exaggeration: "a huge army, as numerous as the sand on the seashore" (Joshua 11:4). "It is easier for a camel to go through the eye of a needle than for someone who is rich to enter the kingdom of God" (Jesus, in Luke 18:25). "The embattled farmers . . . fired the shot heard round the world" (Emerson).

Onomatopoeia is heard when a word approximates the sound of what it describes: "Ding Dong Bell" (nursery rhyme; also Shakespeare). "The bumblebees buzzed, and the rooks cawed" (Bret Harte).

"A Psalm of Life," by Henry Wadsworth Longfellow

Tell me not, in mournful numbers,
　Life is but an empty dream!
For the soul is dead that slumbers,
　And things are not what they seem.

Life is real! Life is earnest!
　And the grave is not its goal;
Dust thou art, to dust returnest,
　Was not spoken of the soul.

Not enjoyment, and not sorrow,
　Is our destined end or way;
But to act, that each to-morrow
　Find us farther than to-day.

Art is long, and Time is fleeting,
　And our hearts, though stout and brave,
Still, like muffled drums, are beating
　Funeral marches to the grave.

In the world's broad field of battle,
　In the bivouac of Life,
Be not like dumb, driven cattle!
　Be a hero in the strife!

Trust no Future, howe'er pleasant!
　Let the dead Past bury its dead!
Act,—act in the living Present!
　Heart within, and God o'erhead!

Lives of great men all remind us
　We can make our lives sublime,

And, departing, leave behind us
 Footprints on the sands of time; —

Footprints, that perhaps another,
 Sailing o'er life's solemn main,
A forlorn and shipwrecked brother,
 Seeing, shall take heart again.

Let us, then, be up and doing,
 With a heart for any fate;
Still achieving, still pursuing,
 Learn to labor and to wait.

"Concord Hymn," by Ralph Waldo Emerson

Emerson wrote this poem — sung as a hymn at a July 4, 1837, ceremony to mark the completion of the Concord Monument — to immortalize the resistance of American Minutemen to British forces on April 19, 1775. The hyperbole "shot heard round the world" is now internationally famous as representing the philosophical importance of the American Revolution for self-determination everywhere.

By the rude bridge that arched the flood,
 Their flag to April's breeze unfurled,
Here once the embattled farmers stood,
 And fired the shot heard round the world.

The foe long since in silence slept;
 Alike the conqueror silent sleeps;
And Time the ruined bridge has swept
 Down the dark stream which seaward creeps.

On this green bank, by this soft stream,
 We set to-day a votive stone;
That memory may their deed redeem,

When, like our sires, our sons are gone.

Spirit, that made those heroes dare
    To die, and leave their children free,
Bid Time and Nature gently spare
    The shaft we raise to them and thee.

"Lepanto," by G. K. Chesterton

This poem memorializes the five-hour Battle of Lepanto, on October 7, 1571, when a fleet of the Holy League of southern European Catholic states, led by "Don John of Austria," defeated the main fleet of the Ottoman Empire near the Gulf of Corinth (then called the Gulf of Lepanto). The Ottoman forces sailed west from Lepanto (on the northern coast of that gulf) and met the Holy League forces, which had come from Messina (in Sicily). The victory helped to block the Ottomans from advancing westward along the Mediterranean flank of Europe. This was the last major naval battle in the Mediterranean fought entirely between galleys.

White founts falling in the Courts of the sun,
And the Soldan of Byzantium is smiling as they run;
There is laughter like the fountains in that face of all men feared,
It stirs the forest darkness, the darkness of his beard;
It curls the blood-red crescent, the crescent of his lips;
For the inmost sea of all the earth is shaken with his ships.
They have dared the white republics up the capes of Italy,
They have dashed the Adriatic round the Lion of the Sea,
And the Pope has cast his arms abroad for agony and loss,
And called the kings of Christendom for swords about the Cross.
The cold queen of England is looking in the glass;
The shadow of the Valois is yawning at the Mass;
From evening isles fantastical rings faint the Spanish gun,
And the Lord upon the Golden Horn is laughing in the sun.
And the Pope has cast his arms abroad for agony and loss,
And called the kings of Christendom for swords about the Cross.
Dim drums throbbing, in the hills half heard,
Where only on a nameless throne a crownless prince has stirred,

Where, risen from a doubtful seat and half attainted stall,
The last knight of Europe takes weapons from the wall,
The last and lingering troubadour to whom the bird has sung,
That once went singing southward when all the world was young.
In that enormous silence, tiny and unafraid,
Comes up along a winding road the noise of the Crusade.
Strong gongs groaning as the guns boom far,
Don John of Austria is going to the war,
Stiff flags straining in the night-blasts cold
In the gloom black-purple, in the glint old-gold,
Torchlight crimson on the copper kettle-drums,
Then the tuckets, then the trumpets, then the cannon, and he comes.
Don John laughing in the brave beard curled,
Spurning of his stirrups like the thrones of all the world,
Holding his head up for a flag of all the free.
Love-light of Spain – hurrah!
Death-light of Africa!
Don John of Austria
Is riding to the sea.

Mahound is in his paradise above the evening star,
(Don John of Austria is going to the war.)
He moves a mighty turban on the timeless houri's knees,
His turban that is woven of the sunsets and the seas.
He shakes the peacock gardens as he rises from his ease,
And he strides among the tree-tops and is taller than the trees;
And his voice through all the garden is a thunder sent to bring
Black Azrael and Ariel and Ammon on the wing.
Giants and the Genii,
Multiplex of wing and eye,
Whose strong obedience broke the sky
When Solomon was king.

They rush in red and purple from the red clouds of the morn,
From the temples where the yellow gods   shut up their eyes in scorn;
They rise in green robes roaring from the green hells of the sea
Where fallen skies and evil hues and eyeless creatures be,
On them the sea-valves cluster and the grey sea-forests curl,
Splashed with a splendid sickness, the sickness of the pearl;

They swell in sapphire smoke out of the blue cracks of the ground, –
They gather and they wonder and give worship to Mahound.
And he saith, "Break up the mountains
    where the hermit-folk can hide,
And sift the red and silver sands lest bone of saint abide,
And chase the Giaours flying night and day, not giving rest,
For that which was our trouble comes again out of the west.
We have set the seal of Solomon on all things under sun,
Of knowledge and of sorrow and endurance of things done.
But a noise is in the mountains, in the mountains, and I know
The voice that shook our palaces – four hundred years ago:
It is he that saith not 'Kismet'; it is he that knows not Fate;
It is Richard, it is Raymond, it is Godfrey at the gate!
It is he whose loss is laughter when he counts the wager worth,
Put down your feet upon him, that our peace be on the earth."
For he heard drums groaning and he heard guns jar,
(Don John of Austria is going to the war.)
Sudden and still – hurrah!
Bolt from Iberia! Don John of Austria
Is gone by Alcalar.

St. Michaels on his Mountain in the sea-roads of the north
(Don John of Austria is girt and going forth.)
Where the grey seas glitter and the sharp tides shift
And the sea-folk labour and the red sails lift.
He shakes his lance of iron and he claps his wings of stone;
The noise is gone through Normandy; the noise is gone alone;
The North is full of tangled things and texts and aching eyes,
And dead is all the innocence of anger and surprise,
And Christian killeth Christian in a narrow dusty room,
And Christian dreadeth Christ that hath a newer face of doom,
And Christian hateth Mary that God kissed in Galilee, –
But Don John of Austria is riding to the sea.
Don John calling through the blast and the eclipse
Crying with the trumpet, with the trumpet of his lips,
Trumpet that sayeth ha!
Domino gloria!
Don John of Austria
Is shouting to the ships.

King Philip's in his closet with the Fleece about his neck.
(Don John of Austria is armed upon the deck.)
The walls are hung with velvet that is black and soft as sin,
And little dwarfs creep out of it and little dwarfs creep in.
He holds a crystal phial that has colours like the moon,
He touches, and it tingles, and he trembles very soon,
And his face is as a fungus of a leprous white and grey
Like plants in the high houses that are shuttered from the day,
And death is in the phial and the end of noble work,
But Don John of Austria has fired upon the Turk.
Don John's hunting, and his hounds have bayed —
Booms away past Italy the rumour of his raid.
Gun upon gun, ha! ha!
Gun upon gun, hurrah!
Don John of Austria
Has loosed the cannonade.

Battle of Lepanto, part of a
nineteenth-century carpet in
museum Kijk-je kerk-kunst, Gennep,
Netherlands (1571)

The Pope was in his chapel before day or battle broke,
(Don John of Austria is hidden in the smoke.)
The hidden room in man's house where God sits all the year,
The secret window whence the world looks small and very dear.
He sees as in a mirror on the monstrous twilight sea
The crescent of his cruel ships whose name is mystery;
They fling great shadows foe-wards, making Cross and Castle dark,
They veil the plumèd lions on the galleys of St. Mark;
And above the ships are palaces of brown, black-bearded chiefs,
And below the ships are prisons, where with multitudinous griefs,
Christian captives sick and sunless, all a labouring race repines
Like a race in sunken cities, like a nation in the mines.
They are lost like slaves that sweat, and in the skies of morning hung
The stair-ways of the tallest gods when tyranny was young.
They are countless, voiceless, hopeless as those fallen or fleeing on
Before the high Kings' horses in the granite of Babylon.
And many a one grows witless in his quiet room in Hell
Where a yellow face looks inward through the lattice of his cell,
And he finds his God forgotten, and he seeks no more a sign —
(But Don John of Austria has burst the battle-line!)
Don John pounding from the slaughter-painted poop,

Purpling all the ocean like a bloody pirate's sloop,
Scarlet running over on the silvers and the golds,
Breaking of the hatches up and bursting of the holds,
Thronging of the thousands up that labour under sea
White for bliss and blind for sun and stunned for liberty.

  Vivat Hispania!
    Domino Gloria!
Don John of Austria
Has set his people free!

Cervantes on his galley sets the sword back in the sheath
(Don John of Austria rides homeward with a wreath.)
And he sees across a weary land a straggling road in Spain,
Up which a lean and foolish knight for ever rides in vain,
And he smiles, but not as Sultans smile,
    and settles back the blade. . . .
(But Don John of Austria rides home from the Crusade.)

"Honky Tonk in Cleveland, Ohio," by Carl Sandburg

It's a jazz affair, drum crashes and cornet razzes.
The trombone pony neighs and the tuba jackass snorts.
The banjo tickles and titters too awful.
The chippies talk about the funnies in the papers.
The cartoonists weep in their beer.
Ship riveters talk with their feet
To the feet of floozies under the tables.
A quartet of white hopes mourn with interspersed   snickers:
"I got the blues.
I got the blues.
I got the blues."
And . . . as we said earlier:
The cartoonists weep in their beer.

"The Second Coming," by William Butler Yeats

Yeats wrote this poem in 1919, soon after World War I, which brought massive destruction and catastrophic loss of life. He uses Christian imagery of the Apocalypse and Christ's second coming as an allegory to describe Europe's atmosphere of despair, disillusionment, and distrust: "The centre cannot hold." Alliteration drives the serious, mysterious tone.

Turning and turning in the widening gyre
The falcon cannot hear the falconer;
Things fall apart; the centre cannot hold;
Mere anarchy is loosed upon the world,
The blood-dimmed tide is loosed, and everywhere
The ceremony of innocence is drowned;
The best lack all conviction, while the worst
Are full of passionate intensity.

Surely some revelation is at hand;
Surely the Second Coming is at hand.
The Second Coming! Hardly are those words out
When a vast image out of Spiritus Mundi
Troubles my sight: a waste of desert sand;
A shape with lion body and the head of a man,
A gaze blank and pitiless as the sun,
Is moving its slow thighs, while all about it
Wind shadows of the indignant desert birds.

The darkness drops again but now I know
That twenty centuries of stony sleep
Were vexed to nightmare by a rocking cradle,
And what rough beast, its hour come round at last,
Slouches towards Bethlehem to be born?

"War Is Kind," by Stephen Crane

The ironic and sarcastic tone of this poem shows that the poet has tongue in cheek.

Do not weep, maiden, for war is kind,
Because your lover threw wild hands toward the sky
And the affrighted steed ran on alone,
Do not weep.
War is kind.

Hoarse, booming drums of the regiment,
Little souls who thirst for fight,
These men were born to drill and die.
The unexplained glory flies above them.
Great is the battle-god, great, and his kingdom —
A field where a thousand corpses lie.

Do not weep, babe, for war is kind.
Because your father tumbles in the yellow trenches,
Raged at his breast, gulped and died,
Do not weep.
War is kind.

Swift blazing flag of the regiment,
Eagle with crest of red and gold,
These men were born to drill and die.
Point for them the virtue of slaughter,
Make plain to them the excellence of killing
And a field where a thousand corpses lie.

Mother whose heart hung humble as a button
On the bright splendid shroud of your son,
Do not weep.
War is kind.

Sounds in Poetry

Terms

Poets choose words to create meanings, using sound effects to create a mood or establish a tone. Sometimes the sounds in poems provide special effects, but often sound is intertwined with meaning, inviting the reader to experience a tone and grasp a meaning: "Once upon a midnight dreary, / while I pondered weak and weary" (Poe).

A *foot* is a unit of measure of poetry: "Tyger" (Poe).

Meter is determined by the *kind* of foot, the regular (or irregular) pattern of accents and number of syllables per line. There are various metrical patterns in poetry:

> *Iambic* is the most common metrical pattern, in which each foot contains an unstressed syllable followed by a stressed syllable. *Iambic pentameter*—one of the most common meters, used in poetry and much of Shakespeare's plays—consists of lines containing five iambic feet (de/DUM de/DUM de/DUM de/DUM de/DUM): "To swell the gourd, and plump the hazel shells" (John Keats).
>
> A *trochee* is a stressed syllable followed by an unstressed syllable (DUM/de): "How they tinkle, tinkle, tinkle" (Poe).
>
> An *anapest* is made up of two unstressed syllables followed by a stressed syllable (de/de/DUM): "'Twas the night before Christmas, when all through the house" (Clement Clarke Moore).
>
> A *dactyl* is a stressed syllable followed by two unstressed syllables (DUM/de/de): "Out of the mockingbird's throat" (Whitman).
>
> A *spondee* is composed of two long or stressed syllables: "*Well-loved* of me" (Tennyson).
>
> For a longer list of metrical patterns, see http://en.wikipedia.org/wiki/Foot_(prosody).

A *caesura* is a short pause within a line, often (though not always) signaled by a mark of punctuation such as a comma: "And he dances, and he yells" (Poe).

Alliteration is repetition of a sound: "Tyger, tyger, burning bright" (Blake).

Consonance (a form of alliteration) is a repetition of consonants: "Dewdrops dilute daisies domain" (Paul McCann).

Assonance (a form of alliteration) is repetition of vowel sounds: "What a world of happiness their harmony foretells!" (Poe).

"The Tyger," by William Blake

Tyger, tyger, burning bright,
In the forest of the night;
What immortal hand or eye
Could frame thy fearful symmetry?
In what distant deeps or skies
Burnt the fire of thine eyes?
On what wings dare he aspire?
What the hand dare seize the fire?

And what shoulder, & what the art
Could twist the sinews of thy heart?
And when thy heart began to beat
What dread hand? & what dread feet?

What the hammer? what the chain?
In what furnace was thy brain?
What the anvil? what dread grasp
Dare its deadly terrors clasp?
When the stars threw down their spears
And water'd heaven with their tears,
Did He smile his work to see?
Did He who made the Lamb make thee?

Tyger, Tyger burning bright,
In the forests of the night;
What immortal hand or eye
Dare frame thy fearful symmetry?

"Don't Delay Dawns Disarming Display," by Paul McCann

The author puts so much effort into consonance by repeating the letter d that he overlooks using apostrophes for possessives. Yet his doodling daringly develops daunting, dashing d-sound demonstration.

Don't delay dawns disarming display.
Dusk demands daylight.

Dewdrops dwell, delicately drawing dazzling delight.

Dewdrops dilute daisies domain.

Distinguished debutantes.

Diamonds defray delivered daylights distilled daisy dance.

"Bells," by Edgar Allan Poe

Hear the sledges with the bells—Silver bells!

What a world of merriment their melody foretells!

How they tinkle, tinkle, tinkle,

In the icy air of night!

While the stars that oversprinkle

All the heavens seem to twinkle

With a crystalline delight;

Keeping time, time, time,

In a sort of Runic rhyme,

To the tintinnabulation that so musically wells

From the bells, bells, bells, bells,

Bells, bells, bells—

From the jingling and the tinkling of the bells.

Hear the mellow wedding bells—

Golden bells!

What a world of happiness their harmony foretells!

Through the balmy air of night

How they ring out their delight!

From the molten-golden notes,

And all in tune,

What a liquid ditty floats

To the turtle-dove that listens, while she gloats

On the moon!

Oh, from out the sounding cells

What a gush of euphony voluminously wells!

How it swells!

How it dwells

On the Future!—how it tells

Of the rapture that impels

To the swinging and the ringing

Of the bells, bells, bells,

Of the bells, bells, bells, bells,
Bells, bells, bells—
To the rhyming and the chiming of the bells!
 Hear the loud alarum bells—
Brazen bells!
What a tale of terror, now, their turbulency tells!
In the startled ear of night
How they scream out their affright!
Too much horrified to speak,
They can only shriek, shriek,
Out of tune,
In a clamorous appealing to the mercy of the fire,
In a mad expostulation with the deaf and frantic fire,
Leaping higher, higher, higher,
With a desperate desire,
And a resolute endeavor
Now—now to sit or never,
By the side of the pale-faced moon.
Oh, the bells, bells, bells!
What a tale their terror tells
Of despair!
How they clang, and clash, and roar!
What a horror they outpour
On the bosom of the palpitating air!
Yet the ear it fully knows,
By the twanging
And the clanging,
How the danger ebbs and flows;
Yet the ear distinctly tells,
In the jangling
And the wrangling,
How the danger sinks and swells,
By the sinking or the swelling in the anger of the bells—
Of the bells,
Of the bells, bells, bells, bells,
Bells, bells, bells—
In the clamor and the clangor of the bells!

Hear the tolling of the bells —
Iron bells!
What a world of solemn thought their monody compels!
In the silence of the night,
How we shiver with affright
At the melancholy menace of their tone!
For every sound that floats
From the rust within their throats
Is a groan.
And the people — ah, the people —
They that dwell up in the steeple,
All alone,
And who tolling, tolling, tolling,
In that muffled monotone,
Feel a glory in so rolling
On the human heart a stone —
They are neither man nor woman —
They are neither brute nor human —
They are Ghouls:
And their king it is who tolls;
And he rolls, rolls, rolls,
Rolls
A paean from the bells!
And his merry bosom swells
With the paean of the bells!
And he dances, and he yells;
Keeping time, time, time,
In a sort of Runic rhyme,
To the paean of the bells,
Of the bells —
Keeping time, time, time,
In a sort of Runic rhyme,
To the throbbing of the bells,
Of the bells, bells, bells —
To the sobbing of the bells;
Keeping time, time, time,

As he knells, knells, knells,
In a happy Runic rhyme,
To the rolling of the bells,
Of the bells, bells, bells—
To the tolling of the bells,
Of the bells, bells, bells, bells,
Bells, bells, bells—
To the moaning and the groaning of the bells.

Poetry in the Bible

The Songs of Moses and Miriam: Exodus 15:1–21

Notice the anthropomorphism as these songs give human characteristics to God as "warrior" with a powerful "right hand," who blasts with his "nostrils," delivers his people, and reigns forever as king. Genesis 1:26–28 says that humans are created in the image of God, and yet God is not a human being. Also there are similes: Pharaoh's army "sank . . . like a stone, . . . like lead." See personification in the phrase "the earth swallows your enemies."

Then Moses and the Israelites sang this song to the LORD:

"I will sing to the LORD,
    for he is highly exalted.
Both horse and driver
    he has hurled into the sea.

"The LORD is my strength and my defense;
  he has become my salvation.
He is my God, and I will praise him,
  my father's God, and I will exalt him.
The LORD is a warrior;
  the LORD is his name.
Pharaoh's chariots and his army
  he has hurled into the sea.
The best of Pharaoh's officers
  are drowned in the Red Sea.
The deep waters have covered them;
  they sank to the depths like a stone.
Your right hand, LORD,
  was majestic in power.
Your right hand, LORD,
  shattered the enemy.
"In the greatness of your majesty
  you threw down those who opposed you.
You unleashed your burning anger;
  it consumed them like stubble.
By the blast of your nostrils
  the waters piled up.
The surging waters stood up like a wall;
  the deep waters congealed in the heart of the sea.
The enemy boasted,
  'I will pursue, I will overtake them.
I will divide the spoils;
  I will gorge myself on them.
I will draw my sword
  and my hand will destroy them.'
But you blew with your breath,
  and the sea covered them.
They sank like lead
  in the mighty waters.
Who among the gods
  is like you, LORD?
Who is like you—

majestic in holiness,
awesome in glory,
   working wonders?

"You stretch out your right hand,
   and the earth swallows your enemies.
In your unfailing love you will lead
   the people you have redeemed.
In your strength you will guide them
   to your holy dwelling.
The nations will hear and tremble;
   anguish will grip the people of Philistia.
The chiefs of Edom will be terrified,
   the leaders of Moab will be seized with trembling,
the people of Canaan will melt away;
   terror and dread will fall on them.
By the power of your arm
   they will be as still as a stone —
until your people pass by, LORD,
   until the people you bought pass by.
You will bring them in and plant them
   on the mountain of your inheritance —
the place, LORD, you made for your dwelling,
   the sanctuary, LORD, your hands established.

"The LORD reigns
   for ever and ever."

When Pharaoh's horses, chariots and horsemen went into the sea, the LORD brought the waters of the sea back over them, but the Israelites walked through the sea on dry ground. Then Miriam the prophet, Aaron's sister, took a timbrel in her hand, and all the women followed her, with timbrels and dancing. Miriam sang to them:

"Sing to the Lord,
   for he is highly exalted.
Both horse and driver

he has hurled into the sea."

David Laments the Death of Saul and Jonathan:

2 Samuel 1:19–27

"A gazelle lies slain on your heights, Israel.
   How the mighty have fallen!
"Tell it not in Gath,
   proclaim it not in the streets of Ashkelon,
lest the daughters of the Philistines be glad,
   lest the daughters of the uncircumcised rejoice.

"Mountains of Gilboa,
   may you have neither dew nor rain,
   may no showers fall on your terraced fields.
For there the shield of the mighty was despised,
   the shield of Saul—no longer rubbed with oil.

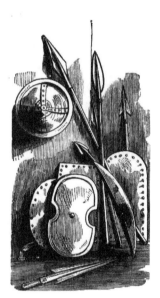

"From the blood of the slain,
   from the flesh of the mighty,
the bow of Jonathan did not turn back,
   the sword of Saul did not return unsatisfied.
Saul and Jonathan—
   in life they were loved and admired,
   and in death they were not parted.
They were swifter than eagles,
   they were stronger than lions.
"How the mighty have fallen!
   The weapons of war have perished!"
"Daughters of Israel,
   weep for Saul,
who clothed you in scarlet and finery,
   who adorned your garments with ornaments of gold.

"How the mighty have fallen in battle!
   Jonathan lies slain on your heights.
I grieve for you, Jonathan my brother;

you were very dear to me.
Your love for me was wonderful,
    more wonderful than that of women.

A Mighty Fortress: Psalm 18

Some metaphors are obvious: "The LORD is my rock, my fortress and my deliverer."

I love you, LORD, my strength.
The LORD is my rock, my fortress and my deliverer;
    my God is my rock, in whom I take refuge,
    my shield and the horn of my salvation, my stronghold.

I called to the LORD, who is worthy of praise,
    and I have been saved from my enemies.
The cords of death entangled me;
    the torrents of destruction overwhelmed me.
The cords of the grave coiled around me;
    the snares of death confronted me.

In my distress I called to the LORD;
    I cried to my God for help.
From his temple he heard my voice;
    my cry came before him, into his ears.
The earth trembled and quaked,
    and the foundations of the mountains shook;
    they trembled because he was angry.
Smoke rose from his nostrils;
    consuming fire came from his mouth,
    burning coals blazed out of it.
He parted the heavens and came down;
    dark clouds were under his feet.
He mounted the cherubim and flew;
    he soared on the wings of the wind.
He made darkness his covering, his canopy around him—
    the dark rain clouds of the sky.
Out of the brightness of his presence clouds advanced,
    with hailstones and bolts of lightning.

The LORD thundered from heaven;
  the voice of the Most High resounded.
He shot his arrows and scattered the enemy,
  with great bolts of lightning he routed them.
The valleys of the sea were exposed
  and the foundations of the earth laid bare
at your rebuke, LORD,
  at the blast of breath from your nostrils.

He reached down from on high and took hold of me;
  he drew me out of deep waters.
He rescued me from my powerful enemy,
  from my foes, who were too strong for me.
They confronted me in the day of my disaster,
  but the LORD was my support.
He brought me out into a spacious place;
  he rescued me because he delighted in me.

The LORD has dealt with me according to my righteousness;
  according to the cleanness of my hands he has rewarded me.
For I have kept the ways of the LORD;
  I am not guilty of turning from my God.
All his laws are before me;
  I have not turned away from his decrees.
I have been blameless before him
  and have kept myself from sin.
The LORD has rewarded me according to my righteousness,
  according to the cleanness of my hands in his sight.
To the faithful you show yourself faithful,
  to the blameless you show yourself blameless,
to the pure you show yourself pure,
  but to the devious you show yourself shrewd.
You save the humble
  but bring low those whose eyes are haughty.
You, LORD, keep my lamp burning;
  my God turns my darkness into light.
With your help I can advance against a troop;

with my God I can scale a wall.

As for God, his way is perfect:
    The LORD's word is flawless;
    he shields all who take refuge in him.
For who is God besides the LORD?
    And who is the Rock except our God?
It is God who arms me with strength
    and keeps my way secure.
He makes my feet like the feet of a deer;
    he causes me to stand on the heights.
He trains my hands for battle;
    my arms can bend a bow of bronze.
You make your saving help my shield,
    and your right hand sustains me;
    your help has made me great.
You provide a broad path for my feet,
    so that my ankles do not give way.
I pursued my enemies and overtook them;
    I did not turn back till they were destroyed.
I crushed them so that they could not rise;
    they fell beneath my feet.
You armed me with strength for battle;
    you humbled my adversaries before me.
You made my enemies turn their backs in flight,
    and I destroyed my foes.
They cried for help, but there was no one to save them —
    to the LORD, but he did not answer.
I beat them as fine as windblown dust;
    I trampled them like mud in the streets.
You have delivered me from the attacks of the people;
    you have made me the head of nations.
People I did not know now serve me,
    foreigners cower before me;
    as soon as they hear of me, they obey me.
They all lose heart;
    they come trembling from their strongholds.

The LORD lives! Praise be to my Rock!
    Exalted be God my Savior!
He is the God who avenges me,
    who subdues nations under me,
    who saves me from my enemies.
You exalted me above my foes;
    from a violent man you rescued me.
Therefore I will praise you, LORD, among the nations;
    I will sing the praises of your name.

He gives his king great victories;
    he shows unfailing love to his anointed,
    to David and to his descendants forever.

Like an Eagle: Deuteronomy 32:10–12

The Lord is "like an eagle."

    In a desert land [the LORD] found [his people, Jacob],
    in a barren and howling waste.
He shielded him and cared for him;
    he guarded him as the apple of his eye,
like an eagle that stirs up its nest
    and hovers over its young,
that spreads its wings to catch them
    and carries them aloft.
The LORD alone led him;
    no foreign god was with him.

Every Knee Shall Bow: Philippians 2:5–11

Paul tells believers, in their relationships with one another, to have the same attitude and mind as Christ Jesus.

In your relationships with one another, have the same mindset as Christ Jesus:

Who, being in very nature God,
  did not consider equality with God
  something to be used to his own advantage;
rather, he made himself nothing
  by taking the very nature of a servant,
  being made in human likeness.
And being found in appearance as a man,
  he humbled himself
  by becoming obedient to death—
even death on a cross!

Christ in majesty, holding up two fingers for his two natures, human and divine, and cradling an orb as ruler of all, Pantocrator, to whom "every knee should bow." Around Christ are four creatures, representing the four evangelists (clockwise, from top left): Matthew (face of a winged man, symbolizing Jesus' incarnation), John (an eagle, presenting Jesus in the soaring light of eternity), Mark (a winged lion, showing Jesus as a figure of courage and monarchy), and Luke (a winged bull or ox, for Jesus as a sacrifice).

Therefore God exalted him to the highest place
  and gave him the name that is above every name,
that at the name of Jesus every knee should bow,
  in heaven and on earth and under the earth,
and every tongue acknowledge that Jesus Christ is Lord,
  to the glory of God the Father.

Student Essays

Beowulf: Medieval Epic Poem

The Anglo-Saxon poem Beowulf is one of the earliest medieval epics that relate the adventures of Beowulf and his encounters with different monsters.

"Lo! praise of the prowess of people-kings of spear-armed Danes, in days long sped we have heard, and what honor the athelings won!" (Prelude). The

Anglo-Saxon poem *Beowulf* is one of the earliest medieval epics that relates the adventures of Beowulf and his encounters with different monsters. Three characters—Hrothgar, Unferth, and Wiglaf—act as foils to develop this hero Beowulf. Hrothgar is the king of Denmark and a descendent of Shield Sheafson. Hrothgar's reign is auspicious until the demon Grendel begins to plunder Hrothgar's kingdom every night. Beowulf, from Geatland, hears of this predicament and resolves to defeat Grendel. He is a great warrior and full of loyalty, courtesy, and pride. Because of his strength and bravery, Beowulf easily defeats Grendel and Grendel's mother.

Soon after Beowulf's victory over Grendel's mother, Hrothgar gives Beowulf a long sermon, warning him of the dangers of success and pride:

> Yet in the end it ever comes
> that the frame of the body fragile yields,
> fated falls; and there follows another
> who joyously the jewel divides,
> the royal riches,
> nor recks of his forebear.
> Ban, then, such baleful thoughts,
> Beowulf dearest,
> best of men, and the better part choose,
> profit eternal; and temper thy pride,
> warrior famous! (§25)

Beowulf, shearing off the head of Grendel From The Death of Grendel in Hero-Myths and Legends of the British Race, by M. I. Ebbutt, illustrated by John Henry Frederick Bacon. Bridgeman Art Library / The Stapleton Collection

Hrothgar cautions Beowulf not to get caught up in pride from his successes because when he ages, he will lose his youthful prowess. A remarkable king is full of honor, nobility, and leadership, not necessarily military aptitudes. Hrothgar's advice helps Beowulf transition from a valiant warrior to a humble king. At the end of the narrative, Beowulf returns to his homeland and eventually becomes crowned king. Beowulf is a successful ruler because he has followed the judicious guidance of Hrothgar.

Hrothgar developed Beowulf for this future as king, but Unferth develops Beowulf for his imminent battle against Grendel. Unferth is one of Hrothgar's courtiers and is extremely envious of Beowulf's bravery.

Unferth spake, the son of Ecglaf,
who sat at the feet of the Scyldings' lord,
unbound the battle-runes. — Beowulf's quest,
sturdy seafarer's, sorely galled him;
ever he envied that other men
should more achieve in middle-earth
of fame under heaven than he himself. (§8)

Unferth therefore tries to strip Beowulf of excessive pride and reduce Beowulf's gallant reputation. However, this only furthers Beowulf's conviction to defeat Grendel. Beowulf replies to Unferth:

". . . 'Twas granted me, though,
to pierce the monster with point of sword,
with blade of battle:
huge beast of the sea
was whelmed by the hurly though hand of mine." (§8)

Unferth is clearly a lesser man than Beowulf and afraid to fight Grendel himself. Unferth's jealousy for Beowulf just helps to accentuate Beowulf's warrior characteristics.
Contrary to Unferth's superficial pride, Wiglaf is the only soldier daring enough to fight side by side with Beowulf against the dragon. In the midst of the battle, Wiglaf encourages his fellow kinsman to join him in helping Beowulf defeat the dragon.

. . . "Now the day is come
that our noble master has need of the might
of warriors stout. Let us stride along
the hero to help while the heat is about him
glowing and grim! . . ." (§36)

However, all the other soldiers are too afraid and run away. Wiglaf remains loyal and risks his life to help Beowulf defeat the fire-breathing dragon. Wiglaf represents Beowulf at his youth. Wiglaf is faithful, audacious, and valorous, just as Beowulf was when he defeated Grendel. Thus Wiglaf serves to show the aging and maturity that Beowulf has gone through. With the "youthful" Wiglaf next to the "aged" Beowulf, it is clearly obvious that Beowulf has greatly changed from his former prowess. Wiglaf serves to be the Beowulf of the next generation.

The Old English poem *Beowulf* is a medieval epic that relates the adventures of Beowulf and his encounters with different monsters. Three characters—Hrothgar, Unferth, and Wiglaf—act as foils to develop Beowulf. Hrothgar's counsel aids Beowulf in the future, Unferth's scornful arrogance contrasts against Beowulf's well-deserved pride, and Wiglaf's fidelity follows Beowulf's example.

Comments on *Beowulf*

The most unexpected quality in Beowulf is its abiding communication of joy. In contrast with the Mediterranean glitter of the *Odyssey*, . . . Beowulf takes place in an atmosphere of semi-darkness, the gloom of fire-lit halls, stormy wastelands, and underwater caverns. It is full of blood and fierceness. . . . Men exult in their conflict with each other and the elements. Even Grendel and his mother are serious in the way Greek demons never are. They may be horrors survived from the pagan Norse world of frost giants, wolf men, and dragons of the waters, but nobody would ever dream of calling them frivolous. They share Beowulf's dogged earnestness; what they lack is his joy. —Kenneth Rexroth

"The Collar," by George Herbert

I Struck the board, and cry'd, No more.
I will abroad.
What? shall I ever sigh and pine?
My lines and life are free; free as the rode,
Loose as the winde, as large as store.
Shall I be still in suit?
Have I no harvest but a thorn
To let me bloud, and not restore
What I have lost with cordiall fruit?
Sure there was wine
Before my sighs did drie it: there was corn
Before my tears did drown it.
Is the yeare onely lost to me?
Have I no bayes to crown it?
No flowers, no garlands gay? all blasted?
All wasted?
Not so, my heart: but there is fruit,
And thou hast hands.

Recover all thy sigh-blown age
On double pleasures: leave thy cold dispute
Of what is fit, and not. Forsake thy cage,
Thy rope of sands,
Which pettie thoughts have made, and made to thee
Good cable, to enforce and draw,
And be thy law,
While thou didst wink and wouldst not see.
Away; take heed:
I will abroad.
Call in thy deaths head there: tie up thy fears.
He that forbears
To suit and serve his need,
Deserves his load.
But as I rav'd and grew more fierce and wilde
At every word,
Me thoughts I heard one calling, *Childe*:
And I reply'd, *My Lord*.

In his 1633 poem about the restrictions and freedoms of the Christian life, "The Collar," George Herbert utilizes two writing techniques: symbolic writing and metaphysical conceit. Both techniques compare vague concepts and ideas with more familiar concepts and ideas; however, metaphysical conceit delves more into the supernatural. In the poem, Herbert uses both of these techniques to describe in understandable terms the boundaries of a Christian life. He compares his freedoms to a road and to wind: both are free but yet have  boundaries. Herbert also uses a harvest to aid in the analogy. By putting the desired concept into understandable terms, Herbert enhances the effect of the poem.

I Struck the board, and cry'd, No more.
I will abroad.
What? shall I ever sigh and pine?
My lines and life are free; free as the rode,
Loose as the winde, as large as store.
Shall I be still in suit?

"The Collar" is a caution against the common mistake that the boundaries on a Christian's lifestyle are far more stringent than is actually the case. Herbert has lived within this imaginary circle of do's and don'ts for long enough. His life, he reasons, utilizing the technique of metaphysical conceit, is akin to a road: open, spacious, and free, but restricted nonetheless. He references the wind, which may blow where it pleases, except for where it is interrupted by a barrier. Herbert is ready to go abroad into this hitherto unexplored land, outside of the conceived boundaries of before.

> Have I no harvest but a thorn
> To let me bloud, and not restore
> What I have lost with cordiall fruit?
> Sure there was wine
> Before my sighs did drie it: there was corn
> Before my tears did drown it.
> Is the yeare onely lost to me?

In his aforementioned conceived circle, the profit of Herbert's time is but a thorn upon which he pricks himself. He could have reaped a goodly harvest of corn and wine, had not his sighs and discontent ruined it. Herbert realizes that to best reap the benefits of the Christian life, one must step outside of imaginary boundaries, else he also restricts the size of his harvest. Again, metaphysical conceit and symbolic writing aid in presenting his insightful observations by comparing them to something as familiar as a harvest.

> Recover all thy sigh-blown age
> On double pleasures: leave thy cold dispute
> Of what is fit, and not. Forsake thy cage,
> Thy rope of sands,
> Which pettie thoughts have made, and made to thee
> Good cable, to enforce and draw,
> And be thy law,
> While thou didst wink and wouldst not see.

Being a Christian does not mean that one must spend all of one's time in sighing and pining, and miss out on pleasure. To make up for what he has lost, bound by his imaginary ropes of sand, Herbert would engage in double pleasure within the wide open road of God's freedoms. No longer does he wish to waste time with do's and don'ts. He wants to enjoy the pleasures that God gave Christians the freedom to partake in, so long as they emerge from their conceptual boundaries.

Herbert employs these examples of symbolism to better enhance the effect of his poem and to make it easier to understand. The symbolism of the road and the wind, and the metaphysical conceit of the harvest—all effectively paint a picture of the compromise of freedom and boundary that "The Collar" addresses. After acknowledging God as Lord, it does not follow that the believer is free to do whatsoever one desires. However, believers reap a better harvest when they partake of the freedom that God has granted, rather than confining themselves with imaginary rules and regulations. There is a balance to be desired, and that balance Herbert discovers in "The Collar."

"The Charge of the Light Brigade," by Alfred Lord Tennyson

"The Charge of the Light Brigade," by Alfred Lord Tennyson, describes a great military blunder by the British in the Crimean War. On October 25, 1854, the men of the 13th Light Dragoons were ordered to charge the Russian gun batteries outside of the town of Balaklava. Many were killed, and Tennyson wrote this poem to commemorate their sacrifice. But is it truly a description of the historical event?

In the poem, Tennyson describes an actual battle of the Crimean War. He romanticizes the glorious charge of the 13th Light Dragoons against unbeatable odds ("Charging an army, while / All the world wonder'd"). He rightly surmises that it was caused by a blunder in the command ("Not tho' the soldier knew / Someone had blunder'd"), and also shows the bravery of the men, who knew that they were going to die, and their willingness to follow orders that would lead to their deaths ("Theirs not to make reply, / Theirs not to reason why, / Theirs but to do and die: / Into the valley of Death / Rode the six hundred").

In the real battle, a miscommunication in orders had disastrous results. The 13th Light Dragoons set off into a coverless valley to capture some Russian artillery on the other side. They did not know that the ridges around the valley were occupied by around twenty battalions of Russian infantry and artillery. William Howard Russell witnessed the charge and reported in the London *Times*:

> They advanced in two lines, quickening their pace as they closed
> towards the enemy. A more fearful spectacle was never witnessed than

by those who, without the power to aid, beheld their heroic countrymen rushing to the arms of death. At the distance of 1,200 yards the whole line of the enemy belched forth, from thirty iron mouths, a flood of smoke and flame, through which hissed the deadly balls. Their flight was marked by instant gaps in our ranks, by dead men and horses, by steeds flying wounded or riderless across the plain.

The poem and the event are similar in some respects, yet the poem is more romanticized than the actual event. The poem is in agreement with the event in that the charge was caused by the commanders' great error. It is also correct in the fact that they were outflanked by cannon, but it greatly exaggerates the losses suffered by the light brigade. Out of 670 men, an estimated 278 were either killed, wounded, or missing. However, Tennyson's poem makes it seem as if none or very few rode back ("They rode back but not, / Not the six hundred"; and later, "They that had fought so well / Came thro' the jaws of Death, / Back from the mouth of Hell, / All that was left of them, / Left of six hundred").

The poem also makes the charge seem glorious and noble, as though the dragoons were the knights of old. This is highly romanticized: one can be sure that the thoughts in the soldiers' minds as their friends and comrades died beside them were not, "How noble and glorious this is!" One can compare it to the charge of the French knights at the battle of Agincourt in the Hundred Years' War. They charged over muddy ground toward the English longbow men, which resulted in hundreds of deaths as the knights, weighed down by their armor, stuck in the mud and were shot down.

While the poem is true to the account in some ways, it is very different in others. It does follow the basic outline of the fight, but it is strongly laced with romanticism. There is nothing glorious about the needless deaths of men. Actually, what was noble was that they followed orders to the death, as it says in Tennyson's poem: "Boldly they rode and well, / Into the jaws of Death, / Into the mouth of Hell / Rode the six hundred." And later: "Then they rode back, but not, / Not the six hundred." On the other hand, the poem does communicate Tennyson's message very well and has solidified the memory of the Light Brigade, the 13th Light Dragoons, in the minds of many for over two hundred years. The order, "Honor the charge they made! / Honor the Light Brigade, / Noble six hundred!" was followed, and for many years after Tennyson and the survivors of the light brigade died, the words of Alfred Lord Tennyson rang on with their cries of honor for the fallen soldiers who rode boldly into the face of enemy fire.

"The Midnight Ride of Paul Revere,"

by Henry Wadsworth Longfellow

This student writes in a robust and forthright style. Henry Wadsworth Longfellow, the poet, accents his poem with many strong literary aspects that make it captivating. At the same time, this student writes with economy and grace: there is no unnecessary verbiage. Next, his transitions are solid, and he restates his argument several times. Finally, his conclusion is informative without being tangential. Before the essay, see here the whole poem, set in 1775:

The Landlord's Tale: Paul Revere's Ride

Listen, my children, and you shall hear
Of the midnight ride of Paul Revere,
On the eighteenth of April, in Seventy-five;
Hardly a man is now alive
Who remembers that famous day and year.

He said to his friend, "If the British march
By land or sea from the town to-night,
Hang a lantern aloft in the belfry arch
Of the North Church tower as a signal light, —
One, if by land, and two, if by sea;
And I on the opposite shore will be,
Ready to ride and spread the alarm
Through every Middlesex village and farm,
For the country folk to be up and to arm."
Then he said, "Good night!" and with muffled oar
Silently rowed to the Charlestown shore,
Just as the moon rose over the bay,
Where swinging wide at her moorings lay
The *Somerset*, British man-of-war;
A phantom ship, with each mast and spar
Across the moon like a prison bar,
And a huge black hulk, that was magnified
By its own reflection in the tide.

Meanwhile, his friend, through alley and street,
Wanders and watches with eager ears,

Till in the silence around him he hears
The muster of men at the barrack door,
The sound of arms, and the tramp of feet,
And the measured tread of the grenadiers,
Marching down to their boats on the shore.

Then he climbed the tower of the Old North Church,
By the wooden stairs, with stealthy tread,
To the belfry-chamber overhead,
And startled the pigeons from their perch
On the sombre rafters, that round him made
Masses and moving shapes of shade, —
By the trembling ladder, steep and tall,
To the highest window in the wall,
Where he paused to listen and look down
A moment on the roofs of the town,
And the moonlight flowing over all.
Beneath, in the churchyard, lay the dead,
In their night-encampment on the hill,
Wrapped in silence so deep and still
That he could hear, like a sentinel's tread,
The watchful night-wind, as it went
Creeping along from tent to tent,
And seeming to whisper, "All is well!"
A moment only he feels the spell
Of the place and the hour, and the secret dread
Of the lonely belfry and the dead;
For suddenly all his thoughts are bent
On a shadowy something far away,
Where the river widens to meet the bay, —
A line of black that bends and floats
On the rising tide, like a bridge of boats.

Meanwhile, impatient to mount and ride,
Booted and spurred, with a heavy stride
On the opposite shore walked Paul Revere.
Now he patted his horse's side,

Now gazed at the landscape far and near,
Then, impetuous, stamped the earth,
And turned and tightened his saddle girth;
But mostly he watched with eager search
The belfry-tower of the Old North Church,
As it rose above the graves on the hill,
Lonely and spectral and sombre and still.
And lo! as he looks, on the belfry's height
A glimmer, and then a gleam of light!
He springs to the saddle, the bridle he turns,
But lingers and gazes, till full on his sight
A second lamp in the belfry burns!
A hurry of hoofs in a village street,
A shape in the moonlight, a bulk in the dark,
And beneath, from the pebbles, in passing, a spark
Struck out by a steed flying fearless and fleet:
That was all! And yet, through the gloom and the light,
The fate of a nation was riding that night;
And the spark struck out by that steed, in his flight,
Kindled the land into flame with its heat.
He has left the village and mounted the steep,
And beneath him, tranquil and broad and deep,
Is the Mystic, meeting the ocean tides;
And under the alders, that skirt its edge,
Now soft on the sand, now loud on the ledge,
Is heard the tramp of his steed as he rides.

It was twelve by the village clock,
When he crossed the bridge into Medford town.
He heard the crowing of the cock,
And the barking of the farmer's dog,
And felt the damp of the river fog,
That rises after the sun goes down.

 It was one by the village clock,
When he galloped into Lexington.
He saw the gilded weathercock

Swim in the moonlight as he passed,
And the meeting-house windows, blank and bare,
Gaze at him with a spectral glare,
As if they already stood aghast
At the bloody work they would look upon.

It was two by the village clock,
When he came to the bridge in Concord town.
He heard the bleating of the flock,
And the twitter of birds among the trees,
And felt the breath of the morning breeze
Blowing over the meadows brown.
And one was safe and asleep in his bed
Who at the bridge would be first to fall,
Who that day would be lying dead,
Pierced by a British musket-ball.

You know the rest. In the books you have read,
How the British Regulars fired and fled, —
How the farmers gave them ball for ball,
From behind each fence and farmyard wall,
Chasing the red-coats down the lane,
Then crossing the fields to emerge again
Under the trees at the turn of the road,
And only pausing to fire and load.

 So through the night rode Paul Revere;
And so through the night went his cry of alarm
To every Middlesex village and farm, —
A cry of defiance and not of fear,
A voice in the darkness, a knock at the door,
And a word that shall echo forevermore!
For, borne on the night-wind of the Past,
Through all our history, to the last,
In the hour of darkness and peril and need,
The people will waken and listen to hear
The hurrying hoof-beats of that steed,

And the midnight message of Paul Revere.

Student Essay

"The Midnight Ride of Paul Revere" is a poem about the Revolutionary War battles of Lexington and Concord near Boston. Henry Longfellow, the author, accents his poem with many strong literary aspects that make the poem captivating. He uses descriptive words to show the emotions and actions of the characters. All of these characteristics make Longfellow's poetry an engrossing poem.

The plot of the poem is laid out nicely. Longfellow opens the poem with Paul Revere's talking to the watchmen at the North Church in Boston, which occupied by the British, but the British had no control of Massachusetts outside of Boston. The two men have made a plan to signal each other if the British regulars should leave the city to confiscate or destroy the military supplies of the colonial militia and arrest rebel leaders. In the rising action, Paul is anxiously waiting for the watchman's signal so that he may warn the people in towns near Boston. The watchman is scanning the city and the ocean. When the climax approaches, the signal, two lanterns hung on the church tower, warns Paul that the British are coming by sea: "One, if by land, and two, if by sea." The anxious feelings of Paul are given to the reader as he rides out of Boston, warning a string of towns. In the falling action and conclusion, Longfellow briefly talks about the battles and ends with saying that Paul Revere's story will last throughout history.

Meanwhile, impatient to mount and ride,
Booted and spurred, with a heavy stride
On the opposite shore walked Paul Revere.
Now he patted his horse's side,
Now gazed at the landscape far and near,
Then, impetuous, stamped the earth,
And turned and tightened his saddle girth;
But mostly he watched with eager search
The belfry-tower of the Old North Church,
As it rose above the graves on the hill,
Lonely and spectral and sombre and still.
And lo! as he looks, on the belfry's height
A glimmer, and then a gleam of light!
He springs to the saddle, the bridle he turns,
But lingers and gazes, till full on his sight
A second lamp in the belfry burns!

311

Throughout the poem, the reader can identify a tone of anxious suspense. Both the watchman and Paul Revere are described with words that relay anxiety. As the poem progresses, suspense builds. The reader wonders when the watchman will give Paul the signal to gallop out of Boston and warn the townspeople to take up arms and resist the British regulars. When the two-lamp signal is given, suspense is still held. Paul rushes to the outlying towns, yelling the warning. A small description of the battles is given, showing the bravery of the townspeople. The tone of Longfellow's poem keeps the reader captivated, even though everyone knows the outcome of the story already.

> So through the night rode Paul Revere;
> And so through the night went his cry of alarm
> To every Middlesex village and farm,—
> A cry of defiance and not of fear,
> A voice in the darkness, a knock at the door,
> And a word that shall echo forevermore!

In "The Midnight Ride of Paul Revere," there is also an evident theme of bravery. Without the bravery of the men who warned the townspeople near Boston, the British would have captured the military supplies of the Patriot militias and thus undercut the rebels' ability to resist the British military threat. The portrayal of this fretful account also shows the bravery of the men in towns near Boston. Since America did not have an actual army at this time, their defense consisted of volunteers briefly trained and ready to operate as local militias (as in the preceding French and Indian War). The bravery of these men showed other Americans that they could, indeed, defeat the British.

> And one was safe and asleep in his bed
> Who at the bridge would be first to fall,
> Who that day would be lying dead,
> Pierced by a British musket-ball.

> You know the rest. In the books you have read,
> How the British Regulars fired and fled,—
> How the farmers gave them ball for ball,
> From behind each fence and farm-yard wall,
> Chasing the red-coats down the lane,
> Then crossing the fields to emerge again

Under the trees at the turn of the road,
And only pausing to fire and load.

All of the characteristics of "The Midnight Ride of Paul Revere" set Longfellow's poetry apart from others. This piece is comprehendible and captivates the reader. It is also an account of an important time in American history. This depiction of Paul Revere's ride also helps the reader to gain insight into the frightful night of April 18–19, 1775.

"I Loved Her Like the Leaves,"

by Kakinomoto no Asomi Hitomaro

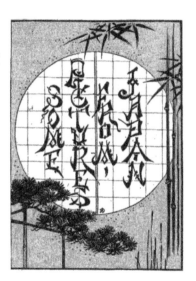

Kakinomoto no Asomi Hitomaro (who lived around 662–710 CE) was a Japanese poet and aristocrat.

I loved her like the leaves,
The lush leaves of spring
That weighed the branches of the willows
Standing on the jutting bank
Where we two walked together
While she was of this world.
My life was built on her;
But man cannot flout
The laws of this world.
To the wide fields where the heat haze shimmers,
Hidden in a white cloud,
White as white mulberry scarf,
She soared like the morning bird
Hidden from our world like the setting sun.
The child she left as token
Whimpers, begs for food; but always
Finding nothing that I might give,
Like birds that gather rice-heads in their beaks,
I pick him up and clasp him in my arms.
By the pillows where we lay,
My wife and I, as one,
The daylight I pass lonely till the dusk,

The black night I lie sighing till the dawn.
I grieve, yet know no remedy:
I pine, but have no way to meet her.
The one I love, men say,
Is in the hills of Hagai,
So I labour my way there,
Smashing rock-roots in my path,
Yet get no joy from it.
For, as I knew her in this world,
I find not the dimmest trace.

Envoys

I

The autumn moon
We saw last year
Shines again: but she
Who was with me then
The years separate for ever.

II

On the road to Fusuma
In the Hikite Hills,
I dug my love's grave.
I trudge the mountain path
And think: "Am I living still?"

Student Essay

"A man is related to all nature." This quote is by the famous Transcendentalist writer Ralph Waldo Emerson. He himself was a Romantic and would not support Naturalism, which developed more after Emerson was dead. Nonetheless Emerson sums up the essence of Naturalism in one statement. Even though Emerson himself lived in the 1800s, the ideas that he espoused in his writings were far from new, even at his time. In many cultures, at some point or another in history, it is possible to observe traces of Naturalistic philosophical and/or scientific ideas that seeped into the civilization. In ancient Japan, what would today be called Naturalistic literary influences are clearly evident in poems such as Kakinomoto no Asomi Hitomaro's "I Loved Her Like the Leaves."

First, the metaphors, similes, and descriptions found in Hitomaro's poem are exclusively related to nature. The first three lines—"I loved her like the leaves, / The lush leaves of spring / That weighed the branches of the willows"—set forth one of the most important analogies in the poem. When studied, this metaphor proves to be quite an ingenious use of the natural seasons. Spring, the season of new life, is when leaves sprout, and Hitomaro wrote that he "loved her like the leaves." But, by putting both the first line and the third line in past tense, he observes that the love, like spring, has faded away and died. The other analogies in the poem, although generally not as deep, are also related to nature. "White as white mulberry scarf / She soared like the morning bird / Hidden from our world like the setting sun." The intensely natural focus of these analogies seem to imply that Hitomaro held somewhat "Naturalistic" views.

Although the exclusively natural metaphors may cause a reader to begin to speculate about the author's Naturalistic worldview, they are not strong enough proof to actually conclude that Hitomaro was indeed a Naturalist. To come to this conclusion, one must examine a couple key phrases in the text. "She was of this world." This concept of everything coming from the world, or from Mother Nature, is an extremely fundamental Naturalistic idea. Thus also Emerson's quote at the beginning of this essay stated, "A man is related to all nature." Second, "man cannot flout the laws of this world." The concept of nature's supremacy and sovereignty is another vital Naturalistic view. To a Naturalist, Nature is the supreme god, and it cannot be swayed. The laws of Nature are set in stone, have not changed since the beginning of the world, and will not change until the world comes to an end. These two key phrases show that Hitomaro viewed Nature as the supreme mother of all life.

According to Hitomaro, not only is Nature a sovereign god; it also is a malevolent force: "The child she left as token / Whimpers, begs for food; but always / Finding nothing that I might give." Nature does not supply what this child needs. Instead of being the one to take in the child left out in the street, Nature is the one turning out the child to die. "I grieve, yet know no remedy." Again, Nature will not alleviate the author's pain. Instead of being the medicine to cure the wound, Nature actually appears to be the one to inflict the wound. "I labour my way . . . / Smashing rock-roots in my path, / Yet get no joy from it." The author tries to fight against Nature but is able neither to defeat Nature, nor to attain joy by allowing Nature to run its course.

From a general look at metaphors and similes, to a careful study of a couple key phrases, to an analysis of the ideas set forth in the last half of the poem—it is obvious that Hitomaro's "I Loved Her Like the Leaves" was influenced by Naturalistic ideas. Ancient Japan was not the first culture to embrace Naturalistic philosophies, but neither was it the last. Maya Angelou, a modern American author, once wrote, "Nature has no mercy at all. Nature says, 'I'm going to snow. If you have on . . . no snowshoes, that's tough. I am going to snow anyway.'" It is interesting to hear ancient Japanese literature, written in a culture that was largely isolated from the rest of the world until modern times, align itself with such seemingly modern ideas.

Poems of Gabriela Mistral

Gabriela Mistral is the pseudonym of Lucila Godoy Alcayaga (1889–1957). As a Nobel Laureate, she is one of Chile's most distinguished writers.

I Am Not Alone

The night, it is deserted
from the mountains to the sea.
But I, the one who rocks you,
I am not alone!

The sky, it is deserted
for the moon falls to the sea.
But I, the one who holds you,
I am not alone!

The sky, it is deserted
for the moon falls to the sea.
But I, the one who holds you,
I am not alone

Tiny Feet

A child's tiny feet,
Blue, blue with cold,
How can they see and not protect you?
Oh, my God!

Tiny wounded feet,
Bruised all over by pebbles,
Abused by snow and soil!
Man, being blind, ignores
that where you step, you leave
A blossom of bright light,
that where you have placed your bleeding little soles
a redolent tuberose grows.
Since, however, you walk through the streets so straight,
you are courageous, without fault.
Child's tiny feet,
Two suffering little gems,
How can the people pass, unseeing.

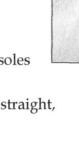

Student Essay

Born and raised in Chile, Gabriela Mistral was a Nobel Prize winner in 1945 and one of her country's most beloved writers. Her poems touch on the themes of childhood, motherhood, sorrow, and love. In many of her poems she offers encouragement to those who are suffering, or have at some point suffered.

The first poem in which she provides encouragement is "I Am Not Alone." With the stanza, "But I, the one who rocks you, / I am not alone!" she alludes to the fact that they have each other. Even though, as she says in three different places and in three different ways, "The night, it is deserted," "the sky, it is deserted," and "the world, it is deserted," she offers herself in sacrificial encouragement in the midst of complete abandonment and desertion.

Throughout her life, Gabriela traveled all over the world representing her country, her concern being for the less fortunate. This concern is manifested in many of her poems, and in many the concern is followed by encouragement. In one poem, "Those Who Do Not Dance," she gives encouragement to the crippled and the invalid who cannot dance or sing:

A crippled child
Said, "How shall I dance?"
Let your heart dance
We said.

Then the invalid said:
"How shall I sing?"
Let your heart sing
We said.

Although she gave encouragement to those alive and suffering, she also cared deeply about doing good for those who had in time past suffered greatly. This is seen in her poem "Death Sonnet I," where she seeks to do honor "with a mother's sweet care" to one dead:

From the icy niche where men placed you
I lower your body to the sunny, poor earth.
And the earth will be a soft cradle
When it receives your hurt childlike body.

This is the beauty of Gabriela Mistral's writing, to comfort the invalid, the crippled, and all those less fortunate than herself, weaving love into all of her poems. To her this was the most vital part of life. As she once said, "We are guilty of many errors and many faults, but our worst crime is abandoning the children, neglecting the fountain of life. Many of the things we need can wait. The child cannot. Right now is the time his bones are being formed, his blood is being made, and his senses are being developed. To him we cannot answer 'Tomorrow.' His name is 'Today.'"

The Song of Roland, an Epic Poem

In history Charlemagne is depicted as a devout Christian and fierce warrior who expanded his Frankish borders until he ruled a Christian kingdom that included large areas of present-day Germany, France, and part of Spain. In *The Song of Roland*, Charlemagne is made larger than life, a vigorous warrior more than two centuries old who has been fighting wearily but unfailingly, continuing to war against paganism wherever he finds it. He is a combination of incredible majesty and touching vulnerability. This king is portrayed as a hero with lasting and unswerving faith until the end.

The nephew of Charlemagne and his right-hand man is Roland, who has conquered vast lands for his "liege lord" and is completely necessary to Charlemagne's efforts during the war. In *The Song of Roland* he is transformed to an epic hero, who models knighthood, during the medieval period. He is bold, daring, and hot-tempered, which provides him with praise and criticism from his friends. But he lacks prudence and wisdom. During the Battle of Roncevaux Pass (in 778), when the rearguard is attacked (by Saracens/Muslims/pagans in the

Song—but in historical fact it was Christian Basques who lived in the mountains), Roland is leading that part of the army. In his pride and false valor, Roland refuses to signal for help, thus leading to the deaths of twenty thousand men, his best friend, and himself. Despite all this, he is the poem's most dazzling hero and holds the most powerful death scenes in French literature as his soul is carried to heaven by saints and angels.

The last of these three glamorous heroes is Roland's best friend Oliver, who is wise, prudent, and much more intelligent than Roland. During the Battle of Roncevaux Pass, he is in the rearguard with Roland. When Oliver sights the enemy coming to attack the rearguard, he pleads with Roland three times to signal for help. He is refused three times, and as a result the entire rearguard, including Oliver and Roland, is killed. But Oliver dies reconciled to Roland, and he is deeply mourned.

The *Song of Roland* was originally to be performed by a skilled juggler (or troubadour), who would recite the poem, accompanied by music and celebration. This allowed this famous piece of French literature to make the heroes of the crusades larger than life. Among them the valiant king Charlemagne, the bold Roland, and the wise Oliver.

The "Rubaiyat," by Omar Khayyám

Omar Khayyám (1038–1141) was "a Persian polymath: philosopher, mathematician, astronomer, and poet. He also wrote treatises on mechanics, geography, mineralogy, music, and Islamic theology" (Wikipedia). The 101 verses of the "Rubaiyat" are

quatrains and were written early in the twelfth century, around 1120 CE. Here are some selected verses as translated by Edward Fitzgerald (fifth edition):

Come, fill the Cup, and in the fire of Spring
Your Winter garment of Repentance fling:
The Bird of Time has but a little way
To flutter—and the Bird is on the Wing. (verse 7)

And those who husbanded the Golden grain,
And those who flung it to the winds like Rain,
Alike to no such aureate Earth are turn'd
As, buried once, Men want dug up again. (v. 15)

The Worldly Hope men set their Hearts upon
Turns Ashes—or it prospers; and anon,
Like Snow upon the Desert's dusty Face,
Lighting a little hour or two—is gone. (v. 16)

I sometimes think that never blows so red
The Rose as where some buried Caesar bled;
That every Hyacinth the Garden wears
Dropt in her Lap from some once lovely Head.
(v. 19)

And this reviving Herb whose tender Green
Fledges the River-Lip on which we lean—
Ah, lean upon it lightly! for who knows
From what once lovely Lip it springs unseen! (v. 20)

Ah, my Beloved, fill the Cup that clears
TO-DAY of past Regrets and future Fears:
To-morrow—Why, To-morrow I may be
Myself with Yesterday's Sev'n thousand Years. (v. 21)

Student Analysis

One category of seekers, the Sufis, "cleanse the rational soul of the impurities of nature and bodily form, until it becomes pure substance. It then comes face to face with the spiritual world, the forms of that world becoming truly reflected in it, without any doubt or ambiguity." This quote is taken from a metaphysical treatise by the Persian poet Omar Khayyám, who lived eleventh and twelfth centuries CE. He is most famous for his poem "Rubaiyat." In the West, this poem labels him as a hedonist and wine lover, unable to believe in an afterlife. To others, many spiritual themes are symbolized throughout the poem, and Seyyed Hossein Nasr claims that Khayyám is "a profound, mystical thinker and scientist whose works are important."

The first theme that Khayyám intertwines throughout the "Rubaiyat" is that of truth and reality. At the beginning of the poem, he gives a strong call:

> WAKE! For the Sun, who scatter'd into flight
> The Stars before him from the Field of Night,
> Drives Night along with them from Heav'n, and strikes
> The Sultan's Turret with a Shaft of Light. (v. 1)

This call begs one not to sleep and is soon backed up by a reminder:

> Whether at Naishapur or Babylon,
> Whether the Cup with sweet or bitter run,
> The Wine of Life keeps oozing drop by drop,
> The Leaves of Life keep falling one by one. (v. 8)

Here Khayyám writes of the reality of the short time one has to live, hinting at the truths of bigger, more beautiful things, and whether one is in a good or bad situation to "WAKE."

To establish this idea of truth, Khayyám writes in the "Rubaiyat":

> Would you that spangle of Existence spend
> About THE SECRET—quick about it, Friend!
> A Hair perhaps divides the False from True—
> And upon what, prithee, may life depend? (v. 49)

It is here that one catches a glimpse of something the author was seeing and the importance of truth that he hints at.

Another theme that shines through Khayyám's mysticism is that of the wine, the life that is given to all through the wine:

> And if the Wine you drink, the Lip you press,

End in what All begins and ends in—Yes;
Think then you are TO-DAY what YESTERDAY
You were—TO-MORROW you shall not be less. (v. 42)

In this stanza, there is a call to imagine all one can be, and the change that can happen, when the wine and the life in the wine, becomes everything. Here again, he is suggesting and giving his reader a brief indication of something beautiful.

In another stanza Khayyám writes:

You know, my Friends, with what a brave Carouse
I made a Second Marriage in my house;
Divorced old barren Reason from my Bed,
And took the Daughter of the Vine to Spouse. (v. 55)

At first this stanza makes Khayyám look like a wine lover. But when the quatrain is taken as meaning that the wine is life-giving, and seeing how in 1 Corinthians 1 Paul writes of the cross of Christ as making foolish the wise, it becomes a meaningful stanza, full of promise.

The last theme that Khayyám stresses throughout his poem is that of the present moment. Too much of one's life is spent in regret of the past and hope for the future, instead of joy in the present:

YESTERDAY This Day's Madness did prepare;
TO-MORROW's Silence, Triumph, or Despair:
Drink! for you not know whence you came, nor why:
Drink! for you know not why you go, nor where. (v. 74)

This symbolizes the trust one must put in living one day at a time with the life-giving drink. But it is not enough just to live day by day. In one stanza, Khayyam gives a warning:

Waste not your Hour, nor in the vain pursuit
Of This and That endeavor and dispute;
Better be jocund with the fruitful Grape
Than sadden after none, or bitter, Fruit. (v. 54)

After reading the "Rubaiyat," the suggestion that Nsar makes is true: Khayyám is indeed a "profound thinker." Throughout his symbolism he brings himself and his readers, "face to face with the spiritual world" and encourages them to become "reflected in it." This reflection happens as the clay, made in the image of the potter, follows the advice of the potter in the "Rubaiyat" when he murmurs, "Gently, brother, gently, pray!"

APPENDIX A: GLOSSARY OF LITERARY TERMS

Adapted from James P. Stobaugh, *Skills for Literary Analysis* (Green Forest, AK: New Leaf Press, 2012)

Allegory: A story or tale with two or more levels of meaning: a literal level and one or more symbolic levels. The events, setting, and characters in an allegory are symbols for ideas or qualities.

Alliteration: The repetition of initial consonant sounds. The repetition can be juxtaposed (placed side by side; e.g., simply sad). Here is an example:

> I conceive therefore, as to the business of being profound, that it is with writers, as with wells; a person with good eyes may see to the bottom of the deepest, provided any water be there; and that often, when there is nothing in the world at the bottom, besides dryness and dirt, though it be but a yard and a half under ground, it shall pass, however, for wondrous deep, upon no wiser a reason than because it is wondrous dark. (Jonathan Swift)

Allusion: A casual and brief reference to a famous historical or literary figure or event: "You must borrow me Gargantua's mouth first. / 'Tis a word too great for any mouth of this age's size" (Shakespeare).

Analogy: The process by which new or less familiar words, constructions, or pronunciations conform to the pattern of older or more familiar (and often unrelated) ones; a comparison between two unlike things. The purpose of an analogy is to describe something unfamiliar by pointing out its similarities to something that is familiar.

Antagonist: In a narrative, the character with whom the main character has the most conflict. In Jack London's "To Build a Fire," the antagonist is the extreme cold of the Yukon rather than a person or animal.

Archetype: The original pattern or model from which all other things of the same kind are made; a perfect example of a type or group. For example, the biblical character Joseph is often considered an archetype of Jesus Christ.

Argumentation: The discourse in which the writer presents and logically supports a particular view or opinion; sometimes used interchangeably with persuasion.

Aside: *In a play, an aside is a speech delivered by an actor in such a way that other characters on the stage are presumed not to hear it; an aside generally reveals a character's inner thoughts.*

Autobiography: *A form of nonfiction in which a person tells one's own life story. Notable examples of autobiography include those by Benjamin Franklin and Frederick Douglass.*

Ballad: *A song or poem that tells a story in short stanzas and simple words with repetition, refrain, and so forth.*

Biography: *A form of nonfiction in which a writer tells the life story of another person.*

Character: *A person or an animal who takes part in the action of a literary work. The main character is the one on whom the work focuses. The person with whom the main character has the most conflict is the antagonist. He is the enemy of the main character (protagonist). For instance, in The Scarlet Letter, by Nathaniel Hawthorne, Chillingworth is the antagonist, and Hester is the protagonist. Characters who appear in the story may perform actions, speak to other characters, be described by the narrator, or be remembered. Characters introduced whose sole purpose is to develop the main character are called foils.*

Classicism: *An approach to literature and the other arts that stresses reason, balance, clarity, ideal beauty, and orderly form, in imitation of the arts of Greece and Rome.*

Conflict: *A struggle between opposing forces; it can be internal or external; when occurring within a character, it is called internal conflict. An example of this occurs in Mark Twain's The Adventures of Huckleberry Finn. In this novel Huck is struggling in his mind about whether to return an escaped slave, his good friend Jim, to the authorities. An external conflict is normally an obvious conflict between the protagonist and antagonist(s). London's "To Build a Fire" illustrates conflict between a character and an outside force. Most plots develop from conflict, making conflict one of the primary elements of narrative literature.*

Crisis or climax: *The moment or event in the plot in which the conflict is most directly addressed: the main character "wins" or "loses"; the secret is revealed. After the climax, the denouement or falling action occurs.*

Dialectic: *Examining opinions or ideas logically, often by the method of question and answer.*

Discourse: *Forms of various modes into which writing can be classified; traditionally, writing has been divided into the following modes:*

> **Exposition**: Writing that presents information.

> **Narration**: Writing that tells a story.

> **Description**: Writing that portrays people, places, or things.

> **Persuasion** (sometimes called **Argumentation**): Writing that tries to convince people to think or act in a certain way

Drama: *A story written to be performed by actors; the playwright supplies dialogue for the characters to speak and stage directions that give information about costumes, lighting, scenery, properties, the setting, and the character's movements and ways of speaking.*

Dramatic monologue: *A poem or speech in which an imaginary character speaks to a silent listener. T. S. Eliot's "The Love Song of J. Alfred Prufrock" is a dramatic monologue.*

Elegy: *A solemn and formal lyric poem about death, often one that mourns the passing of some particular person; Walt Whitman's "When Lilacs Last in the Dooryard Bloom'd" is an elegy lamenting the death of President Lincoln.*

Essay: *A short, nonfiction work about a particular subject; essay comes from the Old French word essai, meaning "a trial or attempt"; meant to be explanatory, an essay is not intended to be an exhaustive treatment of a subject. An essay can be classified as formal or informal, personal or impersonal; it can also be classified according to purpose: expository, descriptive, persuasive/argumentative, or narrative.*

Figurative language: *See metaphor, simile, analogy.*

Foil: *A character who provides a contrast to another character and whose purpose is to develop the main character.*

Genre: A division or type of literature; commonly divided into three major divisions, literature is either poetry, prose, or drama. Each major genre can then be divided into smaller genres. Poetry can be divided into lyric, concrete, dramatic, narrative, and epic poetry. Prose can be divided into fiction (novels and short stories) and nonfiction (biography, autobiography, letters, essays, and reports). Drama can be divided into serious drama, tragedy, comic drama, melodrama, and farce.

Gothic: The use of primitive, medieval, wild, or mysterious elements in literature; Gothic elements offended eighteenth-century classical writers but appealed to the Romantic writers who followed them. Gothic novels feature writers who use places like mysterious castles where horrifying supernatural events take place. Edgar Allan Poe's "The Fall of the House of Usher" illustrates the influence of Gothic elements.

Harlem Renaissance: Occurring during the 1920s, a time of African American artistic creativity centered in Harlem in New York City. Langston Hughes was a Harlem Renaissance writer.

Hyperbole: A deliberate exaggeration or overstatement. In Mark Twain's "The Celebrated Jumping Frog of Calaveras County," the claim that Jim Smiley would follow a bug as far as Mexico to win a bet is hyperbolic.

Idyll: A poem or part of a poem that describes and idealizes country life; Whittier's "Snow-bound" is an idyll.

Irony: A method of humorous or subtly sarcastic expression in which the intended meanings of the words used is the direct opposite of their usual sense.

Journal: A daily autobiographical account of events and personal reactions.

Kenning: Indirect way of naming people or things; knowledge or recognition; in Old English poetry, a metaphorical name for something.

Literature: All writings in prose or verse, especially those of an imaginative or critical character, without regard to their excellence. These can be writings considered as having permanent value, excellence of form, great emotional effect, and so forth.

Metaphor: In this figure of speech, a comparison that creatively identifies one thing with another dissimilar thing and transfers or ascribes to the first thing some of the qualities of the second. Unlike a simile or analogy, metaphor asserts that one thing is another *thing — not just that one is like another. Frequently a metaphor is invoked by the verb to be:*

> Affliction then is ours;
> We are the trees, whom shaking fastens more. (George Herbert)
> Then Jesus declared, "I am the bread of life." (John 6:35)
> Jesus answered, "I am the way and the truth and the life." (John 14:6)

Meter: *A poem's rhythmical pattern, determined by the number and types of stresses, or beats, in each line. A certain number of metrical feet make up a line of verse (thus pentameter denotes a line containing five metrical feet). The act of describing the meter of a poem is called scanning, which involves marking the stressed and unstressed syllables, as follows:*

Iamb: A foot with one unstressed syllable followed by one stressed syllable, as in the word "abound."

Trochee: A foot with one stressed syllable followed by one unstressed syllable, as in the word "spoken."

Anapest: A foot with two unstressed syllables followed by one stressed syllable, as in the word "interrupt."

Dactyl: A foot with a stressed syllable followed by two unstressed syllables, as in the word "accident."

Spondee: Two stressed feet: "quicksand," "heartbeat"; occurs only occasionally in English.

Motif: *A main idea, element, feature; a main theme or subject to be elaborated on.*

Narration: *The way the author chooses to tell the story:*

First-person narration: A character refers to oneself (or one's party) by using "I" (or "we"). For example: Huck Finn in *The Adventures of Huckleberry Finn* tells the story from his perspective. This is a creative way to bring humor into the plot.

Second-person narration: Addresses the reader and/or the main character as "you" (and may also use first-person narration, but not necessarily). One example is the opening of each of Rudyard Kipling's *Just So Stories*, in which the narrator refers to the child listener as "O Best Beloved."

Third-person narration: Not a character in the story; refers to the story's characters as "he," "she," and "they." This is probably the most common form of narration.

Limited narration: The narrator is only able to tell what one person is thinking or feeling. Example: in *A Separate Peace*, by John Knowles, we see the story only from Gene's perspective.

Omniscient narration: Charles Dickens employs this narration in most of his novels.

Reliable narration: Everything this narration says is true, and the narrator knows everything that is necessary to the story.

Unreliable narrator: May not know all the relevant information; may be intoxicated or mentally ill; or may lie to the audience. Example: Edgar Allan Poe's narrators are frequently unreliable. Think of the delusions that the narrator of "The Tell-Tale Heart" has about the old man.

Narrative: Literature in story form.

Onomatopoeia: The use of words that, in their pronunciation, suggest their meaning. For example, when "hiss" is spoken, it is intended to resemble the sound of steam or of a snake. Other examples include these: slam, buzz, screech, whirr, crush, sizzle, crunch, wring, wrench, gouge, grind, mangle, bang, blam, pow, zap, fizz, urp, roar, growl, blip, click, whimper, and, of course, snap, crackle, and pop.

Parallelism: Two or more balancing statements with phrases, clauses, or paragraphs of similar length and grammatical structure.

Plot: Arrangement of the action in fiction or drama, listing events of the story in the order the story gives them. A typical plot has five parts: Exposition, Rising Action, Crisis or Climax, Falling Action, and Resolution (sometimes called Denouement).

Précis: Summary of the plot of a literary piece.

Protagonist: The main character, who is opposed by an enemy (antagonist).

Rhetoric: Using words effectively in writing and speaking.

Setting: The place(s) and time(s) of a story, including the historical period, social milieu of the characters, geographical location, descriptions of indoor and outdoor locales.

Scop: An Old English poet or bard.

Simile: A figure of speech in which one thing is likened to another dissimilar thing by the use of "like," "as," or a similar expression. See Metaphor.

Sonnet: A poem normally of fourteen lines in any of several fixed verse and rhyme schemes, typically in rhymed iambic pentameter; sonnets characteristically express a single theme or idea.

Structure: The arrangement of details and scenes that make up a literary work.

Style: An author's characteristic arrangement of words. A style may be colloquial, formal, terse, wordy, theoretical, subdued, colorful, poetic, or highly individual. Style is the arrangement of words in groups and sentences. Diction, on the other hand, refers to the choice of individual words. The arrangement of details and scenes make up the structure of a literary work, and all combine to influence the tone of the work. Thus diction, style, and structure make up the form of the literary work.

Theme: The one-sentence, major meaning of a literary piece, rarely stated but implied. The theme is not a moral, which is a statement of the author's didactic purpose of the literary piece. A thesis statement is very similar to the theme.

Tone: The attitude the author takes toward his subject. The author's attitude is revealed through choice of details, through diction and style, and through the emphasis and comments that are made. Like theme and style, tone is sometimes difficult to describe with a single word or phrase; often it varies in the same literary piece to suit the moods of the characters and the situations. For instance, the tone or mood of Poe's "Annabel Lee" is very somber.

Adapted from James P. Stobaugh, *SAT and College Preparation Course for the Christian Student* (Green Forest, AK: New Leaf Press, 2011)

The following list represents a fairly comprehensive cross-section of good literature — books, poems, and plays. There are hundreds of other pieces of literature that might be as good for youth. Ask your parents and teachers for suggestions.

Younger Students

Austen, Jane

Emma

Emma Woodhouse is one of Austen's most memorable heroines: "Handsome, clever, and rich" as well as self-assured, she believes herself immune to romance and wreaks amusing havoc in the lives of those around her. A humorous coming-of-age story about a woman seeking her true nature and finding true love in the process.

Sense and Sensibility

Austin tells the story of the impoverished Dashwood sisters, who share the pangs of tragic love. Elinor, practical and conventional, is the perfection of sense. Marianne, emotional and sentimental, is the embodiment of sensibility. Their mutual suffering brings a closer understanding between the two sisters — and true love finally triumphs when sense gives way to sensibility and sensibility gives way to sense. Austen's first novel is a lively tale deftly exploring the tensions that exist in society and force people to be at once very private and very sociable.

Bolt, Robert

A Man for All Seasons

Bolt's classic play is a dramatization of the life of Sir Thomas More, the Catholic saint beheaded by Henry VIII at the birth of the Church of England. More refused to acknowledge the supremacy of England's king over all foreign sovereigns; he was imprisoned then executed in 1535. This is a compelling portrait of a courageous man who died for his convictions.

Bonhoeffer, Dietrich
The Cost of Discipleship

Bonhoeffer pulls no punches as he relates the Scriptures to real life and expounds upon the teachings of Jesus. He plainly teaches that there is a cost to following in the footsteps of Christ, just as Christ himself taught that Christ must be first in believers' lives and that there is no compromise. This work is so intense that even Dietrich himself, later in life, wondered if he had been too blunt.

Brontë, Charlotte
Jane Eyre

This novel tells the story of a proud young woman and her journey from an orphanage to her role as governess in the Rochester household. A heartbreaking love story that is also full of mystery and drama: fires, storms, attempted murder, and a mad wife conveniently stashed away in the attic.

Buck, Pearl
The Good Earth

Pearl Buck depicts peasant life in China in the 1920s—a time before vast political and social upheavals transformed an essentially agrarian country into a world power. Buck traces the whole cycle of life—its terrors, its passions, its ambitions, and rewards—by combining descriptions of marriage, parenthood, and complex human emotions with depictions of Chinese reverence for the land and for a woman's specific way of independence.

Bulfinch, Thomas
The Age of Fable

Love, jealousy, hatred, passion—the full range of human emotions were experienced by the gods and goddesses of ancient Greece. This is a brilliant reconstruction of the traditional myths that form the backbone of Western culture, including those of ancient Greece and Rome that form a great and timeless literature of the past.

Bunyan, John
Pilgrim's Progress

In this allegory, the pilgrim Christian undertakes the dangerous journey to the Celestial City, experiencing physical and spiritual obstacles along the way. *Pilgrim's Progress* captures the treacherous dangers and triumphant victories we encounter as we live the Christian life.

Burdick, Eugene
Fail-Safe

This is a classic novel of the Cold War and the limits we face. Although rather faint and shallow by today's techno-thriller standards, *Fail-Safe* for its day was THE story of the world on the edge of nuclear war. This is a good example of a best seller from the Cold-War-crazy early 1960s.

Carson, Rachel
Silent Spring

Rachel Carson offered the first shattering look at widespread ecological degradation and touched off an environmental awareness that still exists. Carson's book focused on the poisons from insecticides, weed killers, and other common products as well as the use of sprays in agriculture, a practice that led to dangerous chemicals in the food source. Presented with thorough documentation, the book opened more than a few eyes about the dangers of the modern world and stands today as a landmark work.

Christie, Agatha
And Then There Were None

Christie's mystery novel is the story of ten strangers, each lured to Indian Island by a mysterious host. Once his guests have arrived, the host accuses each person of murder. Unable to leave the island, the guests begin to share the darkest secrets of their past, and then, one by one, they begin to die.

Coleridge, Samuel
"The Rime of the Ancient Mariner"

One of the nineteenth century's most enduring narrative poems, "The Rime of the Ancient Mariner" has also been deemed one of the greatest of all English literary ballads. It is a strange and gripping tale of the ancient mariner who killed the friendly albatross and thereby committed an offense against Nature. This is a ghostly adventure of terror, retribution, and penance.

Conrad, Joseph

Heart of Darkness

This story reflects the physical and psychological shock that Conrad himself experienced in 1890, when he worked briefly in the Belgian Congo. Compelling, exotic, suspenseful, and far more than just an adventure story, this vivid picture of the moral deterioration and reversion to savagery resulting from prolonged isolation explores deep into the dark heart of its characters' souls.

Lord Jim

In great depth Conrad explores the perplexing, ambiguous problem of lost honor and guilt, expiation, and heroism. The title character is a man haunted by guilt over an act of cowardice. He becomes an agent at an isolated East Indian trading post, where his feelings of inadequacy and responsibility are played out to their logical and inevitable end.

Cooper, James Fenimore

The Deerslayer

A fine combination of romance, adventure, and morality, *The Deerslayer* follows the adventures of the brave and bold frontiersman Natty Bumppo. The deadly crack of a long rifle and the piercing cries of Indians on the warpath shatter the serenity of beautiful lake Glimmerglass. Danger has invaded the vast forests of upper New York State as Deerslayer and his loyal Mohican friend Chingachgook attempt the daring rescue of an Indian maiden imprisoned in a Huron camp.

The Last of the Mohicans

Hawkeye (Natty Bumppo) and his Mohican Indian friend, Chingachgook, share the solitude and sublimity of the wilderness until the savageries of the French and Indian War force them out of exile. They agree to guide two sisters through hostile Indian country as they search for their father. Cooper incorporates massacres and raids, innocent settlers, hardened soldiers, and renegade Indians into his classic tale of romance and adventure.

Crane, Stephen

The Red Badge of Courage

Crane vividly conveys the terror of battle and the slow-motion torrent of emotions pouring through soldiers under fire through the struggles of a raw recruit, Henry Fleming. Fleming simultaneously lusts for a glorious battle and worries endlessly about the possibility of his own cowardice. When he finally comes face-to-face with slaughter, his romantic notions are stripped away as he witnesses brutal deaths and senseless maneuvers.

Day, Clarence

Life with Father

For everyone who has ever had a father! This is a hilarious book about family life that will make everyone laugh out loud. It was first published by chapters in periodicals and later produced as a Broadway play and a movie.

Defoe, Daniel

Robinson Crusoe

The greatest shipwreck-on-a-deserted-island story ever told in English, *Robinson Crusoe* is a unique fictional blending of the traditions of Puritan spiritual autobiography with an insistent scrutiny of the nature of men and women as social creatures. It reveals an extraordinary ability to invent a sustaining modern myth. The title character leaves his comfortable middle-class home in England to go to sea. Surviving shipwreck, he lives on an island for twenty-eight years, alone for most of the time until he saves the life of a savage—an outcast Polynesian man whom he names Friday.

Dickens, Charles

Great Expectations

Pip, an orphan growing up in Victorian England, is a blacksmith's apprentice who dreams of a better life. Given the means to become a gentleman by an unknown benefactor, he learns from a dangerous escaped convict, a wealthy old woman, and a secret guardian that outward appearances can be deceiving. A mysterious tale of dreams and heartbreak, *Great Expectations* is widely regarded as one of Dickens's greatest novels.

Nicholas Nickleby

This melodramatic novel tells the story of young Nickleby's adventures as he struggles to seek his fortune in Victorian England. Dependent on the so-called benevolence of his Uncle Ralph, Nicholas is thrust into the world to care for his mother and sister. Circumstances force Nicholas to enter the nightmarish world of Dotheboys Hall, a school run by the malevolent Wackford Squeers. Comic events are interspersed with Dickens's moving indictment of society's ill treatment of children and the cruelty of the educational system. Yet, with his extraordinary gift for social satire, Dickens gives us a lighthearted tale in which goodness and joy easily defeat the forces of evil.

Oliver Twist

The story of a street boy on the run is an archetypal adventure. Written shortly after adoption of the Poor Law of 1834, which halted government payments to the poor unless they entered workhouses, *Oliver Twist* used the tale of a friendless child as a vehicle for social criticism. Although the novel is Victorian in its emotional appeal, it is decidedly unsentimental in its depiction of poverty and the criminal underworld, especially in its portrayal of the cruel Bill Sikes.

A Tale of Two Cities

Set in the late eighteenth century against the violent upheaval of the French Revolution, this complex story involves one man's sacrifice of his own life on behalf of his friends. While political events drive the story, Dickens takes a decidedly antipolitical tone, lambasting both aristocratic tyranny and revolutionary excess—the latter memorably caricatured in Madame Defarge, who knits beside the guillotine, encrypting death sentences for the rich. *A Tale of Two Cities* underscores many of Dickens's enduring themes: imprisonment, injustice, social anarchy, resurrection, and the renunciation that fosters renewal.

Doyle, Arthur Conan
The Adventures of Sherlock Holmes

Sherlock Holmes, master of deductive reasoning, and his sidekick, Dr. Watson, solve four classic cases. "A Scandal in Bohemia" finds the sleuth committing a crime of his own to protect a royal reputation. Then in "A Case of Identity," Holmes must unmask a devious disguise to trace a missing person. "The Red-Headed League" and "The Boscombe Valley Mystery" round out a quartet of diabolical deceptions sure to enthrall readers.

Dumas, Alexandre
The Three Musketeers

A historical romance, *The Three Musketeers* relates the adventures of four fictional swashbuckling heroes who lived during the reigns of the

French kings Louis XIII and Louis XIV. The young and headstrong d'Artagnan, having proved his bravery by dueling with each, becomes a friend of Athos, Porthos, and Aramis, members of the King's Musketeers. He is in love with Constance Bonancieux; at her urging, he and his friends head for England to reclaim two diamond studs that the Queen has imprudently given to her lover, the Duke of Buckingham.

Eliot, George

Silas Marner

Silas Marner is a friendless weaver who cares only for his cache of gold. After being wrongly accused of a heinous theft and secluding himself, he is ultimately redeemed through his love for Eppie, an abandoned golden-haired baby girl who mysteriously appears at his cottage.

Eliot, T. S.

Murder in the Cathedral

Eliot's dramatization in verse of the murder of Thomas Becket at Canterbury was written for the Canterbury Festival of 1935. Like Greek drama, its theme and form are rooted in religion and ritual, purgation and renewal. It is a return to the earliest sources of drama.

Fitzgerald, F. Scott

The Great Gatsby

Fitzgerald offers a very human story about a man torn between the various pressures of life: conformity and individualism, facade and substance. Nick is a silent narrator, but he is also a participant as he wades through an insane and typical world, an outsider yet also a member. Fitzgerald makes no judgment of morality, grace, or sin, nor does he favor idealism or cynicism.

Tender Is the Night

Fitzgerald's classic story of psychological disintegration is a powerful and moving depiction of the human frailties that affect privileged and ordinary people alike. The world has recently fallen to pieces in what has become known as the Great War (World War I). Consequently, most of the characters are falling to pieces, too. Hints about this are found everywhere in the book, although Fitzgerald, with his knack for writing about the complicated nature of humans, often hides them in subtle ways.

This Side of Paradise

Here is the story of Amory Blaine in his adolescence and undergraduate days at Princeton. Largely autobiographical, this classic novel of youth and alienation was written with a grace that captures the essence of an American generation struggling to define itself in the aftermath of World War I and the destruction of "the old order."

Foxe, John

Foxe's Book of Martyrs

Foxe recounts the lives, suffering, and triumphant deaths of Christian martyrs throughout history with a sense of immediacy and insight into suffering that few church historians can match. Beginning with the first martyr, Jesus Christ, the book also focuses on such men as John Wycliffe, William Tyndale, and Martin Luther, and it is an exceptional historical record in tracing the roots of religious persecution.

Frank, Anne

The Diary of a Young Girl

In 1942, with Nazis occupying Holland, a thirteen-year-old German Jewish girl and her family fled their home in Amsterdam and went into hiding. Cut off from the outside world for two years, they faced hunger, boredom, the constant cruelties of living in confined quarters, and the ever-present threat of discovery and death. In her diary, Anne Frank records vivid impressions of her experiences during this period. It is a powerful reminder of the horrors of war and an eloquent testament to the human spirit. By turns thoughtful, moving, and amusing, her account offers a fascinating commentary on human courage and frailty and a compelling self-portrait of a sensitive and spirited young woman whose promise was tragically cut short.

Franklin, Benjamin

Autobiography

One of our most inspiring Americans comes to life in this autobiography. Written as a letter to his son, Franklin's account of his life from his childhood in Boston to his years in Philadelphia ends in 1757 with his first mission to England.

Gibson, William

The Miracle Worker

This is the inspiring story of Helen Keller and her teacher, Anne Sullivan, who is *The Miracle Worker*. Deaf, blind, and mute twelve-year-old Helen was like a wild animal. Scared out of her wits but still murderously strong, she clawed and struggled against all who tried to help her. Half-blind herself but blessed with fanatical dedication, Annie began a titanic struggle to release the young girl from the terrifying prison of eternal darkness and silence.

Goldsmith, Oliver

The Vicar of Wakefield

This story, a portrait of village life, is narrated by Dr. Primrose, the title character, whose family endures many trials—including the loss of most of their money, the seduction of one daughter, the destruction of their home by fire, and the vicar's incarceration—before all is put right in the end. The novel's idealization of rural life, sentimental moralizing, and melodramatic incidents are countered by a sharp but good-natured irony.

Hawthorne, Nathaniel

The House of Seven Gables

Set in mid-nineteenth-century Salem, Massachusetts, Hawthorne's gothic masterpiece is a somber study in hereditary sin. It is based on the legend of a curse pronounced on Hawthorne's own family by a woman condemned to death during the infamous Salem witchcraft trials (1692–93). The greed and arrogant pride of the novel's Pyncheon family through the generations is mirrored in the gloomy decay of their seven-gabled mansion, in which the family's enfeebled and impoverished relations live.

The Scarlet Letter

The story is set in a mid-seventeenth-century village in Puritan New England. Hester Prynne, a young woman, has borne an illegitimate child while believing herself a widow, but her husband, Roger Chillingworth, returns to New England very much alive and conceals his identity. Roger finds his wife forced to wear the scarlet letter *A* on her dress as punishment for her adultery, and he becomes obsessed with finding the identity of his wife's former lover. Hawthorne's greatest novel is a philosophical exploration that delves into guilt and touches upon notions of redemption.

Hemingway, Ernest

A Farewell to Arms

While serving with the Italian ambulance service during World War I, an American lieutenant falls in love with an English nurse who tends him after he is wounded on the Italian front. He deserts during the Italians' retreat after the Battle of Caporetto, and the reunited couple flee into Switzerland. By turns romantic and harshly realistic, Hemingway's story of romance, set against the brutality and confusion of World War I, is full of disillusionment and heartbreak.

For Whom the Bell Tolls

Hemingway tells the story of an American in the Spanish Civil War (1930s). Robert Jordan has the assignment of blowing up a bridge, but as he flees, a shell explodes, toppling his horse and breaking Jordan's legs. Thus Jordan faces not only the loss of his life but also the loss of his love for Maria, a woman he met and fell for during his mountain tour of duty.

The Old Man and the Sea

This is a triumphant yet tragic story of an old Cuban fisherman and his relentless, agonizing battle with a giant marlin far out in the Gulf Stream. In this short novel, Hemingway combines the simplicity of a fable, the significance of a parable, and the drama of an epic.

The Sun Also Rises

Set in the 1920s, Hemingway's novel deals with a group of aimless expatriates in the cafés of Paris and the bullrings of Spain. They are members of the cynical and disillusioned post-World War I Lost Generation, many of whom suffer psychological and physical wounds as a result of the war. Friendship, stoicism, and natural grace under pressure are offered as the values that matter in an otherwise amoral and often senseless world.

Heyerdahl, Thor

Kon-Tiki

Heyerdahl had heard of a mythical Polynesian hero, Kon-Tiki, who had migrated to the islands from the east. Further investigation led the scientist to believe that the story of the migration of a people across thousands of miles of the Pacific was fact, not a myth, and he decided to duplicate the legendary voyage to prove its accuracy. Limiting himself to a balsa-log raft, *Kon-Tiki* is the record of his outrageous and daring expedition.

Hilton, James

Goodbye, Mr. Chips

Full of enthusiasm, in 1870 young English schoolmaster Mr. Chipping came to teach at Brookfield, a fictional British boys' public boarding school. It was a time when dignity and a generosity of spirit still existed, and the dedicated new schoolmaster expressed these beliefs to his rowdy students. Nicknamed Mr. Chips, this gentle and caring man helped shape the lives of generation after generation of boys.

Lost Horizon

Hilton's haunting novel takes place in Shangri-La, the valley of enchantment. Amid the towering peaks of the Himalayas, Conway could think only of his crashed plane and the home he might never see again. He couldn't fully realize that he was soon to enter a world of love and peace as no Westerner had ever known.

Homer

Iliad

Although typically described as one of the greatest war stories of all time, to say that the *Iliad* is a war story does not begin to describe the emotional sweep of its action and characters: Achilles, Helen, Hector, and other heroes of Greek myth. The *Iliad* is one of the two great epics of Homer and reveals the history of the tenth and final year of the Greek siege of Troy.

Odyssey

Odysseus wants to go home. But Poseidon, god of oceans, doesn't want him to make it back across the wine-dark sea to his wife, Penelope; to his son, Telemachus; and to their high-roofed home at Ithaca. This is the story in Homer's epic poem written 2,700 years ago. *The Odyssey* is a gripping read.

Hudson, W. H.

Green Mansions

An exotic romance set in the jungles of South America, the story is narrated by a man named Abel who as a young man had lived among the Indians. Abel falls in love with Rima, a girl of a magnificent and mystical race, and is led to discover the greatest joy—as well as the darkest despair.

Hugo, Victor
The Hunchback of Notre Dame

Hugo's haunting and tumultuous tale of the horribly deformed bell-ringer, Quasimodo, unfolds in the shadow of Notre Dame cathedral. The hunchback falls hopelessly in love with the beautiful gypsy girl, Esmerelda; after rescuing her both from hanging and the evil archdeacon Dom Frollo, he reunites her with her mother.

Les Misérables

Set largely in Paris during the politically explosive 1820s and 1830s, this epic follows the life of the former criminal Jean Valjean—an outcast of society—and his unjust imprisonment. Valjean has repented from his crimes but is nevertheless hounded by his nemesis, the police detective Javert. *Les Misérables* is at once a tense thriller, an epic portrayal of the nineteenth-century French citizenry, and a vital drama of the redemption of one human being. Hugo achieved the rare imaginative resonance that allows a work of art to transcend its genre.

Irving, Washington
The Sketch Book

This is a collection of short stories, most of them based on folklore. Of these tales, "The Legend of Sleepy Hollow" and "Rip Van Winkle" are the most famous, both of which are Americanized versions of German folktales. In addition to the stories based on folklore, the collection contains travel sketches and literary essays.

Johnson, Paul
Modern Times: The World from the Twenties to the Nineties

This history explores the events, ideas, and personalities of seven decades following the First World War. It is a superb discussion of the most relevant aspects of the twentieth century—including good discussions on the beginnings of the Soviet Union and its close cousin Nazism, Peronism in Argentina and how it destroyed that prosperous country, and the devastation of the third world by the collectivist ideologues.

Kipling, Rudyard

Captains Courageous

This novel of maritime adventure takes place on the *We're Here*, a small fishing boat whose crew members rescue the son of a multimillionaire, Harvey Cheyne, when he is washed overboard from an ocean liner. The captain refuses to take him back to port and instead makes Harvey a member of the crew, where he quickly learns respect, toughness, and gratitude—and inspires the audience to do the same.

Kim

Kim is an orphan, living from hand to mouth in the teeming streets of Lahore. One day he meets a man quite unlike anything in his wide experience, a Tibetan lama on a quest. Kim's life suddenly acquires meaning and purpose as he becomes the lama's guide and protector—his *chela* (disciple). Other forces are at work as Kim is sucked into the intrigue of the Great Game and travels the Grand Trunk Road with his lama. How Kim and the lama meet their respective destinies on the road and in the mountains of India forms a compelling adventure tale.

Knowles, John

A Separate Peace

Knowles's beloved classic is a story of friendship, treachery, and the confusions of adolescence. Looking back to his youth, Gene Forrester reflects on his life as a student at Devon School in New Hampshire in 1942. Although he is an excellent student, he envies the athleticism and vitality of his friend Finny. Unable to cope with this insecurity, Forrester causes Finny to break his leg, sabotaging his athletic career. *A Separate Peace* looks at this tragic accident involving the two young men and how it forever tarnishes their innocence.

Lewis, C. S.

The Chronicles of Narnia

Lewis's mystical tale of adventure takes the reader on an extraordinary journey to far-off lands. *The Chronicles of Narnia* consists of seven books: *The Magician's Nephew*; *The Lion, the Witch, and the Wardrobe*; *The Horse and His Boy*; *Prince Caspian*; *The Voyage of the Dawn Treader*; *The Silver Chair*; and *The Last Battle*. An allegorical saga great for all ages.

Mere Christianity

In 1943 Great Britain, when hope and the moral fabric of society were threatened by the relentless inhumanity of global war, an Oxford don was invited to give a series of radio lectures addressing the central issues of Christianity. *Mere Christianity* never flinches as it sets out a rational basis for Christianity and builds an edifice of compassionate morality atop this foundation. As Lewis clearly demonstrates, Christianity is not a religion of flitting angels and blind faith, but of free will, an innate sense of justice, and the grace of God. Lewis's lucid apologetics will challenge the faithful and convince those who have not previously heard the gospel.

The Screwtape Letters

Written in defense of Christian faith, this popular satire consists of a series of thirty-one letters in which Screwtape, an experienced devil, instructs his young charge, Wormwood, in the art of temptation. Confounded by church doctrines and a faithful Christian woman, their efforts are defeated when their subject—a World War II pilot—dies in a bombing raid, but with his soul at peace. *The Screwtape Letters* is a classic treatise on a human nature that is as old as the world. Through his satiric use of the demonic narrative persona, Lewis examines the opposing sides in the battle between good and evil.

Llewellyn, Richard

How Green Was My Valley

In this nostalgic tale of a young man's coming-of-age, the Morgan family experiences the simple, vital pleasures of life in the coal fields of South Wales in the late 1800s. However, industrial capitalism takes its toll on the family and community. The Morgan boys are driven from their family home because of the stresses and wild cycles of early industrialism, and the town, once a community of friends, gradually becomes a mean, brutal place. Llewellyn looks critically at industrial capitalism from a conservative point of view.

London, Jack

The Call of the Wild

In his classic survival story of Buck, a courageous dog fighting for survival in the Alaskan and Yukon wilderness, London vividly evokes the harsh and frozen Yukon during the Gold Rush. As Buck is ripped from his pampered, domestic surroundings and shipped to Alaska to be a sled dog, his primitive, wolflike nature begins to emerge. Savage struggles and timeless bonds between man, dog, and wilderness are played to their heartrending extremes, as Buck undertakes a journey that transforms him into the legendary "Ghost Dog" of the Klondike.

White Fang

White Fang is a wolf dog, the offspring of an Indian dog and a wolf, alone in the savage world of the desolate, frozen wilds of the Yukon territory. Weedon Scott rescues the fiercely independent dog from a cruel, ignorant master and trains him to be a loving companion. When an escaped convict threatens violence, a savage beast transformed by human kindness must confront a man brutalized by society.

MacDonald, George

The Curate's Awakening

Originally published as *Thomas Wingfold, Curate* in 1876, MacDonald's tale is retold for today's readers in *The Curate's Awakening*. MacDonald masterfully weaves together an old abandoned house, a frightened young fugitive, a tragic murder, and a sister's love, as the Curate's confidence and faith are shaken.

Malory, Sir Thomas

Le morte d'Arthur

The legendary deeds of King Arthur and his Knights of the Round Table follows Arthur's magical birth and accession to the throne as well as the stories of knights Sir Lancelot, Sir Tristram, and Sir Galahad. Malory's unique and splendid version of the Arthurian legend tells an immortal story of love, adventure, chivalry, treachery, and death.

Maupassant, Guy de

Short Stories

Guy de Maupassant was indeed a great influence. His short stories are considered little masterpieces and have been followed as a model for short-story writers since his time.

Melville, Herman

Billy Budd

It is a time of war between nations, but on one ship, a smaller battle is being fought between two men. Jealous of Billy Budd, known as the "Handsome Sailor," the envious master-at-arms Claggart torments the young man until his false accusations lead to a charge of treason against Billy.

Moby Dick

Melville tells this story through the eyes of Ishmael. A giant white whale took Captain Ahab's leg on a previous voyage, and now, driven on by the captain's obsessive revenge, the crew and the outcast Ishmael find themselves caught up in a maniacal pursuit that inexorably leads to an apocalyptic climax.

Monsarrat, Nicholas

The Cruel Sea

Monsarrat presents the lives of Allied sailors who must protect the cargo ships and destroy the German submarines. He vividly describes the savage submarine battles of the North Atlantic during World War II.

Nordhoff, Charles, and James Norman Hall

Mutiny on the Bounty

In this stirring sea adventure, Nordhoff and Hall tell the story of the historic voyage of the *HMS Bounty*—a journey that culminated in Fletcher Christian's mutiny against Captain Bligh. This unforgettable fictional tale of the high seas is so realistic that it reads like truth.

Poe, Edgar A.

Poems

Poe revolutionized the horror tale, giving it psychological insight and a consistent tone and atmosphere. He invented the modern detective story, penned some of the world's best-known lyric poetry, and wrote a major novella of the fantastic. Some of his more famous works include "The Raven"; "The Pit and the Pendulum"; "Annabel Lee"; "The Fall of the House of Usher"; and "The Murders in the Rue Morgue."

Potok, Chaim

The Promise

This novel follows the story of Reuven Malter in his choices between traditionalism and his feelings. As Potok explores the themes of adolescence, morality, and our collective nature, he captures the essence of Jewish customs and conflicts and puts them in laypeople's terms. This is an uplifting story, realistically and dramatically told.

Remarque, Erich M.

All Quiet on the Western Front

Paul Bäumer and his classmates enlist in the German army of World War II, and they become soldiers with youthful enthusiasm. Yet through years of vivid horror, Paul holds fast to a single vow: to fight against the principle of hate that meaninglessly pits people against each other, especially young men of the same generation but in different uniforms.

Sandburg, Carl

Abraham Lincoln: The Prairie Years and The War Years

The definitive biography of one of America's greatest presidents recounts the fascinating log-cabin-to-the-White House success story. Sandburg aptly describes the complex individual who rose to become an outstanding leader.

Saroyan, William

The Human Comedy

Saroyan's autobiographical story centers around a family whose struggles and dreams reflect those of America's second-generation immigrants. Set in California during World War II, it shows us a boy caught between reality and illusion as he delivers telegrams of wartime death, love, and money, which brings him face-to-face with human emotion at its most raw level.

Scott, Sir Walter

Ivanhoe

Set in twelfth-century England, *Ivanhoe* captures the noble idealism of chivalry along with its often cruel and impractical consequences. It follows the heroic adventures of Sir Wilfred of Ivanhoe as he and his fellow captives are rescued from Knight Templar's castle by Robin Hood; the wounded Ivanhoe's trial by combat with the powerful Knight to save the beautiful Jewess Rebecca from the stake; and King Richard the Lionhearted's aid in Ivanhoe's triumph at evil King John's tournament.

Sebestyen, Ouida

Words by Heart

Hoping to make her adored papa proud of her and make her white classmates notice her "Magic Mind" and not her black skin, Lena vows to win the Bible-quoting contest. Winning does not bring Lena what she expected. Instead of honor, violence and death erupt and strike the one she loves most dearly. Lena, who has believed in vengeance, must now learn how to forgive.

Shaara, Michael

The Killer Angels

This novel reveals more about the Battle of Gettysburg (July 1–3, 1863) — in which fifty thousand people died — than any piece of learned nonfiction on the same subject. Shaara's account of the three most important days of the Civil War features deft characterizations of all of the main actors, including Lee, Longstreet, Pickett, Buford, and Hancock. In the three most bloody and courageous days of our nation's history, two armies fought for two dreams: the Union Army fought to free the slaves and obtain freedom for all people in America; the Confederates fought to preserve a Southern way of life handed down for generations.

Shakespeare, William

Hamlet

This powerful tale of ghosts, murder, and revenge takes on new meaning with each reading. The play begins as a ghost story, full of mystery and suspense. Then in Acts II and III, it becomes a detective story, with Prince Hamlet seeking to find the murderer of his father. Finally, in Acts IV and V, it becomes a revenge story, as Hamlet seeks the ultimate revenge.

Julius Caesar

A crafty and ambitious Cassius, envious of Caesar's political and military triumphs, forms a conspiracy against him. After Caesar's assassination, Antony, seeking retribution against the murderers, drives them out of Rome. *Julius Caesar* is one of Shakespeare's greatest works.

Macbeth

Shakespeare's tragedy *Macbeth* revolves around destiny, ambition, and murder. It is prophesied that the Scottish lord "Macbeth shall never vanquished be / Until great Birnam Wood to high Dunsinane Hill / Shall come against him" (act 4, scene 1). Macbeth luxuriates in his invincibility, knowing that woods don't climb hills. Or do they? As he and Lady Macbeth move from one heinous crime to another, a day of reckoning awaits them.

Shaw, George Bernard

Pygmalion

Behind the popular musical and movie *My Fair Lady* is its inspiration, *Pygmalion*. This is a perceptive comedy of wit and grit about the unique relationship that develops between the spunky cockney flower girl Eliza Doolittle and her irascible speech professor, Henry Higgins. The flower girl teaches the egotistical phonetics professor that to be a lady means more than just learning to speak like one.

Shelley, Mary

Frankenstein

After being rescued from an iceberg, Dr. Frankenstein relates his autobiography to the ship's captain. Dr. Frankenstein has been consumed by his desire to create a fully grown living creature. When he reaches his goal, he perceives his creation as a monster, immediately regrets his work, and promptly abandons it. A story within a story, *Frankenstein* is a subtle and ironic prophecy that raises the question of who exactly is the real monster in this story.

Sinclair, Upton

The Jungle

In Sinclair's book we enter the world of Jurgis Rudkus, a young Lithuanian immigrant who arrives in America fired with dreams of wealth, freedom, and opportunity. And we discover, with him, the astonishing truth about "Packingtown," the busy, flourishing, filthy Chicago stockyards, where New-World visions perish in a jungle of human and animal suffering. Sinclair explores the workingman's lot at the turn of the century: the backbreaking labor, the injustices of "wage-slavery," and the bewildering chaos of urban life.

Steinbeck, John

East of Eden

This sprawling and often brutal novel, set in the rich farmlands of California's Salinas Valley, follows the intertwined destinies of two families—the Trasks and the Hamiltons—whose generations helplessly reenact the fall of Adam and Eve and the poisonous rivalry of Cain and Abel.

The Grapes of Wrath

Here is Steinbeck's epic chronicle of human struggle against injustice and cruelty. It tells the story of the Joads, their flight from the Dust Bowl of the 1930s, and their trek to "the golden land" of California. It is not just the story of one family and one time: it is also the story of the courage and passion of all people throughout history.

Of Mice and Men

This tragic story, given poignancy by its objective narrative, is about the complex bond between two migrant laborers. The plot centers on George Milton and Lennie Small, itinerant ranch hands who dream of one day owning a small farm. George acts as a father figure to Lennie, who is large and simpleminded, calming him and helping to rein in his immense physical strength.

Stevenson, Robert Louis

Dr. Jekyll and Mr. Hyde

Stevenson's supernatural story of good versus evil centers around the well-intentioned, wealthy physician Dr. Jekyll. As he drinks the potion that is the culmination of his research, he unleashes the dark side of his nature, turning into the hideous Mr. Hyde. This book is one of the most horrific depictions of the human potential for evil ever written.

Kidnapped

In this spirited saga, a young heir is seized by his villainous uncle and sold into slavery. Saved ironically in a shipwreck, he travels with a Scot expatriate until they become suspects in a murder. More than just a "boy's story," this is the tale of a brave young man and the amazing odyssey that takes him halfway around the world.

Treasure Island

When young Jim Hawkins finds a treasure map in Captain Flint's chest, he must outwit the dead Captain's collaborators if he is to keep it for himself. Only his two companions, Squire Trelawney and Dr. Livesey, share Jim's secret, and the three decide to set off on a seafaring adventure in this classic tale of exploits on the high seas.

Stone, Irving

Lust for Life

Vincent Van Gogh was a tragic figure in his time, besieged by uncertainty, disappointment, and a tortured mind. The heroic devotion of his brother was the most important sustaining influence on his life. In *Lust for Life*, Stone uses the techniques of a fiction writer and the approach of a biographer in re-creating the storm and stress of this artist's life.

Stowe, Harriet Beecher

Uncle Tom's Cabin

This is a book that changed American history. Stowe was appalled by slavery, and she took one of the few options open to nineteenth-century women who wanted to affect public opinion: She wrote a novel—a huge enthralling narrative that claimed the heart, soul, and politics of pre-Civil War Americans. It is unabashed propaganda and overtly moralistic, an attempt to make whites—North and South—see slaves as mothers, fathers, and people with (Christian) souls. In a time when many whites claimed that slavery had "good effects" on blacks, *Uncle Tom's Cabin* paints pictures of three plantations, each progressively worse, where even the best plantation leaves a slave at the mercy of fate or debt.

Swift, Jonathan

Gulliver's Travels

This four-part, satirical novel is the story of Lemuel Gulliver, a surgeon and sea captain who visits remote regions of the world. Gulliver is shipwrecked on Lilliput, where people are six inches tall. His second voyage takes him to Brobdingnag, where lives a race of giants of great practicality who do not understand abstractions. Gulliver's third voyage takes him to the flying island of Laputa and the nearby continent and capital of Lagado, where he finds pedants obsessed with their own specialized areas of speculation and utterly ignorant of the rest of life. At Glubdubdrib, the Island of Sorcerers, he speaks with great men of the past and learns from them the lies of history. He also meets the Struldbrugs, who are immortal and, as a result, utterly miserable. In the extremely bitter fourth part, Gulliver visits the land of the Houyhnhnms, a race of intelligent, virtuous horses served by brutal, filthy, and degenerate humanlike creatures called Yahoos.

Tolkien, J. R. R.

The Lord of the Rings trilogy

Tolkien's trilogy of fantasy novels, drawn from his extensive knowledge of philology and folklore, consists of *The Fellowship of the Ring, The Two Towers*, and *The Return of the King*. The novels, set in the Third Age of Middle Earth, formed a sequel to Tolkien's *The Hobbit*. The trilogy is the saga of a group of sometimes reluctant heroes who set forth to save their world from consummate evil. At thirty-three, the age of adulthood among Hobbits, Frodo Baggins receives a magic Ring of Invisibility from his uncle Bilbo. A Christlike figure, Frodo learns that the ring has the power to control the entire world and, he discovers, to corrupt its owner. A fellowship of Hobbits, elves, dwarves, and men is formed to destroy the Ring; they are opposed on their harrowing mission by the evil Sauron and his Black Riders.

Tolstoy, Leo

War and Peace

This epic, historical novel is a panoramic study of early nineteenth-century Russian society. *War and Peace* is primarily concerned with the histories of five aristocratic families, the members of which are portrayed against a vivid background of Russian social life during the war against Napoleon (1805–14). The theme of war, however, is subordinate to the story of family existence, which involves Tolstoy's optimistic belief in the life-asserting pattern of human existence. The novel also sets forth a theory of history, concluding that there is a minimum of free choice: all is ruled by an inexorable historical determinism.

Twain, Mark

The Adventures of Huckleberry Finn

Twain's book tells the story of a teenaged misfit who finds himself floating on a raft down the Mississippi River with an escaping slave, Jim. In the course of their perilous journey, Huck and Jim meet adventure, danger, and a cast of characters who are sometimes menacing and often hilarious. This book's humor is found mostly in Huck's unique worldview and his way of expressing himself. Underlying Twain's good humor, however, is a dark subcurrent of cruelty and injustice that makes this a frequently funny book with a serious message.

The Adventures of Tom Sawyer

Twain's story of a mischievous Missouri schoolboy combines humor, terror, and astute social criticism in a delightful tale of life on the Mississippi. Written in 1876, Tom Sawyer became the model for an ideal of American boyhood in the nineteenth century, and many story elements—such as the fence-painting episode—are now woven into the fabric of our culture.

Verne, Jules

Master of the World

"It was seen first in North Carolina, or something was, smoking up from a mountain crater. With blinding speed, it roared past cars on a Pennsylvania road. It skimmed the Atlantic, then at the flick of its captain's will dove beneath the waves. . . . It was the 'Terror' . . . ship, sub, plane, and land vehicle in one and a letter from its inventor claimed that with it, he would rule the world." Long recognized as a truly prophetic science fiction classic, this adventure was also Verne's last novel.

Twenty Thousand Leagues under the Sea

Professor Pierre Aronnax, the narrator, boards an American frigate commissioned to investigate a rash of attacks on international shipping by what is thought to be an amphibious monster. The supposed sea creature, which is actually the submarine *Nautilus*, sinks Aronnax's vessel and imprisons him along with his devoted servant Conseil and Ned Land, a temperamental harpooner. The survivors meet Captain Nemo, an enigmatic misanthrope who leads them on a worldwide, yearlong underwater adventure. The novel is noted for its exotic situations and the technological innovations it describes.

Wallace, Lewis

Ben-Hur

This historical novel depicts the oppressive Roman occupation of ancient Palestine and the origins of Christianity. Judah Ben-Hur, a Jew, is wrongly accused by his former friend, the Roman Messala, of attempting to kill a Roman official. He is sent to be a slave. and his mother and sister are imprisoned. Years later he returns, wins a chariot race against Messala, and is reunited with his now leprous mother and sister.

Washington, Booker T.

Up from Slavery

Illustrating the human quest for freedom and dignity, Washington's American classic recounts his triumph over the legacy of slavery, his founding of Tuskegee Institute, and his emergence as a national spokesman for his race.

Wells, H. G.

Collected Works of H. G. Wells

Wells is the founder of modern science fiction. His stories include "The Crystal Egg," "The Strange Orchid," and "The Invisible Man"—a serious study of egotism.

Wouk, Herman

The Caine Mutiny: A Novel of World War II

Generally books about war fit their stereotype quite well: the hero is the commanding officer, who leads his men courageously into battle. However, Wouk shows that even our most heralded commanders are human and make mistakes, like the rest of us. Captain Queeg is unbalanced, but is he so unbalanced as to warrant a mutiny? That is one of the central themes of *The Caine Mutiny*, along with Willie Keith's change from an immature mama's boy into a man capable of commanding an entire ship in the United States Navy. Wouk shows how most men are vulnerable, and military men are no exception.

Older Students

Bellamy, Edward

Looking Backward

Bellamy's story, first published in 1888, is a passionate attack on the social ills of nineteenth-century industrialism. Bellamy makes a plea for social reform and moral renewal; however, the action takes place in the year 2000. Julian West awakens after more than a century of sleep to find himself in twentieth-century America—a land full of employment, material abundance, and social harmony.

Benet, Stephen
John Brown's Body

This is not the history of John Brown, nor a verse history of the American Civil War, but a narrative of the great and complex struggles between civilizations, where nearly everyone is right and wrong. Benet's saga is an epic poem of the Civil War.

Bronté, Emily
Wuthering Heights

The tempestuous and mythic story of Catherine Earnshaw, the precocious daughter of the house, and the ruggedly handsome, uncultured foundling her father brings home and names Heathcliff. Brought together as children, Catherine and Heathcliff quickly become attached to each other. As they grow older, their companionship turns into obsession. Family, class, and fate work cruelly against them, as do their own jealous and volatile natures, and much of their lives is spent in revenge and frustration. *Wuthering Heights* is a classic tale of possessive and thwarted passion, and it embodies Bronté's philosophy and spiritual quality.

Cather, Willa
My Antonia

Cather's novel honors the immigrant settlers of the American plains. Narrated by the protagonist's lifelong friend, Jim Burden, the novel recounts the history of Antonia Shimerda, the daughter of Bohemian immigrants who settled on the Nebraska frontier. The book contains a number of poetic passages about the disappearing frontier and the spirit and courage of frontier people.

Cervantes, Miguel de
Don Quixote

Humor, insight, compassion, and knowledge of the world underlie the antic adventures of the lanky knight clad in rusty armor and his earthy squire, Sancho Panza. The unforgettable characters they encounter on their famous pilgrimage form a brilliant panorama of society and human behavior.

Dostoyevsky, Fyodor
Crime and Punishment

Dostoyevsky's first masterpiece, this novel is a psychological analysis of the poor student Raskolnikov, whose theory—that humanitarian ends justify using evil means—leads him to murder a Saint Petersburg pawnbroker. The act produces nightmarish guilt in Raskolnikov. The narrative's feverish, compelling tone follows the twists and turns of Raskolnikov's emotions and elaborates his struggle with his conscience and his mounting sense of horror as he wanders the city's hot, crowded streets. In prison, he comes to realize that happiness cannot be achieved by a reasoned plan of existence but must be earned by suffering.

Faulkner, William
The Bear

Faulkner tells the story of a boy's coming to terms with the adult world. By learning how to hunt, he is taught the real meaning of pride, humility, and courage—virtues that Faulkner feared would be almost impossible to learn with the destruction of the wilderness.

Go Down, Moses

This work consists of seven interrelated stories, all of them set in Yoknapatawpha County (a fictional county in northern Mississippi). From a variety of perspectives, Faulkner examines the complex, changing relationships between blacks and whites and between man and nature.

The Hamlet, The Town, and The Mansion

The trilogy follows the origin, rise, and dominance of the Snopes family. The Snopes took root in Yoknapatawpha County and proliferated through and beyond it until they outmaneuvered and overpowered a society that had little defense against their invincible rapacity.

Galsworthy, James
The Forsythe Saga

Galsworthy's saga chronicles the lives of three generations of a monied, middle-class English family at the turn of the century. Soames Forsythe, a solicitor and "the man of property," is married to the beautiful but penniless Irene, who falls in love with Philip Bosinney, the

French architect whom Soames has hired to build a country house. The rest of the saga concerns itself with Soames, Irene, and Philip, and the generations that follow.

Justice

Here is Galsworthy's tragic play about the irony of punishing by rule rather than helping or training the individual. It is full of both irony, justice, and injustice.

Loyalties

This drama treats incidentally the clash of classes and social groups. Its main purpose is to throw up into relief the incessant clash of differing loyalties, which makes the path of right action so difficult.

Hansberry, Lorraine

Raisin in the Sun

When it was first produced in 1959, *A Raisin in the Sun* was awarded the New York Drama Critics Circle Award for that season and hailed as a watershed in American drama. A pioneering work by an African American playwright, the play was a radically new representation of black life.

Hardy, Thomas

Mayor of Casterbridge

This is a classic tale of a successful man who cannot escape his past nor his own evil nature. Michael Henchard is the respected mayor of Casterbridge, a thriving industrial town—but years ago, under the influence of alcohol, he has sold his wife, Susan, and infant daughter to a sailor at a country fair for five guineas. Although repentant and sober for twenty-one years, Henchard cannot escape his destiny when Susan and her daughter return to Casterbridge.

Hersey, John

Hiroshima

When the atomic bomb was dropped on Hiroshima (August 6, 1945), few could have anticipated its potential for devastation. Hersey recorded the stories of Hiroshima residents shortly after the explosion, offering the world firsthand accounts from people who survived it. The words of Miss Sasaki, Dr. Fujii, Mrs. Nakamara, Father Kleinsorge, Dr. Sasaki, and the Reverend Tanimoto give faces to the statistics that saturated the media and solicited an overwhelming public response.

James, Henry
The Turn of the Screw

One of the most famous ghost stories, the tale is told mostly through the journal of a governess and depicts her struggle to save her two young charges from the demonic influence of the eerie apparitions of two former servants in the household. The story has inspired critical debate over the question of the "reality" of the ghosts and of James's intentions. Whether accepted as a simple ghost story or an exercise in the literary convention of the unreliable narrator, this story is classically and relentlessly horrifying.

Lee, Harper
To Kill a Mockingbird

Through the eyes of the six-year-old girl Scout Finch, one of the most endearing and enduring characters of Southern literature, Lee explores with rich humor and unswerving honesty the irrationality of adult attitudes toward race and class in the Deep South of the 1930s. The conscience of a town steeped in prejudice, violence, and hypocrisy is pricked by the stamina and quiet heroism of one man's struggle for justice; the man is Atticus Finch, Scout's widowed father and a lawyer.

Lamb, Charles
The Essays of Elia

Lamb's personality is projected in all his literary work, but in *The Essays of Elia* it shines through. This collection of essays contains a vast deal of autobiographical material, and it is candidly personal in atmosphere and structure.

Lewis, Sinclair
Arrowsmith

Lewis's book follows the life of Martin Arrowsmith, a rather ordinary fellow who gets his first taste of medicine at age fourteen as an assistant to the drunken physician in his hometown. He is forced to give up his trade for reasons ranging from public ignorance to the publicity-mindedness of a great foundation, and becomes an isolated seeker of scientific truth.

Babbitt

A conniving, prosperous real-estate man, Babbitt is one of the ugliest figures in American fiction. A total conformist, he can only receive self-esteem from others and is loyal to whoever serves his need of the moment. *Babbitt* gives consummate expression to the glibness and irresponsibility of the hardened, professional social climber.

Marquand, John P.

The Late George Apley

Marquand presents a wicked, brilliantly etched satire. A portrait of a Bostonian and of the tradition-bound, gilded society in which he lived, it is the story of three generations of Apley men, the maturing America, and the golden era of American security from 1866 to 1933.

Masters, Edgar Lee

A Spoon River Anthology

Masters introduces the reader to a selection of souls who describe their lives and their relationships (or lack thereof) through simplistic, poetic epitaphs. The collection of dramatic monologues by over two hundred former inhabitants of the fictional town of Spoon River topples the myth of moral superiority in small-town America, as the dead give testimony to their shocking scandals and secret tragedies. Masters seems to place readers under Peter's celestial wings, inviting—almost daring—readers to decide eternal placement for his characters.

Maugham, Somerset

Of Human Bondage

Maugham uses the tale of Philip Carey, an innocent, sensitive crippled man in Victorian-era Europe as a front for his own autobiography. Philip was left an orphan at a young age and was continually taunted for his clubfoot and the limp that resulted. His early rejection from society gives him time to seek out his purpose in life and travel across Europe. This book is truly great for the in-depth examination of love and the human animal.

Orwell, George

Animal Farm

A farm is taken over by its overworked, mistreated animals. With flaming idealism and stirring slogans, they set out to create a paradise of progress, justice, and equality. Thus the stage is set for telling anti-utopian satires—a razor-edged fable that records the evolution from revolution against tyranny to a totalitarian dictatorship even more oppressive and heartless than that of their former human masters.

Paine, Thomas

The Rights of Man

This work is clearly one of the great classics on the subject of democracy. Paine's vast influence on our system of government is due less to his eloquence and literary style than to his steadfast bravery and determination to promote justice and equality.

Paton, Alan

Cry, the Beloved Country

Set in the troubled South Africa of the 1940s amid a people riven by racial inequality and injustice, *Cry, the Beloved Country* is a beautiful and profoundly compassionate story of the Zulu pastor Stephen Kumalo and his son Absalom. Everyone can relate to the pathos of Rev. Kumalo in his journey to reunite the tribe and his gradual awakening to the fact that his compassion and tears can do nothing for some major changes that are occurring.

Plato

The Republic

In this work Plato presents a guide to life and living for every person alive. By trying to describe the ideal state, Plato creates the first "Utopia" and in the meantime questions our perceptions of reality. Through Plato's thought we can see that the only way to judge fairness and equality is through the ideal state and what man could be, not what man is. Plato's look on justice and reality is unmatched despite hundreds of attempts to replicate his thought and style in the past few millennia.

Rolvaag, O. E.

Giants in the Earth: A Saga of the Prairie

This refreshingly stark view of pioneer life reflects the hardships, fear, and depression that one women experiences when her husband takes her from her Norwegian homeland and moves her steadily westward across the northern plains of America. This novel is gothic in dimensions—the physical landscape becomes the characters' mental landscape—the vast expanses of snow in winter and grass in summer become a metaphor for boredom and isolation. Rolvaag writes of a lifestyle and of motivations unimaginable to the modern American, and yet he writes of a time that was shockingly recent in the history of the Midwest.

Rostand, Edmund
Cyrano de Bergerac

Set in seventeenth-century Paris, the action revolves around the emotional problems of the noble, swashbuckling Cyrano; despite his many gifts, he feels that no woman can ever love him because he has an enormous nose. Secretly in love with the lovely Roxane, Cyrano agrees to help his inarticulate rival, Christian, win her heart by allowing him to present Cyrano's love poems, speeches, and letters as his own work, and Cyrano remains silent about his own part in Roxane's courtship.

Sophocles
Three Theban Plays: Oedipus Rex, Oedipus at Colonus, Antigone

This trilogy is Greek tragedy and compelling drama. It is the eloquent story of a noble family moving toward catastrophe and dragged down by pride from wealth and power. *Oedipus Rex* raises basic questions about human behavior. *Antigone* examines the conflicting obligations of civic duties versus personal loyalties and religious mores.

Swarthout, Glendon
Bless the Beasts and the Children

Swarthout gives readers an opportunity to view six adolescents whom society has already labeled misfits from the inside out. As the book progresses, readers gradually learn the history of each member of the group from past incidents, namely, unintentional mental abuse by parents. The teenagers set out on a quest to free a herd of buffaloes from a senseless slaughter. Ironically, the freedom and fate of these animals parallel that of the young men. Their freeing the buffaloes symbolizes their own self-discovery, initiation into manhood, and entry into a realm of humanity that transcends the violent, dog-eat-dog society that has excluded them.

Thackeray, William Makepeace
Vanity Fair

This novel is a story of two heroines—one humble, the other a schemer and social climber—who meet in boarding school and embark on markedly different lives. Amid the swirl of London's posh ballrooms and affairs of love and war, their fortunes rise and fall. Through it all, Thackeray lampoons the shallow values of his society, reserving the most pointed barbs for the upper crust. What results is a prescient look at the dogged pursuit of wealth and status—and the need for humility.

Turgenev, Ivan
Fathers and Sons

Turgenev deals with the inevitable conflict between generations and between the values of traditionalists and intellectuals. The physician Bazarov, the novel's protagonist, is a nihilist, denying the validity of all laws save those of the natural sciences. He scorns traditional Russian values, shocks respectable society, and for the young, represents the spirit of rebellion. Uncouth and forthright in his opinions, Bazarov is nonetheless susceptible to love and by that fact doomed to unhappiness.

Vonnegut, Kurt
Cat's Cradle

Here is Vonnegut's satirical commentary on modern humans and their madness. An apocalyptic tale of this planet's ultimate fate, it features a midget as the protagonist; a complete, original theology created by a calypso singer; and a vision of the future that is at once blackly fatalistic and hilariously funny. These assorted characters chase each other around in search of the world's most important and dangerous substance, a new form of ice that freezes at room temperature.

Wharton, Edith
Ethan Frome

Although Ethan Frome, a gaunt, patient New Englander, seems ambitious and intelligent, his wife, Zeena, holds him back. When her young cousin Mattie comes to stay on their New England farm, Ethan falls in love with her. But the social conventions of the day doom their love and their hopes. Ethan is tormented by a passionate love for Mattie, and his desperate quest for happiness leads to pain and despair.

APPENDIX D: INDEX OF SUGGESTED WORKS

General Literature

This index is arranged in canonical sequence. Brief illustrative citations are not listed here.

CPSIA information can be obtained at www.ICGtesting.com
Printed in the USA
BVOW101217050613

322514BV00001B/1/P